ORIGINS,
ORIENT
AND
ORIANA

The ORIANA in dry-dock in Falmouth.

ORIGINS, ORIENT AND ORIANA

BY

CHARLES F. MORRIS

Seen within the perspective of the development of the ship from earliest times, this is the history of the Orient Line, one of the most notable passenger liner companies, from its sailing ships through its century of passenger steamships in all its aspects, including the story of the families who guided its fortunes and, finally, all the problems—likely and unlikely—of the design and building of the very last of the great liners seen, unusually, through the eyes of the Company's Chief Naval Architect.

WITH AN INTRODUCTION BY

SIR COLIN ANDERSON, K.B.E

TEREDO BOOKS LTD
BRIGHTON
SUSSEX

MCMLXXX

ISBN 0 903662 07 8

Filmset by Photocomp Ltd., Birmingham, England.
Printed in Italy by
International Publishing Enterprises, Rome

FOREWORD

I feel sure that a great many people will find this book to be full of absorbing and unusual information about its rather specialised subject, of which a great deal will have been unknown to them hitherto. Indeed, when I came to read the text, I never imagined that, having been so closely concerned with so many of the matters about which Charles Morris has written in it, I should find so many fascinating things of which I had not previously been aware. Naturally, I am not thinking of his more personal reminiscences; still less of his *bêtes noires*, though I would not have wished him to have withheld these, for they make the book both human and personal, which is quite a feat when dealing with so potentially 'heavy' a subject.

There is a now rapidly dwindling body of people who have worked their lives in the building or running of the great passenger liners. They will, I am sure, be grateful with me that, while there was still time to do so, someone with first-class, first-hand knowledge should have sat down and recorded in such detail what he knew of the designing, construction and service problems of a certain group of these ships. It was, indeed, the eleventh hour.

This book will prove to be a mine of information on what will, all too soon, become thought of as a very specialised, and even obscure, industrial -historical subject.

Colin S. Anderson

CONTENTS

LIST OF ILLUSTRATIONS

Plate numbers for coloured pictures in **bold** fount
Plans and diagrams given in *italics*

ACKNOWLEDGEMENTS

As might be expected, the author received valuable help to enable him to write this book, and he wishes to express his gratitude.

Sir Colin Anderson and Mr. Ford Geddes, who were Managers of the Orient Line, read the typescript, corrected many points and offered much encouragement and guidance to improve what had already been written, and I also thank Sir Colin Anderson for writing the Foreword.

Earl Inchcape, Chairman of the P. & O. Steam Navigation Company, graciously authorized access to the library and historical records of the P. & O. and Orient Companies, together with the provision of very many of the photographs reproduced in this book.

Sir Leonard Redshaw, Chairman of Vickers Shipbuilding Group Ltd., before his retirement, arranged for the supply of drawings and technical information, and Mr. William Richardson, the present Chairman of that Group, read the typescript of the book and added further good advice and suggestions.

I should also like to thank the following persons and institutions for their kindness and help in contributing matter to this work:- Mr. Montague Poiney for supplying the monograph by the late Mr. William Fenton Hird on the Company's finances, which has formed the basis for Chapter VIII: Mr. Alex. Hurst, who has not only established many useful and helpful contacts throughout the world, but has added considerably to my knowledge of the Anderson, Anderson clipper ships of which I have written in Chapter II and has also provided unstintingly of his collection of pictures of passenger liners: to Mr. A. R. C. Osmond, of South Australia, for all his help in obtaining further pictures and information and for the time which he so unstintingly gave to the project and for tracking down yet more pictures, and to Miss Penny Osborn and Mr. Stephen Rabson, of the P. & O. Company, for such enormous co-operation in so many matters.

My quest for illustrations spread far and wide and met with a magnificent response. Indeed, although my publishers have included far more than I had had reason to hope or to expect, there are still very many which could not be included, and a large number were duplicated from different sources and, in some instances, the same pictures arrived from three different continents! It is thus difficult to be specific in acknowledging all the sources, but I should like to express my thanks to all those involved, whether or not it has proved possible to use the actual prints provided in the event. Thus, for example, the National Maritime Museum at Greenwich provided some pictures from the Orient Guide of 1880, of which I was subsequently presented with a copy and, in the same way, pictures by the late Mr. F.C. Gould were provided both from this source and from Mr. O.A. Lundgren. I should, however, like to thank Mr. Denis Stonham of the National Maritime Museum for all his assistance, and also, in particular, I should like to detail the following:- The Barrow News and Mail (plates 196–199): The Adelaide Advertiser (plates 49, 62 and 63): The State Library of South Australia for plates 20/23, 25, 29, 33/4, 70, 84 and 85 from the A.D. Edwardes Collection, The National Maritime Museum for plate 103, and Captain R.H. Turner, previously master in the P. & O. Company, for his own negatives of plates 2, 3, 6, 7 and 9, besides much other help and assistance with pictures, since he kindly put his collection at my disposal.

Mr. C-H. Friberg, of Saltsjö-Boo has most kindly allowed me to use reproductions of some of his magnificent oils, which comprise plates 4, 5, 10, 11, 14, 15, 16, 27 and has provided his photograph of the *Oriana* which is plate 153. These are quite splendid pictures which, I feel, enhance any book. The picture of the *Preussen*, plate 17, was provided by the late Mr. K.G. Holm of Varberg, and is reproduced from one of his fine water-colours.

Finally, I am bound to mention all the help which has come to me from my daughter, Anne, and my son, Peter, in the form of drawings and typing required in the preparation of this work. Indeed, I should like to add to the foregoing list all those who have so actively encouraged me and made such helpful suggestions and, not least, Dr. Anthony Hordern, whose persuasion prompted me to put pen to paper in the first place.

Charles F. Morris
1979

INTRODUCTION

SOME PEOPLE ARE too young when a crucial moment arises in their lives, while others are too old, but I was one of the lucky ones and I think that this brief Introduction will make this fact apparent.

The firm of Vickers, Shipbuilders and Engineers, is situated in Barrow-in-Furness, Cumbria, where I was born. Like the majority of boys in the town at that time, I started my working life in the Shipbuilding Company as soon as I was old enough, becoming a draughtsman and, later, training in one or other of the two ship design offices. Early in 1944, whilst the second World War was still in progress, I was invited by my chief, Stanley Redshaw, to apply for a position as assistant to the Naval Architect of the Orient Steam Navigation Company in London. It is well known that, when an employer invites an employee to apply for a job in another company, there is only one acceptable answer and, a few days later, a colleague of similar experience and qualifications to my own and to whom the same proposal had been made, was travelling to London with me. I believe that I am correct in stating, after all the lapse of years, that neither of us really wanted the job and that we did not wish to leave our home town. However, we were interviewed by the Senior Management of the Orient Company and, after a short time, I was selected for the post.

Although I did not appreciate the fact at the time, this was the point in my life when the first sentence of this page became relevant and now, more than thirty years later, I can look back and realize that I then entered the most happy, interesting and absorbing period of my life.

Hitherto, my work in designing ships had been done from the Shipbuilder's point of view, but now it was to be done from the Shipowner's entirely different standpoint. The Shipbuilder can only know what happens to a ship after she leaves his hands if the Shipowner keeps him informed, and this rarely happens in practice. If it does happen, the 'feed-back' of information is not in sufficient depth to be of significant value and, in consequence, short-comings in ship design are often repeated by the Shipbuilder in ship after ship.

During my first interview with the management of the Orient Steam Navigation Company, the managers told me that I should have to work closely and amicably with the Marine Superintendent, Superintendent Engineer, the Decorative Architect, and with others. Furthermore, I was to be on a sort of acceptance period of twelve months, after which I should either be retained by them or returned to my former employers, whilst it was equally open to me to return whence I had come at the end of the same period. I was satisfied with these conditions and would accept the same ones from the same company today, were it still in existence. The Orient Company was held in high esteem by Shipbuilders and others at that time, and my own chief in Barrow had told me, before I went to London for the interview:- *'Don't worry about pension particulars and so on: they will see you right.'* I never had any doubts about the truth of this at the time, nor subsequently from the day I joined the Company.

The point made by the managers that I should have to work amicably with the Marine Superintendents, the Superintendent Engineer and the Decorative Architect was not only very true, but not too easy to observe at times, since interests of responsibility clashed all too often. I do not know, and cannot remember, whether the managers said that I had to work with them, too, but they should have done so because they were the most important influence on the future design of ships for the Company, and I have always been impressed with their inherent understanding of the really important factors which produce a good passenger and cargo ship.

From some of the foregoing remarks, it will be apparent that I have described a procedure for employing and for being employed which no sensible modern society would propose or accept but, having given the matter much thought, I know that I am lucky and happy to have lived through that period in time, and would not wish to change it for the new world in which we live today.

The text that I have written in this book is not technical in nature. If the reader wishes to read a technical book on ships, there are many already in existence which are far more profound than I intend this one to be. My own interest in the highly technical aspects of ships diminished after I left the Vickers' Shipbuilding Works at Barrow, because I soon found that details of ship design and building, together with many and diverse subjects, such as the lasting qualities of materials: comfort of passengers and crew; painting, floor finishes and so forth, were of great importance in my work. The cost of maintenance of a ship during her life after leaving the Shipbuilder's yard is a significant part of her total cost to the Shipowner. Only a keen observation of this principle, and the subsequent installation of improvements into new ship construction by the Naval Architect, can make his employment by a Shipowner worthwhile. There is not the same incentive for a Shipbuilder's Naval Architect to take this interest in ship maintenance and, in fact, it could be argued that the reverse might be true, although I cannot believe that this would ever be the case.

I shall end this Introduction by explaining that the reason that this book has been written is because I have a very domineering, persuasive and good friend called Dr. Anthony Hordern who said to me one day, and on many subsequent days: *'There aren't many of you left. You'd better write a book on the subject of large passenger ships before they and you die'*. Sir Colin Anderson, a former Director of the Orient Steam Navigation Company, has read the text of this book and, in a colloquialism, described it as a *'proper rag-bag of a book*!—a description which I cannot better, for it has no plot and may appear to wander about in a confusing fashion. However, I have touched on many aspects of vessels which are seldom considered in print and, if what I have written interests and amuses the reader, I will be happy and contented.

1. *The head of a ship-building berth in Vickers-Armstrong's yard at Barrow-in-Furness, 1929, when fabrication was by erecting small units on the berth. The cranes could lift 2-5 tons, depending how the lift was made. (Etching by the author.)*

I. ORIGINS

As might be expected, the words 'boat' and 'ship' are both used frequently in this book. A ship carries boats, but a ship is often called a 'boat' as, for example, in the case of a 'Cross-Channel *boat*'. A purist would say—correctly—that a 'boat' is open and undecked, unless used in conjunction with another descriptive word (e.g. 'Fishing boat'). However, common usage is not necessarily that of the purist and a ship is usually larger than a boat, but the point when a boat becomes a ship is impossible to define. For instance, in past centuries a vessel was termed a ship even if she was only—say—thirty feet long because, at that time, a craft of such size was considered to be large. Nowadays we speak commonly of R.N.L.I. Lifeboats and canal boats which are much longer than other vessels which we deem to be ships.

The large and vague area through which 'boat' sizes pass before becoming 'ships' is so indefinable as to beggar description and, in consequence, the writer requests his readers to accept 'ship' or 'boat' in this book to mean either or both and, indeed, in a most cowardly manner, has sometimes dodged the issue by using the all-embracing words 'craft' or 'vessel'.

The history of ships is probably almost as old as that of mankind, but the stages of improvement in ways and means of construction, in design and in the infinite variety of types of vessel have proceeded at widely varying rates of change over the centuries in all parts of the world. Local evolution produced more types of boat than have been recorded but, as world travel has developed, especially in the last two or three hundred years, there has been a great interchange of

2.

3. *Whether known as Serendip, Taprobane, Ceylon or Sri Lanka, these local dug-out canoe type fishermen, here seen near Colombo, have not changed their form for centuries.*

knowledge and of ideas resulting from the borrowing of methods of building: rigging; sailing and hull design. Naturally, as has been seen in the car industry, there has often been a loss of identity of types of boats over the years, but the change has been more gradual and, in spite of this, some boats have still retained their original characteristics and will do so until 'civilization' engulfs those parts of the world where such craft still survive.

Often local operating conditions, such as those found in fishing, have produced special features in sailing boats, while availability of materials and the primitive nature, prosperity or otherwise, of the community had a great influence on the sort of craft which became used in that locality. The number of ingenious fittings and devices contrived for the handling and sailing of such craft were, and still are, legion, but manufactured articles are being used more extensively. The traditional fittings and gear will disappear completely or, perhaps, survive only as museum pieces. It is quite common today to see pictures of the most primitive dug-out canoe or traditional boat being propelled by a modern type of outboard motor unit. Preposterous as it may look, this conforms with the trend of using corrugated iron to roof a mud hut in Africa or elsewhere in what are now termed the 'developing countries' of the world, and the reader must be aware of numerous incongruities of the same sort. Perhaps we are witnessing a change which will settle down to a different level in a few years or, perhaps, it will be like London and other cities: always 'being built', but never finished.

The stages of improvement in design of ships in all particulars proceeded at different rates in all areas of the world, as has been noted, but the emphasis varied, depending on the interest in seaworthiness, prevailing sea and wind conditions, together with the requirements of usage—in other words, the craft's fitness for her purpose. As the focus of interest influenced design, so, for instance, progress in the design and skills in the use of sails seems to have been better in the ships of the eastern Mediterranean, and possibly further eastwards, than it was in the west European areas in the early centuries, but the interest in the hull and sea-keeping qualities of ships in the west developed quicker than elsewhere, while the beautifully-built and shapely hulls of the Scandinavian ships showed how they had progressed in the period from the fourth century A.D. onwards.

Much earlier the Greeks were transporting men and horses to the siege of Troy, and the evidence is that there was nothing very novel about their craft at that time. In the reign of Solomon there was active trade in cargo in both the eastern end of the Mediterranean and down the Red Sea—probably even to the south of Cape Gardafui—and a Phoenician expedition is said to have circumnavigated Africa, by stages, around 600 B.C. It is certainly not my object to examine all the beginnings of seafaring nor all the craft, but, within the general period 500–200 B.C., the Greeks and Phoenicians had developed a form of craft propelled by oars and, as a rather secondary motive power, a large rectangular sail hung from a yard secured to a single mast amidships. The oars were pulled by men sitting on each side of these galleys, of which there were two outstanding types, namely: Biremes and Triremes, having two and three banks of oars respectively.

Some of the larger triremes were approximately 130 feet in length and pulled by about 170 oars, which were kept in correct timing of their strokes by the playing of a sort of flute. The sight of such a ship, with its oars rising and falling rhythmically as it passed across the calm seas of the Mediterranean, must have been an inspiring and exciting one. (Their voyaging was normally confined to the summer sailing season.) However, although history and research infers that these vessels were fast, they could not have exceeded ten knots and were probably much slower than that. The oarsmen must have been rather miserable and hopeless creatures and, furthermore, could not have been very keen on their work but, having said this, it must also be stated that these galleys were the fastest craft of their times.

The Greeks had adapted the bireme from the penteconter, devised in the city of Phocaea in Asia Minor, which had twenty four oarsmen each side and two steering oars, making fifty working men. These craft had proved to be fast, but they were over-long; somewhat unseaworthy, difficult to manoeuvre and were expensive to build. Thus the bireme, which was about one third shorter in length, came into being, with the same number of rowers in two banks. (There were smaller types at the same time.) The triremes had first appeared almost two centuries later, roughly at the time of the Graeco-Persian wars, but each type was primarily a fighting ship, usually with a ram in her bow. Although sometimes used for military transport or for transmitting messages quickly, they were not used as ordinary merchant craft and, indeed, were normally beached at night whenever circumstances permitted. In fact, it is broadly true to say that all of the fast vessels were used for military or warlike purposes until almost the middle of the nineteenth century.

Almost a millennium after the era of the triremes and similar ships, the Norsemen were ravaging and pillaging all the countries around them, from Russia in the north to places far to the west and south of their land. Hardy, fearless and adventurous men, their climate and living conditions were severe, but these Northmen were accustomed to hardship and exposure to the elements. Quite independently of the thinking which had brought about the development of the triremes, and also without any means of knowing anything of such vessels as were then being used in the Mediterranean, they had been devising their own methods of mastering the waters around their own coasts. Their ships and boats had been devised for their owners' way of life and for the purposes for which they were to be used.

For many hundreds of years past, shipbuilders of the Western World and elsewhere have constructed ships in wood, iron or steel by first of all making drawings to scale—sometimes from a model in the case of wooden vessels—and then enlarging their drawings to full size and drawing them on a mould loft floor. This full scale drawing, or Lofting, was then used by shipwrights to make templates from which the frames of the vessel were shaped. The frames were then taken to the building berth and erected in their correct positions. Afterwards the planks or plates of the hull were fitted over, and secured to, the frames. The order of construction was, therefore: a) a model (perhaps): b) a drawing: c) the shaping and erection of frames on the building berth and, d) the fitting of the hull planking or plating over the frames.

Scientific study of the remains of ships built in wood by the Greeks and others, particularly the Norsemen, during the approximate period 500 B.C. to A.D. 1000 shows that an entirely different method was used. No drawings were made of a vessel, since the skilled eye of the master builder was all that was required. The planks of the hull were shaped and fitted together in place on the building berth, and then the frames were shaped by eye and fitted inside the hull planking *afterwards*. This method of construction is almost impossible for modern shipbuilders to accept, but the evidence revealed by careful investigation of ancient ship finds is almost irrefutable. Indeed, it is true to say that boat-builders in Western Norway today use very much the same methods of construction as the Vikings, using the eye instead of drawings for their work.

Ancient Greek ships were often carvel-built with the planking of the hull fitted flush: that is—each plank was fitted edge to edge with its neighbouring one by using wood dowels or tree-nails to join them. The Viking ships, on the other hand, were clinker-built, each plank being riveted to its neighbouring one's overlap by iron nails clamped over clinch plates. There were, of course, details of construction and of the shapes of the hulls which were selected by the Norsemen to suit the particular needs of the users, for only a small proportion were raiding or fighting ships. For example, their earlier ships, which were the prototypes for the trend to larger craft at the time of Olaf Tryggvason and the later 'giants' of the Danish Knut (Canute) often had to be carried or hauled overland between rivers or between parts of rivers where rapids intervened with the normal navigation. Thus the vessels had to be of light construction and shaped for the purpose.

Moreover, their ships had to be resilient to withstand rough use and wild waters and, to achieve these ends, were built to be beamy and shallow and with a high measure of flexibility. After the edges of the hull planking had been riveted together, the ribs were inserted and secured to the planks by lashings of spruce roots or some other suitable material, these being passed through cleats formed on the inner sides of the hull planks during their manufacture by the plank cutters (*filungr*.) Since these cleats were integral with the planking, the consequence was that much wood had to be cut to waste in the forming of each plank and, for this reason, the Scandinavian oak forests were used up in a few hundred years in much the same way as in England during the building of our 'wooden walls'. The construction of the

4. A fine study of Viking 'snekkja' off the coast. The spears and tjald were not normally to be seen when the vessels were under way, but are depicted with a purpose in this picture.

Viking ships was ideal for its purpose and resulted in the beautiful ships which can be seen restored in Scandinavian museums today.

The lines of these low hulls are quite beautiful and have not been bettered by any craft built since their time, whilst the manner of attaching the ribs gave them a flexibility in their build which allowed them to 'give' to the waves and not to break up, which would have been the case had they not had this inbuilt resilience.

The early Viking ships were not so large as those of the Greeks a thousand years previously, but they were more seaworthy. Although certain craft built for other purposes were larger, the majority were about 75 feet long and, although they had a single square sail right amidships, the evidence is that it not only could be, but frequently was, trimmed almost fore-and-aft. Certainly the Norse were good seamen and better oarsmen, while more dedicated to their task than those poor wretches who pulled the Greek galleys and, allowing for these points and assuming that there were generally 32 oars in a Viking ship, and estimating the total effort which the oarsmen would generate for a short burst in a calm sea, it can be adduced that they would have achieved a speed of about five knots. Research into records has shown that the usual sea speed of a voyaging Viking vessel would have been three or four knots under oars and up to eight or nine knots under sail.

In 1893, an exact copy of the famous Gokstad ship was sailed from Marstein, near Bergen, to Newfoundland, and it was claimed that this vessel, named the *Viking*, occasionally sailed at ten and eleven knots during the voyage. It must, of course, be acceded that the Gokstad ship was probably the private yacht (or barge) of a queen* and, perhaps, more lightly built than the fighting and trading ships, but her construction was similar to them. It is not without significance, when considering the lines of these craft, that no wake is apparent until a speed of three or four knots is achieved. Although they could be trimmed close up to the wind, there is no question that they *did* make a lot of leeway.

These vessels had no rudder and were steered by a large oar fitted on the starboard side, which has led to the supposition that the word 'starboard' derives from the 'steerboard', or steering oar. Notwithstanding the qualities of their vessels, the conditions aboard on long voyages must have been poor and uncomfortable for the men concerned, and only the fortitude and strength of character of the Norse would have prevailed for them to have accomplished the voyages they are known to have made. In the course of their predominence during the eighth and ninth centuries they harrassed the continent of Europe, parts of Asia minor, the British Isles, Iceland, Greenland and, finally, remote parts of Eastern North America. They were warlike and ruthless but, like most civilizations, ended by fraternising and settling in the lands they had invaded.

It was generally those from Norway and Denmark who went 'west-viking', but those from Sweden generally took the *Austrvegr*—

* Probably Queen Aasa, mother of the ynglinge Halfdan the Black.

5. *The stern of a Norse dragon ship, showing the 'styrboard' (Starboard).*

the Eastway—and, from Lake Ladoga, sailed southwards on the rivers of what is now Russia, generally along the Dvina and Dnieper, finally decanting into the Black Sea and proceeding thence to Micklagarda, as they called Byzantium, and sometimes proceeded on into the Mediterranean. One of the early invaders, who settled in Holmgard, was one Rus, who would doubtless have been astonished had he had any inkling of the vast expanse of the world's land-mass which was to come to bear his name.

At this period, little, if anything, was known of navigation as we know it today. Like the ancients in the Mediterranean, they generally confined their seafaring to the summer months and, whenever possible, they beached their ships at night, hauling them ashore on rollers

6. *Stern of a dhow at Karachi.*

7. *An Indian dhow under a settee sail (a lateen with a square leading leech) entering Colombo.*

which were standard equipment of their craft. Then was the *tjald*, or tent, spread over the lowered yard.

There are those who think original thoughts and who devise new ideas, and there are also those who are quick to copy and improve on the work of others. Some peoples of the earth became civilized before others, and their inquisitive minds enabled them to discover new things and spread their knowledge afar. If there was a need for something, such people would endeavour to find the answer to that need. Centuries ago, astronomy was amongst the interests of scientific people in the middle East, and it seems that this interest led to the development of the art of navigation by the Arab seamen who sailed their dhows on ocean voyages in days long past. They are known to have used a crude form of compass long before the adventurous seamen of Spain and Portugal made their first epic voyages, and the Arabs displayed a far superior knowledge of navigation at this time.

Although the emphasis of popular interest has always lain in the Viking 'long-ships'—the *snekkja, skuta* and *skeida*—which were built for raiding, the majority of the Norsemen's vessels were *kaup*—or cheaping (trading) ships, which ranged from the *knarr* (which might be used in raiding) though the *buja* and the *bydingr*, all these having a lower length-beam ratio; a higher freeboard (for bailing was the bane of the dragon ships) and being sailed rather than rowed. In fact, it was really only possible to row them from positions well forward and well aft, where there were oar-holes in the hull which did not exist in the midship (cargo) space.

Before these developments, the Mediterranean peoples had also built improved trading ships which, again, had a lower length-beam ratio than fighting ships (since, generally, the higher the length-beam ratio, the easier to drive the ship, although other factors can influence this greatly) and, in the early days of the Roman Empire, the *corbita*, which carried the Egyptian grain to Ostia, were becoming relatively large. Indeed, they did build a few outsize freak ships to bring back to Rome some of the Egyptian obelisks which weighed, in some cases, 500 tons and had a length of 130 feet, and also some 800 tons of lentils as ballast, which presumed a deadweight tonnage not achieved in Europe generally for nearly a millennium. In passing, it should also

8. A model of a Roman Corbita.

be remarked that, in days before heavy-lifting cranes, these obelisks not only had to be loaded into the vessels, but also discharged at Ostia—before being transported overland to Rome itself. It might be interesting to observe twentieth century man attempting such feats with the same equipment!

Speed in merchant ships was not held to be of paramount importance but, gradually, from the Roman *corbita*, with its single square sail, sometimes surmounted by *seppora* or, as we should term them, split raffees, and with its *artemon*, which was the forerunner of the spritsail, skills in using sails had become more sophisticated and embraced many varieties, some of which now had three masts and were capable of working better to windward. However, little or no scientific investigation had been made into ways to improve ships' forms, and nothing was known about the reasons why ships sailed upright. Indeed, some did not fulfil this function, and turned over!

Prior to 1746, the forces keeping a ship upright were believed to be the weight of the vessel herself acting through the Centre of Gravity in a downward direction and, of course, the forces of buoyancy acting upwards through the Centre of Buoyancy, which was supposed to be above the Centre of Gravity. After some thought on the part of those interested in this problem, it was realized that the Centre of Buoyancy was invariably *below* the Centre of Gravity of the ship and, therefore, that this simple and obvious theory on stability was false. Indeed, the problem remained unsolved until 1746, when Pierre Bouguer produced a theory which later became the basis of one of the most important aspects of ship design.

Until this time, ship-builders had coped with the mysterious and unknown problem of stability by simply copying ships which had already been built and which had proved to be successful in practice, but there were frequent disasters to prove that things could go wrong. A method frequently used to improve a vessel, which was found to be defective in regard to her stability, was to fasten a thick band of wood around her about the waterline. This band was quite deep both above and below the waterline and was called a 'wale'. It improved the stability and reduced the possibility of the ship capsizing. No doubt this practice was born of 'trial and error', simply because the true method of assessing stability had not been devised. There have been many instances of disasters caused by instability recorded, one of these being the *Wasa* and another the *Royal George*.

The ill-fated *Wasa* was a large new Swedish warship built in Stockholm, which was being moved out from a quay near the Royal Palace on Sunday, 10 August, 1628, to start her maiden voyage. It was a calm day with only a light breeze blowing as she moved across the harbour towards Södermalm. As she neared this place, a squall swept down and, although only a small number of sails were set, the ship heeled and, within minutes, sank, carrying with her almost all of those on board. The exact number of men aboard is not known, but the *Wasa* was a large ship of about 1400 tons displacement and some 180 feet long—twice as long as the *Mayflower* of 1620 which was estimated to be of about 400 tons displacement. The *Wasa's* complement is estimated to have been about 130 sailors and 300 soldiers, but it is also believed that there were considerably more people aboard than that. This terrible maritime disaster was witnessed by many people walking around the area, because it took place on a Sunday afternoon which must have been an occasion of festivity with one of the King's ships—and a large one for her day—leaving on her maiden voyage.

After over three hundred years, the *Wasa* has been raised from the floor of the harbour and has become a most interesting subject for researches into maritime history. A fine museum has been built around the hull where it now lies on the shore of Stockholm harbour, and the recovery is a story of great interest and demonstrates the ingenuity and dedication and courage of those who accomplished it.

The other well-known ship disaster, about which I recall singing when a boy at school, was the loss of the *Royal George*, with 'twice four hundred men'. This vessel, a large British warship, was lying at anchor near Portsmouth and was heeled in order to enable the crew to clean the ship's side below the water-line. This practice was a common one at that time and is still done today. To carry it out, ballast or weights, such as cannons, aboard the ship were moved across to one side in order to produce a suitable amount of 'heel', 'list' or angle of the centre-line with its normal vertical position, thus exposing part of the side normally below the water-line. When in this position, the side can be cleaned, repaired if necessary, and re-painted. This was the position in the case of the *Royal George* in a calm condition of wind and sea when, without any warning, she rolled over and sank. Nearly all her complement of 900 were lost, including her captain who, so the song went, '*was not lost in battle, his fingers held the pen*'.

These disasters could only have been due to lack of stability, or loss of it caused by sea water entering the ship through gun ports or other openings. Since 1746, knowledge has been gained and made available to the world on the subject of stability of ships, but this has not eliminated disasters from this cause. There have been several

9. A Chinese junk off Dalniy (Dairen) in 1921.

cases in this century when ships have capsized during launching, and of others which have turned turtle during service. These accidents have usually been caused by human error or neglect of duty.

Leonardo da Vinci (1452-1510), that genius of so many parts, painter and inventor, experimented with models of ships to try to improve the performance of their hulls. His deductions were not strictly true, but it took over four hundred years for anyone else to realise that his was a method which could be developed and used to reduce the resistance of water to ships' hulls. Hitherto, there had been many theories about how hulls should be shaped to produce the maximum speed through the water, and one form which had had a great deal of support for many years was fish-shaped, having what is sometimes termed the 'cod's head' and 'mackerel tail stern'. This implied that the forward under-water form should be rather full-lined (Cod's head) and fine-lined in the after part of the vessel. This theory was followed during the years in which it was in vogue, quite regardless of the speed with which this form could be associated. The fundamental laws for ideal ship forms were not discovered until the middle of the nineteenth century. For hundreds of years before that, ships were being constructed to various beliefs held by the different peoples of the earth and, for the most part, these beliefs differed as much as the peoples themselves. If a vessel had been built which had proved faulty in some way, the ship which was built after her was corrected in the manner thought to be most proper by those building her, but it did not necessarily follow that the second was any better than the first, because no knowledge was then extant on the subject of ship design, and such little as was known was based rather on experience and a certain mystique.

In 1768 a remarkable man named Fredrik Henrik af Chapman published in Stockholm a book he had written called *Architectura Navalis Mercatoria.* Chapman had been born in 1721 in Sweden, the son of Thomas Chapman who had emigrated there from Yorkshire and worked in the Göteborg Naval Dockyard. Fredrik Chapman's book on naval architecture covered his scientific approach to the design and construction of ships of all types, and was recognized to be outstanding in character, being translated and printed in French in 1779: in English in 1813; later in Russian and, finally, in German in 1864. He had enabled a very much better understanding of the subject to be spread through Europe and, although some of his work was not quite correct or developed in line with modern thought, he started a scientific approach to the problems which had lain almost dormant for centuries before his own time. Chapman summed up the matters he was trying to solve by saying (from the English translation):-

> *'In the construction of ships, people usually make attempts at different times to improve the form, each person according to his own experience; thus after the construction of one ship, which has been tried and found to possess such or such a bad quality, it seems possible to remedy this defect in another. But it often (not to say generally) happens, that the new ship possesses some fault equally as great, and frequently even that former defect, instead of being removed, is increased. And we are unable to determine whether this fault proceeds from the fault of the ship, or from other unknown*

circumstances. It thus appears that the construction of a ship with more or less good qualities, is a matter of chance and not of previous design, and it hence follows that, as long as we are without a good theory of shipbuilding, and have nothing to trust to beyond base experiments and trials, this art cannot be expected to acquire any greater perfection than it possesses at present.'

If Chapman had said nothing more than this in 1768, he would have benefited ship design and construction enormously, but he had much more to tell the civilized world about the subject, and he did so. His book is illustrated with extremely good drawings of such ships, with their lines and rigging, as were commonly to be found in the waters around Europe in his day. His thoughts on the construction of ships: methods of assessing displacements; ships' lines and stability and so forth are all clearly laid down. It is a fascinating book, which should be read by everyone interested in the subject of the history of ship design and building.

It must not be thought that no-one else was thinking about the science of shipbuilding at that time, but Chapman was one of the outstanding men of his day and has therefore been singled out for mention. Wooden ships were built to 'rule of thumb' or in the light of experience of those that had preceded them, been successful and had proved themselves to be adequately strong for their purpose. Investigations into requirements of strength became necessary when building in iron started at the beginning of the nineteenth century. Due to its use, ships could be made longer and more slender, whilst still retaining adequate strength. Furthermore, with the coming of steam a new need had arisen. The true resistance of water to ships had to be assessed in order that the power of the engines required to propel them at their required speed could be known. Many theories were put forward and, often, followed faithfully until disproved by later developments.

J. Scott Russell, who was the naval architect for the famous *Great Eastern* laid down in 1854, had a theory which was known as the Wave Line principle and was related to the shape of ocean waves. Alas! The theory was groundless, but it had many devoted followers until it was proved to be wrong. This period of faulty theorizing, experience and comparison with other ships, together with simple empirical methods, continued until there was a monumental breakthrough by William Froude in the latter part of the nineteenth century. He found methods of assessing the resistance encountered by ships by using models in a tank specifically designed for the purpose.

First of all he had experimented with clockwork-propelled models on a river and on a lake in the Lake District of England, and later used a tank near Paignton. Eventually he deduced a law of comparison between an actual ship and a model of her. This had been one of the greatest problems which had not been solved by anyone before the discoveries of William Froude. From that point he, aided by his son, R. E. Froude, developed and methodically recorded experiments on the friction of water over graded surfaces: on propellor design; the rolling of ships, and on other related aspects of the science of ship design and shipbuilding which, hitherto, had not been investigated in sufficient depth to be of real use.

It is now nearly a century since Froude produced his findings, but they have not been shown to be wrong and, indeed, whilst many have refined his methods, none have produced anything to replace his fundamental theories. Thus, unlike his predecessors in this field, he has been shown to have been correct in his tenets, even if certain small details were lacking and have been modified by a succession of followers. The model experimental tanks produced by Froude have been copied and improved upon in a number of places in the world, and these have become technical wonders backed by large, highly specialised staffs and fine workshops. Sophistication has become the vogue, but one could query why there is such a pursuit of the ultimate in refinement of ship hull shapes when one of the major causes of resistance remains unsolved. The increase of skin resistance due to barnacles and other marine growths on the underwater skin of a ship, together with the roughness caused by accumulations of bad painting, creates growth of resistance in service and a considerable slowing of the ship or, alternatively, a serious increase in the power required. In either case, the resulting deficiencies cause appreciable increases in cost, either directly or indirectly.

As the part of the total resistance to the movement of a ship through the water expressly due to skin friction (or 'working' of the sea against the hull) is about three-quarters of the total resistance in the case of a modern cargo ship, one can easily imagine how great a part the cleanliness of the hull plays in the cost of propelling her. It should be noted that skin resistance forms a smaller part of the whole in the case of a ship designed for, and travelling at, higher speeds than those usual for cargo ships.

The growth of fouling on the underwater hull and appendages of a ship takes place whether the vessel is moving, at anchor or tied up to a quay but, as one would expect, the speed of growth is greater when she is not moving. The growth is also quicker in warm waters than in cold and varies in different seas of the world. Some fouling is caused by the growth of sea-weed on the hull and other fouling by marine life such as barnacles and limpet-like creatures. Some of these, such as goose-barnacles, are tubular-shaped growths which festoon the lower part of the hull. A green weed, often called 'grass' by sailors, hangs on the ship's side below her waterline and grows profusely where it is lit by daylight passing down through the water. The effect of fouling on the speed of a ship is deleterious and expensive, and nowadays ships are dry-docked regularly to enable the hulls to be cleaned and painted; the intervals between such dockings varying, dependant on the conditions of service and the opportunities for carrying out the operation.

Sailing ships with wooden hulls were often sheathed with copper or lead, not only as a protection against the teredo*, but also to reduce the rate of growth of fouling, since the leaching of chemicals from the sheathing material killed much of the life in it. Today anti-fouling paints are applied to ships' hulls, and these usually contain copper-based chemicals which leach out of the paint and reduce the rate of fouling.

In the early days of the development of the West Indies, the sailing ships of the times were, of necessity, away from home ports for many months, and often for years at a time. In those waters, the fouling of bottoms became very bad in such long periods of service, and so an elaborate method of cleaning was used which was termed 'careening'. This operation is described in the *Glossary of Nautical Terms* at

* A mollusc which bores into the underwater hulls of wooden ships.

the end of this book, under 'Careen'. There was another and less efficient, if much easier, way of cleaning off the 'grass' below the water-line which was properly called a 'Parliamentary Heel', and it is this which has already been described briefly in connection with the loss of the *Royal George*.

Some readers may be coming to the private conclusion that much of the so-called science of ship design and construction consists more of mysticism or of a sort of witchcraft than of scientific thought. Perhaps, in truth, it *is* more of an art than a science. We have heard the simple explanations given for the writing of grand classical works by such giants as Beethoven, Brahms, Mozart and other composers. Those who analyse such works know exactly how it is done, but they cannot do it themselves. A brilliant surgeon knows how to take a body apart, but he cannot manufacture the parts and build one. There are many similar examples of this curious phenomenon. Many can explain how something is done, but few can do it.

It is certainly true that most of our knowledge of ships has been gained by the technique often called, in laymen's terms, 'suck it and see', 'trial and error', or, more fashionably, 'of empirical origin', but this could be true of almost everything which man has ever devised since he first existed. Evolution of animals, plants and of the very world itself has led to a condition which we accept as normal today but, equally, everything we use today is an expression of the evolution of that object itself, and ships fall into the same category—they are developments from ages gone by. Ship design is still something of an art, expecially in the more sophisticated ships, and the artist in man can still be seen in very small sailing craft. Reverting again to the Viking ships, the entirely non-functional but artistic serpent design can be seen in the high stern—the tail—and the higher, curving stem—the head of the serpent. There were so many ships with figureheads and stern and other carvings and, still used today after many centuries, we can see in sampans and junks of the East the sinister, or all-seeing, *oculi** painted on the port and starboard sides of the stem. Sailors are superstitious and religious by nature, and the adornment of their vessels through the ages has reflected these characteristics.

The sailor—and I refer to the man who worked his ship across

* Eyes.

the oceans—saw the elements at close range, and the dangers of the sea and storms were never far from his thoughts. He respected and feared them, and always prayed to his Gods for protection against these forces. Thus the figureheads and decorations about ships were generally vestigial indications of artistic endeavours by the sailor to placate and propitiate the gods in which he believed, to ward off the evils and dangers which threatened him and his ship. This decoration finally ceased to have any quasi-religious function and reached a stage in the seventeenth century when 'ginger-bread', as that elaborately painted carving is commonly known today, became overdone in its ornate and blatant extravagance. This excessive decoration on sailing ships persisted through the period of the Napoleonic wars on ships in European waters, but gradually decreased and only reached reasonable proportions at the beginning of the twentieth century.

Today, little decoration in the form of figureheads or the like can be seen in ships other than in such traditional craft as may be found in remote fishing harbours around the seas of the world, and in the craft of the more primitive peoples of the Earth.

I have now considered the beginnings of the scientific approach to naval architecture but, from these beginnings, refinements of methods and detail have been taking place constantly as time has gone by, and the skills have now reached a high standard of competency.

The steam engine was first used in ships to drive paddle wheels. This method of propulsion is very inefficient and, when a ship is at sea, the paddles become poorer as a means of propulsion as the state of the sea becomes worse.* Then, of course, the screw propeller was discovered and developed: its design and construction having improved with the improvement in knowledge and as better materials and manufacturing methods became available. Nowadays much more power per unit area of blade, together with improved design, have made the screw propeller reasonably efficient.

The transition from sail to steam was no 'overnight' affair, for the first steam engines and methods of transmitting power to propel the ships were very crude, unreliable and inefficient. In consequence, the first ocean-going vessels with steam used it as an auxiliary power to that of the sails. These early transition vessels did not carry enough

* Masters of the early screw tugs said they preferred the (older) paddlers, because they always had half their power in the water. This was true, but it was not so much power!

10. The figurehead of the latter-day square-rigger BEATRICE (ex ROUTENBURN).

coal to enable them to complete long sea voyages, which were only accomplished by using the sails when the winds were favourable, and the steam engine when they were unfavourable or non-existent. Another problem was the arrangement of coaling stations on, or close to, their routes and, often, these could only be arranged where islands were conveniently situated. The random positions of some of these stations usually necessitated the ship being diverted from the course she would have taken had the need for coal not been present.

When a ship with auxiliary steam power working a screw propeller was using her sails, the unused propeller created resistance to the sea and reduced the speed of the ship. Something had to be done, therefore, to allow this resistance to be reduced or removed altogether. The propeller could be allowed to revolve freely with the movement of the water over its blades or, better still, it could be lifted out of the water. This latter arrangement obtained in some ships, the screw being drawn up into a water-tight trunk built above it. A device of this sort was fitted in the famous Antarctic ship *Discovery* when she was built as late as 1901 for Polar research. The ship still survives, and the propeller and the means of stowing it can be seen easily, although this particular method was designed primarily to avoid damage to it when the ship was in ice. Nevertheless, the two-bladed propeller would have been raised when the ship was proceeding under sail in clear water.

The period of auxiliary steam sailing ships was at the time when the sailing clippers had been developed to their greatest peak of efficiency. They made long voyages and, at that time, completed them as quickly, and often more quickly, than these steam-sail competitors, but this state of affairs did not last. The reliability of the steam engine was improved and, as the output of power also increased, it followed that ships were soon being designed specifically for the use of the steam engine and only carried sails as an insurance against some unexpected mechanical failure. Another serious problem connected with the use of steam-engines in the earlier ships was the not infrequent fracture of the propeller shafting, or loss of propeller blades. This danger was reduced by the introduction of twin screws in later ships, whilst improvements in materials used in the construction of engine parts and associated shafts and propellers were taking place constantly.

Wrought iron was produced in 1782, but a few years elapsed before it was used to build a water-borne craft. John Wilkinson, an Iron-master and Engineer, in the face of strong criticism, made a barge of iron plating secured over a framework of elm wood which weighed about eight tons and was launched on 16 July, 1787. He must have been a very strong-minded and determined man, because the iron plating had to be fashioned by forging the plates from cast iron bars to a thickness of about 5/16ths of an inch. This barge, named the *Trial*, was used to carry castings on the river Severn and the Birmingham canal. It was so successful that Wilkinson built two more of iron. This venture did not start an immediate trend in the business of shipbuilding, but a claim could be made that Wilkinson had fathered iron ships. Indeed, iron was not accepted generally as a shipbuilding material until about 1850, although the first iron ship to be classed in Lloyds Registry was the *Sirius* in 1837. Incidentally, Lloyds first *Rules for Iron Shipbuilding* was published in 1855.

Iron had pronounced advantages over the traditional timber for the construction of ships. It permitted larger vessels to be built and the scantlings for an iron hull could be calculated with a degree of accuracy not possible with a wooden one. The iron ship offered a saving of weight of about 25% as compared with an equivalent wooden vessel. So the construction of iron ships continued to grow in volume and replaced wood altogether for the building of large vessels.

Steel production developed with the growing ability of industry to make steel from iron, and it was hardly surprising that a steel ship should have been built in Britain in 1858. Steel was costing about six times as much as iron per ton at that time, but enabled a further weight-saving to be made, for a steel ship was about 20% less in weight than an iron one of the same size. The appreciably higher cost of steel as compared with iron caused delay in the use of the former but, in 1877, Lloyds Register issued their *Rules for the Building of Steel Ships*. By this time, steel was roughly twice the cost of iron. Lloyds *Rules for the Building of Iron Ships* was issued with those for steel ships until 1894, but was then discontinued.

The introduction of iron and, later, steel into ship construction developed with some caution on the part of shipbuilders except in the case of a few adventurous spirits such as Isambard Kingdom Brunel, (1806-1859), whose name is known in so many spheres of engineering history and who, above all others, made history in the first half of the eighteenth century by building the iron vessels *Great Britain* and *Great Eastern*.

Brunel was a man who must have been arrogant, thrusting and fairly ruthless, but he had great imagination and thought in a most original way how to devise means to achieve the right answer to the engineering problems which always arose when contemplating the great works he initiated. He was the principal designer for all sorts of

11. *The SAVANNAH, of 300 tons, was the first steamer to cross the Atlantic in 1819 – with some assistance from her sails!*

pioneer engineering projects, including railways, bridges, tunnels, docks and harbours. I say 'principal designer' because I do not believe that any one man can design the whole of a large project. It must be the work of many assistants as well as the principal.

A man born in Canada but probably now a citizen of the United States, John Kenneth Galbraith, is a greatly respected and admired author and lecturer on social sciences and allied subjects. He is quoted as saying, in answer to the statement that he was a man

> *'with the courage to think big', 'Oh, but the world is not short of generalizers. We are cannibals and scavengers on the hard, detailed work of people in the specialised fields . . . . We owe them an immense debt of gratitude.'*

There is a saying that *the man who never made mistakes never made anything*, and so it is true to say that Brunel made mistakes and, because he was a 'big' man, he made big mistakes. He was also wise in that, if he saw a good and original idea, he did not disdain to copy it and, if possible, to improve upon it. When he was about to undertake the building of a large wooden ship in 1838, he saw and examined a small paddle steamer named the *Rainbow* when she called at Bristol. Her hull was built of iron. Brunel was impressed with this ship and so he changed the material from wood to iron in the vessel he was about to build, and at the same time increased her size. He later changed the method of propulsion, for which paddle wheels had been planned. Whilst the new vessel was in course of construction, the keel having been laid in 1839, a ship called the *Archimedes* visited Bristol, being propelled by a screw designed by Sir Francis Petit Smith. Evidently the performance of this vessel also impressed Brunel, because he then scrapped the planned use of paddles and decided to fit a screw propeller. Thus Brunel did not hesitate to adopt new ideas, and this is what any good designer should do. Incidentally he found that no shipbuilding company wanted to take the responsibility for building such a large iron ship—she was to be the largest in the world at that time—so he forced through the building of shipyard workshops and a dry-dock in order to build the ship, which was to be the *Great Britain*. It could therefore be claimed that Brunel was the man responsible for the building of the first workshops in the world for the construction of large iron ships. He was a great man but, no doubt, a difficult one with whom to work. This may be a suitable moment to refer in more detail to the ship which Brunel built at this time.

The *Great Britain* was a remarkable achievement in her day and created new standards in the design and methods of building of ships. There were innovations in her design such as the balanced rudder, the fabricated six-bladed propeller, a large tubular fabricated propeller shaft, and the four-cylinder steam engine and its toothed chain drive on to the propeller shaft. There were many other features of interest in this vessel which was so far ahead of her times. She had a commercial life of great variety and never failed to draw forth attention and admiration wherever she went. For many years of her active life she was a steam-sail ship, her sailing rig being changed on several occasions, having at different times six, five, four and three masts: she had one funnel, then two side by side, and then again only one. For most of her life she was basically a passenger ship, but became a cargo sailing ship with three masts after her machinery and passenger accommodation had been removed. She also changed ownership on a number of occasions.

The *Great Britain* was almost lost in her early days when she ran ashore in Dundrum Bay in County Down, Ireland. Her strong construction and the skill and ingenuity of a Scot named James Bremner, with others, enabled the vessel to be re-floated and sailed to Liverpool to be repaired. She sailed seven times to New York from Liverpool and thirty one times from Australia to England, also becoming a troop-ship during the Crimean War and Indian Mutiny.

As a cargo-carrying sailing ship she sailed round the Horn to San Francisco with coal and returned with wheat but, on the following voyage, she had the misfortune to run into very bad weather near Cape Horn and sustained damage to her rigging and hull, after her cargo had shifted and caused a bad list. She put into Port Stanley in the Falkland Islands for shelter and examination, but repairs were considered to be too expensive and too difficult, so the ship became a hulk for the storage of wool and coal. She lay there for fifty years before being moved a few miles to shallow water in Sparrow Cove in 1937. Here some holes were cut in the ship's bottom to allow her to sink to the sea-bed and become captive against further movement.

In recent times Dr. Ewan Corlett, a well-known Bristol Naval Architect, has taken a keen interest in the salvage of the *Great Britain* and, in 1967, wrote a letter on the subject which was published in *The Times*. From this letter began a movement to save the ship. She was surveyed by Dr. Corlett, who reported favourably on her condition. She had been strongly built and had survived the ravages of the sea and weather over the many years she had been lying derelict and neglected in the inhospitable Falklands. After much planning and effort, the vessel was brought back to England in 1970 and now lies in the Great Western drydock where she was built between the years 1839 and 1845 in Bristol. It should be noted that the normal life of a ship today is between twenty and thirty years! The *Great Britain* is being repaired and fitted out as a permanent exhibit to the public of one of the great ships of the past built by the famous engineer Brunel: a vessel which provided many of the basic ideas on which modern ships are designed and built.

The epic of the salvage of the *Great Britain* and her return to England and the original port of her building could be the subject of a very large, interesting and illuminating book.

Brunel had built the *Great Western*, a wooden steamship, to carry Atlantic passengers in 1838, but he followed that ship with the *Great Britain* in 1845 and with his other famous iron steamship, the *Great Eastern*, which was larger than the *Great Britain* and, indeed, the largest ship in the world at the time of her building: a position which she retained for forty one years until a longer vessel, the *Oceanic*, appeared. The displacement of the *Great Eastern* was not exceeded by any other ship for forty eight years after her launch!

This vessel was built at John Scott Russell's shipyard at Millwall on the Isle of Dogs by the River Thames. She was laid down in 1854 on a berth running roughly parallel with the river and about 330 feet from its edge. Originally the name of the ship was to have been *Leviathan*, but it was later changed to *Great Eastern*. She was 693 feet long overall: 83 feet beam; 118 feet wide over her paddle-boxes, and 58 feet in depth. Her gross tonnage was 18,915 and her loaded draft 30 feet. It was said that she carried four thousand passengers when full, but there is some doubt whether this figure was ever achieved.

The means of propulsion were interesting, being sails, paddle wheels and a single screw. She had four boilers raising steam to drive engines of 1,000 nominal horse-power which, in turn, drove a pair of paddle wheels. Six more boilers provided steam for the engine of 1,600 nominal horse-power driving a four-bladed screw 24 feet in diameter. There were five funnels and six masts which carried 6,500 square feet of sail. The *Great Eastern* was rated to have a speed of 14 knots.

Her building and fairly long life of service as a ship were marred too frequently by death, misfortunes and financial troubles. Perhaps 'misfortunes' could be better described as 'disasters'. As a passenger ship she seemed to be incapable of being financially successful in spite of the popularity which followed her throughout her life. Some ships seem to be dogged with misfortune or bad luck, and this vessel seemed to come into this category. Several men lost their lives during the building stages and, in 1856, there was financial trouble caused by under-estimated costs in construction. As a result, control was taken from Scott Russell and Brunel took charge of finishing the ship, although Scott Russell was still involved.

The launch was to take place on 3 November, 1857, and, as has already been stated, the vessel lay parallel to the banks of the Thames, for she was to be launched sideways. Because of her great length, there were many launchways and, to control the speed of launching and also to prevent one end of the ship sliding away quicker than the other, Brunel had arranged near each end of the hull a huge drum and its frame. These were called 'checking drums' and were wrapped with massive chains, the ends of which were attached to the ship herself. These checking drums were equipped with brakes operated by workmen. The launch was to be conducted by Brunel himself from a launching stage and a young lady, Miss Hope, the daughter of one of the owners, named the ship. As events turned out, 'Hope' was a suitable name for the sponsor for, as soon as the vessel started to move, there was disaster. The forward end moved away immediately, leaving the stern behind, but then it moved, in turn, causing the checking drum at the stern end to revolve and fling

12. Isambard Kingdom Brunel beside the checking drum which caused the trouble.

13. The first attempt to launch the GREAT EASTERN at Millwall.

the men attending the winch into the air. Five were injured, one fatally.

Brakes were applied and the ship stopped, only to become stuck on the ways, having moved about four feet. From then on there were many attempts made to launch the great vessel, as a result of which she finally entered the water on 30 January, 1858, ending an unfortunate chapter in her life, which was only the forerunner of many which were to follow.

On 9 September, 1858, the *Great Eastern* started her trial trip from the Thames along the English Channel, and was off Hastings when disaster struck her. There was a terrible explosion, apparently caused by steam valves which had been shut off in error, and a forward funnel and its surrounding deck were blown skywards, with a resulting loss of life and hideous burns from scalding steam.

Repairs were made, and the maiden voyage started on 17 June, 1860. The ship had been designed and built to operate to Australia, but her owners decided to run her to New York initially. In the event, this was found to lack viability financially, and the ship lost money. In 1866, her accommodation was taken out to stow telegraph cable, and she was used as a cable ship and laid 2000 miles of cable across the Atlantic to the United States. This was the first trans-Atlantic cable, and it seems that the *Great Eastern* had proved herself to be an excellent ship for this purpose. After this operation, she was chartered by the French Government to transport passengers from the United States to France for the Great Exhibition in London of 1867 and she left Liverpool for New York to this end. However, instead of returning with some thousands of passengers, as was hoped, she had to sail for Brest with less than two hundred, and the operation proved to be another financial disaster.

In the meantime, her original purpose of entering the Australian service was largely vitiated by the fact that the Suez Canal, which had been opened in 1869, was too narrow for her to pass through it, which put her at a great disadvantage since all the competing steamers on the same run were able to use this short cut. So the *Great Eastern* suffered her worst humiliation, and became an exhibition ship in the Mersey. There were fun fairs, side shows, advertisements, music hall shows, and the great vessel had become dilapidated to a point where (had she had life and feelings) her heart would have been broken.

Isambard Kingdom Brunel had died of a stroke in 1859 before the *Great Eastern* sailed on her maiden voyage. The troubles he encountered whilst the ship was being built cannot have helped him physically. As for the ship herself, she was finally broken up in 1888.

About that time, others were making haste more slowly than Brunel. Composite ships were being built: that is to say, vessels having a mixture of iron and wood in their construction. Often the hulls would be built of wood planks and the frames (or ribs) would be of iron angle bars or bulb angle bars bolted to the wood planking. The famous tea-clipper *Cutty Sark* was built in this manner, and can be seen today lying in her specially prepared dry-dock at Greenwich, where she lies preserved. This peerless vessel was launched in 1869 from her builder's yard, Scott and Linton at Dumbarton, but, since they became bankrupt, she was never finished by them but by Denny's, of the same town. Unfortunately she was built too late for the tea trade for which she was intended and in which she was not engaged for very long, because the Suez Canal was opened in the year of her launch and its advantages for steamers bound to the East shut out the competitive use of sailing ships for that purpose. However, she was used most successfully in the Australian wool trade from 1883 to 1895 and for ten of these years, with her famous master, Capt. Woodget, in command, was never beaten homeward bound to England by any other ship in the trade.

Sailing ships had carried passengers and cargo in competition with steam vessels but, latterly, they traded only in cargo and, in their last years, mostly bulk cargo, such as saltpetre or grain.* The Scandinavians (notably Gustaf Erikson of Mariehamn) and Laeisz of Hamburg, ran fine square-rigged ships until 1939, but the hey-day of such ships ended in the early nineteen-twenties with the post-war slump. These last big sailers could—sometimes—sail home from Australia in less than ninety days, but such performances were unpredictable and, often, their voyages exceeded one hundred and fifty days. This was acceptable for some cargoes but, obviously, passengers preferred to travel in ships which sailed to a tight schedule than in those which could not be relied upon to arrive on time. The sailing ships' days

* I use the term 'bulk' cargo in distinction from 'general' cargo. Of course, sailing ships did not carry grain or saltpetre in bulk, but in bags (though coal was carried in bulk). Generally such cargoes represented the sole commodity in any one voyage.

14. The GREAT REPUBLIC – the largest square-rigger ever to be built in the U.S.A. She caught fire loading her first cargo and was re-constructed in a less grandiose fashion.

15. The CUTTY SARK.

were numbered, and the era of the supremacy of the 'white swans' had ended when steam engine propulsion achieved reliability at sea.

The use of iron as a shipbuilding material continued whilst the making of steel was developed. The plates and bars of iron were joined together by riveting, and the sizes of plates were limited by the iron-makers' primitive means of manufacture. Because of the use of these small plates, the appearance of a ship's hull in those days, as compared with modern vessels, was almost as if postage stamps had been used instead of iron plates! Welding of pieces of iron was carried out by hammering them together after being heated in a furnace to the proper temperature.

This method of joining plates and bars, particularly the latter, had been used ever since iron was first discovered and smithed or forged. The same method continued to be used when steel replaced iron in the building of ships. For instance, to form a corner piece in a watertight riveted deck, an angle bar would be mitred and bent to the shape of the corner piece and then hammered, whilst heated to the correct temperature, so as to weld the cut flanges together. This angle-smithy work, as it was called, was only discontinued after the general introduction of electric welding in shipbuilding between 1930 and 1945.

The castings made in iron were unreliable because the material was inconsistent in quality and 'blow-holes' (or gas bubbles) formed during casting could seriously weaken the finished product, whilst not revealing the weakness to those examining them. At that period, the failure of bridges, locomotives and other engineering works carried out in iron was commonplace. However, this state of affairs did not last because vast strides were being made in the development of steel processing and, as steel became more available, it was used in shipbuilding. The rolling mills were built so as to produce plates bigger and more consistently to the required thicknesses, while, concurrently, shipbuilding processes were constantly improving.

Just before the second World War, a new method of joining steel parts together was devised and developed: welding by electric arc. Some shipbuilders were quick to adopt this and to apply it to their work but, as is usual with new ideas, there were failures, and the

16. The SOVEREIGN OF THE SEAS – a famous American clipper.

17. The PREUSSEN – the only five-masted full-rigged ship ever built.

successful use of electric welding was achieved only by sensible application or by the copying of the successful methods used by others. Nowadays, there are few shipbuilders who do not use welding in the building of steel ships. At one time, shipbuilding towns rang with the noise of riveting hammers, but this is now a thing of the past and shipyards now cause no more noise than would be heard near any other steel construction works. Other materials are also now used in the building of ships, particularly aluminium alloys, to which I shall refer later in this book. The design and building of ships to carry a large number of passengers only became a reality less than a hundred and fifty years ago. Before then there had been little demand for the movement of large numbers of people by sea, unless they were required to serve as soldiers or sailors to man the guns and muskets on board ships, or for other purposes of offence. In all these cases, the people being carried would live in great discomfort and, often, in deprivation. One hundred years ago, the so-called 'first-class' passenger would be provided with a certain amount of comfort but, from today's standpoint, of a poor standard. The second class, third class and, particularly, the steerage, had a miserable time but, because they usually came from conditions of poverty and were leaving their homeland to seek wealth or to better themselves elsewhere, the discomforts were accepted by stoical and, often, unhappy people. Apart from this compelling need to leave Britain or Europe, there were the gold rushes in the mid-nineteenth century to California and to Australia which created a great movement of would-be gold prospectors together with the ever-present 'hangers-on' who invariably make their appearance at such times.

It is hardly likely that the passenger on board ship today, using hot and cold fresh water from the taps over his wash-handbasin, his bath or from his shower fitting, ever pauses to think about where it comes from. Perhaps he never thinks about the source of water he uses and drinks when ashore, but possibly this is just as well. In modern passenger vessels, fresh water is usually made by a distilling plant in the machinery spaces, some seven hundred tons being produced each day from sea water in large passenger vessels. In the early sailing passenger ships, canvas rain-sails were arranged to catch the

18. *The brig-rigged Union Castle liner NORHAM CASTLE, built in 1863, taking the mails at Kingswear, opposite Dartmouth.*

rain, which was conserved in tanks and used very sparingly. Indeed, sea-water was used extensively for washing purposes for certain processes, such as potato peeling in the galleys or kitchens, in order to conserve the supplies of fresh water.

In the Atlantic between Europe and North America in the early nineteenth century, a sailing ship carrying passengers would provide cabins for only a few of the more wealthy of them and for the officers. These would also be fed by the Company, but the other passengers had to bed down wherever they could find room in the 'tween decks, and they also had to carry their own provisions for the duration of the voyage of some twenty days, more or less. There was no such aid to comfort as refrigeration to enable unsalted food to be carried for long periods, and it was usual on long voyages to carry live chickens, cows and other animals: some for the provision of eggs and milk: others to be slaughtered as the passage progressed, but these were only for the first-class table. Vegetables and fruit were eaten in varying stages of freshness or rottenness but, if the voyage was a long one, this difficulty could be alleviated by calls at ports *en route* to pick up fresh stores. In practice, this was seldom resorted to in the days of sail, and although it occurred with the rise of steam, would probably not have done so had there not been a need to make port to replenish the coal bunkers.

The development of water-making in ships was not good until after the second World War and, until then, the conservation of fresh water was of paramount importance. Water was distilled principally for use in ships' boilers because, strange as it may seem, boiler water requires much more care in its making than that for human consumption. This point is particularly true today, due to the greatly improved performance of steam plants and their boilers.

Until the 1950's, fresh water could be bought in quantity and quality at prices acceptable to ships at many of their ports of call. The generous use of fresh water for domestic purposes ashore had not become common in many parts of the world until that time but, as demands ashore increased and piped fresh water was developed on land, its availability for sale to ships diminished. This was particularly true of the smaller ports used by the very large cruising ships, because

19. The 42,348-ton Canadian Pacific liner EMPRESS OF BRITAIN sported the largest funnels and tallest masts of her generation.

large resorts for tourists were growing at these places, and the hoteliers were demanding the fresh water which had, hitherto, been available for ships. The consequence was that the ships had to find their own means of providing fresh water.

At that time, it was commonplace for large passenger vessels to carry 3,000 tons or more fresh water in their own tanks, but these would need to be replenished within a week. Supplies were becoming very difficult from the shore in many places, and prices were rising steeply while, in some ports, the water provided was brackish and unpalatable to the passengers, even when it had been treated and cleansed by the ships' purifying plants. Marine engineers quickly met the need and ships were provided with economical fresh-water making plants, using the sea water in which they sailed.

This can only be done so long as the sea water itself is not contaminated and, for this reason, distillation usually takes place when the ship is a suitable distance from land. (Storage tanks are built in the ships to provide a reserve for contingency purposes.) These water-making plants can only operate economically when the vessel is steaming at about ten knots or more and, the nearer to her cruising speed, the more effective is her water-making.

This chapter has only touched very briefly on the subject of ships and their development, and very much more could have been written. To have done so would have diverted the reader from the main purpose of this book, which is to describe the events which led up to the formation of a famous shipping line: of its fleet, of the design and building of a Queen—the *Oriana* and, finally, of the end of an era—namely: the reign of the great passenger liners. The dominant period lasted for about seventy-five years and, although some of them remain in service, few are fulfilling the purpose for which they were originally designed on regular routes, but are usually trading as 'cruising' ships. (A 'liner' is a vessel which, when in service, follows a regular programme of time on a given trade, and can be a cargo 'liner' or a passenger 'liner'.)

It would seem that all great things have an end, and I have lived through a period in which has ended the eras of the beautiful and graceful 'wind-jammers'; the magnificent and handsome steam locomotives, and now the dying phases of the great and very beautiful passenger liners. They are sad times for many of us.

II. THE ORIENT LINE—UNTIL 1939

As mentioned in the previous chapter, passenger ships in the nineteenth century were first of all sailing ships and followed by sailing ships with auxiliary engine propulsion and these, in turn, gave way to vessels primarily propelled by steam engines with auxiliary sail power until, finally, when steam engine propulsion had become reliable, they were propelled entirely by this means. The Diesel engine arrived on the scene at a later date, but that innovation does not affect the story of the Orient Line because their ships never used internal combustion engines.

Sailing ships were run to the West Indies and to Australia in the first part of the nineteenth century by the Andersons, though never in any recognizably regular pattern. This enterprise had been started by the London firm of James Thomson and Company which had, during the course of years, become Anderson, Anderson and Company and, finally, Anderson, Green and Company. I shall weave the threads of the family connections in another chapter but, in 1853, the Company had built a three-masted full-rigged ship of 1,030 tons called the *Orient*, which made a number of record-breaking trips to Australia and became the pride of their fleet.

Since the theme of this book is the Orient Steam Navigation Company, I am loath to divert myself into discussion of the sailing ships of the Orient Line which preceded it and which was a lineal forebear of the passenger steamship company. Nevertheless, these vessels were too illustrious to be passed over without any mention at all, and the *Orient* herself was a marvellously successful vessel. Like several of the Orient Line sailing ships, she was built at Rotherhithe (on the Thames) in the Nelson Dock by Bilbe and Perry, the former partner being the designer who was pioneering the use of diagonal framing in composite-built ships.

The Nelson dry- and wet-docks at Rotherhithe were, in fact, owned by Anderson, Anderson & Co., and James Anderson was an owner of the old school who took a very personal interest in his ships in much the same manner as 'White-hat' Willis who owned the *Cutty Sark* and other famous clippers. Bilbe's methods of construction were unusual insofar as the midship frames were perpendicular to the keel and quite conventional, whilst those extending forward and aft were increasingly raked away from the vertical, progressively more forward and aft respectively and at greater angles to the upright. Lloyds' surveyors were doubtful of this method, which the same builders applied to various other vessels at the same time, and they were offered varying classifications: that for the *Orient* being 7A1, which was declined by James Anderson and the ship was never classified.*

That did not alter a most successful career. Although intended for the Adelaide run, she was taken up for trooping at the start of the Crimean War as soon as she was completed and, after landing the 88th Connaught Rangers at Alma in 1854, successfully rode out the terrible gale which wrecked some 34 allied ships at Balaklava with the loss of over 1,000 lives. The next year she was being utilized as a hospital ship in the operations around Odessa and Kinburn, and it was not until the following year that she was released from Government service and finally on the berth for Adelaide, whither she ran regularly for the next twenty one years, making passages which varied from 72 days (in 1866) to 86 days (in 1870 and 1871) with the exception of the last of these, in 1877, when she was 104 days out. Her homeward trips were normally round the Cape, calling at Cape Town and St. Helena, though even then she averaged some 95 days for the passage over the span of the years.

In 1861 she caught fire at sea coming up from the Cape, and her passengers were taken off by a Dutch vessel which stood by her. After a long fight, the fire was got under control and she made Ascension Island where part of her cargo was discharged. On arrival back in

* In fact, Lloyds entered their classification in the Registers, and she was 5A1 in 1856, later C2, etc.

20. *The Anderson, Anderson clippers YATALA (left) and ORIENT (alongside, right) in Adelaide in 1871. The locally owned brigantine WILLIAM, built on Prince Edwards Island, is on the right of the ORIENT.*

England, a quantity of her timbers and deck planking had to be replaced but, otherwise, she had a very trouble-free life, despite her proposed classification and, on one occasion, in 1873, created quite a stir when Jock Willis (White-hat) came aboard before she sailed to ask Captain Mitchell, her master, to deliver the carpenter's chest, which had been left behind, to his clipper *Lammermuir* in Adelaide. Captain Mitchell said that he would not do that, but that he would deliver it before he reached the Line—a proud, vain and empty boast as one might think, since the *Lammermuir*, which was a noted flyer, had already been ten days at sea. Willis evidently thought so and immediately bet the master £5 that he would not succeed, but the fact of the matter was that the *Orient did* overhaul the *Lammermuir* some 300 miles north of the Line and duly delivered the chest, finally reaching Adelaide six days before the Willis vessel and beating her on passage by sixteen days!

In 1879 the ship was sold to Cox Bros, of Waterford and survived for many years as a coal hulk off Gibraltar.

Another famous Orient clipper was the *Heather Bell*, bought in from Brown & Co, for whom she had been built by Hall of Aberdeen in 1855. She was only 479 registered tons and measured 155′ × 28.3′ × 17.5′, and was running mainly to Melbourne and Sydney. (Most Orient sailing ships were on the South Australian run). It is recorded that this little vessel once ran from Port Phillip Heads, outside Melbourne, to the Horn in 26 days, which was truly remarkable for so small a ship. (The record for that run is held by the big Black Baller *Lightning* in 19 days), but she then ran up to the Line in 21 days, which was then a record and has only been since surpassed by the much bigger *Cutty Sark* and *Thomas Stephens*. She was not broken up until 1894, when she was in Sydney, after nearly 40 years of hard driving.

The last Orient ship to be built entirely of wood was the *The Murray*, also built by Hall at Aberdeen in 1861. This was a vessel of 903 tons, 180.3′ on her keel, with a beam of 33.3′ and a depth of 20.8′. Costing some £17 per ton, she was very sharp in her ends, although carrying a good cargo, and was also a fast vessel. Then, between 1863 and 1866, six lovely composite-built vessels were launched for the

21. The HEATHER BELL.

Company—the *Coonatto, Borealis, Yatala* and *Argonaut* by Bilbe and Perry in London, of 633, 920, 1,127 and 1,073 tons respectively, and the *The Goolwa* and *Darra* of 717 and 999 tons by Hall of Aberdeen. These were all out-and-out clippers of the times, and are said to have been driven hard and to have been very wet, but they *did* make fine passages and were most successful.

Those who are interested in sailing ship performances will not fail to be impressed by, for instance, the *Coonatto's* run from the Thames to the Semaphore (off Adelaide's River Torrens) in 66 days, nor by another of her outward passages of 70 days, despite broaching to off St. Paul's Island in the Southern Ocean *en voyage* when she lost her two helmsmen and her wheel overboard. These bare facts tell the tale of the sort of hard sailing which was involved. This vessel piled up just west of Beachy Head in 1876. The *Darra*, another vessel which seems to have achieved small space in the history books, also ran out in less than 70 days, and

22. The THE MURRAY.

the *Yatala* held the London to Adelaide (pilot to pilot) record of 65 days until it was finally eclipsed by the famous *Torrens*: a vessel in which Joseph Conrad later served as mate. The *Yatala* was lost in 1872 when she went ashore on Cape Gris Nez with a wool cargo.

Of course, there were others. Structurally, one of the most interesting was the *Red Riding Hood* which had been built by Thomas Bilbe in 1857, for she was the first that he constructed under a new patent which he had taken out in which the frames and beams were formed of two angle-bars set opposing each other to form a 'U' section and with timber laid between them. Indeed, she was probably the first of the composite ships* to be built in the yard and measured 709 tons, being run initially as a China tea clipper on Bilbe & Perry's own account and becoming very well known in that trade. With an under-deck block coefficient said to be 0.66, she was clearly very fine, and the composite vessels of this period proved able to take much

* Vessels with iron frames, beams, etc. but wooden planking.

23. *The COONATTO drying and sending down her sails.*

24. The THE GOOLWA, fresh from her builders yard.

more driving than their wooden predecessors. She was sold to Anderson, Anderson & Co. in 1876 but they re-sold her to Arab owners for £2,100 two years later and she was re-named *Iscandria*. By 1886, she was owned in Batavia as the *Barend-Christiaan* and was broken up in 1890.

There was the *Anglo-Indian*, built by Briggs of Sunderland in 1858 and owned in Shanghai by 1884: the *Belle-Isle*, built by Symons & Co. at Bristol and hulked in Dunedin in 1893: the *Eden* which, unusually for the vessels of this fleet, had been built in Quebec (by Baldwin & Co.) and which passed to Norwegian colours in 1884: the *Tropic*: the *Florence Nightingale*, another of Bilbe's creations: the *Witch of the Wave* which had been built at Teignmouth in 1858; the *Holmesdale*, built by Reid & Co. and commanded by Capt. Daniel Bolt until he took over the *Harbinger,* was not sold until 1897, and one of the most famous of all—the *White Eagle*—which had originally been

25. The s.v. ORIENT (left) and the WHITE EAGLE – two Anderson, Anderson cracks.

built by Alexander Stephens in 1855 and run by them on their own account. Indeed, this vessel had various owners in the course of her career, changing hands for nearly £16,000 when only just over a year old. She was very sharp forward and made some excellent passages, but was sold by Anderson, Anderson & Co. to the New Zealand Shipping Company who re-named her *Pareora*, in 1877, and she ran in the New Zealand trade until she was broken up in 1885. This vessel was built of iron.

The *Veronica*, a 332-ton barque had been built by Brocklebanks at Whitehaven for their own account in 1860 and had had a fairly colourful career before coming under the Anderson, Anderson house-flag. When running out to Hong Kong in 1862, she was only some 50 miles from port when the pilot spotted a pirate junk close to her in the moonlight. The captain fired a rifle through her mainsail and thus gained the element of surprise, whereupon the junk made off. The consequences could have been disastrous, particularly as she was carrying shot and ammunition. On arrival, a gunboat was sent south and brought in the junk, whereupon those aboard the *Veronica* had the satisfaction of seeing the pirates hanged in quick succession from the bough of a tree just opposite their anchorage. She had also been in the Hughli trade for Brocklebanks, who sold her to P. Walsh of Liverpool in 1874, and she only came under the Anderson, Anderson ownership in 1884. Doubtless she was rather too small for them, because they sold her two years later for £2,100 to W. Robertson of London but, in 1888, she was sunk in collision with the barque *Marquis of Worcester* off Port Nolloth on the South African coast.

This is just the bones of the story of the sailing ships of the company. They, alone, could fill a book, and it will be noted that, as is so often the case, many bore names which were carried by other vessels, so that it is easy for confusion to arise. The company also owned a small screw schooner-rigged craft of 97 tons in this period, named the *Woodburn*. Little seems to be known of her, though it is a safe presumption that she was used on the Australian coast.

Oddly, some sailing ships seem to have caught the popular imagination of historians whilst others, whose performances and successes were just as good, seem to have avoided mention in the Rolls of Fame. Certainly the passages of these vessels compared very favourably with, for example, the much bigger and heavily publicized Black Ballers and also with the great run of superlative clipper ships trading to Australia at that period, and in appearance they were the equals of any of them. However, the Orient was a relatively small company and, doing very well, possibly saw no need to court publicity in the manner practised by some owners.

The last of their vessels to survive in trade is probably the best known, if for somewhat different reasons. This was the iron clipper *Hesperus*, built of iron by Robert Steele in 1873 with her sister, the *Aurora*. Regrettably, this latter vessel was lost on her first homeward passage, since she caught fire in the North Atlantic when fire broke out due to the spontaneous combustion of her wool cargo, and had to be abandoned after her fore and mainmasts had crashed down and the ship was well alight, during August, 1875. Both she and the *Hesperus*

26. The saloon of the HARBINGER.

were magnificently fitted and maintained, with a great deal of brass-work and teak fittings, almost like yachts, and, although it is said that the *Hesperus* was never driven, she was indubitably a very fast vessel but, in the light of the reputation for driving which had accrued to her predecessors, it seems most likely that this story has grown up chiefly because she invariably made the Cape passage home, rather than via the Horn, although it does appear that the later (iron) clippers were sailed more easily with more thought given to the passengers' comfort. These two vessels were of 1,773 tons and, therefore, much bigger than their predecessors, and were also lofty in their sail plans. The *Hesperus* crossed skysails in the tropics, but did not normally keep the yards crossed at other times. Three years later, in 1876, Anderson, Anderson & Co., went to the same builders for the *Harbinger*, which was slightly smaller, at 1,506 tons, and which was the last sailing ship to be specifically built for the passenger trade. This was another very

27. The HESPERUS became well-known as a Devitt & Moore training ship.

fast vessel, and one with a good deal of character, for she, too, was extremely lofty, even by the standards of much later and larger square-riggers, since her main truck was 210 feet above the water-line, and she, unlike the *Hesperus*, did keep her skysail yards crossed. She was also iron-built, and is supposedly the only iron ship to have had outside channels, whilst, unlike the majority of British vessels, she carried a large hoisting spanker (which was so common in American square-riggers) but no sail bent on the crossjack yard. She was easily recognisable for these features alone, but she also had a flying jibboom, which was unusual in vessels of her date, and set a whole battery of headsails. For all her height and large sail plan, and like the *Hesperus*, she proved to be very stiff and was also a potentially fast vessel. Indeed, Frank Bullen, the well-known sea-author, served in her as second mate and some of his writings refer to her. He recorded, *inter alia*, that she was the only vessel in which he had had any experience that would stay* under reefed topsails and reefed foresail in a gale of wind, and he reckoned her to be a beautiful vessel to handle.

Both the *Hesperus* and the *Harbinger* are far better known than most of their predecessors in the Company, though this is possibly because they were both bought by Messrs. Devitt & Moore† in 1890 to operate under the training scheme which they operated and which had been proposed by Lord Brassey. These were some of the most successful sail-training ships ever run—and I use the word in contradistinction to the modern 'school-ships' which are merely 'drill' vessels, for the sail-training ships still carried cargo (though not passengers) and thus gave a number of boys an excellent grounding for a career at sea in a way a that was normally denied to the run-of-the-mill apprentice. The *Harbinger* was commanded by Capt. Daniel Bolt, who had formerly been in the Black Ball Line, both before and after her sale, and she still continued on the Australian run until she was sold to Raumo owners in Finland in 1898 and re-named *Solglimt*, finally being broken up in Antwerp in 1910.

The *Hesperus* was sold by Devitt & Moore a year later, in 1899, to the Odessa Navigation School and run as a Russian training ship in the Black Sea with about 160 cadets and no cargo but, after the first world war, she made some more commercial passages, being named

* i.e. 'Tack.'

† Thomas Lane Devitt, son of one of the two founders of Devitt & Moore, and who was known as the 'Grand Old Man of the City of London', had been a partner of Frederick Green & Co. for some forty years when they amalgamated with Anderson, Anderson & Co. and continued to play a major part in the fortunes of the Orient Line.

Grand Duchess Maria Nikolaevna while under Russian ownership, and made one passage from Quebec to England with lumber in which the well-known marine historian F.W. Wallace was passenger and subsequently wrote a book about this short voyage*. Soon after this she was sold to a London based firm and re-named *Silvana*, being sent to load salt in Spain for the Argentine, after which she brought maize home. Both loaded voyages were very long, the outward one finishing with a long and expensive tow, and, much cut down in her rig by now, she took 117 days from Buenos Aires to Bordeaux, after continuous calms, and was being quoted on the re-insurance market. Her owners had lost money on the voyage and the slump was gaining ground on the world economy, so she was towed from her discharging port at Bordeaux to Genoa, where she was broken up. It was a sad finale to a very glorious career, brought about by a financial condition and through no failure of the ship, which had been thoroughly re-fitted at Wallsend in 1913.

These splendid clipper ships set a standard of performance and reliability which must have formed a basis from which the Orient Steam Navigation Company (Orient Line), as I knew it in the 1950's, eventually emerged and, of course, although this book does not set out to deal with sailing ships except to round off the whole picture, it will not escape notice that the early steamships of the company were running in parallel with its clippers. The newly constituted Line had been named after the favourite ship of one of the two founding firms of shipowners.

The first interest of Anderson, Anderson & Co. in running steamships to Australia came to the public notice long before the founding of the Orient Line, when they advertised in *The Times* on 7 February, 1874, that the 1,489 tons wooden auxiliary *Easby* was to be sent via the Cape to Port Phillip in Australia on 28 March, 1874. This ship was followed about seven months later by another, the 3,541 ton *St. Osyth*, an iron screw vessel, which completed her voyage to Melbourne in 42 days after calling at Plymouth and the Cape. Thus the first essay of the firm in steam vessels became known to the world.

Amongst the other firms of sailing shipowners which was

* *Under Sail in the Last of the Clippers*

examining the potential of steamships for the Australian trade was that of Frederick Green and Company, which had a close association with R. & H. Green, shipowners and shipbuilders on the Thames at Blackwall and who, as will be mentioned, had become famous for their so-called Blackwall Frigates. In 1872, Frederick Green & Co, in their own name but acting on behalf of R. & H. Green, loaded and despatched to Sydney their first steamship, the 1,255 ton *Siracusa* from London. Two years later they formed an association with Anderson, Anderson and Company to send the *Easby* to Australia.

This voyage of the *Easby*, with that of the *St. Osyth* which followed, evidently satisfied the charterers and led to the formation of the Orient Steam Navigation Company in 1878. Prior to that date, however, Anderson, Anderson & Co. and Frederick Green & Co. in 1877 jointly approached the management of the Pacific Steam Navigation Company, which had a substantial fleet of steamships trading to the West Coast of South America. At that time the South American trade could not employ their whole fleet and some of its units were actually losing money. The outcome of this meeting was that the P.S.N.Co. agreed to turn over some of their surplus tonnage to a new passenger and emigrant service via the Cape to Australia, while Anderson, Anderson & Co. were to load the four steamships which had been earmarked for this purpose for a voyage each to Australia and back, with a guarantee of earnings and an option to purchase if the project proved itself to be successful.

The first three of these vessels, s.s. *Lusitania* (3,825 N.R.T.); s.s. *Chimborazo* (3,847 N.R.T.) and the s.s. *Cuzco* (3,845 N.R.T.), were advertised in March, 1877, to sail in June, August and September respectively from London to Melbourne and Sydney, Australia. They were advertised as 'Orient Line', and as . . .

> '*magnificent, full-powered steamships belonging to the Pacific Steam Navigation Company.*' The steamers were: '. . . . *of 3,000 horse power effective and are expected to make the passage in 40 days. Their accommodation for passengers is unsurpassed and their appointments throughout are of the completest character. Passengers will be embarked by steam tender at Gravesend and Plymouth.*'

The *Lusitania* was the first ship away and *did* make the outward

28. *The CUZCO lying off Gravesend.*

voyage in 40 days and 6 hours, which was quite a feat at that time since she beat the previous record by ten days. The ships returned home through the Suez Canal, which had been opened in 1869. As a result of these three voyages (the fourth ship had not, in fact, been provided by the P.S.N.Co. and her place had been temporarily filled by the Dutch steamer *Stad Amsterdam),* it was decided by the associates, Anderson, Anderson & Co. and Frederick Green & Co., to exercise their option to purchase the four vessels from the P.S.N.Co. and, to achieve this, the Orient Steam Navigation Co. was formed with a capital of £44,642 in 1878.

The fourth ship, the s.s. *Garonne* (3,876 N.R.T.), did not sail for her new owners until after the new company was formed and was thus the first vessel of the Company to fly the new Orient houseflag. A decision was made to run a monthly service but, in order to ensure

29. The GARONNE with . . . . . .

30. . . . and without her mainyards crossed.

regularity against breakdown or other contingencies, yet another steamer, the s.s. *Aconcagua* (4,105 N.R.T.) was chartered from the P.S.N.Co., though she retained her registration with her owners and her own company officers throughout the period that she was operated by the Orient Line. In 1879, the service became four-weekly instead of monthly, and the P.S.N.Co. began to take a greater part in the service.

The slang word 'Posh' was, until recently, popularly used in reference to the 'grand' manner of living and its philological origin is not only apt to be overlooked, but is quite interesting, since it is formed from the initial letters of the words: '*Port Outwards, Starboard Home.*' Experienced travellers through the Red Sea and Indian Ocean had quickly learnt that the conditions of heat aboard would be more endurable if they had a cabin on the Port Side outward bound and on the starboard side coming home since, at the time that the word 'Posh' was coined, passengers had little, if any, mechanical ventilation to improve their lot in the ships of the time.

None of the vessels being used for this Australian service had been specifically designed to meet its needs, but in 1879 the Orient Line placed an order for a vessel to be built to their own requirements and, as a result, the s.s. *Orient* was delivered by her builders, John Elder & Co., in that year. She was equipped with a complete outfit of sails, although by that time the reliability of steam propulsion had improved to the point where sails could be regarded as being of secondary importance. She was a large vessel and second in size only to the *Great Eastern* which was still the largest ship afloat in the world at that time. Moreover, the *Orient* was not only the first vessel to be equipped with electric light, but the first one in the Australian trade with refrigeration facilities. She also had a promenade deck for passengers, which represented an innovation, whilst her oval drawing room, which was rather wasteful in space, had a well looking down into the dining room which had heavy tiles let into its ceiling. It seems that, when the ship first struck bad weather, some of these became dislodged, to the peril of the diners, who completed the voyage under a net canopy into which the odd tile occasionally dropped!

In this year, by agreement, the P.S.N.Co. introduced additional

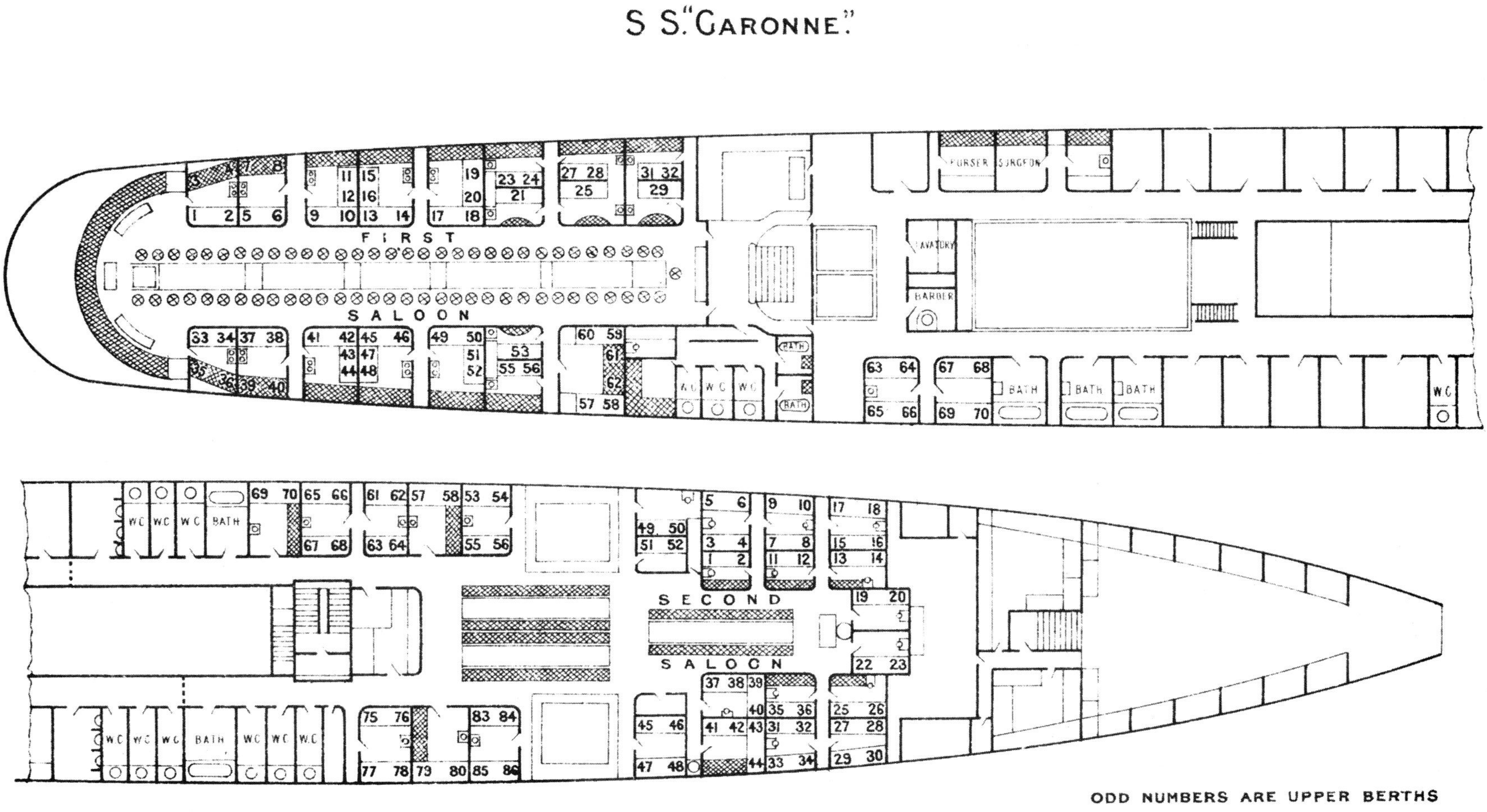

31. Cabin plan of the GARONNE.

32. s.s. ORIENT off Gravesend.

steamships into the trade, carrying their own house-flags and retaining any earnings, while the Orient Line acted as brokers and managers for this joint service. These additional vessels made it possible to run a fortnightly service, and the first sailing under this new arrangement was in December, 1879.

Two years later, in 1881, a new vessel, the *Austral* (5,524 N.R.T.) was built to join the fleet, being the first steel ship in the Company and outclassing her predecessors. Unfortunately, she had an unlucky second voyage, because she suffered engine trouble on the way south to the Cape and, when she arrived there, was detained for a week due to an outbreak of smallpox ashore. There was more engine trouble after she left South Africa and, for once, the sails were set to enable the ship to continue whilst repairs were effected. (Sails were normally set with a fair wind to provide additional 'push' or for steadying purposes, but it was rare for them to be providing the sole motive power.) The ship's misfortunes continued and, when in Sydney on 11 November, 1882, she developed a list which caused flooding through her coaling ports, as a result of which she sank on an even keel to the bottom of the harbour with the loss of four lives. However, she was raised in

February of the following year and, after temporary repairs, sailed back to the Clyde for a major re-fit, after which she was chartered to the Anchor Line for a short period.

Hitherto, the Orient Company had operated without the valuable aid of any mail subsidy, but this position changed in 1883 when, after negotiations with the Government of New South Wales, it won a share of the Australian mail contract. From then on, their mail steamers were sent through the Suez Canal, both homeward *and* outward bound, in order to save time and to meet the stringent delivery requirements of this mail contract. In this connection, it had been shown that steamships with auxiliary sail power had found little difference in sailing time to Australia between the Suez Canal and Cape routes, although there was about 550 miles greater distance using the latter. The fairly equal time in sailing to Australia was due to the favourable winds and the Westerly Drift across the southern part of the Indian Ocean, but this state of affairs was far from true when coming in the opposite direction, and it was for this reason that, until the mail contract was gained, Orient ships travelled out by way of the Cape and home through the Suez Canal. Another factor which came to favour Suez was the possibility of picking up valuable freight at Colombo, homeward bound.

Since the mail contract required the regular and timely delivery of mail, no delays could be permitted by the Company, and their first problem in this respect revolved round the matter of obtaining coal supplies at Aden. The P & O Company, which at that time was a rival of the Orient in the Australian trade, controlled the coal supplies at Aden which they had founded, both as a port and coaling station. Naturally, they were not prepared to be very helpful to their opposition! To overcome this difficulty, the Orient Line arranged to have its own bunkering station on Diego Garcia, an atoll in the Chagos Archipelago some 2,000 miles to the south-east of Aden, and this arrangement lasted for the period 1882-8, after which it became more convenient to use Aden, which became available to the Company when the Australian mail service came to be shared between the two companies. A regular call was also made at Colombo for coaling purposes. It is, perhaps, worth noting that the P & O mail

33. The ORMUZ with her square yards crossed and . . . . .

contract was with the British government, and that of the Orient with the Australian government.

Another problem associated with fulfilling the mail contract on time lay in the Suez Canal itself, since delays could be encountered there. After representations to the Post Office authorities, the 'Royal Mail' pendant was instituted so that it could be flown by mail steamers to enable them to obtain priority in their passage through that stretch of water.

In 1883, the Orient Line signed a contract with the Government of New South Wales to carry emigrants from the United Kingdom, and its main terms are of interest today, for the Company was paid £15 per head for numbers up to four hundred, and £14 10s for numbers between four and six hundred. Five years later, in 1888, it was reported in a London periodical that an Orient liner had landed in London a consignment from South Australia consisting of apples, pears, grapes, oranges, quinces, lemons, melons and pomegranates, and it is clear that all this must have been carried in cold storage or it would otherwise have putrefied through the tropic passage.

The *Ormuz* was built for the Company in 1887 and was some 500 tons larger than the *Austral.* Both ships were luxuriously decorated by Stevenson* and, in the light of the recent resurgence of interest in

* see p.323

34. . . . . later in life when she no longer bent auxiliary sail.

Victorian painters, it is interesting to note that her deck saloon (measuring 42′ × 20′) contained original works by such artists as W.L. Wyllie, John O'Connor, J. Pettie, Colin Hunter, J. MacWhirter and Napier Hemy, etc. Then a new ship called the *Ophir* entered the service in 1891, and was of 6,800 tons register having, amongst other interesting features, twin screws, two funnels and two light pole masts.

It has been stated that the boiler rooms of this vessel were spaced widely apart so that, for reasons of safety, the engine rooms could be fitted between them. This was a half truth, since the fact of the matter was that the *Ophir* was one of the first vessels designed—if not the very first—for possible conversion to an armed merchant cruiser in time of war, and her boilers were so separated in order to reduce the possible effects of shell fire if and when acting in this role, which finally did come about in 1915. This practice has been perpetuated in naval vessels to this day.

When seen in profile, the effect of having her two funnels so wide apart, together with the marked rake of her pole masts, made her look very different from other vessels of her time. Beauty is a matter of taste, but I consider that she was a very handsome vessel. She had been designed to be able to do without sails, for the improvement in engine design, coupled with her twin screws, had dispensed with the

35. The first class dining saloon on the upper deck of the ORMUZ.

need for sail power once and for all, and this was amply demonstrated on her first voyage when she developed some machinery trouble but was nevertheless able to continue on her way with one propeller shaft until the necessary repairs had been made.

The mail contract had been reduced to a time of 31½ days by 1898 and, in this period, the *Ophir* had proved to be a very popular vessel on the Australian run, attracting a big following of passengers and being known as the 'Queen of the Indian Ocean'. On the other hand, she was not successful economically because she consumed over 120 tons of coal a day when she was at sea. In 1901, she was chosen to be the 'Royal Yacht' to take the Duke and Duchess of York* to Australia for the opening of the first Commonwealth Parliament.

The combined service to Australia run by the Orient and the P.S.N.Co. used the Orient name until it was called 'Orient-Pacific Line'

* Later, of course, King George V and Queen Mary.

36. The ornate and heavy furnishing in the drawing room and library of the first ORMUZ.

in July, 1901, and this title remained until 1906 when the P.S.N.Co. sold its Australian fleet to the Royal Mail Steam Packet Company, and the Australian service was re-named 'Orient-Royal Mail Line'. It is abundantly evident from the records that the new partnership was an unhappy one. The Royal Mail Company evidently wanted a large share in the organisation and, finally, in July, 1907, gave notice that they intended to withdraw all the former P.S.N.Co. ships from the Orient-Royal Mail fleet in eighteen months time. This withdrawal was undertaken in order that the Royal Mail Company could tender against the Orient Line for a mail contract, which they duly did, although they were not successful.

The Orient Steam Navigation Co. was now faced with a most serious decision, since it was confronted with the alternatives of either having to cease to provide the mail service or, indeed, any regular form of service to Australia, or of having to provide, through its own resources, ships to replace those which its former partner was withdrawing. A huge, sudden capital outlay was required if the second course was to be pursued and, with commendable courage, whilst taking a grave risk, the Orient Line decided to take this bold step but, because new capital could not be raised quickly on the scale required, the directors even pledged their personal credit in order to build no less than five passenger steamships of 12,000 registered tons*. It will have been observed how the size of ships had been gradually increasing, but these were to be bigger by far than the largest vessel in the fleet at the time. The Orient Line managers also persuaded one of the shipbuilders to construct one of the ships free of all charges. This additional credit helped to finance the other vessels and, finally, to pay for the one supplied free of charges. This information was provided recently by Ford Geddes, who had learned of it from his father, Irvine C. Geddes, one of the managers of the Company involved in this venture.

This firm decision on the part of the directors of the Orient Company enabled the regular fortnightly sailings of the Line to continue when the Royal Mail Steam Packet Company withdrew their ships from the Orient service. The last sailing of a Royal Mail vessel in the Orient-Royal Mail Line took place when the *Ortona* left London on 30th April, 1909. Thereafter the Orient Line reverted to its original name.

The five new ships set new standards in passenger accommodation and were both larger and, with a speed of 18 knots, a little faster than their P. & O. rivals (and partners) in the Australian mail service. They had twin screws, two masts without yards and two funnels which, for the first time in the fleet, were fitted with the Admiralty-type black cowl tops which distinguished ships of the Company until the Line lost its identity in 1960. Then another vessel was ordered, and sailed on her maiden voyage in November, 1911. Named the *Orama*, she was of 12,927 gross tons and bigger than the previous five vessels, with three screws but the same service speed of 18 knots. The machinery of the *Orama* was of the 'combination' type: the triple expansion engines on each of the outer shafts exhausting their

* *Orsova, Otway, Osterley, Otranto* and *Orvieto*

steam into a direct-coupled low-pressure steam turbine on the centre propeller shaft. The *Orama* was the only unit of the fleet which ever used this type of machinery, because improvements in the steam turbine caused the latter to be chosen for vessels built for the Line from then onwards.

By this time the Company had nine ships of which only one, the *Ophir*, was over twelve years old. The service had earned a splendid reputation for reliability and was very popular with passengers on the Australian route. About this time, the usual itinerary was from Tilbury to Plymouth, Gibraltar, Marseilles, Naples, Port Said, Colombo, Fremantle, Adelaide, Melbourne and Sydney. (Tilbury had been used as the London terminal since 1887.) The fortnightly sailings, alternating with the P. & O. ships, continued for the three years before the Great War which started in 1914 and brought with it the inevitable interruption of services and involvement with hostilities.

The first of the fleet to go into war service was the *Orvieto*, which was commissioned as a mine-layer, though later converted to an armed merchant cruiser. The *Otranto* and *Orama* were also commissioned as armed merchant cruisers before the end of 1914, and the *Ophir* and *Otway* followed in 1915. This left only four ships under the control of the Company but, unfortunately, the Australian government wanted the *Orsova* for trooping in mid-1915 and, although she was returned to her owners in May, 1916, the British government requisitioned her again at the end of that year. The *Orontes* was also taken over later in 1916 for trooping and then, in January, 1917, the *Orsova* was torpedoed in the English Channel, but she was able to be beached in Cawsand Bay and was later taken into Plymouth where repairs were completed in 1919.

In June, 1917, a scheme was introduced by the British government for liner requisition, and two more of the Orient fleet were taken into service as troopers. This left the Company without any vessel in the Australian service. At the same time, as could be expected, their ships suffered losses in government service. In addition to the damage to the *Orsova*, the *Otway* was sunk in July, 1917 while the *Orama* met the same fate in October of that year when off the south coast of Ireland, and, in May, 1918, the *Omrah* was sunk off

Sardinia when serving as a troop-ship. Later in 1918 the *Otranto* was in a convoy bound from New York towards Liverpool and came into collision with the P. & O. steamer *Kashmir* in the Irish Sea. The *Otranto* was very badly damaged and, without power, drifted on to the shore of Islay, where she became a total loss with a very heavy loss of life—four hundred and thiry one souls, including American servicemen.

The *Ormonde* was on the stocks, building, when the war started, but work had been discontinued at that time. However, by 1917, the loss of merchant tonnage had brought about such a shortage of ships that work was re-commenced and she was hurriedly completed as a troop-ship and entered service in that role in June, 1918. The *Ormonde* was of 14,982 gross tons and the first ship in the Company to be fitted with geared turbines, and also the first in the fleet to have a 'cruiser' stern. After coming through the final stages of the war unscathed, she was fitted out with accommodation as a passenger liner.

Peace came in November, 1918, but, like all shipowners at that time, the Orient Company had to wait many months before their regular service to Australia could be resumed for, until September, 1919, all passenger accommodation remained under government control. After that time there was a gradual improvement in conditions and the Company struggled to its feet again.

The structure of the Orient Company was changed in 1919 as, in that year, the controlling interest was purchased by the Peninsular and Oriental Steam Navigation Company. After this, the Anderson partners held 49% of the ordinary stock, whilst the remaining 51% was taken up by the London shipbrokers, Gray, Dawes & Co., on behalf of the P. & O. group. There was no outward change in either the ships or the operation of the Orient Line, and its management continued to be vested in the hands of Messrs. Anderson, Green and Company, as it continued to be called.

After the first Great War was over, the Orient Company had only five steamships of the original fleet so they bought from the Government three ships taken as prizes which had formerly belonged to the Norddeutscher Lloyd, as an interim measure. The *Köningen*

37. The newly completed ORMONDE, camouflaged with dazzle-painting, leaving the Clyde in 1917.

38. The OTRANTO (II) built in 1925.

Luise (11,103 G.R.T.) became the *Omar*; the *Prinz Ludwig* (9,764 G.R.T.) the *Orcades*, and the *Zeppelin* (14,588 G.R.T.) became the *Ormuz*, these three vessels being used in the Orient Line for between five and eight years until replacements could be built to suit the Company's service and requirements. Orders were, in fact, placed in 1922 for three new ships, each of about 20,000 gross tons.

Two of these vessels, the *Orama* and the *Otranto*, were ordered from Vickers Ltd. of Barrow-in-Furness: a firm which had never built passenger ships for the Orient Line and whose experience in the building of large passenger liners was very limited, although the firm had become widely known as builders of warships for the Admiralty and for foreign navies. In 1922, Vickers had no ships on their order books and desperately wanted to obtain the work of building these vessels for the Orient Line. The townsfolk of Barrow were practically destitute, because they relied for their living on the work provided by Vickers, and hundreds of workers had been unemployed for four years because that firm had no work for them.

In order to obtain work, the shipbuilding company put in a very low tender price for the ships the Orient Company planned to build. Messrs. John Brown, of Clydebank, had previously built vessels for the Company and were good and reliable builders who also tendered

39. The first class dining saloon of the OTRANTO (II) – a popular conception in height which is no longer permissable under modern regulations.

for these new ships, while there was also an unsuccessful tender from Messrs. Cammell Laird, of Birkenhead. The Orient Line managers had the choice of an unknown—to them— shipbuilder offering a very attractive price for the ships, or a good and tried one with a much less attractive tender, so they made something of a 'belt and braces' decision by placing an order for two ships with Vickers and an order

40. First class reading and writing room in the ORAMA.

for a third vessel, the *Oronsay*, with John Brown. At least one of the ships would be a good one! As events proved, the decision to build at Barrow was significant for both shipowner and shipbuilder and started a long association between the two companies which resulted in the building of ten large passenger liners for the Orient Line, and was probably indirectly responsible for the building of many P. & O. vessels at the same shipyard.

Some shipbuilders adopted an attitude towards the shipowner of knowing more than he did about what is needed in a passenger ship. This was not the case in the relationship between Vickers and the Orient Company in 1922, possibly because Vickers were trying to learn the business of passenger liner building, but they were prepared to adopt new ideas and methods, and to try to meet the needs of the

41. First class lounge in the OTRANTO (II) – a fine conception for a tropic passage.

shipowner. This they continued to do until the completion of the last Orient liner at Barrow in 1960.

The first of the three ships to be delivered was the *Orama* in November, 1924, and was of 19,777 gross tons with geared turbines and twin screws, and was designed for a service speed of 18 knots, although she could provide 20 knots if required. Her accommodation was for 592 first class and 1,244 third class passengers.

It is worth mentioning that the *Orama* was the first ship in the world to be fitted with the new (at that time) gravity davit. Hitherto, since the demise of the old radial davit, ships' davits had been of a simple 'turn-out' type, or 'Welin' davit, which was a form of large vertical lever at each end of the boat and from the tops of which the boat was suspended by the lowering blocks and falls. The levers were turned out manually by turning handles before the boat could be lowered*. If the ship was listing at an angle, this procedure could be very hard work. The gravity davit was invented by a Scotsman, Colin Donald McLachlan, who devised twin fixed sloping tracks on which ran wheeled arms and from which the boat was suspended at each end by hooks and a wire. When released, the arms ran down the tracks by the force of gravity and brought the boat into the embarking position, whence it could be loaded and lowered into the sea. This davit invention was a tremendous step forward in the safety of life at sea. It became known as the Welin-McLachlan davit because, for manufacturing purposes and for the benefit of Welin (whose davit had become out-dated by this new invention), an arrangement was reached between the parties concerned. McLachlan's son, Donald, designed the special gravity davits fitted in the *Oriana* and the *Canberra* in 1960.

The other two ships ordered with the *Orama* in 1922 were the *Oronsay* (20,001 G.R.T.) which was delivered in February, 1925, and the *Otranto* (20,026 G.R.T.) which was delivered in the following January (1926). These three ships were similar in most aspects and, in appearance, were something like the *Ormonde* and had 'cruiser' sterns, which had first appeared on passenger liners just before the outbreak of war†. Some vessels have unspectacular but successful careers and others seem destined to encounter trouble. The *Otranto* certainly had her adventures. For instance, whilst cruising in the Mediterranean in May, 1926, she sustained serious hull damage forward when, in heavy rain and poor visibility, she struck some cliffs near Cape Matapan, in Greece. There was no radar in those days, of course. Fortunately the ship was able to continue and returned to Britain for repairs under her own steam.

In 1928 she was again in trouble when she became involved in a collision with a Japanese steamship, the *Kitano Maru*, off the mouth of the Humber, while outward bound from Immingham on a cruise to Scandinavia. This accident occurred in broad daylight on a fine, sunny day, with nothing but the blue sky and a wide and rather empty ocean. The Rule of the Road at sea involves an understanding of the roles of the 'stand on' ship and the 'give way' ship in much the same way as that of road traffic at cross-roads and roundabouts in some

* Moreover, many passenger ships had been equipped with two boats for each pair of davits so that, when the first boat was away, the boat fall had to be hoisted up again *without fouling*—an operation which was not so easy and, indeed, virtually impossible in practice.

† e.g. The s.s. *Missanabie, Metazama, Alasatian, Calgarian.*

countries where there are rules which give the right of way (stand on) to vehicles approaching from the right-hand side. When ships are on crossing courses with their relative bearings remaining unaltered, one must give way—to the vessel approaching from the starboard side (the 'stand on' ship), but the next requirement is the most dangerous one. The 'stand-on' ship must keep her course *until* it is observed that the 'give way' vessel is NOT giving way, and then, and then only, is it incumbent on her to take avoiding action.

Those on the bridge of the *Otranto* finally concluded that the *Kitano Maru* was not going to give way and thereupon took avoiding action. As a result, the two ships collided, because the *Kitano Maru* turned at the same moment as the *Otranto*. In all, there were three court hearings: the Admiralty court; the Court of Appeal and, finally, the House of Lords, first one ship being held to blame, then the other and, finally, from the House of Lords came the judgement of Solomon—that both ships were blameworthy! The *Otranto*, in a last minute effort to avoid the collision, was turned to port and made the impact more difficult to avoid—in the circumstances as they arose. In the light of considered judgement it seems that, had she turned to starboard, the collision could have been avoided or, at worst, its effects could have been reduced. Fortunately, there was no loss of life and neither ship was seriously damaged.

After these three ships were delivered, the Orient Company was once again able to introduce fortnightly sailings to Australia, but these were confined to the peak season between October and March. Sailings were phased at four-weekly intervals in the remainder of the year and, during these periods—the summer of the Northern Hemisphere—the new vessels were used for cruising in the Mediterranean and to Scandinavia.

The next addition to the fleet, the *Orford* (19,941 G.R.T.), joined the Company in October, 1928, and she was followed by the *Orontes* (19,970 G.R.T.) the following year, this latter vessel making her first voyage to Australia in October, 1929. Prior to that, the *Orontes* had cruised in the Mediterranean in place of the *Ormonde* which had been disabled by machinery trouble.

The *Orontes* differed in appearance from the other four vessels of

42. *Third class dining saloon in the ORAMA. This was still the age of 'long tables'. It will be seen that there is no deck-head decoration.*

the 20,000 ton class, being the most beautiful of them all. This was due to subtle changes in her exterior details, some of which were fortuitous. For example, her stem was raked a little more and made 'soft-nosed' of conically-rounded plate construction, as compared with the stem bar of rectangular section fitted on the other four ships. This form of plate construction is almost universal today, but was uncommon at the time of the construction of the *Orontes*. It should be noted that both the *Orford* and the *Orontes*, together with all later passenger ships for the Orient Line, were built by Vickers at Barrow-in-Furness.

These 20,000-tonners were fitted with accommodation for nearly 600 first class passengers and over 1,200 third class, the latter being somewhat austere and suitable for people who wanted to travel as cheaply as possible, mainly as emigrants to Australia. This need became less and less and, in the 1930's, the recession in world-wide trade and its effect on shipping and emigration to the Antipodes caused great difficulties for the managers of the Orient Line. They had forecast the needs of the trade to the best of their ability as, indeed, all good shipowners must work on close estimates based on their experience if they are to prosper and survive the recessions which inevitably occur in the life of a successful company.

Unfortunately, the accommodation for the third class passengers had been arranged to suit the demands of maximum numbers, travelling as cheaply as possible during the rush of migration to Australia after the first Great War, but this situation had changed dramatically within a very few years, so the Orient management started to alter the third class accommodation to try to suit the new needs. Ships were taken out of service as the opportunity presented itself, and the third class was altered to what was known as 'Tourist B' standard, which led to a certain improvement in the trade, whilst at the same time other steps were taken. For instance, calls were made at Palma, thus allowing holidaymakers to travel by an Orient liner outward bound to Majorca, have a vacation there, and then travel back in one of the Company's homeward bound vessels at a suitable time. The fleet managed to survive this bad time, and trade gradually improved.

About this time, an experiment was made in the external colouring of the Orient ships, as the *Orama's* hull was painted corn colour instead of black, and the boot-topping was painted green instead of red, in order to test public reaction and enable the Company to decide the colours to be used for the *Orion*—their new ship of 23,696 gross tons which was under construction at Barrow-in-Furness.

It is not recorded why the corn colour was chosen specifically but, because the ships passed through the Tropics, it was a sensible choice since it reduced the heat absorbed into the hull by the fierce rays of the sun, and it was decided that new vessels built for the fleet should be painted as the *Orama* was experimentally, although she then reverted to her original colour scheme.

At about the time that the *Orion* was ordered, a big change took place within the Orient Company regarding the arrangements for the design of their new ships. A new figure came to the fore in the person of Colin Skelton Anderson, the son of Sir Alan Garrett Anderson and a junior director of the Company. He was young and very artistic and, rightly, thought that something should be done to bring new ships of the company more into line with contemporary thought, not only in the architectural arrangement of the public spaces, but externally, too. He put his views to the Board of Management and they gave him the responsibility for carrying out his ideas in the *Orion*, which was about to be built.

His first step was to find an architect who had the right qualifications and the same feelings about design as he had himself, and a great partnership was formed when he found a young New Zealander, Brian O'Rorke, who, at that time, was working in England. That partnership of two kindred spirits, so far as the interiors of Orient ships were concerned, endured throughout the period which followed the building of the *Orion* between 1933 and 1935 until the closure of the company in 1960. In an article entitled *Ship Interiors** which he wrote in 1969, Sir Colin Anderson stated that his hand-written and very short 'brief' to Brian O'Rorke in October, 1933, regarding the design work in the *Orion* was:-

1) *Escape from period decoration without going extremely in opposite direction. Hints of Period are not objected to.*
2) *Produce rooms which will bear sitting in:*
   a) *Every day and night for 5 weeks.*
   b) *Through the Tropics.*
   c) *Through the English winter.*
   d) *Highest possible seating capacity.*
   e) *Every seat in a light suitable for reading at night.*
   f) *Flooring not very slippery.*
3) *Decoration as fire-resistant as can reasonably be produced.*
4) *Taboos;*
   Curtains, (unless they have a real use, as opposed to being merely decorative).
   Close carpeting.
   Fireplaces.
   Squeak-and-chatter producing decoration.

* *About Ourselves*, June 1969, No. 28

Surfaces of decoration or fabric requiring constant upkeep or showing dirt freely.

And so it went on—but only for four more paragraphs.

The result of this close collaboration between Colin Anderson, Brian O'Rorke and the builders, Vickers at Barrow-in-Furness (who worked well with them, as we are told by Sir Colin in his article), was that the *Orion* came into service in 1935 and created a great sensation in all the leading shipping and architectural papers and periodicals of the time. She was a splendid ship and was still equal to, or ahead of, most other passenger vessels afloat at the time of her breaking-up in her 29th year in 1963.

Her outer appearance was very different to that of her predecessors in the Orient Line, for she had one funnel and one mast, and her service speed was 21 knots. With her corn-coloured hull, which was inspired by Colin Anderson, she looked more like a large private yacht than a passenger liner, since the proportions of the ship belied her size. Indeed, the *Orion* set a pattern which was to be followed by all other vessels built for the Company after that time and, not only that, she influenced almost all subsequent liners and had a recognized influence on the interior decoration of hotels. Sir Colin Anderson spear-headed the team designing and building all the additions to the fleet from the *Orion* until the completion of the *Oriana* in 1960.

The decoration and design of the public rooms and interiors of the *Orion's* passenger accommodation was due to Brian O'Rorke and created new standards at that time. Air-conditioning was employed for the dining rooms and some special cabins in the vessel. There was also a feature which received great publicity at the time she took the water, as the Duke of Gloucester named and launched the *Orion* by radio-telephone from Brisbane, Australia, in December, 1934.

The success of this vessel, and her popularity in Australia, was such that an order was placed in 1936 for a similar ship to be built. This was the *Orcades (II)* of 23,456 gross tons, which was delivered in October, 1937, being slightly larger than the *Orion* and, as always, incorporating some improvements brought about by the experience of her predecessor. The *Orcades* was possibly a little more popular with

43. Both the inside and outside appearance of the ORION caused a sensation when she made her debut in 1935.

the Australian sea-travellers and was nick-named by them 'The Big Tug', perhaps because she had one mast and one funnel, which made her look smaller than she really was, and (slightly) to resemble a tug.

The system of nomenclature of the Orient ships may have been exercising the minds of some readers, for it is well-known that some shipping companies have maintained a standard system of naming their ships, which would all be called after Gods and Goddesses in one: constellations in another, Scottish counties in a third, and so forth. In the Anderson, Anderson clippers there had never been any standard system although the last three, the *Aurora, Hesperus* and *Harbinger* had beautiful names and seemed to be developing a common theme, but this was not continued in the steamships. The P.S.N.Co. vessels which were purchased already had names which were prudently not changed (though the temptation to re-name the *Aconcagua*, or even the *Cuzco* and *Chimborazo*, may have been considerable!)

The *Orient*, as already stated, was named after the successful clipper, and the name *Austral* might seem to be obvious enough when considering the trade of the Company. From then onwards, the Management never attempted any more exacting practice than to start

44. *The first class Library and . . . .*

45. *. . . . the first class lounge in the ORION.*

46. Games deck of the OTRANTO (II). (note the clutter of ventilators, funnels and awning supports.)

the names of its vessels with the letter 'O', following the lead of the first *Orient* and, of course, of the Company itself. If a name commencing with 'OR' commended itself by—say—phonetic appeal, so much the better, but otherwise there was no limit to the field from which a name might be chosen, although names such as *Ophir* and *Otranto* demonstrated that there was no immutability about the 'OR' to start the name. It was felt that the names should not be too difficult to pronounce or to spell, which is why the Roman name *Orcades* was chosen instead of the more modern equivalent 'Orkney', since it was considered to be a finer-sounding word but, in the event, it *was* often mispronounced *Orcādes* instead of *Orcădes*, whilst the *Oronsay* was also generally mispronounced, since the accent should be on the first syllable, and not on the second. On the other side of the scale, some intending passengers would pronounce the *Austral* as if her name began with 'OR'!

47. *Games deck of the ORION, still with a clutter of ventilators near the funnel but the awning supports improved by the use of wire instead of woodwork.*

Examination of the names of the fleet will demonstrate that although geographical ones took precedence, there was no real rhyme or reason about them. The one rule was that no further ships should be named *Orient*, for two good reasons: first, if there should be a disaster to such a vessel, it would involve the Company's name too deeply and, in the second place, whilst such a ship was new and the 'pride and joy' of the fleet, it was well enough for her to carry the Company's name but, when she became 'long-funnelled and tiresome', she would be bad for their name and image. There is so much logic in this illogicality that no more need be said unless to note that ships are much like humans and that it is small wonder that they are referred to as 'she'!

It may not be generally known that, nowadays, it is no longer always possible in Great Britain to christen a ship with whatever name one may prefer, since the Registrar of Shipping will not accept a name which is already in use by another British vessel. Thus, if some 'liner' name, such as *Majestic*, happens to be registered already and used by—say—a small paddle-steamer, the owners of the great new liner must find another name, since *Majestic* would be barred to them unless they can procure the sole right to it by bribing the owners of the paddle-steamer to change her name and release *Majestic* to them. A very similar thing did, in fact, occur in the case of the great Cunarder—*Queen Mary*.

The Orient Management had determined that the first of the two new vessels previously discussed should be named *Orion*, but this was shortly after the new rule had been made and it was objected that there was already a sailing barge, owned in Essex, with this name. This led to a somewhat amusing, if ironic situation. The Thames barge was a highly efficient type of local craft with a character all her own, but clearly ranked amongst the humbler echelons of working vessels in the eyes of deep-water sailors and owners and, even then, was fighting a losing battle against the tide of economics. This particular *Orion* was well-known in the Thames estuary and was often referred to as the 'little barge-yacht', since she had been built as a coasting barge, was only of 90 tons and, by that date, was not a very viable proposition. A tale was told of her that, when freights were becoming difficult to find, her owner was approached and asked to sell her as a lighter—or so he interpreted the proposal—and he agreed to do so for the relatively low sum of two or three hundred pounds. In due course, he received his cheque and, after an interval of some three months, a similar cheque arrived in the post, which he promptly queried. He then learnt, to his delight, that the firm which had approached him had not intended to purchase the barge, but to *charter* her, and that the sum agreed was, in fact, the amount to be paid each quarter!

Whether this story, which used to be in common currency, found its inception from a riverside bar or from fact I cannot determine, but it is abundantly certain that the barge's owner was fully alive to his opportunity when approached by a company of the status of the Orient Line to buy the name of his craft, and there is little doubt that the managers of that company felt that they had had to 'pay through the nose'! The sum is believed to have been in the region of £500. As for the barge, she was re-named *Gold Belt*, appositely enough, and, rather oddly, actually did become a barge-yacht in the course of the years.

The new liner was duly registered *Orion* but, of course, the Registrar of Shipping has no control over names of vessels which are owned outside the United Kingdom. This fact was amusingly demonstrated on the occasion of one of the new vessel's first visits to Tilbury when there was a Swedish cargo ship named *Orion* berthed within view at Northfleet, a Finland Line steamer named *Orion* passed down the river on her way to sea and, lying at the buoys just below the Gravesend pilot pier and also within view, by strange coincidence, was *H.M.S. Orion*! Nor were these the only vessels named *Orion* afloat at that time, so that the objection based on a Thames barge might be argued to have been an unreasonable one. Had the Board of the Orient Line been present on that summer morning, they might have had some trenchant comments to make about that regulation!

Indeed, one might wonder why they had not considered naming the new vessel *Orvandel-Egil*, which would have been much cheaper and would have achieved much the same result. Orvandel-Egil is, of course, the old Norse name for the constellation Orion and, like the Greek mythological hunter, he was a great archer before being translated into the heavens. Certainly *Orvandel-Egil* is more of a mouthful than *Orion* (even if it does start with the magic 'OR') but it should certainly have held a relevant connotation in a ship which might find herself cruising in Northern waters, much as the Aberdeen White Star Line of clippers, which customarily named its fleet after proper names in ancient Greek history, influenced the Jewish trade by naming some of them, instead, *Patriarch, Maid of Judah, Jerusalem* and the like. However, this must remain a matter of idle speculation and, had the Company not opted for the rather expensive name *Orion*, they would certainly have deprived the East Coast barging fraternity of much merriment!

It is a strange thing that those who are immediately connected with ships, from their masters downwards, seldom display much interest in the origins of the names of those in which they serve, and few members of the staff, whether ashore or afloat, in such a company as the Blue Funnel Line (as it used to be called—or the 'Blue Flue' within shipping circles!), have any idea of the stories of the characters, mainly drawn from the *Iliad* or from the *History of Herodotus*, which formed the inspiration of the nomenclature of that fleet, and most had difficulty enough to pronounce them, whilst ships christened with Maori names created an even greater aura of mystery. However, those who are interested in the history and literature of the sea have much more interest in the subject, and for their benefit it may be pertinent to write a little of the names in the Orient fleet although, in all conscience, it is difficult enough to present any common denominator which links them over the years—a fact which has been confirmed by both Sir Colin Anderson and Ford Geddes, the advice of both of whom I have sought on this question. As already remarked, most (but not all) were of geographical origin but, beyond that, there is little overall connection.

Ophir strikes an immediate chord, since we know that it was a city (and land) of much wealth from the references to it in the Old Testament which records that both King Solomon and Hiram of Tyre sent fleets there to pick up gold, jewels and precious woods, though no-one knows precisely where it was. Named after Ophir, a descendant of Shem, it was unquestionably a great emporium and *entre-pôt* port (had such a term been invented in those days!) for the Indian trade, but whether it lay on the coast of Arabia or in India (as it was) is a matter for conjecture. Certainly it lay along the northern coast of the Indian Ocean, but it does not seem to have fallen to the spades of the archaelogists. The word 'Omrah' occurs very little in English and then usually, with variant spellings, in the writings of early travellers to describe a grandee of a Mohammedan court who might be equated with a mediaeval baron. The *Orontes*, of course, took her name from the largest river in Syria, called by the Arabs Nahr-el-Asy. This seems to be a safe enough assumption, although it is conceivable that he who first devised the name for an Orient ship might have been thinking either of the mountain to the south of the Caspian or, alternatively, of an Assyrian tribe!

The following ships of the Company are, perhaps, a little easier, though why the *Orsova* should have been named after an Hungarian market town on the Danube where it passes through the Iron Gates will probably never be answered, although *Otway*, named after an Australian cape not far from Melbourne, has much more relevance. Osterley, at the time the ship was named, was a relatively small place a few miles west of London, noted only for a fine country house, and even more insignificant when the ship was launched than it is today, with its housing estates crowded round a trunk road which skirts it. Otranto is a town on the heel of Italy which fronts the straits of that name which separate the country from Albania, whilst Ormuz is an alternative spelling for the Straits of Hormuz which lead from the Gulf of Oman into the Persian Gulf. Orvieto leads us to Umbria, in Northern Italy, where a town of that name is situated, but I suspect that few natives of the State of South Australia would identify Orama as being a small township within their boundaries! The *Ormonde* took her name from an almost equally obscure place in Ireland and, despite the Latin version of Orcades for the Orkneys, another ship was simply named *Oronsay* after a very small island in the Hebrides, opposite the entrance to the Caledonian Canal.

Orford, as British readers will know well enough, is a town on the Suffolk coast of no great importance, but at least it is possible to assign a reason for it, since some of the managers of the Company had connections in the area—a reason which can scarcely be advanced in respect of Orsova! From the foregoing, it will be seen that there is an ever-present temptation to search for origins of Orient names in a gazetteer and, although there is a little known place called Omar in West Virginia, it seems more likely that the ship was named for Omar Khayyam, whose quatrains were being translated by Edward Fitzgerald to such public acclaim at that time. It is difficult to believe that she was named for the famous Mohammedan Caliph who lived from 581-644. I have already dealt with the *Orion*, for which there was no precedent in the fleet, while *Orient* needs no explanation.

Readers may conclude that names for ships did not come readily to the Orient Management, and it is certain that a public suggestion scheme to this end was once held in Australia. This was the occasion when the name of an Australian town Orbost was put forward, whilst someone else even suggested 'Orstralia'—perhaps a descendant of one of those who so mispronounced the poor *Austral*!

The last name, which will occur more and more in this book, was that of the *Oriana* which, as will be explained in connection with her badge, was the name given to the first Queen Elizabeth by the poets of the day, who drew their inspiration from the leman of Amadis of Gaul—a romance which was so popular in Tudor times. Thus, at the start of what was hoped would prove to be a new 'Elizabethan Age', with a young queen of the same name—Elizabeth—upon the throne, was the last and greatest of the Orient fleet called *Oriana*, and I shall deal with this vessel in much greater detail in the last part of this book.

However, reverting to the story of the Company and completing all that need be said in this chapter, it should be recorded that an experimental service was started by the Orient Company in conjunction with that of the P. & O. in which both lines ran extensions to their services to Australia by proceeding on from Sydney to New Zealand, thus providing opportunities for Australians to have holidays in that latter country, whilst providing an alternative route for travellers from Britain to New Zealand. Unfortunately, due to the outbreak of hostilities within a year, this new service was brought to a halt.

III. THE ORIENT LINE

FROM THE OUTBREAK OF THE SECOND WORLD WAR

AT THE OUTBREAK of war in September, 1939, the Orient Line had eight ships, the oldest of them being the *Ormonde*, 14,982 G.R.T., which was built in 1917 and had seen service in the previous war. The most recently-built vessel was the *Orcades (II)*, but these eight ships were all requisitioned as troop-ships and were used in almost every theatre of the war, taking part in some of the major landings and other operations. Inevitably, there were losses, but it did not follow that it was the oldest units of the fleet which were sunk, and the *Ormonde* came through hostilities unscathed as she had through the previous ones. However, the *Orford* was bombed and set on fire in Marseilles harbour on 1 June, 1940, having to be beached and abandoned as a total loss. Fourteen of her crew were killed and twenty five wounded, but the majority of her complement escaped from the vessel and made their rather adventurous way across France back to England.

The *Orama* was the next casualty. She was *en route* to evacuate troops from Narvik, in Norway, and was sunk by a German task force which included the cruiser *Admiral Hipper* with the notorious *Scharnhorst* and *Gneisenau*, 20 of her crew being killed and 280 being picked up and taken prisoner by the *Admiral Hipper*. The *Oronsay* had had some luck when one of her consorts, the *Lancastria*, was sunk, but she herself escaped, albeit with a certain amount of damage. (2,800 odd lives were lost in the *Lancastria*.) Her luck began to run out a few months later when she was damaged by a bomber off Ireland and, finally, on 9 October, 1942, she was sunk by the Italian submarine *Archimede* some 500 miles south-west of Freetown, when she was returning after carrying Free French troops to Madagascar. The passengers and crew were able to get away in the boats and, under the command of Captain Savage, nine of them covered some 250 miles in eight days before they were picked up—the bulk of the men (nearly 300) by a British warship, but the remaining 30 were taken to Dakar by a French sloop, and were interned there for the rest of the war. Captain Savage was awarded the C.B.E. for his courage and the exceptional judgement which he had exercised.

Then, the day after the *Oronsay* was lost, the *Orcades (II)* was homeward bound from Cape Town with 1,000 passengers, comprising civilians and troops, when she was struck by two torpedoes from the U-172. Her master, Captain Fox, concluded that the ship would keep afloat and was still navigable, so turned back for Cape Town, but shortly afterwards a third torpedo hit her, and the passengers and most of the crew were put in the boats, while about 53 men remained aboard with the intention of saving the vessel which was by then scarcely manageable and making about five knots. However, three more torpedoes found their mark after the submarine had reloaded her tubes, and she sank with the loss of some 50 lives, the survivors all being picked up by the Polish steamer *Narwick*. Captain Fox was also awarded the C.B.E. and Lloyds' War Medal for his bravery during the tragic loss of the vessel.

Thus, by the end of the war, the Orient Line was reduced to four vessels—the *Ormonde, Otranto, Orontes* and the *Orion*. Of these, the *Orion* was the first to be released from government service and, in 1946, was extensively refitted by Vickers, her builders, at Barrow-in-Furness, and was able to re-enter the Australian service in 1947, being fitted out to carry 546 first class and 706 Tourist class passengers.

The *Ormonde*, now an ageing vessel, did not return to the Orient Line main passenger service, but was taken over by the British Government Ministry of Transport for a scheme to take emigrant passengers out to Australia, and sailed on the first of these voyages in October, 1947, after being fitted out in Birkenhead to carry 1,052

48. *The ORONSAY evacuating troops from St. Nazaire and picking up survivors from the sinking LANCASTRIA. (From a painting by Chas. Pears.)*

passengers in rather plain accommodation. During the ensuing five years she carried nearly 18,000 government-assisted passengers to their new homes in Australia. When homeward bound, she carried smaller numbers of Tourist class passengers on the Orient Line account but, in November, 1952, she completed her final voyage after 35 years service in which she sailed on 75 voyages to Australia and back and had made her contribution to her country in two major wars in waters all over the world. So, on 1 December, 1952, the *Ormonde* sailed to Dalmuir on the Clyde, not very far from her builder's yard, where she was broken up—a ship with a very fine and long record.

The *Orontes* was released by the government next, and was refitted at Southampton by John I. Thornycroft Ltd. with berths for 489 First class and 608 Tourist passengers, after which she re-entered the Company's service in June 1948. The last of the four remaining vessels to be refitted was the *Otranto*, which sailed up the Mersey on 8 June, 1948, when Messrs. Cammell Laird went to work on her and, after 12 months, she was ready for sea with accommodation for 1,400 Tourist class passengers—a one class ship. She sailed from Tilbury for Australia on 4 July, 1949.

If the *Ormonde* be ignored, since she had not entirely returned to Orient service, the three remaining vessels were not capable of maintaining the sort of service expected of the Company and steps had to be taken to put this deficiency right. The Chairman, Mr. Irvine C. Geddes, in a *Message to members of the staff of the Orient Line* in April, 1948, at the time of ordering two new vessels, wrote:-

> *In normal times it is possible to foretell with some certainty the type of cabin required by passengers, how much they are prepared to pay for it, and also how many will travel in each year. Today, however, times are not normal and there is complete uncertainty as to the level of fare passengers will be able to afford during the next 20-25 years—that is, during the life of a new ship. We have also to take into account the competition of air travel, which—although it existed before the war—is now in a more intensive form. It is true to say that for business or family reasons some passengers must travel, but these, so far as first class is concerned, are relatively few in number and could be largely accommodated by aeroplane. On*

the other hand, there are now vast numbers of potential passengers—both in England and Australia—who will travel if they can be made comfortable and carried at rates which suit their pockets. Individuals have different tastes and different cash resources, so we provide a range of cabins from top-grade accommodation in first class right down the scale to the most spartan cabins in tourist class and, as compared with pre-war in certain grades, we have purposely sacrificed some comfort so that cost may be kept down. There is one point which should not be overlooked, and it is that a ship really sells to passengers not only transport and cabin space but also amenities (victualling, service, public rooms, deck space etc.) and it must provide this combination at prices which passengers can afford. This is a point that is often ignored by first class passengers who have booked in minimum rate cabins. They complain about the lack of space in cabins—forgetting that they have the advantage, at a cheap rate of passage money, of a full share in the other first class amenities.

In assessing the charge to be made for different types of cabin, no strict logical formula can be relied upon. For instance, the higher graded cabins are on a fare level where the passenger may wonder whether it would be a better bargain for him to travel by air. At this point it should be said that the Orient Company and all those who pay taxes either directly or indirectly to the British Government contribute to the cost of the National Air Lines, and this contribution enables them to carry passengers below the actual cost of transport; in fact, all of us are subsidizing competition against ourselves. This is quite unfair.

Forty years ago, a ship of the size then suitable for the trade had to be planned to accommodate the crew and three classes of passengers in much less comfort than today. Larger ships, combined with developments in Marine Engineering and the skill of the Naval Architect, have brought great changes. Space required by boilers, engines and fuel to give the same, or even greater, speed has been considerably reduced, especially during the last twenty five years. Then, too, Naval Architecture has contributed its share in progress by improving the lines of the ships, so making them easier to drive through the water, even with a greater beam. It is the gains in space and economy in propulsion arising from all these improvements which has made it possible to provide better accommodation for all on board. The elimination of one of the classes of passengers has also helped. One of the great problems in design is to make a fair allotment of space between the different cabins. Ideal comfort would be for every soul on board to have a single berth cabin with a private bathroom attached. If such a ship were built today, it would land the owner in the Bankruptcy Court, although something approaching that standard may be economically possible in the lifetime of our grandchildren.

Meantime, we must advance by stages, and it is the responsibility of management to keep a fair balance in the allocation of space between the different interests on board the ship. As already indicated, economies can be obtained from keeping the number of separate classes down to the minimum, and obviously every passenger thinks he would prefer to have the run of the whole ship. We believe, however, that the amount people are prepared to pay for different standards of cabins, feeding, service, etc., varies so much it would be impracticable to deal with the whole traffic in a service of one class ships. We are, however, moving as far as we can go in this direction by making it as easy as possible for people with limited means to travel first class, and this entails adopting a somewhat lower standard than pre-war for our minimum rate cabins and saloon feeding. At the same time, we are endeavouring in Orion, Orcades *and* Oronsay *to provide more elaborate meals, for those who wish them, in the restaurant on payment of an extra charge.* By these means, and by fitting* Otranto *as a one class ship (and conceivably by running other ships as one class in the off-season) we hope to be able to cater for all tastes, and so ensure the large numbers which are necessary to make big ships pay.*

The present position in the Australian trade is this:-

1) Australia wants to increase her population and this is right nationally. It also suits the personal interest of all those connected with the Orient Company, for it will mean more passengers for us to carry in both directions.

* See page 108.

2) Taxation is high and will likely remain so for many years. Therefore, we must guess at the level of fares our potential passengers will be able to afford in the future.

3) The cost of building ships has risen to giddy heights. In 1906 we built ships at about £25 per ton; in 1923-37 at about £45, today Orcades *and* Oronsay *will cost us about £110 per ton.**

4) The cost of running ships also shows a spectacular rise and is about 100% up over the pre-war figure.

So, we are today faced with three difficult problems—uncertainty as to the volume of traffic, as to the level of fares at which it can be tempted to move and as to whether this revenue will produce sufficient cash to cover the costs. The Australian passenger trade is very difficult to cater for economically for two reasons. First, because the traffic (other than migrants) only wants to travel in large numbers in a few months in the year in each direction. This is especially true of first class homewards. Secondly, because migrants provide only an outward load with the result that the Tourist accommodation has much bigger demands made on it outwards than homewards. We hope, by keeping our minimum first class fares low, to induce a number of Australians, who travel home Tourist, to book outwards in first class, thereby avoiding being overcrowded themselves and also making more room for migrants. This should not inconvenience those who travelled home first class, as past experience shows they spread over a greater number of sailings outwards than homewards. If this can be achieved, it will be a great advantage to the economics of our business, since we can afford to keep our fares at a level which will attract still more people to travel.

The rise in fares as compared with the pre-war figures is as follows:-

First class maximum single rate up 42.3%
First class minimum single rate up 16.9%
Tourist class maximum single rate up 52.6%
Tourist class minimum single rate up 47.5%

Cargo is unlike passengers in that its 'stowage factor' cannot be materially varied; the percentage increase in freight rates is therefore

* These were intended as approximate figures. Costs were changing constantly.

equivalent to that in running costs, namely 100%.

These percentages do not quite reflect the whole story because the quality of minimum rate first class accommodation has been depressed, and this explains the low percentage increase in this rate. It should be added that at present no return tickets are issued. Increased cost of building ships is a very serious matter, and we must aim to limit its effects as much as possible. Thus by building larger and faster ships (capable, therefore, of more frequent voyages with heavier loads), we count on having to build fewer ships. But, for this policy to be successful, the ships must make the greatest predictable number of voyages within the year, so the speed of turn-round here and in Australia is of great importance, for each day a ship lies idle beyond what is physically necessary increases the difficulty of making her pay her way. Anyway, she cannot live on passage earnings alone: she depends on earning freight, too, and so her speed of loading and discharging cargo, baggage and stores is of the utmost importance to all of us . . . . . .

' . . . . In ordering two new ships costing over £3,000,000 each, we are entering into an adventure as great as the Company has ever embarked upon. The severity of our war losses has forced us to do this. No substitute ships are available and it would be equivalent to going out of business to leave the berth uncovered. We shall not be able to say whether this adventure has been a wise one for a good many years . . . . .

' . . . . The owner of capital who lends it for an enterprise expects to have its value preserved and not only to receive interest for its use. If he puts £3,000,000 into building a ship, it is not enough for her merely to pay him his annual interest, for in twenty to twenty-five years he will find that his £3,000,000 ship has become a tired old hull worth only the scrap value of metal of which it is composed. Unless, therefore, in the meantime, she has secured sufficient earnings in excess of running costs to make good the depreciation in value of the ship, he would judge that he had made a very bad bargain. If this happened generally, no more capital would be available for building ships. So, our adventure will only prove to have been justified if, at the end of the effective life of the

49. A 'ticker-tape' send-off was part and parcel of sailing day from Australia.

ships, they have earned enough passage money and freight to provide:-

a) The running voyage expenses and repairs.
b) A share of the general expenses of the organization.
c) Depreciation.
d) Interest on the capital cost.

It is only after all these charges have been met that one can begin to talk of profits. Experience shows that ships of our type, when they are new, are more attractive to passengers than older ones running alongside them, and that they tend to give better results in earnings in the early years of their life . . . . If, therefore, these earlier years do not give better results than the average required throughout the ship's life, the start will be unfortunate.

On present day prices, and provided the ships can be turned round fast enough to do four voyages a year, we estimate that we shall need to secure a steady £300,000 of earnings for every voyage that Orcades *and* Oronsay *make to cover the various costs detailed above. If the turn round is slower, this estimate will have to be increased . . . . Every act towards efficiency or increased economy is a step towards ensuring the successful life of these ships. This is the desired result and it is an object which is in the personal interest of every one of us to pursue in every way.'*

The foregoing extracts from Mr. Irvine C. Geddes' message to the staff in 1948 give the thoughts of a man wise in the expertise of providing a first class passenger line service. If his words are read carefully, they tell us all that is required to be known in the conception of the design of a passenger ship for the guidance of naval architects and marine engineers. The skills and knowledge of the latter should furnish the rest of the answer to the problem. It is interesting to note how Mr. Geddes helps his staff to understand the problems facing the management in deciding what sort of ship should be built to cater for the requirements of the travelling public at that time. There is much written today about the faults in employer-worker relations and participation; about how deficient they used to be, and how much better they are today. Such comment was not true of the Orient Line organization, and I will quote two facets of their procedure to demonstrate this.

During the period between the arrival and departure of each of their vessels, the Orient Line board held a meeting with senior staff of the Company to discuss the estimated revenue and expenditure for the forthcoming voyage, and these were compared with the actual results of the corresponding voyage for the same ship in the previous year. Officially, these were called 'Heads of Departments Meetings', but unofficially 'In the Red Meetings', the latter title having been coined by some wag on the staff or . . . . was it given by some member of the Board, because they were not lacking a sense of humour? The estimated expenditure included a small percentage of the profits to be kept for the purchase of a replacement ship, but this figure was usually woefully inadequate to meet the rocketing prices of shipbuilding.

The voyage accounts during the 1950's were often disappointing and depressing, so the nickname for the meetings was apt enough, since all too frequently red figures appeared on the copies of estimates of voyage accounts circulated at them. It is possible that one or two readers may ask themselves: 'Why introduce this matter of Meetings of Heads of Departments as an example of employer/worker relationship?'. It so happened that I attended these meetings myself and, so far from being of a confidential nature, it was the intention that the information emanating from them should be deseminated right through the Company. Indeed, although I ranked as 'senior staff', I was in fact as near to the 'shop-floor' as any shop-steward, and it was my experience that the relation of this sort of thing was both appreciated and created confidence and that, if there was a breakdown of communications, it invariably occurred at a lower level amongst the 'in-betweens' who usually spring from the ranks of the workers. Use of this latter word leads me to register a question which has perpetually exercised my mind, namely: 'At what point in the hierarchy does one cease to become a worker and become a drone?' Within my own observation, the Directors and the senior staff usually work much harder than the so-called 'workers', and certainly take a great deal more responsibility.

The Orient Line also had a practice, which might almost be described as a ritual and may well have been unique, but was certainly unusual. On the evening before every sailing day of each of their ships, whether at Tilbury or Southampton, there was what was called a 'Sailing Night'. Some members of the Board, together with many members of the staff and their guests, would go straight from their offices to the ship, where they would have dinner. Afterwards, many of them would return home, but others would go on an inspection of the ship, and then stay on board overnight before returning to their offices. These inspections, both of the ship and of work which had been done on repairs, maintenance, and modifications, were attended by senior staff, ships' officers and others concerned, and were led by the interested member of the Board. The benefits to the Management, staff and ships' companies in these opportunities to meet one another, get to know one another and to exchange views, were quite incalculable.

Another practice of the Orient Line Board which had originated many years ago—probably in the very beginnings of the Company, was known by the staff as 'The March Past', and took place either in December or January of each year. It was an occasion when every employee from the office boys to the most senior management met one of the members of the Board, and when no-one else was present at the interview. The salary to be paid to each member of the staff was stated but, beyond that (which is common enough), he or she could talk about conditions of employment; problems associated with work, salary, or any other aspect to do with his or her position in the Company. This practice, which was extended to the staff at Tilbury, was a very good one and not one with which I was familar before I joined the Orient Line. Perhaps it was almost unique and only possible in a relatively small firm, but it does illustrate that the Board were interested in the men and women and their ships: and were trying to communicate with their employees and to establish good relationships with them. As a result, the men took a pride in their work and in the ships, and were 'kept on their toes'. Any 'remoteness' of a Board of Directors can indicate lack of interest in staff which, in turn, earns disloyalty from them.

Conditions have changed since 1948 and a few things said in the 'Message' by Mr. I.C. Geddes are not true today. For instance, his remarks that naval architecture had developed the lines of a ship '*making her easier to drive through the water, even with a greater beam*'. Ships before the 1914-18 war had, on the whole, been very narrow, partly as a legacy of the 'length-beam' ratio to speed, inherited from the days of sail, but, due to various reasons and requirements, beams of ships were increased, and the fact of the matter is that we could no longer build the narrow ships of those times today even if we wished, because they would not meet modern safety requirements, apart from any other considerations.

After the second World War greater attention was given to the safety of ships, and precautions against the sinking of passenger vessels became extremely strict. The Rules for the Safety of Life at Sea applied by the British Ministry of Transport, like those of other countries which are signatories to International Agreements

50. *It is no longer possible to build the 'narrow-gutted' ships like the old – and peerless – MAURETANIA.*

formulated by I.M.C.O.*, require that passenger ships are required to remain afloat after side damage has occurred and take account of the size of the vessel, specifying the length of penetration and its height and depth into the ship's side. The point of damage is assumed to be at any one of the worst places along the length of the ship. After the flooding takes place as a result of each of these selected positions of imagined damage, the vessel must not exceed a specified maximum angle of heel.

* Inter-Governmental Maritime Consultative Organisation.

51. *The ARUNDEL CASTLE as originally built. Later, with two broader and squatter funnels and various structural alterations, she would hardly have been recognised.*

One implication of the foregoing regulations is that the amount of damage assumed grows bigger with larger ships until—when we consider those of the size of the *Queen Elizabeth*—we are bound to wonder what could cause such large holes in the extremely heavy steelwork. The reader can appreciate readily that asymmetrical flooding causes heeling of a ship and that, therefore, in order to restrain the list to conform with the Rules, a vessel must be designed wide enough to have reserve stability to meet these requirements. Thus it is that we find that ships have become beamier since these regulations were framed, and this is the reason why the old 'narrow-gutted' passenger liners could not be built today.

Most large passenger ships are built with water-tight bulkheads spaced so that any two compartments can be flooded by the sea and that they will still remain afloat and only list to an angle equal to, or

52. *Built in 1911, the OLYMPIC of 46,479 tons was the largest vessel afloat in Britain before the QUEEN MARY was launched. She was broken up in 1935.*

53. *Damage to the OLYMPIC after collision with H.M.S. HAWKE, which was held by many to have been caused by attraction between two such large vessels. When the TITANIC (pl. 201) left on her maiden voyage, she 'sucked' the liner NEW YORK away from the quay at Southampton, carrying away her mooring lines. The OLYMPIC and TITANIC were near-sisters.*

less than, that required by the Rule. These vessels are now fitted with navigational aids of the most sophisticated kind. At first there was one form of radar, but this was quickly followed by improved installations: there are extremely good radio sets; lifeboats to take all the passengers and crew, and every soul on board must have a lifejacket. The width of stairs up to the lifeboats was controlled by the Rules to ensure quick access to them but, after the war, a big increase in this width of stairs was made.

It is interesting to note that, in October, 1942, the *Orcades (II)*, with a complement of a full crew and 1,000 passengers in the form of civilians and troops on board, was attacked and later sunk by a submarine which fired six torpedoes into the ship over a period of hours. All of these people, except for those who were killed in the attack, took to the boats and were saved. So far as I am aware, there was no story of narrow stairs from those who returned, and one cannot but wonder why stricter rules were introduced to require stairs to be made wider still in passenger ships.

There is a reference in Irvine Geddes' Message to the Company's staff to '*the restaurant on payment of an extra charge*', marked with an asterisk. The P. & O. and Orient ships ran a similar service for many years, and their designs tended to follow similar patterns, particularly after the 1930's. They differed in a few ways noticeable to the passengers travelling in them as, for example, in the fact that the P. & O. vessels had a preponderence of coloured members of the crew, whereas those in the Orient were all white. Then the P. & O. ships were fitted with 'Tourist A' accommodation, which was slightly roomier and more comfortable than the 'Tourist B' of the Orient Line. These Tourist A and Tourist B distinctions were later discontinued, and the Orient tourist cabins were improved with later refittings and 'face-lifts'.

In 1947, the *Orion* sailed on her first post-war voyage with a restaurant which had been built over the after end of the boat deck, and this was fitted with its own lounge and bar for passengers who wished to have a meal away from the first class dining room, in which each person had an allotted seat. In this restaurant they could entertain friends; have birthday or other anniversary parties, or just

54. The Silver Grill in ORIANA (see p. 367).

get away from the routine of the main dining room for a while. There was a small extra charge for the added luxury of a meal individually cooked and served in a beautiful room overlooking the sea through large windows, and this facility was added to all the ships built for the Company thereafter. Like many amenities, such as a swimming pool, no earning power could be attached to these restaurants, but they did seem to give inestimable pleasure to passengers. P. & O. vessels did not have such restaurants and they were taken out of the Orient ships which sailed under the P. & O. house-flag after the merging of the two companies in 1960.

The *Orcades (III)* was the first unit of a new class designed and built to meet the envisaged needs of the future Australian service, and we can imagine the turmoil of thoughts in the minds of the Orient managers at that time. There is a simple factor of economy which is probably true of all forms of transport, whether of freight or of human cargo: that the larger the unit used to carry the freight, the cheaper it is to carry that cargo per unit load, providing that the freight is there to be carried. Hence the emergence, in recent years, of the huge oil tankers, bulk carriers and, to a lesser extent, of passenger liners.

After the second World War, discussions on the considerations of the size of the new ships for the Orient Line went on at great length. Another factor of economy linked to the size of the ship was her speed, for the economical speed is closely allied to her length and, the longer she is, the higher is the economical speed. At that time (1945) when these investigations were taking place, the ports of call on the Company's route were not so good in terms of size and quality as they are now, and thus the size of vessel which could use some of them was limited, since the manoeuvring space available had to be taken into account. Another crucial question which entered into the discussions was the maximum power which, at that time, could be passed through two propellers.

The Company did not wish to increase the number of turbines and shafts, for reasons of economy of first cost, fuel consumption and the inevitable increase in engine room staff. Eventually the *Orcades* became the first of a new 28,000 G.R.T. class, and she could provide satisfactory answers to all the points which had been raised. Plans of sample cabins were prepared, together with schemes of passenger cabin layouts: their public rooms and spaces: galleys; pantries, laundries and ancillary associated spaces and, of course, plans of the crew accommodation. Many such schemes were devised and the potential earnings, based on four voyages a year, were estimated by the passenger departments of the Company. To their estimates were added the potential earnings of freight, the estimated costs of the ship; fuel; crew, port dues and so forth. From the sum total of these calculations, the management had to decide whether the vessel was going to be a viable unit of their fleet.

It should be noted that this procedure was repeated a number of times before anything like a final decision was reached. Then, at that point, larger and more detailed drawings of the accommodation were made so that they could be sent to the Builder's drawing office. Some new information must have caused the Management to give new thoughts to the Tourist accommodation, since a radical change in standards was approved. Up until that time, this had been laid out as simple and plain cabins, mostly six, eight or ten berth ones, in order to carry large numbers at the smallest possible fare. The new arrangement, to which the ship was built, consisted of much better Tourist cabins, but it meant that the sums regarding her potential earnings had to be revised drastically.

Originally there had been accommodation planned for over 1,000 Tourist and about 730 First class passengers, but the revisions brought the numbers almost equal—some 700 in each class. Moreover, open-deck space had to be improved for the tourist class and, although this was done, it was realized after the *Orcades* had been in service for a short time that it was still not as good as was desirable with the result that, in subsequent ships, further improvements were made. There is a great need for generous open deck areas for passengers and crew in vessels operating through tropical waters, in order to provide space for exercise and relaxation in the open air. This point received a great deal of consideration, and the passenger games decks had to be planned so as to provide the maximum of good games layouts, for deck quoits and quoit tennis in particular.

In the previous, slower vessels, these open spaces had been arranged so that the sea breezes could help to temper the blazing tropic sun, but this new class of ship was to operate at 22½ knots service speed as compared with the 16 or 18 knots of most of their pre-war predecessors. In consequence, the wind created merely by the ship's own speed was a force to be considered, and the new class had their superstructure shapes designed with this point in view. Artists like to depict ships' superstructures with 'swish' shapes, 'streamlined' like the shapes of aeroplanes or racing cars. This is utterly wrong in a vessel where people want to use the open decks. If a shape is properly streamlined, it follows that the wind should follow the contour of the shape. If this happened in practice, the lives of the passengers using the decks would be an unending misery of wind-buffeting. I knew one such vessel, but mercifully the beautiful streamlining was ruined by a subsequent and terrible growth of ventilators and of other excrescences which, in the event, offered some wind protection and helped the passengers to enjoy what would otherwise have been a sort of purgatory.

During the planning of the *Orcades*, the managers had an idea (as they often did) and passed it on to the naval architect for examination. They suggested that the navigating bridge of the new vessel be moved aft from the usual position at the forward end of the boat deck and superstructure, to make a combination with the funnel casing, and thus provide a large, uninterrupted and square deck space forward of it for the use of the passengers. This arrangement would move the navigating bridge to a position close to, and over, the point about which a ship turns—an arrangement which a mariner might consider to be an improvement. This suggestion was put to members of the Marine Department of the Company, but it received quite a lot of adverse criticism and only few words of support. This did not surprise me, because I have always found that a majority of seamen dislike change.

However, working in the office was Capt. G.G. Thorne, R.D., R.N.R., an ex-commodore of the Orient Line who was then retained by the Company rather in the role of a consultant on marine matters. He was a gentleman whom I already admired greatly both as a knowledgeable helpmate and for his open-minded and unbiased attitude, and he now gave his blessing to the new idea, with the result that we did move the bridge aft to form part of the funnel casing—and no-one ever regretted doing so. In so moving the navigating bridge to this new position it became possible for the officers to observe both the fore and after ends of the ship from the wings of the bridge, which was an invaluable help when moving in confined waters or when entering and leaving harbour.

The appearance of the ship was altered considerably by the change and the forward end of the boat deck, vacated by the navigating bridge, became an observation point for passengers. With this in mind, a high, curved front had been fitted across the forward end of the deckhouse and given tall, closely spaced windows and a roof about sixteen feet in height from the deck to deflect wind from forward over the heads of the passengers sitting in deck chairs or playing quoits. Sliding screens were also built into the sides of the deck and thus was formed a very large and attractive deck area. Unfortunately, when the ship went into service, we found that the wind, which had been deflected upwards by the screen at the forward end of this space, curled down again just forward of the bridge front; struck the deck and was deflected up again—to the infinite dismay of the ladies and great amusement of the more uninhibited males present! This difficulty was overcome by the addition of a large horizontal screen about six feet wide built across the bridge front over the 'arena', as the new games deck was called. This deck space, together with others elsewhere in the ship, provided the passengers with what must have been the best deck areas of any vessel of her size afloat at that time.

Ships have had sheer and camber ever since time began. The reason for sheer is obvious enough: it provides reserve buoyancy forward and aft to enable the vessel to be more seaworthy, ride well and lift to and keep the seas from running over her in stormy weather. Camber, the upwards curvature of decks from the sides to the centre-line, provides a means of running loose water to the scuppers, besides being a reserve against the sagging of wooden decks, in particular, which can take place as a ship ages. It is also a structurally stronger shape than a flat deck. However, sheer and camber cause difficulties and expense in the building of ships, especially in the accommodation within them. Every bulkhead, door and window has to be shaped to suit the camber or sheer, and sometimes both of them, so it will be apparent that the cost of the work involved must be appreciably greater than if the decks were flat.

In days gone by, ships had elaborate mouldings fitted around every cabin door and window, so one can imagine the work entailed in fitting these alone, since none could be mitred as in the case of right-angled window- or door-frames. In the Orient ships before the second World War, no decks other than the weather ones had any camber, which had thereby reduced the joinery work required. When the *Orcades* was planned, another step was taken to reduce the cost of the installation of accommodation. Above the bulkhead deck, which was

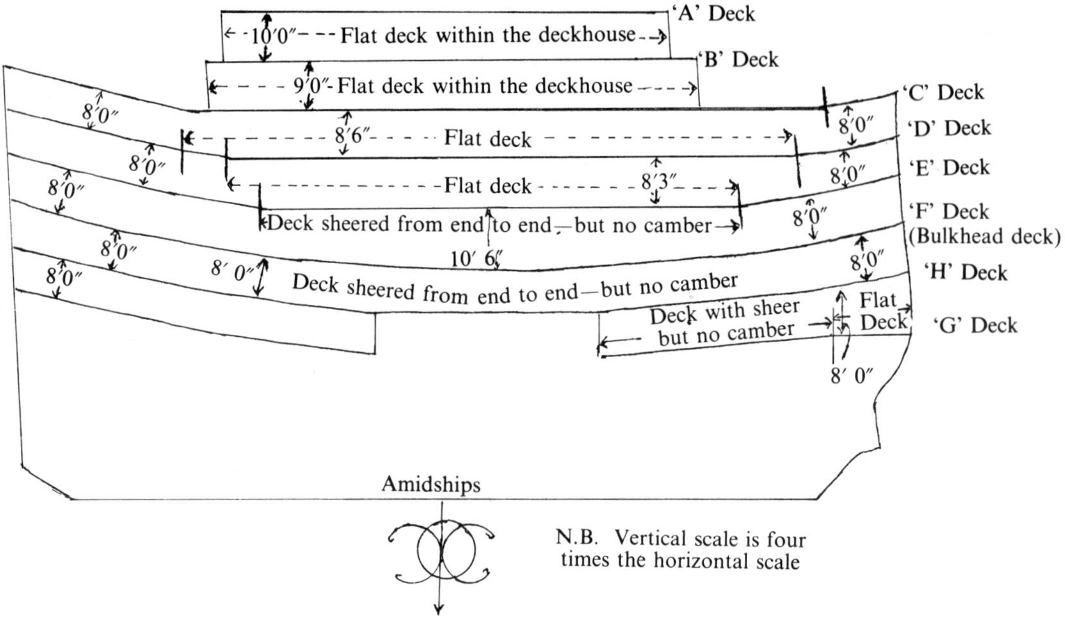

55. The method of arranging flat decks in the ORCADES (1948).

sheered to suit the International Rules for Freeboard and Subdivision, there was need for a greater height between decks in the midships section of each deck than towards the end of the ship, because services, such as ventilation trunking, are larger amidships than those required towards the ends of the decks. The practice of the Company was to provide a minimum 'tween deck height of 8 feet from top of deck beam to top of deck beam for both passengers and crew. In the Dining and other public rooms, 10 feet 'tween deck height was provided. In other amidship passenger accommodation, greater height was needed to cater for the increased size of services fitted above the cabin ceilings. This was usually 8 feet 6 inches, but was occasionally 8 feet 9 inches or even 9 feet.

In order to increase the area of accommodation without sheer or camber, we resorted to the scheme shown in the figure*, from which it will

* See Plate 55.

be seen that the uppermost decks under the main public rooms on 'B' deck were flat from end to end. This resulted in a saving in building cost of some consequence. One small result of this was that we did not have to fit sills on some cabin doorways to cater for the sloping decks. In earlier vessels, many passengers, unused to the ways of the sea and ships, must have stumbled or even measured their lengths whilst passing through doorways and forgetting about the sills.

Of 28,164 tons gross, and 32,200 displacement, the *Orcades* was a large ship, over 700 feet overall and, with her two sets of Parson's geared turbines which developed 42,500 s.h.p., achieved an average of 24.74 knots on trials. With her 22½ knots service speed, she could reduce the time of passage from London to Melbourne from 36 to 28 days. When she first went into service she had air-conditioning in many of her public rooms and special cabins but, in a re-fit in 1959, she was air-conditioned throughout her passenger and crew accommodation. She sailed on her maiden voyage on 14 December, 1948, and had cost £3,000,000. It may be of interest, for purposes of comparison, to quote some costs of other ships of the Company. For instance, when the Orient Steam Navigation Company was founded in 1878, the fleet of four ships bought from the P.S.N.Co., each of which was of a little less than 4,000 tons gross, cost less than one quarter of the price of a single *Orcades* in 1948. When one considers that these ships were seven years old at the time, and were more than half the tonnage of the *Orcades* in aggregate, the reader may well express surprise that the figures were so very similar (taking account of their age), especially having regard to the comment made in Mr. Geddes' 'Message' to his staff to the effect that building costs had virtually doubled since before the second World War. The *Orient*, of 5,386 tons gross, cost £150,000— or £27.85 per gross ton (against £106.52 per gross ton for the *Orcades*,) representing an increase of 3.82 times, of which a factor of two must be accounted for by the inflation in prices between 1939 and 1945, so, bearing in mind the immense extra sophistication of the modern ship, the costs were not, perhaps, so unreasonable. However, the *Orion*, in 1935, cost £950,000, which is again explicable, since this was £40.65 per gross ton which, doubled, becomes £81.30, and much of the remaining 23.68% might be attributed to the additional sophistication, stabilizers, etc.

These figures could only be compared equitably by resorting to a most extraordinary—and somewhat fruitless—investigation, involving computers, but it is quite clear that, while ship-building costs had gradually increased over the years until 1939, they had not done so unreasonably where ships of this sort were concerned, and bearing in mind that 'gross tons' do not tell the whole story of the equipment and services built into them. However, the really fascinating figures follow, since the *Oronsay (II)*, which was basically similar to the *Orcades (III)* cost £4,000,000 three years later (an increase of 25%) and the *Orsova (II)* in 1954, cost £6,500,000. In other words, costs had increased by over 116% in a period of six years. Last, the *Oriana*, of 41,925 gross tons, cost £14,000,000 in 1960—a cost of £333.93 per gross ton. It may be said 'All right, but she was more sophisticated still', and so she was, but in other ways great economies had been effected (as I have already shown), and the matter of the building of the *Oriana* is dealt with in some detail in Part 3 of this book. One thing which emerges is abundantly clear: those who have managed our government and economy in recent years have much to answer for, and, with the staggering and continuing rate of inflation (at the time of writing) the mind boggles to think how much a vessel like the *Oriana* would cost today.

As was customary with all new Orient Line ships, representatives of all departments of the Company sailed for some part of the maiden voyage of each, in order to make observations on the behaviour of parts of the vessel with which they were concerned. I was in the *Orcades* on her maiden voyage and, one morning, when we were in the Red Sea, I went up to the boat deck after an early breakfast to enjoy the soft, warm air and beautiful sunshine. There was a slight breeze from the port beam—(Port Out!)—and, as I looked up at the haze of hot gases rising from the top of the funnel, I could see large, soft soots falling slowly down by the funnel casing on to the wood deck. These soots looked like immense black snowflakes and were rather oily, and I knew that they contained sulphuric acid and were very corrosive in nature. Knowing that our Superintending Engineer was having breakfast in the dining room, I dashed down to ask him to have a look at this problem. He and I returned as quickly as possible to the boat deck but . . . too late! Two ladies in long white summery dresses were just sitting down on a seat against the funnel casing on which some of these large soots had already fallen. There was nothing we could do at that moment so . . . we silently stole away!*

Funnel soots have always been a nuisance since steam first appeared in ships, but nowadays they are much worse than they were before the use of oil as fuel for ships' boilers. The quantity of soot has increased greatly, due to the greater power developed by ships' engines and, in recent times, the quality of oil being used is of a type remaining after nearly everything useful, such as aviation spirit, petrol, paraffin and so on has been extracted from it. The residue is glutinous, difficult to burn, and requires very special equipment to force it through the nozzles into the boiler furnaces. I believe that the next grade below some ships' bunker oil is tar—or so it would seem—and goodness knows what goes into the atmosphere from the funnel tops. At all events, this problem of getting rid of funnel gases remains to be solved by marine engineers and naval architects. The trouble was a real scourge for all who went to sea in passenger ships with boilers, since the acid in the soots destroyed awnings, deck surfaces and the clothing of passengers and crew, while the cost to the shipowner was considerable. Today the degree of nuisance has been reduced considerably, and may not be noticeable to most passengers.

Very many interesting technical papers have been written on the subject of wind over the decks and funnels of ships and on how to reduce or eliminate entirely the fall of smoke and soot from ships' funnels. Many of the earlier papers were almost useless because they presumed that winds at sea flow over a ship from forward to aft in a sensible and predictable way. This is rarely true and, from personal observation, I can testify that the winds around a vessel are often turbulent, variable in intensity and behaving in extraordinary and deplorable ways. Often the wind blows forward along corridors in a ship, and it is not unusual to find an exhaust ventilator, positioned some distance aft of a supply ventilator, feeding foul air into that supply one! This was shown clearly during an investigation into the cause of foul air in the accommodation of one vessel, for a long ribbon

* Of course the Company knew very well about the likelihood of beam winds in that area and elsewhere, but there was extreme ignorance in shipping circles about the behaviour of winds over ships and falling soots at that time.

was tied to the exhaust grills of the vent, which was fitted some twenty feet or more abaft the air intake of the fan feeding the offending foul air into the quarters. Although the vessel was moving forward at speed, the end of the ribbon soon entered the air intake into the fan!

Much more is known today of the behaviour of wind over ships and their funnels and, as a result, there has been an outbreak of very interesting, and sometimes hideous, fashions in ships' funnels and funnel tops.

At the beginning of the 1950's the P. & O. Company introduced the Thornycroft funnel top on their two ships *Chusan* and *Himalaya*. This type of funnel top was designed and produced by J. I. Thornycroft, shipbuilders and engineers in Southampton, and consisted of a number of horizontal slots below the top of the funnel which, in theory, were supposed to induce streams of air from forward of the funnel to pass through the slots and to carry away the smoke and soots clear of the deck.* This theory may have been correct but, soon afterwards, the Orient Company, who were also being plagued with the nuisance of soots from funnels, made a completely separate investigation into the ways of reducing or curing the problem and tried in a wind tunnel a model Thorneycroft funnel design on a large model of the *Orcades*. It was a failure in that, if the slots in the model funnel were covered, the behaviour of the funnel gases over the ship remained unchanged! It could be argued that the scale effect on the slots of the model funnel was such as to render them useless but, if this be accepted, why bother to look at the Thornycroft model funnel test at all?

The Orient Company made its own contributions to the fashions in funnel tops, as a result of many experiments made for it with large waterline models of their vessels in wind tunnels. Probably the best of these was produced in the National Physical Laboratory at Teddington in a tunnel which had been used originally for aeronautical research. The first step to be taken in such experiments is to establish the outline of the envelope of turbulent air which travels with a ship, wheresoever the source and whatever the power of wind relative to her. This first step is necessary because, if a funnel is not high enough to poke up through the top of this envelope of turbulent

* See Plate 135.

56. *Smoke and smuts were problems common to all companies. Here is the Nord Deutscher Lloyd COLUMBUS (built 1922) . . . . .*

57. *. . . and the White Star MAJESTIC (built in 1914 as the Hapag BISMARCK). (The third funnel was a dummy).*

air, the smoke and soots from it will not pass outside the boundary, but will remain and travel with the ship, and slowly fall to the decks. Having, by wind tunnel experiments, raised the funnel top to clear the boundary, the next step is to find a suitable shape for it to ensure that funnel gases move clear away from the funnel and into the upper air, free from the ship's boundary air.

The falling of soots witnessed in the *Orcades* was caused by a wind from the beam of the ship. The funnel was streamlined and about thirty feet long in a fore-and-aft direction and twenty feet wide in a transverse direction. The problem created by streamlined shapes is that, whilst they look nice and are suitable for use when pointed in the right direction, generally they are very inefficient when pointed in any other way. For this reason, probably the best type of funnel for slow ships is a circular, cylindrical shape of the smallest diameter that the volume of the rising boiler gases will permit. In faster vessels, on the other hand, where the speed is, on average, equal to, or more than, the average wind speeds, some streamlining of the funnel seems to be sensible. The shape of the *Orcades*' funnel presented a large, rather flat and tall surface against the beam wind, and this created a reduction in ambient air pressure on the lee side of it (away from the wind) and thus pulled the soots from the funnel top down into the area of lower pressure. In this context, it should be noted that the funnel gases are forced up from the funnel by fan pressure, but when these hot gases enter an atmosphere of warm air, the reduced mass weight of their particles does not carry them far, and they are therefore more easily drawn down against the funnel side. This is why, incidentally, punka louvre ventilators are less effective in the tropics.

The wind tunnel experiments on the *Orcades*' funnel showed that it was high enough to clear the boundary or turbulent air and that, if we fitted a tubular extension of about eight feet diameter by ten feet high to the top of the existing funnel, the soot trouble should be cured. This was done and was successful for most conditions. (Nothing of this sort can be *entirely* perfect.) The same sort of arrangement was fitted on subsequent funnel tops of Orient ships, and it was popularly known as the 'Welsh Hat', for obvious reasons. The diameter of the

58. The ORCADES (III) with her 'Welsh hat', which was fitted after she went into service.

extension to the top of the funnel was the smallest which could be effective without increasing the speed and power of the fans pushing the funnel gases out of the boiler uptakes. To the uninitiated, it should be pointed out that the outside skin of a funnel encloses many other things besides boiler uptakes. The ten foot extension, therefore, could not be fitted lower down without other problems arising from the change.

Although the *Orcades*, *Oronsay* and the *Orsova* were of one class of so-called 28,000 tonners, each was a little different in external appearance from her sisters, and very different in details of structure and internal arrangements—a fact to be taken into some account when considering relative costs earlier in this chapter. The *Oronsay* was an improvement in many ways on the *Orcades*, and the *Orsova* was better still. At the time of the building of these vessels, improved welding techniques and allied constructional methods, particularly of prefabrication and the erection on the berth of large parts of the vessel, were being developed by Vickers-Armstrong at Barrow-in-Furness, and all these things were very progressive.

References are made in this book both to Vickers and to Vickers-

Armstrong Ltd. The explanation of this is that the firm was Vickers Ltd. in 1924, when the *Orama* was built but, in October, 1927, amalgamated with the shipbuilding firm of Armstrongs, and then became known as Vickers-Armstrong Ltd. Subsequently it became Vickers (Shipbuilders) Ltd, but this was after the *Oriana* was built and beyond the time scale of this book. The firm no longer builds passenger liners but, whether under the one name or the other, it had improved the quality of its work to such a degree that, at the time of the building of the *Oriana*, it was as good as any shipbuilding and marine engineering company in the world.

Certainly I know of no other passenger ship that can compare in quality of building or of marine engineering with the *Oriana*. There was only one serious fault made in the choice of installation in that vessel, which was the decision to use direct electrical current instead of alternating. There were, of course, other minor faults but, over the past eighteen years of service, the ship has proved herself to be excellent. Incidentally, the builders were not responsible for the choice of electrical installation, and cannot be blamed for it. The story is rather a tangled one and not worth setting forth here.

The Orient management had always been anxious to adopt any new building methods which could improve their vessels and, for this reason, coupled with the fact that we were ordering ships in a climate of rather rapidly changing welding methods and other techniques, they took advantage of these in each new ship as she was built. In the *Orcades* (1948), the vertical keel plate and side girders in the double bottom were welded direct to the shell plating and inner bottom plating, and the butts of the shell plating were welded. The bossed shell-plating seams and butts were welded, as was the bossed framing direct to the bossed shell plating. The watertight bulkheads, deck girders, deck plating seams and butts, engine and boiler seatings, generator and auxiliary machinery seats were all welded, too. In the *Oronsay* (1951), in addition to all the welding which had been done in the *Orcades*, large areas of the shell were pre-fabricated with welded seams and butts of the shell plating. These pre-fabricated parts were then assembled on the building berth and welded together. The *Orsova* (1954) was all welded except for the few fore-and-aft seams of riveted connections which were demanded by Lloyds, the Classification Society.

These lines of riveted connections were known as 'crack arresters' at that time, because there had been evidence of failure in the structure of some welded ships in which cracks had started and gone on until they had even broken in two and foundered. This was due to the use of unsuitable steels and to bad design in many instances. The 'crack arresters' were really thick bands of overlapping riveted plates, or doubled plates, to stop tears or cracks going any further. This procedure was said by many to show the weakness of welding, but others (and I number myself amongst the latter) believe it shows how welding is capable of creating a homogeneous structure which is only weak if the design of materials (or both) are faulty.

The failure of welded ships is worthy of a short diversion from the subject of the Orient Line. Many pre-fabricated welded ships, particularly cargo vessels constructed in the United States during and immediately after the second World War, had structural failures of various kinds, some of which were very serious and caused losses of the ships themselves. The United States set up a Maritime Commission to enquire into this outbreak of casualties under the official designation of '*The Design and Methods of Construction of Welded Steel Merchant Vessels.*'

Between 1942 and 1946, investigations were made into 4,694 welded ships, those found to have had structural failures being recorded in three categories: Class 1 being of fracture so serious as to cause the ship to be in a dangerous condition or to be lost. The other two categories are not important to this chapter. Of the 4,694 ships, 1,442 casualties were recorded, of which 127 were in class 1 (2.71% of the whole!). Eight of these ships broke in two and were lost. Four others broke in two but were salved.*

The outstanding case which could be investigated in detail, because it happened in harbour in known conditions, was the all-welded tanker *Schenectady.* nearing completion at her builder's yard at Swan Island in the United States. On 16 January, 1943, she was lying alongside the outfitting quay in still water, with the weather clear and the air temperature 26°F, which was cold, but not unduly so.

* A writer in *Sea History* recorded seeing large concrete blocks in the J.R. Jones yard at Panama City during the war, with the numbers '25', '50', '75' etc. painted on them, these denoting their weight in tons. Each morning the ways foreman inspected the hull being built and measured the rise of the (designed) flat keel ends off the blocks. When they reached 1½-2″ from the true, the blocks were put on the ends of the hull to force them back, and the welding sequence was reversed!! In due course, each light Liberty ship arriving in New York was sent to a yard to have an endless (welded) belt of steel, 2 feet deep, riveted along her sheer strakes. *Sea History, No. 12, p.29.*

Then, according to the records:

'Without warning and with a report which could be heard for at least a mile, the deck and sides just aft of the bridge' (centre) *'superstructure fractured. The fracture extended almost instantaneously to the turn of the bilge*, port and starboard. Only the bottom plating held. The vessel jack-knifed, with the centre portion rising so that no water entered the hull.*

Investigations showed that there was only a small stress in the plating of the deck at the time of the failure. Other examinations into ship failure of this sort showed similar features, especially the low stresses.

Most of the ships lost were 'Liberty' class, which were being mass-produced to replace war-losses. They were dry-cargo vessels with five holds and the bridge fitted roughly amidships. Fractures usually took place in the vicinity of the hatches near the bridge. The *J. L. M. Curry* suffered in this way, and was lost. The *Valerie Chkechov* broke in two but was not lost. The investigations showed that the stresses at the time of fracture were low and that, therefore, the failures must have been caused by discontinuities or notches in the structures and/or brittleness in the make-up of the steel. Of these two reasons, the former should not have happened and could be, and would be, corrected, but the latter called for the development of suitable steels and their specifications. This was done and, by the late 1950's, steelmakers were producing consistent qualities of notch-ductile steels to be used in ships of all-welded construction. That is to say, in simpler terms, steels that are pliant and not brittle, and not liable to fracture at discontinuities in structures, whilst being suitable for welding.

This enquiry held in the U.S.A. had its counterpart in the United Kingdom, where the findings were in close accord with those in America. As can be readily understood, interchange of developing information on the subject was constantly taking place, and the Classification Societies for ship construction were not only informed but involved, so that eventually specifications were printed in their rules. The major societies in the world are Lloyds Register (Great Britain): American Bureau of Shipping (U.S.A.): Nippon Kaiji

* The bottom rounded corners of the hull at amidships.

59. The ORSOVA (II) of 1954.

Kyokai (Japan): Bureau Veritas (France); Registrano Italiano Navale (Italy), Germanischer Lloyd (Germany) and Det Norske Veritas (Norway).

Nowadays, the incidence of serious structural failure in ships has largely disappeared, but cargo ships, especially large bulk carriers, can be loaded badly and this can cause serious damage, or even disaster.

The *Orsova* was the first all-welded passenger liner to be built in Britain and, possibly, in the world.

These improvements brought about smoother hulls by reducing the areas of exposed edges of shell plating and the large numbers of slightly raised heads of rivets. In the *Orsova*, there were no edges of shell plating and very few raised rivet heads to cause unnecessary friction and turbulence in the flow of sea water about the ship's hull. Although the officially recorded performances of the three 28,000-ton Orient ships varied because of different conditions of weather at the times of their sea trials, and because other factors caused minor differences, there is no doubt that the advances in welding methods and techniques largely improved the trial results. The *Orcades* achieved a mean speed of 24.74 knots on the measured mile in November, 1948. In May, 1951, the *Oronsay* achieved a mean of 25.23 knots and, in March, 1954, the *Orsova* recorded a mean speed of 26.07 knots. Another improvement which followed from the increased use of welding was the reduction of weight made in the *Oronsay* and, more particularly, in the *Orsova.*

When the *Orcades* was built in 1948, there were serious shortages of all sorts of materials which had been readily available before the second World War. One of these was teak wood, which had long been used in ships for weather decks, handrails and external ladders. Teak is oily in nature and very resistant to rot in wet conditions of use. It is very hard wearing; long grained, has no knots or shakes in the grain, and is a wood without peer in the normal uses to which it is put in ships. Due to the ravages of the recent hostilities in the Far East, where teak grows, it was difficult or impossible to procure after the war was over.

But for the foresight of the shipbuilders in Barrow, there would have been no teak to sheath the steel decks of the *Orcades*, but Vickers had bought before the war and put into store enough of it to lay the decks of a large passenger liner. Fortunately, this wood was not lost by enemy action and was offered to the Orient Line when the *Orcades* was built and, of course, laid in the ship. By the time the *Oronsay* was ordered, there was no more teak and she became a guinea-pig for woods available as substitutes for it. We were offered a bewildering selection under the most exotic of jungle names—Iroko, Sekondo, Obeche, etc.—but the one most highly recommended was Serayah, a white wood which grows in Borneo and looks very like bleached teak, and which had been used in many ships of the Royal Navy at that time.

We used Serayah extensively on the decks of the *Oronsay*, and some types of mahogany as well. None of them were very much good, and some of the mahogany-type woods went completely rotten throughout their thickness within a few years of service. One could write a large book on the subject of deck coverings and substitutes, but very little of its contents could contain anything really constructive except to say:- 'Stick to old and tried materials'.

The problems created by using new materials to replace traditional deck coverings inside and outside a ship are legion, and some of them are insoluble. In the mid-1950's a new and costly difficulty was caused by a new ladies' fashion in footwear—the 'stiletto' heel. This was a high heel with a very small base of about a quarter of an inch diameter which, depending on the wearer's weight, could bring to bear one to one and a half tons per square inch impact pressure on the deck covering.* This new form of assault was experienced not only in ships but also on the floorings of concert halls; museums; assembly halls, dance floors and even palaces throughout the world. It was a silly fashion which was also found to be harmful to the ankles of those who wore them. Some reduction in the extent of damage was only achieved by the banning of the wearing of these particular heels on the floors of some public places. It would have been interesting to have seen an estimate of the aggregate damage done, were that possible. The trouble only abated when the fashion became outdated again—probably due to the silent prayers of a multitude of the despairing menfolk responsible for the good condition of floors in general.

The realization of the damage wreaked by stiletto heels on the Orient Line floor coverings became apparent one day when members of the shore staff had gone aboard one of the ships which had just returned from Australia. In those days, a popular floor covering was a high quality linoleum about a quarter of an inch in thickness, and this was laid throughout corridors, stair and embarkation halls and in some public rooms and, in this particular vessel, was of a polka dot pattern, consisting of dark dots about a quarter of an inch in diameter, spaced about an inch apart, on a paler ground colour. We were mystified by a multitude of small indentations about the same diameter as the polka dot and, when I say a 'multitude', I mean—possibly—millions. The mystery was quickly solved, however, since, as we looked around, we could see a young lady of our staff in animated conversation nearby. She was standing on one leg with the other leg pushed out and, poised on one of her deadly heels, her out-thrust foot was being waggled busily back and forth so that the heel was screwing itself into the linoleum which had softened a little, anyway, with the heat of the tropical passage which the Company's ships made, and it was clear that stiletto heels had ruined the floor covering of this vessel in one single voyage!

It should also be said that some of the beautiful and expensive

* This is a far greater pressure per square inch than is exerted by a standing elephant.

parquetry floorings of the ships were damaged at that time and, if anything be engraved on my heart when I die, it will be 'Deck Coverings', because that sums up in two words what has proved to be to me the most worrying and difficult part of my life as the naval architect of a shipping company.

The choice of materials is mainly confined to finding those which will stand up to the wear and tear of a constantly changing usage through all the climates of the world. The materials must look well and must wear well, not only in these altering conditions, but must be proof against the rough treatment they receive from both passengers and crew. It is a strange attitude found in human beings that they seem to enjoy despoiling any area except, perhaps, that which they actually own themselves. For instance, they will throw down lighted cigarette ends and extinguish them by screwing them underfoot into the carpet—that is, if they bother to extinguish them at all. Incidentally, as a result of carefully kept records over a period of years, it has been found that the cheapest way of carpeting areas used by the travelling public is to put down the most expensive carpets for the roughest passengers (if one wants that carpet to last), or, alternatively, to lay the cheapest possible carpets and to replace them frequently as they become shabby.

The fashion nowadays seems to be to have one class travel and, from personal observation, I can state unequivocally that this seems to have resulted in a general lowering of standards of behaviour. The treatment of accommodation has deteriorated markedly, and a new viewpoint on the part of a section of the travellers seems to be that, because they have paid their fares, they should leave everything worthless when they leave the ship. There are rough and thoughtless people in any community and, because the days of discipline and self-discipline seem to have gone, I believe that the return of the two class system is long overdue. It should be possible for those who like quietness and time to think to be able to indulge themselves.

Some years ago, I had reason to go into an occupied crew cabin in a ship which was to sail the following day. The crew accommodation had been cleaned throughout by shore labour a few hours before the crew joined her, and was therefore clean and tidy for occupation.

I will draw a veil over what I found. Suffice it that I so understate the case as to remark that it was far from neat and tidy by then. Unfortunately, it is a fact of life that there are people in all grades of society who are natural 'louts', and only firm discipline can control them from spoiling the lives of others. In the days of this incident, the lower ranks of the crew were berthed in four and six berth cabins and, therefore, one badly behaved man could cause unhappiness for several of his cabin-mates. In this context, it is worth mentioning that the pre-war seamen's union in Australasia not only achieved very exceptional conditions for their men (by the then standards of the times), but they *did* also make sure that their men were not only competent to do their jobs, but respected the accommodation and so forth which they had achieved. It is an unhappy reflection on the National Union of Seamen in this country that they have never, at any time, taken a similar stance and, although they have demanded (and usually achieved) a great deal—and I speak of British ships as a whole and not just of the Orient Line—there has never been any sense of 'Give and Take', whether in ensuring that their members are competent to fulfill the tasks likely to be required of them*, or in making sure that they respect the accommodation and so forth provided for them. Perhaps one may amend that remark, by saying that they have a well developed sense of 'Take', but little, or none, of 'Give'.

In 1955, the management of the Orient Line decided that the crew should have much better accommodation than was usual at that time, and that no members of it, apart from a small number of boys, should be berthed more than two men to a cabin. The boys were in four-berth cabins. Each cabin had a wash-basin with hot and cold running water and the furniture was of polished mahogany. It was not supposed that abuse of facilities would be eliminated, but that its effect on other members of the crew would be reduced, and might be the more easily controlled by periodic inspections by the officers at sea.

There was a gentleman at the Ministry of Transport who was in charge of the department dealing with Crew Regulations. For a long time he had been very difficult to deal with in discussions about the

* Many so-called 'A.Bs' who have spent most of their time in passenger ships know little of sailor work, which is normally carried out by shore gangs. Some cannot even steer—let alone splice wire.

crew accommodation planned for our new vessels and, when comparing our experiences with the naval architects of other shipping companies, I realized that all of them were having the same problems with him, and that he was labouring under a delusion, born many years before, that shipowners were a grasping lot and that they totally disregarded the 'poor seamen'.

Finally, I invited this fellow to lunch aboard one of the newer Orient ships on the morning of her arrival from an Australian voyage and, afterwards, we visited the crew accommodation. In the same way as it takes only a few rowdy 'fans' to spoil a football match, so it takes only a few badly-behaved members of the crew to wreak havoc in their accommodation, and many of these fellows wait till the night before arrival to do their worst. This gentleman from the Ministry was a much wiser man after his visit, and we were friendly and understanding of each other's problems after that time.

The reader could ask, with some logic:- 'Why do shipowners not provide the crew with single-berth cabins?' Indeed, this is done very commonly nowadays in cargo ships but, as I have stated elsewhere in this book, the deck space of most freighters is not so precious and capable of earning its keep as that of a passenger ship. The minimum area of a cabin required by a single member of the crew is nearly the same as that needed for a two-berth one, and the result of putting all personnel into single-berth cabins in a passenger ship would reduce the passenger numbers appreciably. Thus, such a move could only be paid for by increasing the rates of passenger travel or by reducing the crew numbers or wages. Neither of the latter would be acceptable and, incidentally, the potential passenger would probably not be prepared to pay a higher fare. In other words, cargo ships and passenger vessels are very different in their economics, and should not be compared with one another.

Plastics became a new material to be considered for application to all sorts of items for use in ships in the 1930's, and many of these were found to be unsuitable until the mixtures used in their manufacture, or the manufacturing methods, were changed. The Orient Company pioneered the use of many of these products when fitting out the *Orion* in 1934. There were plastic door furniture; hat and coat hooks,

60. The ORONSAY (II) in P. & O. colours passing under Sydney bridge.

curtain rails and other items of equipment in their thousands, but it was found that the heat of the tropics caused havoc with these untried materials as they aged. Most of these items had a light metal matrix, or interior strengthening frame, which remained fairly constant in size, but the plastic shrank and, in doing so, cracked and often splintered off the matrix. It also changed in colour from the chosen pale cream to a rather nasty brown colour. Sheet plastic was also used extensively to cover furniture tops and, to a lesser extent, as wall coverings.

This latter use was shown by experience to be a worthwhile means of protecting surfaces against the nail-polishes and other spirits usually used by ladies. However, we had an unexpected and very expensive experience with sheet plastic in 1951. In order to save the great expense of the maintenance of painted bulkheads, it was decided to use hard-faced plastic sheets measuring about 8′ × 4′, by approximately one twentieth of an inch in thickness, to cover the bulkheads of corridors in crew and tourist passenger accommodation. As can be imagined, this entailed the use of thousands of sheets, which were stuck to the plywood bulkheads by an impact adhesive. One thing which we did not know, and I would hazard a guess that the average reader of this does not know it either, is that some, if not all, of these hard-faced plastics absorb moisture to a low degree which, together with changes in temperature, causes them to shrink and expand, depending on the humidity of the atmosphere.

The *Oronsay*, the new ship which was nearing completion, was fitted with these sheets of plastic in a very cold winter, and her crew accommodation was being tested with heating to satisfy the relevant rules of the Ministry of Transport at that time. Unfortunately, there was no humidifying arrangement being used in the steam-heating system, and the very cold air from outside was being drawn into the ship by fans, heated, and then blown into the crew quarters. Atmospheric cold air has little moisture in it and, when heated to fairly high temperatures, is extremely dry and arid. These were just the conditions that the sheet plastic and mahogany furniture in the accommodation could not stand. Moreover, there was a further misfortune. The temperature control failed to stop the heating of the accommodation rising over the required limit, and subjected it to more heat than was necessary.

The resulting chaos almost beggared description. The woodwork curled up with the heat and drying effects but, and this was infinitely worse, the sheets of plastic contracted and either curled off the bulkheads or shattered from top to bottom in about the middle of their width, each with a noise like a gun blast. A curious feature of the impact adhesive was that it softened with the heat, often in the middle areas of the sheets, and this permitted them to behave like the strings of a bow until their limits of strength were reached, when each shattered. This damage was eventually repaired, but the end of this story has not yet been reached. Some time later, the ship entered the port of Vancouver during a very cold period, meeting the same conditions again.

Once again, the outside air, which was very cold, was drawn by fans into the ship, heated up to a high temperature, and blown into the accommodation. During the night there was a frightful noise of plastic sheets being broken by unusual contractions, as before, due to the drying conditions of the heated air in the passenger spaces. Incidentally, when the disaster—for no other word will do—was being investigated, it was found that the plastic sheets had contracted one eighth of an inch in the four feet width of each sheet, a fact which the manufacturer would not believe at first, and of which he was only convinced when his own eyes had seen the marks left on the bulkheads*. So much for the problems of those who seek to pioneer new materials. As far as plastics are concerned, great improvements have since taken place, not only in their own quality, but also in the adhesives used to fix them.

Finally, on this matter of materials, our experience in the use of plywood is worthy of mention. The Company had decided to investigate the possibility of using pre-formed plywood sheets to build deck chairs. The strong sunlight in the tropics plays havoc with materials such as canvas, which can be used successfully, and which endure for years of usage, in temperate climates. We had found that sheet plastics and plastic coat hooks and like fittings did not last longer than about six months when fitted in spaces exposed to tropical sunlight, and that they crazed into brittle fragments in that time.

The first plywood deck chairs were constructed using pre-formed mahogany- and teak-faced plywood. Because we had suffered failures when using materials which had proved satisfactory over long usage in Britain, we warned the excellent furniture makers whom we had employed of the effects which we had experienced when using such materials in tropical conditions. In consequence, heeding this advice, they consulted the best experts they could find about adhesives for the plywood and about the best makers of the plywood itself whom they should employ for the supply of their raw material. In the event, they selected a good type of 'Marine' plywood regularly employed in the manufacture of boats and dinghies, which could lie for months in the waters around the coasts of Britain.

So, the deck chairs were made and duly supplied to one of our vessels, which then voyaged to Australia and back to Tilbury, when

* It may seem to be strange that the same disastrous set of circumstances could arise twice in the same company—let alone in the same ship. Suffice it to say that it should not have occurred and was occasioned by a personality problem and consequent lack of communication which could not have been foreseen.

they were found to be a complete failure! The plywood had opened like the leaves of a book! It was our belief that the sea-water used for washing down the decks (and rain water, too), had gradually seeped up the end grain of the plywood and that, when a strong sun had heated up the damp wood, it had formed steam and burst the layers of ply asunder. Certainly, the appearance of the chairs supported this view, which was one with which forestry experts and plywood manufacturers concurred as being the cause of the trouble. The next step was to involve the makers of adhesives, who worked on the solution of the problem, and who finally produced a special adhesive which would withstand the forces developed in plywood when boiled in water and then dried quickly in an oven, repeatedly for weeks on end. Finally, plywood was made using this new and expensive adhesive, after which more chairs were made and tested through the tropics with great success. Indeed, they are still being used after more than twenty years of service.

Over the years, the Orient Line vessels had carried passengers of various denominations, such as 'steerage'; 'third', 'second' and 'first' class, together with 'emigrants'. These titles of classes varied as time went by, and the standards of accommodation, feeding and service varied and improved in each class. Between 1909 and 1910, five of the 12,000 ton class of Orient ship were delivered and carried about 230 first class passengers, 200 second class and 700 third class. In the period 1924 to 1929, five ships of a new class, of 20,000 tons, were put into service, and these carried 600 first class, and 1,200 third class. The *Orion* and the *Orcades*, built in 1935 and 1937 respectively, carried about 460 first class and 600 tourist passengers. These titles for passengers of 'First' and 'Tourist' were used by the Company from that time until the end of its trading under the Orient houseflag. The only change was made in the standard of 'Tourist', which for a short time was known as 'Tourist A' and 'Tourist B', but after a short time this differentiation became just 'Tourist'.

The 28,000-tonners were a successful class of ship and three vessels of this size, the *Himalaya, Iberia* and the *Arcadia*, were built for the P. & O. Company by Vickers at Barrow-in-Furness, Harland & Wolff at Belfast and by John Browns of Clydebank respectively, and

61. *The P. & O. ARCADIA had the same dimensions to her hull as the Orient 28,000-tonners, but her profile and interior was very different. She is here seen in Hamburg.*

used to run on an agreed programme of sailings with the three similar ships of the Orient Line from Britain to Australia.

On 1 January, 1954, the *Oronsay* left Sydney and sailed across the Pacific, calling at Auckland, Suva, Honolulu, Victoria, B.C., Vancouver and San Francisco, before returning and calling at the same ports as on the outward journey, thus pioneering a new route for the Orient Company ships. On the 17 September of the same year, the *Orion* made a similar voyage. These new ventures were explorations into the commercial possibilities of this route, which had been planned and advertised in 1953, following the withdrawal of the Canadian-Australasian Line's motor ship *Aorangi*, which had maintained a service linking Sydney and Auckland with Vancouver until that time, and after the previous withdrawal of the American Matson Line vessels *Monterey* and *Mariposa*, which had also run a trans-Pacific passenger route.

In 1955, the *Orsova* left Tilbury on 27 April and called at

62. The Matson liner MARIPOSA.

63. The $18\frac{1}{2}$ knot AORANGI, built in 1924.

Gibraltar,, Naples, Port Said, Aden, Colombo, Fremantle, Adelaide, Melbourne and Sydney before sailing across the Tasman Sea to Auckland and thence across the Pacific to Suva and Vancouver in Canada. Thence she proceeded to San Francisco and Los Angeles before returning to Tilbury via the Panama Canal, and calling at Trinidad and Cherbourg *en route*. She reached Tilbury on 1 July, 1953, after making a complete circumnavigation of the world.

The *Orcades* followed a similar route, but in the reverse direction, when she left Tilbury on 22 August, 1955. These voyages proved to be popular with passengers and to be financially sound, so the development of the joint P. & O.-Orient Australian/Pacific Far Eastern network of services followed from this pioneering and adventuring of the Orient Company. This expansion of interests of the two companies was introduced as the Orient and Pacific Lines in January, 1958. The operations of the P. & O. and Orient Companies had been similar for many years and had grown closer since the end of the second World War. Their ships had a certain similarity in appearance and were designed to operate through the tropics on the same sort of service and, indeed, the P. & O. had built their *Himalaya* precisely on the lines of the *Orcades (III)* so far as hull and machinery were concerned, although the two companies had different ideas about the accommodation and so forth, and in the view of those responsible for the design and building of the vessels of the two companies they were very different in details and outward appearance. There were, indeed, a number of instances which could be quoted in which the P. & O. had followed the Orient lead.

As a result of the fact that there were now fewer, but larger and faster vessels in each company and of the closer liaison between them in the joint venture across the Pacific and, finally, round the world, it was an inevitable act of rationalization for them to have amalgamated as, indeed, they did in 1960 when, on 2 May, they became known as the P. & O.-Orient (Passenger Services) Ltd. This move was the beginning of the end of the Orient Company and, through various stages, it finally came in October, 1966, when the title was dropped in favour of 'P. & O.' The Orient Line, we might say, had sunk without trace as an entity, after a glorious history had been written. There will never be a better passenger shipping line within its routes or orbits of interest.

64. *Commodore J. L. Dunkley hauls down the Orient house-flag for the last time on 30 September, 1966.*

IV. ORIENT STEAM NAVIGATION COMPANY FLEET LIST

The following schedule shows all those vessels owned or chartered by the Orient Line from its beginning in 1878 until its end between 1960-5, together with those few vessels which were operated by Anderson, Anderson & Partners under steam and before the actual formation of the Orient Steam Navigation Company, together with those which were managed by the Orient Line managers (Anderson, Green & Co. Ltd.) on behalf of the British government during and immediately after the two World Wars. It should be noted that Orient liners carried cargo and were, therefore 'passenger-cargo' vessels, although their capacity for carrying cargo became relatively smaller in the vessels built towards the end of the Company's life.

Vessels wholly owned by the Orient Line are shown in **BOLD CAPITALS**
P.S.N.Co. vessels chartered by the Company are shown in PLAIN CAPITALS.
Other chartered vessels are shown in bold small case, viz: **Stad Amsterdam**
o.a. denotes 'length overall'.
b.p. denotes 'length between perpendiculars'.
Gross Registered Tonnage (G.R.T.) is generally given as built. This tonnage did tend to change, due to alterations, in the life of ships.

1) **Siracusa**
Iron hull. 1,255 G.R.T. 12 knots.
Managed by Frederick Green & Co. Made one return voyage to Sydney, Australia on 12 November, 1872 to explore the potential worth of the trade route.

2) **Easby**
Single screw steamer. Iron hull. 1,489 G.R.T. Built S. Stockton 1873. 250.7 × 32.0 × 21.4′.
Owned by Fraser & Fulton of Dunedin, New Zealand.

3) **St. Osyth**
Single screw steamer. Iron hull. 3,541 G.R.T. Built 1873 by Mitchell, Newcastle-upon-Tyne for Watts, Milburn & Co. 12 knots.
Managed by Anderson, Anderson & Co. Made one return voyage from London to Cape Town and Melbourne to explore potential worth of the trade route.

4) **LUSITANIA**
Iron hull. Built 1871 by Lairds at Birkenhead. 3,877 G.R.T. 384.2′ o.a. 379.9 × 41.3 × 35.2′. 12 knots. Compound engine, coal-fired boilers. 454 passengers (84 first class; 100 second and 270 third class or emigrants.) Re-engined in 1886 after which she carried 155 first and second class, but no emigrants. Speed then 15 knots.
Built for P.S.N.Co. for South American Service. Chartered by Anderson, Anderson & Co. in 1877. First voyage London to Melbourne and Sydney 12 August, 1877. Bought by O.S.N.Co. in 1878. Commissioned for six months as armed merchant cruiser in 1885 for Crimean War. Last voyage to Australia 10 December, 1897. Sold to Beaver Line 1900. Wrecked off Cape Race 26 June, 1901.

5) **CHIMBOROZO**
Single screw steamer. Iron hull. Built 1871 by John Elder, Glasgow. 3,847 G.R.T. 384.0′ b.p. × 41.3′ × 35.3′. 12 knots. Compound engine, coal fired boilers. Passengers: approx. 72 first class; 92 second class and 265 third class or steerage.
Built for P.S.N.Co. for South American service. Chartered by Anderson, Anderson & Co. 1877. First voyage London to Melbourne and Sydney 12 August, 1877. Bought by O.S.N.Co. 1878. Last voyage to Australia 12 May, 1887. Cruised to Norwegian fjords 1889. Sold to P.J. Pitcher, Liverpool, 1894 and re-named *Cleopatra* 1895. Transferred to Ocean Cruising and Highland Yachting Co. 1897. Broken up at Preston 1897.

6) **CUZCO**
Single screw steamer. Iron hull. Built 1871 by John Elder, Glasgow, 3,898 G.R.T. Dimensions, engines, speed, and passenger accommodation as for **Chimborozo**. *Re-engined with triple expansion engine 1888. Then 15 knots, but no longer carried third class passengers.*
Built for P.S.N.Co. for South American service. Chartered by Anderson, Anderson & Co. 1877. First voyage London to Melbourne and Sydney 25 September, 1877. Bought by O.S.N.Co. 1878. The *Cuzco* and *Orient* carried the first frozen meat from Australia to England in 1881*. Last voyage to Sydney 23 May, 1902. Broken up at Genoa in 1905.

7) **GARONNE (1)**
Single screw steamer. Iron hull. Built 1871 by R. Napier, Glasgow. 3,876 G.R.T. 382.1′ b.p. × 41.4′ × 35.7′. 13 knots. Compound engine, coal-fired boilers. Passengers: approx. 60 first class; 60 second class and 320 third class.
Built for P.S.N.Co. for South American service. Chartered by Anderson, Anderson & Co. 1877 and bought by O.S.N.Co. in 1878. First voyage London to Melbourne and Sydney 17 April, 1878, when she became the first Orient ship to fly the new house flag of the O.S.N.Co. Last voyage to Australia 7 June, 1889. The *Garonne* then cruised for eight years. Sold to V. Porter of Liverpool in 1897, and immediately re-sold to F. Waterhouse of Seattle, U.S.A. Broken up at Genoa in 1905.

8) **Stad Amsterdam**
Single-screw steamer. Iron hull. Built 1874 by Inglis, Glasgow. 2,714 G.R.T. 349.7′ × 38.4′ × 28.0′ 12 knots. Compound engine.
Built for the Royal Netherlands Steamship Co. One return voyage from London to Melbourne and Sydney 24 October, 1877.

9) ACONCAGUA
Single screw steamer. Iron hull. Built 1872 by John Elder, Glasgow. 4,105 G.R.T. 404.9′ × 41.5′ × 35.4′ 13 knots. Compound engine, coal-fired boilers. Similar ship to **Cotopaxi.**
P.S.N.Co. vessel built for South American service. First voyage London to Melbourne and Sydney 17 May, 1878. Last voyage to Australia 11 May 1881. She then sailed on the Liverpool-Valparaiso service of the P.S.N.Co. Bought by Verdeau & Cie. of Bordeaux in 1895 and re-named *Egypte*. Broken up in 1896.

* This is true. The s.s. *Northam* preceded them, but never carried any meat as her refrigerating plant was unsatisfactory. Of 1,537 G.R.T., she had been built in 1858 and was owned by Sir J. Malcolm, Bt. Messrs. McIlwraith and McEarchan had chartered the s.s. *Strathleven* from Burrel & Son of Glasgow to carry a consignment (as distinct from a cargo) of 28 tons of frozen food from Australia in 1879, but this was 'chilled' rather than refrigerated. This ship was of 2,436 G.R.T. and built in 1875.

10) JOHN ELDER

Single screw steamer. Iron hull. Built 1869 by John Elder, Glasgow. 4,152 G.R.T. 406.4′ × 41.5′ × 35.2′ 12 knots. Compound engine, coal-fired boilers.

P.S.N.Co. vessel. First voyage London to Melbourne and Sydney 27 January 1879. Last voyage to Australia 27 May, 1886. She then sailed on the Liverpool-Valparaiso service and was wrecked off the Chilean coast 16 January 1892.

11) **City of London**

Single screw steamer. Iron hull. Built 1856 by Connell, Glasgow. 3,212 G.R.T. 11 knots.

Built for George Smith's 'City' Line. Chartered by O.S.N.Co. for a few voyages. First voyage London via Suez to Melbourne and Sydney July, 1879. Later owned by Inman Line.

12) **Sultan**

Built 1873 by Green's at Blackwall. 2,502 G.R.T. 319′ × 37.6′ × 27.7′

Built for the Indian trade of R. & H. Green. Made one round voyage on charter to O.S.N.Co. from London via Suez to Melbourne and Sydney, 28 July, 1879. Sold to the Marquis de Campo of Cadiz 1879 and re-named *Asia.*

13) **ORIENT**

Single screw steamer. Iron hull. Built 1879 by John Elder, Glasgow. 5,386 G.R.T. 460.0 o.a. 445.5′ b.p. × 46.3′ × 35.0′. 15 knots (service speed); 17 knots (on trials). Compound engine, coal-fired boilers. Passengers: 120 first class; 130 second class and 300 third class or emigrants. She had two funnels and four masts to carry sails if required. She could carry 3,000 tons of coal and steam from London to Australia without re-coaling. During a refit in 1898 triple expansion engines were fitted and her service speed increased to 16½ knots, with a trial speed of 17½ knots. Her tonnage increased to 5,453 gross; her 2nd and 3rd masts were removed and a single, tall funnel replaced the two shorter ones.

Named after the famous sailing ship *Orient*, she was the first ship ordered by, and built specifically for, the O.S.N.Co. First voyage from London to Melbourne and Sydney, 3 November, 1879. An outstanding ship, she was the largest (excluding the ill-fated *Great Eastern*) in the world at that time. Used as a transport for the Boer War between 1899 and 1902. She and the *Cuzco* carried the first frozen meat from Australia to England in 1881* and the *Orient* was fitted with electric

* See previous note.

light in 1884. Last voyage to Australia 23 July, 1909. Sold to Italian shipbreakers and sailed to their yard as the *Oric*.

14) SORATA

Single screw steamer. Iron hull. Built 1872 by John Elder, Glasgow. 4,014 G.R.T. Dimensions similar to the **Cotopaxi**. *13 knots. Compound engine. passengers: approx. 60 first class, 90 second class and 335 third class.*

P.S.N.Co. vessel. First voyage London to Melbourne and Sydney 13 February 1880. Last voyage to Australia 29 April, 1886. She then sailed on the Liverpool-Valparaiso service. Broken up at Tranmere in 1895.

15) COTOPAXI

Single screw steamer. Iron hull. Built 1873 by John Elder, Glasgow. 4,622 G.R.T. 402.2′ b.p. × 42.8′ × 24.2′. 13 knots. Compound engine. 420 third class passengers.

P.S.N.Co. vessel, built for West Coast of South America service. First voyage to Australia from London to Melbourne and Sydney 14 April, 1880. Last voyage to Australia 28 December, 1882. She then sailed on the Liverpool to Valparaiso service of the P.S.N.Co., but was beached in the Magellan Strait after collision with the German s.s. *Olympia*. After being careened she was re-floated but immediately struck another reef and sank on 15 May, 1889. The crew and passengers rescued by the German s.s. *Setos*.

16) LIGURIA

Single screw steamer. Iron hull. Built 1874 by John Elder, Glasgow. 4,666 G.R.T. Similar dimensions to the **Iberia.** *14 knots. Compound engine. Passengers: approx. 90 first class; 150 second class and 340 third class.*

P.S.N.Co. ship built for West Coast of South America run. First voyage to Australia from London to Melbourne and Sydney 12 May, 1880. Last voyage to Australia 9 May, 1890. She then sailed on the Liverpool-Valparaiso service of the P.S.N.Co. except for a single voyage to Sydney via the Cape on 12 July, 1895. Broken up in Genoa in 1903.

17) POTOSI

Single screw steamer. Iron hull. Built 1873 by John Elder, Glasgow. 4,218 G.R.T. 421.6′ b.p. × 43.3′ × 33.5′. 13 knots. Compound engine. Passengers: approx. 80 first class; 110 second class and 350 third class.

P.S.N.Co. vessel on West Coast of South America service. First voyage

65. The AUSTRAL of 1881 ready for sea. (The old Tilbury hotel can be seen under her stern.)

from London to Melbourne and Sydney 7 July, 1880. Last voyage to Australia 20 May, 1887. She then reverted to the Liverpool-Valparaiso service of the P.S.N.Co. and was broken up in Genoa in 1897.

18) **AUSTRAL**

Single screw steamer, steel hull. Built 1881 by John Elder, Glasgow. 5,524 G.R.T. 456.0′ b.p. × 48.2′ × 33.9′. 15 knots (17 knots designed). Compound engine. 550 passengers, of which 120 were first class; 130 second class and 300 steerage. She could set 28,000 sq. feet of sail on her four masts.

First voyage London to Melbourne and Sydney via Suez 18 January, 1882. On her second voyage she flooded through coaling ports and sank on an even keel in Sydney harbour on 11 November, 1882., but was salvaged in February, 1883 and returned to the Clyde for refit, when she had electric light installed and her funnels were lengthened. In 1884 was chartered by the Anchor Line and made seven voyages between Liverpool and New York, alternating with the *City of Rome*. Resumed Orient service to Australia 12 November, 1884. Did 4 months trooping in the Boer War in 1900. Last voyage to Australia 21 November, 1902. Broken up in Genoa in 1903.

19) **Cephalonia**
Single screw steamer. Iron hull. Built 1882 by Laird at Birkenhead. 5,517 G.R.T. being biggest ship then built on the Mersey. 430.6′ × 46.5′ × 34.5′. 14 knots. Compound engines 4,000 i.h.p. Passengers: 200 first class; 1,500 steerage. Lit by electricity and accommodation heated by steam.
Built for Cunard Line. One return voyage London to Melbourne and Sydney via Suez 11 January, 1883.

20) IBERIA
Single screw steamer. Iron hull. Built 1873 by John Elder, Glasgow. 4,689 G.R.T. 435.5′ b.p. × 45.0′ × 35.1′. 14 knots. Compound engine. Passengers: approx. 113 first class; 150 second class and 340 third class. Refrigerating machinery fitted 1881. Electric light fitted 1884. Re-boilered and re-engined 1890.
P.S.N.Co. vessel. First voyage to Australia from London to Melbourne and Sydney via Suez 25 January, 1883. Last sailing to Australia 31 January, 1890. Then reverted to P.S.N.Co. Valparaiso service until broken up in 1903 at Genoa.

21) **Belgravia**
Single screw steamer. Iron hull. Built 1882 by Henderson, Glasgow. 4,977 G.R.T. 400.0′ × 44.8′ × 33.0′. 13 knots.
Built for the Anchor Line. One round voyage from London to Cape Town, Melbourne and Sydney, 7 March, 1884.

22) ORIZABA
Steel hull. Built 1886 by Barrow S.B.Co. at Barrow. 6,077 G.R.T. 460.0′ b.p. × 49.5′ × 35.3′. 15 knots service speed (16 knots design). Triple expansion engines. 680 passengers, of which 126 first class, 154 second class and 400 steerage or third class. Two funnels and four masts.
P.S.N.Co. ship. First Australian voyage from London to Melbourne and Sydney via Suez 30 September, 1886. Ran ashore on Garden Island near Fremantle in poor visibility and became a total loss 16 February, 1905.

23) **ORMUZ (1)**
Single screw steamer. Steel hull. Built 1886 by Fairfields, Glasgow (formerly John Elders). 6,031 G.R.T. 465.5′ b.p. × 52.1′ × 34.1′. 15½ knots service speed (18 knots designed). Triple expansion engine. Passengers: approx. 106 first class, 170 second class and 120 steerage.
First voyage via Suez 3 February, 1887. Represented O.S.N.Co. at

66. The first class smoking room in the ORIZABA and OROYA.

Spithead review 3 August, 1889, and was first Orient ship to be painted in the new colours of buff funnels and vents; white superstructures and black hull in 1906. Last voyage to Australia 18 August, 1911, when sold to the Cie. de Nav. Sud Atlantique in 1912 and re-named *Divona*. Sold to Lefevre-Despeaux for breaking up in 1922.

24) OROYA
Single screw steamer. Steel hull. Built by Barrow S.B. Co., Barrow. 6,057 G.R.T. 460.0′ b.p. × 49.3′ × 35.3′. 15 knots service speed ($16\frac{1}{2}$ knots designed). Triple expansion engine. 692 passengers, of which 126 first class, 154 second class and 412 third class or steerage. Her tonnage increased to 6,277 G.R.T. and her funnels were lengthened during a re-fit.
P.S.N.Co. ship designed for Australian service. First voyage to Australia via Suez 17 February, 1887. Stranded in the Bay of Naples and seriously damaged in 1895. P.S.N.Co. Australian interest bought out by Royal Mail S.P.Co. in 1906 and the *Oroya* was transferred to this

67. *The ORIZABA making the passage through the Suez Canal.*

68. The second class dining saloon in the OROYA.

company. Last voyage to Australia 16 April, 1909, after which she was broken up in Genoa.

25) OROTAVA

Single screw steamer. Steel hull. Built by Barrow S.B. Co., Barrow. 5,857 G.R.T. 430.0′ b.p. × 49.3′ × 34.2′. 15 knots service speed. ($16\frac{1}{2}$ knots design). Triple expansion engine.

P.S.N.Co. vessel built for Valparaiso service. First voyage from London to Australia via Suez 6 June, 1890. She capsized in Tilbury while coaling in 1896 when four men were lost, but was salvaged and resumed service to Sydney 5 February, 1897. She was chartered for trooping in the Boer War, 1899-1903, and was transferred to the R.M.S.P.Co. in February, 1906. Last voyage to Australia 5 March, 1909. In 1914 was purchased by the British Admiralty and fitted as armed merchant cruiser, being broken up in 1919.

69. The unusual profile of the OPHIR, with her widely spaced funnels.

26) ORUBA

Single screw steamer. Steel hull. Built by Barrow S.B. Co., Barrow, 1889. 5,852 G.R.T. Other details similar to **Orotava.**

P.S.N.Co. ship built for Valparaiso service. First Australian voyage from London via Suez 4 July, 1890. Last Australian voyage 16 October, 1908. Transferred to R.M.S.P.Co. in February, 1906 and sailed in their West Indies service from 1909. Was bought by the Admiralty in 1914 and converted to a 'dummy' replica of *H.M.S. Orion.* She was scuttled to form a breakwater in Mudros Harbour in the Aegean in 1915.

27) **OPHIR**

Twin screw steamer. Steel hull. Built 1891 by R. Napier, Glasgow. 6,814 G.R.T. 482.0′ o.a. 465.0′ b.p. × 53.5′ × 34.1′. 16 knots service speed. 18.8 knots on trials. Triple expansion engines. Passengers: 220 first class, 150 second class and 520 third class or emigrants. Her main machinery fitted between two boiler rooms. This meant that the funnels were very wide apart and these, together with two pole masts, raked more than usually, giving the ship a striking appearance. She carried little cargo and her coal consumption was very uneconomical—some 125 tons per diem.

Sometimes called the 'Queen of the Indian Ocean'. First voyage from London via Suez 6 November, 1891. Last voyage in Orient service 20 June, 1913. First twin-screw vessel on Australian run. Her accommodation for passengers was excellent. The *Ophir* was chartered to be a royal yacht from March to November, 1901, to take the Duke and Duchess of York to Australia, the vessel being painted white and manned by naval personnel for this voyage. January, 1915, commissioned as an armed merchant cruiser. Purchased by the Admiralty in 1918 and converted to a hospital ship. In 1919 the ship was laid up in the Clyde and broken up at Troon in 1922.

28) **OMRAH**
Twin screw steamer. Steel hull. Built 1899 by Fairfields, Glasgow. 8,130 G.R.T. 507.0′ o.a. 490.7′ b.p. × 56.7′ × 26.0′. to main deck. 16 knots service speed. (18 knots design). Triple expansion engines. Passengers: 350 first and second classes, 500 third class.
First voyage via Suez 3 February, 1899. Last voyage to Australia 3 November, 1916. Then requisitioned as a troop transport. Torpedoed and sunk off Sardina 12 May, 1918.

29) ORTONA
Twin screw steamer. Steel hull. Built 1899 by Vickers Naval Construction Co. at Barrow. 7,945 G.R.T. 500.0′ b.p. × 55.3′ × 33.7′. 16 knots service speed (18 knots design). Triple expansion engines. Coal-fired boilers. Passengers: 130 first class, 162 second class and 300 third class. 1910 converted to be the first regular cruising liner and re-named **Arcadian** *(see infra), tonnage being increased to 8,950 G.R.T. and converted to carry 320 first class passengers.*
P.S.N.Co. ship built for Australian service. First voyage from London via Suez 24 November, 1899. Used as troop transport for nine months from June, 1902 (to South Africa). Last voyage to Australia 30 April, 1909, after which the R.M.S.P.Co. used her in their West Indies service, the O.S.N.Co. and P.S.N.Co. partnership having ended. (She was transferred to the R.M.S.P.Co. in 1906, and in 1910 was re-named *Arcadian* and used as a cruise ship (*supra*).) Became a tróop transport in the First World war and was torpedoed and sunk off Milos on 15 April, 1917, whilst carrying 1,300 troops. 279 lives were lost.

30) VICTORIA
Twin-screw steamer. Built 1902 by Harland & Wolff, Belfast. 5,549 G.R.T. 14 knots. Quadruple expansion engines.
P.S.N.Co. vessel built for the South American coastal trade. Made one return voyage from London to Melbourne and Sydney via Suez 12 September, 1902. Sold to Dutch shipbreakers in 1923.

31) **ORONTES (1)**
Twin-screw steamer. Built 1902 by Fairfields, Glasgow. 9,028 G.R.T. 513.7′ b.p. × 58.2′ × 34.4′. 16 knots service speed. Maintained 18.18 knots for 24 hours on trials. First Orient vessel with quadruple expansion engines. She had one funnel and two pole masts. Passengers: 640, of which 320 first and second class, and 320 third class.
First voyage from London via Suez 24 October, 1902. Requistioned as a

70. The ORONTES.

troop transport October, 1916. Returned to O.S.N.Co. service October, 1919. Last voyage to Australia 19 February, 1921. Laid up off Southend early 1921, and in 1922 sold as an exhibition ship and re-named *British Trade*. Resold to O.S.N.Co. August, 1922 and re-named *Orontes*, but she did not sail again in the Company's service and was broken up in 1926.

32) ORITA
Twin-screw steamer. Built 1902 by Harland & Wolff, Belfast. 9,231 G.R.T. 14 knots. Quadruple expansion engines.
P.S.N.Co. ship built for their South American service. Made one round voyage from London to Australia via Suez 8 May, 1903.

33) **Asturias**
Twin-screw steamer. Built 1908 by Harland & Wolff, Belfast. 12,002 G.R.T. 535.0′ o.a. 520.0′ b.p. × 62.0′ × 31.0′. 15 knots. Quadruple expansion engines. 300 first class passengers.
R.M.S.P. Co. ship built for the River Plate service. First voyage from London to Melbourne, Sydney and Brisbane via Suez, 24 January, 1908. Last voyage to Australia 5 February, 1909. Converted to hospital ship in 1915 but torpedoed in the Channel and beached. Later salvaged and re-fitted as a cruise ship, being re-named *Arcadian* in 1922. Broken up in Japan in 1933.

34) **ORSOVA (1)**
Twin-screw steamer. Built by John Brown, Clydebank. 12,036 G.R.T. Similar dimensions to **Otway.** *(This 12,000 gross ton class were the*

first Orient ships to be fitted with black Admiralty cowls on their funnel tops. This fashion henceforth became a feature of the Company's ships.) 16 knots service speed (18 knots design). Quadruple expansion engines.
First voyage from London to Melbourne, Sydney and Brisbane via Suez 25 June, 1909. Requisitioned as a troop transport May, 1915. Made two commercial voyages to Australia in 1916. Torpedoed near Eddystone Lighthouse and beached in Cawsand Bay 14 March, 1917. Subsequently re-floated and repaired at Devonport. She resumed Orient Line service 22 November, 1919. Was converted to a one class ship (660 tourist class) in 1933. Made her last voyage to Australia 20 June, 1936, having outlived her contemporary ships of the 12,000 ton class and made 70 voyages to Australia. Sold and broken up at Bo'ness in October, 1936.

35) **OTWAY**
Twin-screw steamer. Built 1909 by Fairfields, Glasgow. 12,077 G.R.T. 535.9′ b.p. × 63.2′ × 34.2′. 16 knots service speed (18 knots design.) Quadruple expansion engines. Passengers: approx. 400 first class and 700 third class.
First voyage to Australia via Suez 3 July, 1909. Commissioned as armed merchant cruiser 1915. Torpedoed and sunk in the Minches 22 July, 1917.

36) **OSTERLEY**
Twin-screw steamer. Built 1909 by London & Glasgow Shipbuilding Co. on the Clyde. 12,129 G.R.T. 535.9′ b.p. × 63.0′ beam. 16 knots service speed (18 knots design). Quadruple expansion engines.
This vessel stuck on her launchways for a week. First voyage to Australia via Suez 6 August, 1909. On this passage she collided with a Russian steamer. Requisitioned as a troop transport June, 1917. Resumed Orient service to Australia January, 1919. Stranded in Australian waters 1924. Cruised to Norway in the latter part of her career. Last voyage to Australia 3 August, 1929. Sold for scrap and broken up 1930.

37) **OTRANTO (1)**
Twin-screw steamer. Built by Workman Clark, Belfast, 1909. 12,124 G.R.T. 535.3′ b.p. × 64.0′ × 38.6′. 16 knots service speed (18 knots design). Quadruple expansion engines. Passengers: 235 first class, 186 second class and 696 third class.
First voyage from London to Melbourne, Sydney and Brisbane

71. The OSTERLEY.

72. The ORAMA, of 1924, first of the 20,000-tonners.

1 October, 1909. Commissioned as armed merchant cruiser 1914. Was part of Rear-Admiral Cradock's squadron at the Battle of Coronel but had not got the necessary speed and was useless in a battle between warships, leaving soon after the action began. During a storm on 6 October, 1918, when in convoy, she was in collision with the P. & O. *Kashmir,* being disabled and drifting ashore on the Isle of Islay where she became a total loss. 431 lives were lost.

38) **ORVIETO**
Twin-screw steamer. Built 1909 by Workman Clark, Belfast. 12,133 G.R.T. Same details as **Otranto (1).**
First voyage 26 November, 1909. Converted to a minelayer and later to an armed merchant cruiser 1914, she became the flagship of the 10th Cruiser Squadron. Resumed Orient service to Australia 1 November, 1919. Last voyage to Australia 30 August, 1930. Broken up in 1931.

39) **ORAMA**
Triple-screw steamer. Built 1911 by John Brown, Clydebank. 12,927 G.R.T. 551.0′ b.p. × 64.2′ × 39.0′. 16 knots service speed (18 knots design.) Triple expansion engines on port and starboard shafts. L.P. turbine on centre line shaft. 6th and last ship of the 12,000 ton class.
First voyage to Australia 10 November, 1911. Commissioned as armed merchant cruiser 1914. Sank the German store ship *Navarra* in the South Atlantic. Whilst escorting a convoy off the South Irish coast she was torpedoed and sank after four hours on 19 October, 1917. The only triple-screw steamer built for the Orient Line.

40) **ORMONDE**
Twin-screw steamer. Built 1913-1917 by John Brown, Clydebank. (Work stopped on outbreak of war). 14,853 G.R.T. 580.0′ b.p. × 66.0′ × 40.0′. 16 knots service speed (18 knots design). First O.S.N.Co. ship fitted with geared turbines and the first in the fleet to have a 'cruiser' stern. Passengers: 278 first class, 195 second class and 1,000 third class. Originally fitted with coal-fired boilers but was converted to burn oil in 1933 and, at the same time, her accommodation was changed to turn her into a one-class ship for 777 Tourist class passengers.
Order for the *Ormonde* placed in 1913 but, due to the war, she was not completed until 1917, when she was requisitioned and fitted as a troop transport in 1918. First Orient Line sailing to Australia 15 November, 1919. Requisitioned as a transport in 1939 and took part in the

landings in North Africa, Sicily and Salerno. 1944 based on Bombay for Far East trooping. After 1946 she was converted by the Ministry of Transport to carry 1,052 emigrant passengers, her first voyage (under Orient management) to Australia 10 October, 1947. She completed her 75th and last voyage to and from Australia in November, 1952, after a long and distinguished career, including service in two World wars. Sold for scrap and broken up at Dalmuir on the Clyde December, 1952.

41) **Indarra**
Twin-screw steamer. Built 1912 by Wm. Denny at Dumbarton. 9,735 G.R.T. 451.0′ b.p. × 60.0′ × 37.0′. 13 knots service speed. Quadruple expansion engines.
Chartered from Australian United Steam Navigation Co. First voyage from London to Sydney 20 December, 1918. Third voyage planned for September, 1920, was cancelled and the *Königin Luise* was used in her place. The *Indarra* was too slow for the Orient Line service. She was sold to the Lloyd Royal Belge (Gt. Britain) Ltd. and re-named *Pays de Waes*. Later she became the Japanese *Horai Maru* and was sunk in Singapore when acting as a troop transport.

42) **OMAR** ex *Königin Luise*
Twin-screw steamer. Built 1896 by Vulkan AG. Stettin. 11,103 G.R.T. 523.1′ b.p. × 60.1′ × 54.9′. 14 knots service speed claimed, but records show that she could not better 13 knots in service. Quadruple expansion engines. Rated as 'intermediate' ship of the Orient fleet, and sailed independently of the main part of the Line.
The *Königin Luise*, of the Norddeutscher Lloyd Line, was surrendered to Britain at the end of the war. Managed by the Orient Line 1919 and made her first voyage to Australia as the *Königin Luise* 4 September, 1920. Bought by the O.S.N.Co. she was refitted for 170 first class and 757 third class passengers and re-named *Omar*, making her first voyage to Australia under this name 29 January, 1921. Last voyage to Australia 9 February 1924, after which she was sold to the Greek Byron Line and re-named *Edison* in 1924 and employed in the carriage of emigrants to the U.S.A. Transferred to National Steam Navigation of Greece in 1929. Broken up in Italy 1935.

43) **ORCADES (1)** ex *Prinz Ludwig*
Twin-screw steamer. Built 1903 by Vulkan AG, Stettin. 9,764 G.R.T. 492.0′ b.p. × 57.6′ × 35.0′. 15 knots service speed. Quadruple expansion engines. Rated as 'intermediate' vessel of the Orient Line and sailed independently of the main fleet.

73. *The ORCADES (I), ex-PRINZ LUDWIG.*

Surrendered by Germany to Britain as the *Prinz Ludwig*, previously owned by the Norddeutscher Lloyd Line and placed under Orient Line management in 1919. Purchased by the O.S.N.Co. and refitted for 123 first class and 476 third class passengers and re-named *Orcades* in 1921. First voyage to Australia 8 October, 1921; last 20 September, 1924. Broken up in Germany 1925.

44) **ORMUZ (II)** ex *Zeppelin*
Twin-screw steamer. Built 1914 by Bremer Vulkan, Vegesack. 14,588 G.R.T. 570.0′ o.a. 550.0′ b.p. × 67.0′ × 35.0′. 15 knots service speed. Quadruple expansion engines. As built for the N.D.L. she carried 500 first class, 500 second class and 1,500 third class passengers but under the Orient flag she carried 293 first class and 882 third class, with 300 crew. Surrendered by Germany as the *Zeppelin* in 1919, she was bought by the O.S.N.Co., refitted, including refrigerating installation, and re-named *Ormuz* in 1920. First voyage to Australia 12 November, 1921. Last voyage 27 November, 1926. She was the best of the three ex-German ships (*Omar, Orcades (1)* and *Ormuz (II))* and sailed in the regular schedule of the Company. Sold back to the Norddeutscher Lloyd in 1927 and re-named *Dresden* for their New York service. Wrecked after hitting a rock off the Norwegian coast during a cruise 20 June, 1934.

(In fact, she was beached, but turned over on her side and became a total loss.)

45) **ORAMA (II)**

Twin-screw steamer. Built 1924 by Vickers, Barrow. 20,026 G.R.T. 658.0′ o.a. 630.0′ b.p. × 75.0′ × 47.0′ depth to 'E' deck. 18 knots service speed (20 knots design). Oil fuel, 19,500 S.H.P., S.R.G. Turbines. Passengers: 592 first class and 1,244 third class. First passenger ship to be fitted with gravity davits.

First vessel of 20,000 ton class. First voyage 15 November, 1924. Refitted in 1935 for 484 first class and 498 Tourist passengers and hull painted corn-colour as an experiment. This colour carried for two voyages only, after which she reverted to her black hull. One Australian voyage extended to New Zealand ports in 1939. Requisitioned as a troop transport in 1939. Sunk by gunfire from a German Naval surface force including the *Admiral Hipper, Scharnhorst* and *Gneisenau*, 300 miles off the Norwegian coast, 8 June, 1940. 19 men were lost and 280 survivors picked up by the *Admiral Hipper.*

46) **ORONSAY (I)**

Twin-screw steamer. Built 1925 by John Brown, Clydebank. 20,001 G.R.T. 637.5′ b.p. × 75.0′ × 47.0′. 18 knots service speed (20 knots design). Oil fuel. 20,000 S.H.P. S.R.G. turbines. Passenger accommodation similar to Orama (II).

First voyage 7 February, 1925. Made the first call at Hobart as a regular passenger ship call in 1936, and one voyage was extended to New Zealand ports in December, 1938. Requisitioned as a troop transport in 1939. Took part in the evacuation from St. Nazaire 16 June, 1940 and received damage from bombing by aircraft. Resumed trooping after repairs but was torpedoed by an Italian submarine off the coast of West Africa 9 October, 1942, when returning to England from Madagascar.

47) **OTRANTO (II)**

Twin-screw steamer. Built 1925 by Vickers, Barrow. 20,026 G.R.T. (Displacement 27,624 tons). Details, when built, as for **Orama (II).** *The Welin-MacLachlan davits fitted to the* **Orama (II)** *were successful and fitted to all subsequent Orient Line vessels. After refit in 1948 her cargo capacities were: Insulated cargo 151,750 cu. ft. General cargo (bale) 109,044 cu. ft.*

First voyage 9 January, 1926. In 1926, when cruising, she struck high land off Cape Grosso near Cape Matapan during heavy rain and poor visibility, but freed herself, although her stem was badly damaged. She sailed back to England for repairs. Collided with Japanese s.s. *Kitano Maru* off Hull and damaged her stem, 1928. Refitted to carry First and Third class passengers as for *Orama (II)* in 1935. Requisitioned as a troop transport September, 1939. Converted into assault ship November, 1942, and took part in North African landings, and at Sicily and Salerno. Released from Government service in 1948 and re-conditioned at Birkenhead 1948-9. During this period she took a list whilst lying in a partially flooded dry-dock, but this was corrected. She was re-conditioned as a one-class ship to carry 1,416 Tourist passengers. Made first post-war Australian passage 14 July, 1949, and her last (via Cape Town) 13 February, 1957. Broken up at Faslane in 1957.

48) **ORFORD**
Twin-screw steamer. Built 1928 by Vickers, Barrow. 19,941 G.R.T. Details as for **Orama (II).** *Officers and crew about 440.*
First voyage 13 October, 1928. Two voyages extended to New Zealand ports 1938/9. Requisitioned as a troop transport 3 September, 1939. Bombed and set on fire at Marseilles 1 June, 1940, and although beached had to be abandoned. 14 men killed. Refloated and broken up at Savona, 1947.

49) **ORONTES (II)**
Twin-screw steamer. Built 1929 by Vickers Armstrong, Barrow. 19,970 G.R.T. 664.0′ o.a. 630.0′ b.p. × 75.0′ × 30.2′ draft. 26.650 tons displacement. Deadweight 8,941 tons after 1947. 18 knots service speed (20 knots design). 6 large and 2 small Scotch boilers delivering steam at 215 lbs. per sq. inch. Oil fuel. 20,000 S.H.P. S.R.G. turbines. Passengers: originally 500 first class and 1,125 third class but, about 1935, during a refit, the passenger numbers and classes were changed to 463 first class and 528 Tourist. She was slightly different from the other ships of her class, her bow being raked and built of plate (instead of a thick bar) and well-rounded at the top. She was the best-looking of these sisters. After 1947 her cargo capacities were: Insulated cargo, 149,789 cu. ft. General cargo (bale) 134,173 cu. ft.
She made several cruises before her first voyage to Australia on 20 October, 1929. One voyage extended to New Zealand ports in 1939. Requisitioned as a troop transport in 1940. Took part in landings in North Africa (at Oran), Sicily and Salerno, and for a time was a trooper in the Far East. Returned to her owners in 1947. Refitted by J.I. Thornycroft at Southampton 1947/8 to accommodate 489 first class and 608 Tourist class, with 464 officers and men. Her tonnage was then

20,186 G.R.T. Resumed Orient Line service 17 June, 1948. Converted to a one-class ship for 1,410 Tourist class passengers in 1953. Last voyage to Australia 25 November, 1961. Broken up at Valencia 1962.

50) **ORION**

Twin-screw steamer. Built 1935 by Vickers Armstrong, Barrow. 23,371 G.R.T. 665.2′ o.a. 630.0′ b.p. × 84.6′ extreme beam (82.0′ moulded beam) × 47.6′ depth to 'E' deck. 28,700 tons displacement at 30.2′ draft. Passengers (originally): 486 first class and 653 Tourist. Air-conditioned in some public rooms and first class cabins. Officers and men 466. 19 knots service speed. 21.66 knots on trials. 24,000 S.H.P. S.R.G. turbines. 6 watertable boilers, 425 lbs/sq. inch pressure. Oil fuel. The cargo capacities after 1947 were: Insulated cargo 193,466 cu. ft; General cargo (bale) 186,660 cu. ft. Her funnel was lengthened after experience had shown that the original short one caused serious smoke and soot problems. She was the first one-masted vessel in the Orient Line and the first to have only one funnel since the **Orontes** *in 1902. Her hull was the first in the O.S.N.Co. to be painted in the corn-colour tried in the* **Orama (II)** *experiment in 1935, New Orient ships were painted as the* **Orion** *from that time.*

Launched by the Duke of Gloucester, in Brisbane, by radio, December 1934. Made a short 'shake-down' cruise to the Mediterranean before her first voyage to Australia, 18 September, 1935. On her maiden voyage, she embarked the passengers of the White Star Liner *Doric*, which was cruising off the Portuguese coast after she had been in collision with the French s.s. *Formigny*. (The *Doric* was badly damaged and broken up). Requistioned as a troop transport September, 1939. Damaged in collision with battleship *H.M.S. Revenge* in the Indian Ocean in 1941. She carried 7,000 U.S. troops on each of two trooping voyages and remained in Government service until she was refitted at Barrow in 1946/7 to accommodate 546 first class and 706 Tourist class passengers and 563 officers and men, her gross tonnage being increased to 23,696. Resumed Orient Line sailings 25 February, 1947. Her first Pacific service voyage 17 September, 1954. Refitted to accommodate 342 Tourist 'A' (Cabin class) and 722 Tourist 'B' class passengers 1958. Last voyage to Australia 28 February, 1963. Chartered as hotel ship in Hamburg for four months in 1963. Sold for scrap and broken up in Belgium 1963.

51) **ORCADES (II)**

Twin-screw steamer. Built 1937 by Vickers Armstrong, Barrow. 23,456 G.R.T. Dimensions as for **Orion.** *Passengers: 463 first class and 605*

74. The ORCADES (II).

Tourist. 19 knots service speed (21 knots design). 22.3 knots on trials. Parsons S.R. turbines. 4 large and 2 small Babcock & Wilcox water-tube boilers. Steam pressure 450 lbs. per sq. inch. Oil fuel. 8 decks. 12 watertight bulkheads. 6 holds. Air-conditioned in some public rooms and first class cabins as for **Orion.**

First voyage (to Australia) 9 October, 1937. Requisitioned as a troop transport September, 1939. One day's steaming from Cape Town she was torpedoed by the German submarine U.172 in daylight. The *Orcades* sank after two attacks over a period of several hours 10 October, 1942. There was a small loss of life (48) from a large number of passengers (1,300 including women and children) and crew. The Polish ship *Narvik* picked up the survivors from the boats and landed them at Cape Town.

52) **ORCADES (III)**

Twin-screw steamer. Built 1948 by Vickers Armstrong, Barrow. 28,164 G.R.T. 708.8′ o.a. 668.0′ b.p. × 90.6′ moulded beam × 50.0′ depth to 'E' deck. 32,210 tons displacement. 11,140 tons deadweight. Passengers: originally 733 first class and 772 Tourist class. 617 officers and men. 22½ knots service speed. 24.74 knots on trials. 42,500 S.H.P. (max.) Parsons geared turbines. 4 Foster-Wheeler watertube boilers, 525 lbs. per sq. inch pressure at 850°F. temperature. Oil fuel. 6 cargo holds. 12 watertight bulkheads. Funnel, tripod mast and bridge grouped amidships

75. The ORCADES (III).

in a single structure. Cargo capacities after 1959: Insulated cargo 162,540 cu. ft. General cargo (bale) 219,000 cu. ft.
First of the 28,000 ton class. First voyage to Melbourne and Sydney 14 December, 1948. She reduced the pre-war voyage time to Melbourne by 10 days to 28 days and could make four complete round voyages in a year. Fitted with Denny Brown activated-Fin Stabilizers soon after entering service. Partially air-conditioned originally, she was completely air-conditioned for passengers and crew in 1959. Transferred to P. & O. ownership in 1964. Re-classified as a one-class ship in May, 1964. Left Southampton 6 December, 1972 and was handed over to Mitsui & Co. at Kaohsiung on 6 February, 1973, to be broken up.

53) **ORONSAY (II)**
Twin-screw steamer. Built by Vickers Armstrong, Barrow 1951. 27,632 G.R.T. Dimensions as for **Orcades (III).** *32,237 tons displacement, 10,704 deadweight. Passengers: 668 first class and 833 Tourist. 630 officers and men. Engines and steam pressure as* **Orcades (III).** *Cargo capacities after 1959: Insulated cargo 222,990 cu. ft; General cargo (bale) 151,920 cu. ft.*
First voyage to Australia 16 May, 1951. Had suffered bad fire when fitting out. Fitted with Denny Brown activated-fin stabilizers soon after entering service. Refitted by Harland & Wolff in Liverpool and fully air-conditioned throughout passenger and crew accommodation in

1959. The *Oronsay* initiated the Orient trans-Pacific service from Sydney to Vancouver and San Francisco 1 January, 1954. Transferred to P. & O. ownership in 1964. Last voyage to Australia August 1975. She left Southampton, crossed the Atlantic to Port Everglades and through Panama to Los Angeles, San Francisco, Honolulu, Auckland and Sydney, whence she sailed for Hong Kong and left her passengers and most of the crew before leaving for Taiwan to be broken up.

54) **ORSOVA (II)**

Twin-screw steamer. Built 1954 by Vickers Armstrong, Barrow. 28,790 G.R.T. 722.1′ o.a. 668.0′ b.p. × 90.6′ moulded beam × 67.3′ depth to 'C' deck. 32,140 tons displacement, 11,610 deadweight. 22½ knots service speed. 26.07 knots on trials. 42,500 S.H.P. (max.) Parsons geared turbines. 3 Foster-Wheeler watertube boilers, 525 lbs. per sq. inch steam pressure at 850°F. temperature. Oil fuel. After 1959 cargo capacities were as follows: Insulated cargo, 94,060 cu. ft; General cargo (bale) 209,570 cu. ft. Passengers: 681 first class and 813 Tourist class. 646 officers and men. Partially air-conditioned passenger accommodation. The **Orsova** *had one funnel built on top of a midship structure housing the navigating bridge and officers accommodation. This funnel carried aerials and radar scanners and no mast was fitted in the ship. Her stem curved forward (unlike her sister ships) and, in consequence, she was longer overall.*

Maiden voyage to Australia 17 March, 1954. On 27 April, 1955 she sailed from Tilbury to Australia and thence across the Pacific and back to Tilbury via Panama. She started in the Orient Pacific service in 1958. Refitted by Vickers Armstrong at Walker, Newcastle, and fully air-conditioned throughout the passenger and crew accommodation in 1959. Transferred to P. & O. ownership in 1965. Left Southampton 14 December, 1973 for breaking up in Taiwan.

55) **GARONNE (II)**

Single-screw oil tanker. Built 1959 by Vickers Armstrong, Walker-on-Tyne. 24,513 G.R.T. 40,057 tons deadweight. 690.2′ × 90.4′ × 36.3′. 15 knots. 2 steam turbines double reduction geared, 2 water tube boilers, steam pressure 700 lbs. per sq. inch.

One of the P. & O. group tankers and the only one built for the O.S.N.Co. Her buff-coloured funnel had a black admiralty type cowl but the hull was painted light grey. Operations of the *Garonne*, with all other P. & O. Group tankers, taken over by Trident Tankers Ltd. December, 1962. Registry of ship transferred to P. & O. S.N.Co. in 1964.

76. *The ORIANA.*

56) **ORIANA**

Twin-screw steamer. Built 1960 by Vickers Armstrong, Barrow. 41,923 G.R.T. 804.0′ o.a. 740.0′ b.p. × 97.0′ moulded beam (100.0′ beam extreme) × 31.6′ load draft. 38,400 tons displacement, loaded. Passengers: 688 first class and 1,496 Tourist class. 899 officers and men. $27\frac{1}{2}$ knots service speed. 30.64 knots on trials. D.R.G. turbines 80,000 S.H.P. (max.) 65,000 S.H.P. in service. 4 Foster-Wheeler watertube boilers. 700 lbs. per sq. inch at 950°F. Oil fuel. 4 main generators each of 1,750 kws. 2 solid propellers each 20′ diameter and weighing 29 tons. Insulated cargo capacity 55,520 cu. ft. General cargo (bale) 150,541 cu. ft. (including hatch trunks). The **Oriana** *was the biggest passenger liner ever built in England. Her cargo capacity was reduced from that of previous Orient Line ships to suit trade demands and 'turn-round' times in ports on the new route across the Pacific. Her lifeboats were lowered over 27 feet as compared with the usual position on previous Orient vessels, by use of the under-deck davits.*

Maiden voyage 3 December, 1960 ($3\frac{1}{2}$ years after the laying of her keel). Return round voyage from London to Sydney, San Francisco and Los Angeles. Reached Sydney from Southampton in 27 days. Transferred to P. & O. ownership in 1965.

77. *The AUSTRAL (from a drawing by W.L. Wyllie.)*

SHIPS MANAGED BY THE ORIENT LINE

In addition to the running of their own fleets, it often happened that shipping companies would manage vessels for the Ministry of Shipping or for some other Government service in time of war. The Orient Steam Navigation Co. managed the vessels in the following list in these circumstances, viz:-

Huntsgreen, ex *Derfflinger*
Twin-screw steamship. Built 1909 by Schichan. 9,060 G.R.T. 463.5′ b.p. × 57.4′ × 35.5′. Passengers: 292 cabin class and 519 third class. 14½ knots. Coal-burning boilers. Reciprocating engines.
ex-German ship *Derfflinger* captured in 1914, previously owned by the Norddeutscher Lloyd Line. Manned and managed for the Ministry of Shipping from 1915 until 1920. Re-sold to original owners in 1920, and continued to serve with them, under her original name, until 1934.

Rio Negro
Single-screw steamer. Built 1905 by Tecklenborg, Wesermunde. 4,556 G.R.T. 361.2′ b.p. × 46.7′ beam. 12 knots. Triple expansion engine.
Built for the Hamburg Sud-Amerika Line. Manned and managed for the Ministry of Shipping at the end of the 1914-18 war.

Rio Pardo
Single-screw steamer. Built in 1905 by Tecklenborg, Wesermunde. 4,588 G.R.T. 361.1′ b.p. × 46.7′ beam. 12 knots. Triple expansion engine.
Built for the Hamburg Sud-Amerika Line. Manned and managed for the Ministry of Shipping at the end of the 1914-18 war.

Friedrichsruhe
Twin-screw steamer, built by Fairfield's, Glasgow 1903. Quadruple expansion engines. 8,332 G.R.T. 469.2′ × 35.1′ × 29.7′.
Managed and manned for the Ministry of Shipping at the end of the 1914-18 war.

78. The JOHAN VAN OLDENBARNEVELDT off Cape Town.

Cordoba

Single-screw steamer. Built 1895. 4,889 G.R.T. 376.5′ b.p. × 46.3′ beam. Quadruple expansion engine.

Built for the Hamburg Sud-Amerika Line. Managed and manned for the Ministry of Shipping at the end of the 1914-18 war.

Christiaan Huygens

Twin-screw steamer. Built 1928. 16,287 G.R.T. 551.4′ × 68.8′ × 36.2′. 17 knots.

Built for the Nederland Royal Mail Line. Managed by the Orient Line with Dutch crews for war-time only, 1940-45.

Johan van Oldenbarneveldt

Twin-screw steamer. Built 1930 by Nederland S.B. Co. at Amsterdam. 20,314 G.R.T. 587′ × 75′ beam × 27.9′ draft (36.1′ depth). Service speed 16½ knots. 2 × 10 cylinder Sulzer diesels. Built for 1,210 single class passengers and carried no cargo.

Built for the Nederland Royal Mail Line. Before the war was running round the world eastabout, through Mediterranean to Australia, then across Pacific through Panama (with calls *en route*) to Port Everglades and New York and back to Europe. Managed by Orient Line with Dutch crews for war time only from 1940-45. 1954, chartered by owners to Trans-Ocean Steamship Company (Netherlands Government) to run between Rotterdam and New York or Canada with emigrants and, later, with students until 1958, when she was largely re-built and employed cruising until 1963 when she was sold to the Greek Line and re-named *Lakonia*. After a major and hurried reconstruction, again for cruising, she caught fire four days after leaving Southampton on the first cruise and burnt out with heavy losses amongst the passengers.

Marnix van St. Aldegonde
Details similar to the Johan van Oldenbarneveldt.
Running pre-war in conjunction with the *Johan van Oldenbarneveldt*. Managed by the Orient Line from 1940 until she was sunk in the Mediterranean in 1943.

Johan de Witt
Twin-screw steel steamer. Built 1920. 10,474 G.R.T. Length 482.2′. 17 knots.
Nederland Royal Mail Line, managed by Orient Line with Dutch crews from 1940-45.

Samkansa
Single-screw steamer. Built 1943 by the Bethlehem Shipbuilding Co., U.S.A. 7,218 G.R.T. 10,573 deadweight. 441.5′ o.a. 416.0′ b.p. × 57.1′ × 37.3′. 11 knots service speed (13.6 knots on trials). Triple expansion engine. Oil fuel.
Manned and managed by the Orient Company for the Ministry of War Transport, 1943-1947. Bought by Hadley Shipping Co. in 1947 and re-named *Cerinthus*.

Sameveron
Single-screw steamer. Built 1944 by Bethlehem Shipbuilding Co., U.S.A. Details the same as the **Samkansa.**
Manned and managed by the Orient Line for the Ministry of War Transport from 1944-1947. Bought by Andrew Weir & Co. in 1947 and re-named *Ericbank*.

Empire Orwell ex *Empire Doon* ex *Pretoria*
Twin-screw steamer. Built 1936 by Blohm & Voss at Hamburg. Built as 16,662 G.R.T. but 18,036 G.R.T. after 1948. 574.4′ o.a. 541.4′ b.p. × 72.2′ moulded beam × 44.55′. Displacement (load) 18,950 tons. 16½ knots service

speed (17.65 knots on trials). S.R.G. turbines, 11,000 S.H.P. 2 Foster-Wheeler watertube boilers. 530 lbs. per sq. inch pressure at 850°F. temperature. Oil fuel. These particulars relate to the ship after 1948.
Built for German East Africa Line and named *Pretoria.* Handed over to Great Britain in 1945 on cessation of hostilities and re-named *Empire Doon.* She was used as a trooper for the Ministry of War Transport and manned and managed by the Orient Line. There were great difficulties caused by faults in the main machinery, particularly the boilers, and in consequence the ship was extensively refitted in 1948 by J.I. Thornycroft at Southampton. She was re-boilered and her accommodation was changed, after which she was re-named *Empire Orwell.* She and the *Empire Fowey*, manned and managed by the P. & O. Line, were the most modern troopers of their day. The *Empire Orwell* was returned to the Ministry of Transport in 1957 and was then chartered to the Pan Islamic S.S. Co. of Karachi. The next year she was sold to the Blue Funnel Line and was refitted by Barclay Curle at Glasgow to carry 106 first class and 2,000 third class passengers. A compartment on 'B' deck was fitted out as a mosque. She was not only unique in the Blue Funnel Line in having two funnels and a white hull, but the only one with a mosque, which was created in accordance with the wishes of the Indonesian authorities. In March, 1959, she made her first pilgrim voyage from Indonesia to Jeddah as the *Gunung Djuti.* In 1962 she was bought by the Indonesian Government and passed into private hands in 1965. In 1966 she was acquired by PT Perusahaan Pelajaran Arafat. In 1973 her main machinery was changed to 12,000 b.h.p. M.A.N. diesels.

V. HULL AND FUNNEL COLOURS OF THE ORIENT LINE

Prior to 1906	The ships' hulls and funnels were painted black and the upper-works were white.
In 1906	The Funnels were painted yellow ochre; the hulls remained black and the superstructure white.
In 1935	The *Orion* and subsequent ships of the Company had hulls painted in corn colour, while the funnel remained yellow ochre and the superstructures white. Existing ships in 1935 retained the black hulls, except that the *Orama* made two voyages in 1935 with a corn-coloured hull prior to the commissioning of the *Orion*. Ships with black hulls usually were painted red on the waterline with a special paint to withstand the heavy scouring of the passage through the sea. However, a dull green boot-topping was used in association with the corn-coloured hulls after 1935.

After the ships were transferred to the P. & O. S.N.Co., the corn-coloured hulls became white.

79. *The head of a shipbuilding berth at Vickers in 1930, before the days of welding. The workman in the foreground carries a template embodying all the details of the shape and rivet holes of a steel plate. (Etching by the author.)*

VI HOUSE-FLAGS

REFERENCE TO PLATE No. 81 will show the various house-flags known to have been worn by the various companies with which the Anderson family were associated and which finally blossomed into the Orient Steam Navigation Co. Ltd.

Basil Lubbock, the sailing ship historian, has recorded his belief that, prior to the St. Andrew's Cross, and for a period in the 1870's, the Anderson, Anderson sailing ships flew a house-flag which consisted of a rising sun in yellow on a white field, but it seems impossible to verify whether this was, in fact, the case. However, it is certain that they had adopted this motif and that the clipper *Harbinger*, which was not launched until 1876, had this device carved on her stanchions, bollard heads and that it also appeared on all her plate and crockery. Since a contemporary lithograph of the *Orient* arriving at Gibraltar with troops from the Crimean War most certainly shows her flying the St. Andrew's Cross, and since the rather poor photograph of both this vessel and the *Yatala* in Adelaide in 1871* is not very clear as to their house-flags, which could well be the St. Andrew's Cross and are definitely *not* a rising sun on a white field, it seems to be a fair assumption that this latter device was never used as a house-flag and that Lubbock was incorrect in his belief. I have not, therefore, taken any account of it in the following list:-

1) Prior to 1878.
   A white saltire on a blue field—the St. Andrew's Cross. This was the house-flag of Anderson, Anderson & Co., formerly Anderson, Thomson & Co., and flown by the Orient Line of sailing ships. In 1877 it was the first house-flag flown by steamships in the joint Australian service run by the Orient Line.
2) House-flag of F. Green & Co.
   This was the house-flag when the company joined with Anderson, Anderson & Co. to form the joint Australian service.
3) In 1878.
   The Orient Steam Navigation Company devised their own house-flag—a combination of the Anderson, Anderson and the Frederick Green flags. This was flown until about 1880.
4) *Circa* 1880-1892.
   A flag similar to the house-flag of the Pacific Steam Navigation Co. was flown by

* Plate 20.

ships of the Orient Line. The only difference between the two companies' house-flags lay in the lettering P.S.N.C. and O.S.N.C. in the quarterings. (Since the paint-work of the ships was also similar, and some vessels of the two companies had not dissimilar names, this arrangement was certainly not designed to obviate confusion!)

5) *Circa* 1892-1908.
The 'C' in the lower quartering of the fly was amended to 'Co.'
6) From *c.* 1908 until the closure of the O.S.N.Co.
The letters in the quarterings of the flag were omitted when the Company became independent of the P.S.N.Co. and the R.M.S.P.Co.

80.

THE ORIANA BADGE

This badge was featured prominently in the ship, particularly on the bow searchlight door and as a general motif in decorations, curtain fabrics, floor coverings, tableware, ashtrays, bookmatches, soap wrappings and so forth. It was conceived by Sir Colin Anderson in conjunction with Mr. Milner Gray, R.D.I., who executed the design.

Since the name 'Oriana' had been applied to Queen Elizabeth I by the poets of her day, it was decided that the *Oriana* badge should link the name of Elizabeth I with the present Elizabethan era. The double 'E' was therefore used as a monogram symbolising the two Elizabethan eras, and surrounded by the letter 'O' for Orient, whilst the whole was surmounted with a formalized interpretation of an Elizabethan pearl crown.

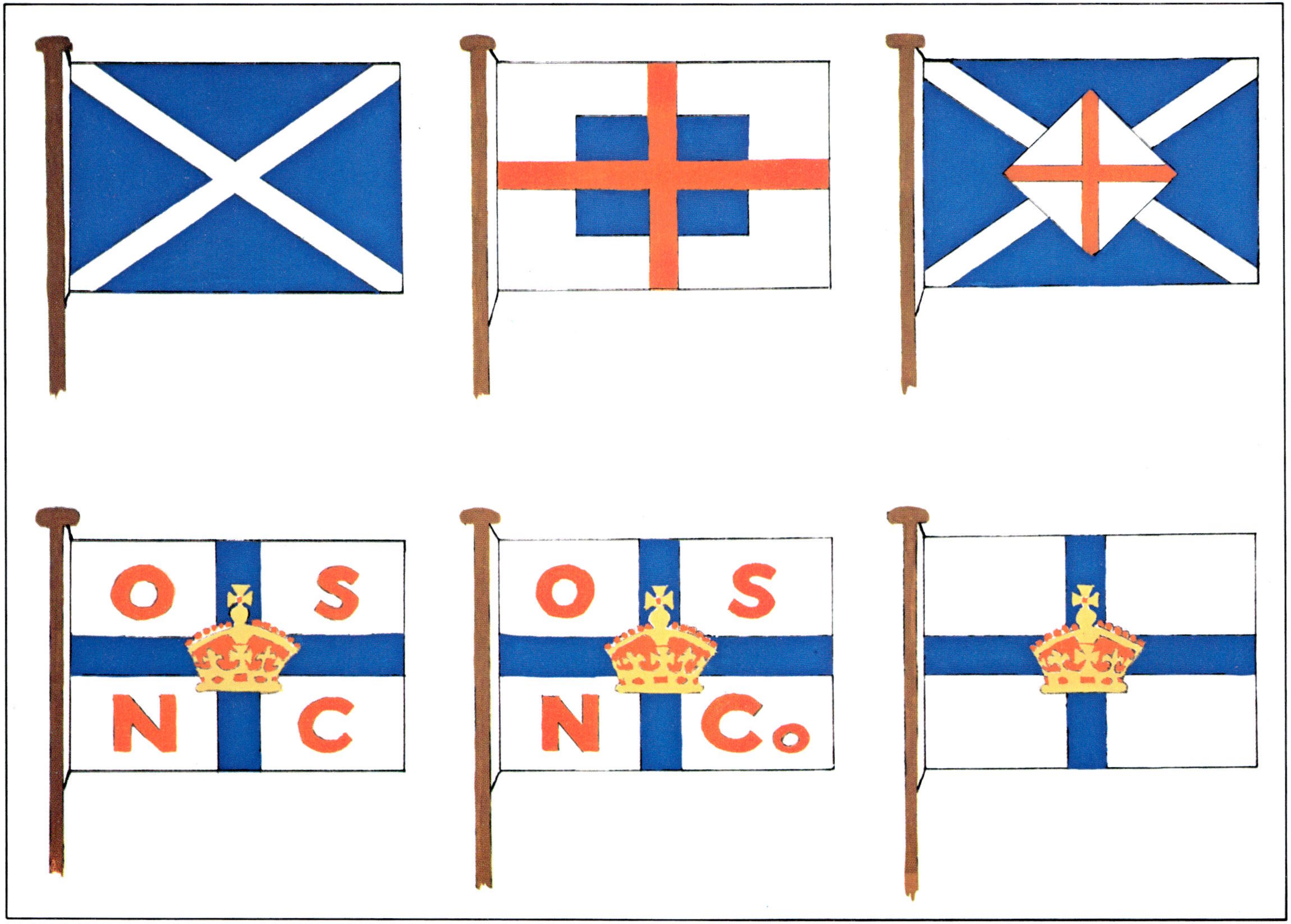

81. *The House flags of the Orient Line.* *(See pp. 171/2 for text.)*

82. *The Anderson, Anderson clipper COONATTO (from a lithograph after Dutton).*

83. *The YATALA, (from a lithograph by John Chr. Legoe, after Dutton.)*

VII. THE ORIENT FAMILY BACKGROUND

SINCE THE ORIENT Line and its fleet have already been discussed, it is pertinent to discuss its inceptions and the family which provided its life blood. Although I spent the most enjoyable part of my life as its Naval Architect during its last years (for the reader will already be aware that it was founded over a century ago), I can write without bias that it was a singularly fine concern, although it could be said, obviously, that there were other companies within the history of its period which were equally fine in their conception.

In order to start a company of any worth, there must be one or two persons, or perhaps a family, with vision, quality and drive—certainly not a committee. The Orient Line owed its creation and continuance to a family tree of which the branches had exceptional managerial abilities which had not only founded the enterprise many years ago, but had blossomed and flourished under its shadow.

It seems to me, as an interested observer, that the Line was overtaken by events and merged with the P. & O. Company in 1960 due to outside pressures and influences which were in no way related to the skills and qualities of its management. There is a saying in the North of England:- '*From clogs to clogs in three generations*'—a generalization which is often true, but which certainly did not apply to the family which built the Orient Line.

About 1560, a child was born in Northern Scotland who went to sea and became Captain Anderson and who, for his service to King James V of Scotland, was given Scots Mill in the parish of Peterhead.

Later, this same sea-captain, who had become a miller, acquired another mill: the so-called 'English Mill', near Inverugie Castle.

This erstwhile ship-master had a son, born about 1600, who continued to run the mills. Later there was a grandson and, in order to confuse the reader, it should be noted that his name, like so many of the branches of this family tree, was Alexander. Indeed, this grandson, who lived between around 1640 and 1715, had, in turn, a son called Alexander, who was born in 1676 and died in 1754, during which time his wife bore him five children, of whom one, born in 1721, was also named Alexander. This latter Alexander Anderson died in 1794, but his wife had had ten children, of whom the oldest was James (1746-1828) and the second another Alexander (1747-1806). It was from this last Alexander that the branch which founded the Orient Line was to spring.

James was a great sheep farmer, first at Brora, in Sutherland, and later at Kealdale, whilst he also became factor to Lord Reay, who owned the land in the area where he lived. Indeed, he prospered and built his own house, which he called Rispond, thereafter being known as 'James the First of Rispond'. Later, he had large sheep farms in Sutherland, Cromarty and on the Orkney mainland. In the course of his life, James had three wives, the last of whom had a daughter named Elizabeth who married a George Geddes (1786-1840). If, at this point, the reader should wonder at the introduction of the name Geddes, it will become apparent that the family names of Anderson and Geddes were closely associated through marriage over the years which followed.

James the First of Rispond had a son, also named James, who inherited Rispond and, naturally, became known as James the Second of Rispond (1776-1854). The house lay at the mouth of Loch Erriboll, which provided a good, sheltered harbour and the last calling point for ships sailing north-about the British Isles. It should be mentioned that, during that period of the Napoleonic Wars, the common route for shipping to and from the East coast of the British Isles and countries lying to the east of them and the English Channel was around the north of Scotland and, since this was a long way round and prolonged the voyages, Loch Erriboll was an excellent place at which to call for re-storing, maintenance and repair of ships before they proceeded any further. Since James became involved in all this business brought to the Loch, in addition to his sheep-farming and acting as factor to Lord Reay, his prosperity increased and he also became a ship-owner, running his vessels mainly in the North European trade but also from ports on the East Coast of Britain to Ireland.

His uncle, Alexander, who was the younger brother of James the First of Rispond, lived from 1747 till 1806 and became a doctor of medicine, serving in the Royal Navy for a time as a surgeon and, after retiring from the navy, practiced as a doctor at Peterhead. He had two sons: John Ford Anderson (1784-1812) who followed him as medical practitioner in Peterhead, though he died at the age of twenty-eight, and Alexander (1791-1865) who, after entering the navy as a midshipman, left the service with the rank of lieutenant and then still followed the sea as master of merchant ships.

John Ford Anderson's wife was the daughter of a well-known Peterhead shipowner named Skelton, and her father, brothers and a cousin formed a business relationship with her brother-in-law, Alexander Anderson, the sea-captain. The Skelton family and Captain Anderson agreed that he should buy a prize vessel taken in the Napoleonic wars, and he duly did so with the financial help of the Skeltons. He himself went as master of her and kept her in the West Indian trade from 1815 till 1841, and it seems that this was the beginning of the Andersons' interest in deep-sea trading which ultimately blossomed into the Orient Line.

Since Dr. John Ford Anderson died when still quite a young man, his young wife was left to bring up her four small children, so she moved to the house of her uncle, the Rev. Francis Nicoll, who was the principal of the University of St. Andrews. These four children, and their progeny, shaped the course of the future and, if I sometimes dwell on members who were not directly connected with ships and shipowning, it is to demonstrate that we are considering a rather remarkable family. The oldest of these four children, another Alexander (1808-1884) graduated as a Master of Arts at St. Andrews University and entered the church, but in 1848 he became the founder

84. The HOLMESDALE in tow.

and headmaster of Chanonry House—a boarding school in Old Aberdeen. In fact, he became a leader in modern (at that time) education for boys, stating that his school was intended to promote the improvement of the preparatory education of youths proceeding to University—principally St. Andrews. He was widely known as 'Govie', being short for Governor Anderson, and the school became widely respected throughout Buchan.

James Anderson (1811-1897), his younger brother, was interested in everything to do with ships and was thus fortunate in having relatives in the world of shipping. His mother's family, the Skeltons, were shipowners, and his uncle Alexander was captain of the ship owned jointly with them. In consequence, James became the London agent for that vessel, as junior partner with a Mr. Thomson of the firm of James Thomson & Co. in their premises at 8, Billiter Square in the

85. The DARRA after passing from Anderson, Anderson ownership.

City of London. Being well-educated and keen, James soon became a keystone in the business of the company to a degree that the name was finally changed to Anderson, Thomson & Co. The firm prospered and, in 1854, James' nephew, James George Skelton Anderson (1838-1907), son of 'Govie' Anderson, joined the business, to be followed in 1865 by his younger brother William (1844-1895). Mr. Thomson retired in 1869 and the firm once again changed its name: this time to Anderson, Anderson & Co.—James Anderson and his two nephews being by now the partners. In 1870, Gavin Anderson (1833-1892), another son of 'Govie', joined the firm, which had become established in the London shipping community by this time.

Hitherto, the ships run or managed by the company, in its various names of Thomson and Anderson, had been sailing ships, and it would seem that Thomson had been involved in the Australian trade prior to being joined by James Anderson. However, as I have already outlined briefly in 'The Orient Line' chapter, they became shipowners with their own fleet of ships on this run, and these ranked high, both in appearance and performance, in the golden age of the clipper era. The name 'Orient' Line took its inception from their very successful full-rigged ship *Orient*, of 1853, which was so famous and popular, but despite the successes of their clippers, the rise of steam was inevitable and the Partners experimented with the use of steamships to Australia.

In February, 1878, as previously mentioned, the Orient Steam Navigation Company was founded jointly by Anderson, Anderson & Co. and Frederick Green & Co. whose background was similar, albeit possibly more distinguished since they had acted as brokers for the closely associated shipowners, R. & H. Green. This partnership of Frederick Green & Co. and R. & H. Green was well-known, not only for the 'Blackwall clippers', but more especially for their shipyard at Blackwall on the Thames, which had been in existence since 1611. Until the 1830's, this yard had been building vessels to a design based on a man-o'-war sailing ship, which became known as the 'Blackwall Frigates'. These tended to be rather 'tubby' ships which were good, seaworthy craft, but rather slow. However, passage times did not necessarily reflect the abilities of their ships, since so many were built for the Hon. East India Company which, enjoying a monopoly trade, tended to make leisurely voyages and to reduce sail each evening for the night. However, the 'Frigates' were followed in the mid-nineteenth century by the 'Blackwall clippers' which returned much faster passages, not only because they were built with more extreme lines, but because many were being used on the Australian run where free competition obtained and, in any case, the East India Company had already lost its monopoly. These faster Blackwall vessels only lost their popularity when steamships finally came into their own.

In 1887, Gavin Anderson retired and, in the following year, Kenneth Skelton Anderson (1866-1942), son of James Anderson (1811-1897) joined the firm. His father retired two years later and died in 1897.

Kenneth Skelton Anderson became a distinguished name in shipping, but he was also interested and active in the fields of art and education. During the first World War he was called away from the

86. A view of the promenade deck of the OROYA and ORIZABA.

Company to do special work connected with the war, becoming a member of the Shipping Control Committee. Later he became President of the Chamber of Shipping and, in recognition of his services, he became Sir Kenneth Skelton Anderson, Bart., K.C.M.G.

James Anderson had another son named Hugh Kerr (1865-1928), who had an outstanding scholastic career for, having had a classical education, he went to Cambridge where he became Professor of Physiology, Master and Fellow of Gonville and Caius College. In due course he became Sir Hugh Kerr Anderson, F.R.S., M.D., M.A. and was chairman of the University Press at Cambridge. If he had no association with shipping, he is yet another example of the calibre of this family.

Meanwhile, James George Skelton Anderson had married Dr. Elizabeth Garrett (1836-1917), who was a lady of great distinction and achievement, for she had fought against the prejudices of the age in which she lived; against the obstacles that then stood in the way of the education of girls and women, and most particularly against the barriers put up by men to prevent the advancement and employment of women in the field of medicine. She had decided, when little more than a child, to become a doctor and, in the face of all manner of difficulties, had gained her M.D. to become the first woman to qualify as a doctor in England. She became a practitioner dealing mainly in women's illnesses, was consultant in a hospital for women in Shadwell (in East London), and ran clinics for poor people elsewhere in London. Eventually, she was instrumental in the founding of what came to be known as the 'Elizabeth Garrett Anderson Hospital' for women in Euston Road, London—an institution which, as I write this, is in the process of being 'phased out' under the nationalised scheme for medical services. She was also a great fighter for the liberation of women, but not in the destructive militant sense, although she knew and associated with many of the militant suffragette characters in the drive for women's freedom at the time of the Pankhursts.

Two of her other distinctions—and she had many—were that she became the first woman to hold the position of mayor, which she held for a number of years in her home town of Aldeburgh in Suffolk, and also that she became the first dean of the London School of Medicine for Women, now merged with that of the Royal Free Hospital. She had met James George Skelton Anderson, who was one of the governors of the hospital at Shadwell, when she was applying for a position on the staff.

Alan Garrett Anderson (1877-1952) was the only son of their marriage. He joined the Company of Anderson, Anderson & Co. in 1897 and more is to be told of him, but this must be deferred until others have been introduced to this story in the order in which they appeared.

'Govie' Anderson had a daughter named Nellie* (1850-1914), who married a distant cousin, Acland (later Auckland) Campbell Geddes (1831-1908), a descendant of James Anderson, the First, of Rispond. They had a family of two girls and three boys. Auckland Geddes had a very successful engineering career, mostly in India, and

* Christina Helen McLeod, to give her full names.

87. Punkahs over the aspidistra-decorated tables in the first class saloon of the OMRAH.

retired early to Edinburgh to look after the education of his children.

After the family had grown up, Nellie turned her thoughts to the question of the education of girls and, about 1887, with a Miss Guthrie Wright, organised a school of 'Cookery and Domestic Economy' at No. 3, Atholl Crescent in Edinburgh. From this small beginning developed the 'Edinburgh College of Domestic Science', known throughout the world as 'Atholl Crescent' or, more simply, 'A.C.' Unfortunately, the College has now moved to a new building and is called 'Queen Margaret's College', thereby losing a measure of its identity.

Nellie must have been a lady of boundless energy, because she then turned her attentions to other activities. With the advice and help of others, including her sister-in-law, Dr. Elizabeth Garrett Anderson, and her own sister, Dorothy Mary Marshall, she started a movement to create the Edinburgh School for the Medical Education of Women. Nellie had the supreme pleasure and pride of seeing her daughter Mona made the first woman medical graduate of Edinburgh in 1894 and, four years later, Mona (1872-1936) became the first woman to be made 'M.D., Edinburgh'. During the first World War, by her initiative and drive, Mona Geddes brought about the formation of women's services commanded by women. At first they were all volunteers and Mona, by that time married and named Chalmers-Watson, became the first 'Chief Controller, Women's Army Auxiliary Corps' in 1917. Afterwards the W.R.N.S. and W.R.A.F. were formed. In 1918, when she resigned, she was made a C.B.E.

The other children of Auckland Campbell Geddes were Eric Campbell (1875-1937); Margaret, Auckland Campbell (1879-1954) and Irvine Campbell (1882-1962). (If confusing to the reader on first impact, I have consciously given all the family Christian names in full, due to the constant repetition in nomenclature.) Eric Geddes was born in Agra and educated at Merchiston Castle School, Edinburgh, after which he went on to the Oxford Military College at Cowley, but he was high-spirited and athletic rather than studious and decided not to join the Royal Engineers, as had been intended for him.

Instead, when aged 17, he went over to the United States of America where he worked as a brakesman on the freight trains of the

88. The solidity of the panelling and stairways in the OMRAH and her contemporaries.

Baltimore and Ohio railroad, as a lumberjack and as a labourer in steel works, finally returning to Scotland after four years in 1895 with no more money in his pocket than he had had when he started. His next move was to India, where he became the manager of a forestry estate, clearing jungle and building light railways, obtaining a certain experience in that field which led him to return to England in 1906, when he took a comparatively lowly post in the North-Eastern Railway Company but, by 1914, before he was forty, he was its deputy manager.

On the outbreak of hostilities with Germany, he took charge of the mobilization movement in Northern Command and also raised a battalion from employees of the North-Eastern Railway, which became the 17th Northumberland Fusiliers. His big chance came, however, in 1915, when he was asked by the Director-General of Munitions Supply to report on the obstacles impeding the flow of munitions to the front, and his report was such that it won him the friendship and confidence of Lloyd George. In consequence, he became Director-General of Transportation on the staff of the Commander-in-Chief of the British Army in France and, later, inspector-General of Transportation for all theatres of war, with the honorary rank of Major-general, in 1917. However, in May of that year, it was considered that the ports and general transport arrangements were working well, and Eric Geddes was then appointed to be Controller of the Navy and an additional member of the Board of Admiralty with the temporary honorary rank of Vice-Admiral but, since Field Marshall Sir Douglas Haig had stipulated on releasing him that he should be liable to recall to his staff, he became one of the very few men to hold senior naval and military rank simultaneously.

He contested the bye-election for Cambridge as a Unionist successfully at about this time (and held his seat in the next general election) and, shortly afterwards, was made the First (Civil) Lord of the Admiralty. After the 1918 general election, Admiral Beatty urged Lloyd George to retain Eric Geddes as First Lord in the interests of the navy, but instead he was appointed to the Imperial War Cabinet and was the first Minister of Transport—a subject on which he was expert—and it was he who rationalized the various British railways into four main groups.

After the war, he was made Chairman of the famous committee which was charged to formulate plans for reducing Governmental spending and it proposed some very unpopular measures, most of which were promulgated. In fact, it made firm recommendations for the saving of £86,750,000, with further suggestions which brought the total to above £100,000,000—a very much larger sum in those days than it might appear in these times of wanton government. The consequences of this committee were known as the ‘Geddes Axe’ (as many naval officers, whose careers were cut short, will remember only

89. *There was a certain opulance about the smoking room in the OMRAH which is missing in more modern décor.*

too well), and Eric Geddes himself became disenchanted with politics and left Parliament in 1922 to turn his attention to industry, in which he then built up another notable career, being, *inter alia*, Chairman of the Dunlop Rubber Company in the years of its great expansion, and also Chairman of Imperial Airways, which he expanded enormously and during the course of which he must be given the lion's share of the credit for the inception of the 'all-Empire' Air Mail which revolutionized the post between Great Britain and her colonies and dominions. He was not always an easy man with whom to work, but it was said of him that he asked a great deal, but never more than he gave himself. He was knighted in 1916, appointed K.C.B.(Mil.) in 1917 and, in the same year, G.B.E. and then, two years later, the G.C.B. (one of the odd instances of promotion from military to civil ranks) and he finally died in his country house at Albourne Place, near Hassocks in Sussex, on 22 June, 1937. It was an extraordinary career after so unpromising a start.

Margaret, his sister, never married, but devoted her life to the care of others and particularly, in later life, to that of children. She engaged in social work for the mentally handicapped and for orphaned children in Edinburgh and became a Baillie, or Town Councillor, of that city.

Educated to be a doctor, Auckland Geddes graduated with honours as M.D. and became Professor of Anatomy in the Dublin Royal College of Surgeons. He was very interested in military matters but, due to bad eyesight which eventually blinded him, he could not serve effectively in the Army. He saw some active service, however, in the Boer War and in France in the First World War until 1916, when he came to London to enter the War Office as Director of Recruiting with the rank of Brigadier-General. He became a minister of the Crown in Parliament in 1917, and subsequently held many important positions in Government, including some during the second World War while he was, at one time, H.M. Ambassador to the United States of America. As a result of his work he was created Baron Geddes, G.C.M.G., K.C.B.(Mil.), M.D. in 1942.

Irvine Campbell Geddes was the brother in his generation of Geddes who brought an interest in ships and shipping to the family.

90. *Sir Alan Garrett Anderson, G.B.E.*

91. *Irvine Campbell Geddes.*

Educated in Edinburgh, he was the youngest in the family and, after leaving school, wanted to follow the law as a career and entered a Law Office to this end. However, quite unexpectedly, he was invited to join his Anderson cousins in the firm of Anderson, Anderson & Co., the managers of the Orient Line, and to follow a career in shipping. In consequence, in 1901, Irvine moved from Edinburgh to London and took up his appointment, thus coming into close contact with his cousin, Alan Garrett Anderson, who had joined the firm in 1897. Irvine had been a keen rugger player at school and, when living in London, played for the London Scottish and, in 1908, captained the Scottish side against England. He had become a partner in the firm in 1906.

From all that has been written already in this chapter, it will be apparent that the personalities who had built up the firm were people of substance and culture: in short, the sort that are necessary to create a shipping company of World class with ships of outstanding merit. We have now reached a point where the individuals of the family which founded and built the Orient Line were known personally and, in some cases, still are known, to the writer.

Alan Garrett Anderson, the only son of Elizabeth and James George Skelton Anderson, became a partner in the firm in 1900, and his career was one of achievement and excellence. He became the Deputy Governor of the Bank of England and Controller of Railways in the first World War and Chairman of the Railway Executive Committee in the second. He was also the Member of Parliament for the City of London from 1935 to 1940. These are but a few of the important positions and duties which he held and carried out during his long career and for which he was knighted and awarded the G.B.E. I met him frequently when he was an old man, still intensely interested in ships and, particularly, in those which were being designed and built for the Orient Line just after the end of the second World War, for he often visited the Naval Architect's office to talk about the design work. Sir Alan was over six feet tall, broad in the shoulders and upright in carriage. Indeed, he was a gentleman of imposing and commanding presence who drew an instant respect from all who met him.

92. *The s.s.* **ORIENT** *with sail set in a fair wind to enhance her speed. (From a lithograph after Dutton.)*

93. *The s.s. ORVIETO. (From a water-colour by W. M. Birchall.)*

To me, he appeared almost fearsome, having a craggy, handsome face with eyes almost shrouded with heavy eyebrows. This characteristic was to be seen in his two sons, about whom more is written in due course. Sir Alan's interest in ships occasionally caused some disquiet amongst many of the staff, both ashore and afloat. He was knowledgeable in the skills of navigation and used to visit the bridge of the Orient vessels and often ask questions which taxed the imagination and knowledge of the officers there. He also taxed my own knowledge very often and, on occasions, suggested some useful ideas as well.

The other elderly member of the Orient management and of Anderson, Green & Co. Ltd. whom I knew, liked and respected probably more than any other, was Irvine Campbell Geddes. He was the senior manager of the Company when I joined it in 1944, having become a partner in Anderson, Anderson & Co. in 1906, and being Chairman of the Orient Steam Navigation Co. Ltd. for seventeen years until he retired in 1952. In appearance he was thick-set, but this disguised his height, for he probably stood over six feet in his socks and was powerfully built. He was one of the most kindly, gentle and considerate men whom I have ever known, and at no time in the frequent meetings I had with him did he ever show rancour or unkindness of any sort. When discussing ship designs, he had a hesitant way of suggesting changes, but in many ways he influenced the design and building of the Orient Line passenger ships and certainly, in my personal experience, introduced many new ideas into the detailed planning of new vessels. The period of building new units for the fleet which followed the second World War was most difficult for shipowners, and Irvine Geddes held the chairmanship during that crucial and worrying period. The fleet had been sorely depleted by sinkings during the war, and the selection of ships suitable to the needs of post-war travellers was a task perhaps best accomplished by the use of a crystal ball! A good selection of ship type was made, however—without the aid of clairvoyance, so far as I know!

Sir Hugh Kerr Anderson had a son, Austin Innes Anderson (1897-1973) who, after being educated at Harrow and Kings College, Cambridge and serving in the army in the 1914-18 War, joined

Anderson, Green & Co. Ltd. in 1921, to become a director of the Orient Steam Navigation Co. in 1950. He became Chairman of the Company after the retirement of Irvine C. Geddes in 1952, being knighted in 1956. He held many positions of responsibility during his career, amongst which were Chairman of the Refrigerated Cargo Research Council; President of the Chamber of Shipping (1955-6), Chairman of the General Council of British Shipping (1955-6) and a member of the Ministry of Transport Committee on the Application of Nuclear Power to Marine Purposes (1956-62). Sir Austin was Chairman of the Orient Company until its merger with the P. & O. Company in 1960, while his son, Keith Royse Anderson (born 1926) became a senior member of Anderson, Green & Co. and, later, a manager in one of the divisions of the P. & O. Company.

Ships can be owned by one company and managed by another or, alternatively, can be owned and managed by one company. Often it will be found that a company (such as Anderson, Anderson & Co.) starts in business by managing vessels for other firms and then, later, buys ships for themselves to form their own shipping line—in their case, The Orient Steam Navigation Co. It follows that, in such an arrangement as this, the Directors of the managing company are also on the board of the shipping line, and this was so of these firms after the managers became Anderson, Green & Co. Ltd.

In 1919, the business of Anderson, Anderson & Co., whose partners were at that time Sir Kenneth S. Anderson, Sir Alan G. Anderson and Mr. Irvine C. Geddes, was dissolved and the business was amalgamated with Frederick Green & Company: the new company being called Anderson, Green & Co. Ltd. The three former partners of Anderson, Anderson & Co. acquired a half interest in the new Company, and the other half interest was bought by Gray Dawes & Co. on behalf of Lord Inchcape, acting for the Peninsular & Oriental Steam Navigation Co. Ltd. This new company became the managers of the Orient Steam Navigation Company as a result of this transaction. The directors of the new company were the three partners of the old Anderson, Anderson & Co. and Lord Inchcape, Sir Duncan Carmichael and Mr. W. Longridge, representing Gray Dawes & Co. Sir John Beale* joined the board in the same year. At the

* A director of Guest, Nettlefold & Keen Ltd.

94. Sir Austen Innes Anderson.

same time the P. & O. S.N.Co. Ltd. bought from the former managers of the Orient Line a large part of their holdings of deferred shares in that company which meant that it (the P. & O) then held more than 50% of the deferred capital of the O.S.N.Co. and thus gained a controlling interest in the latter company.

Sir Alan Garrett Anderson had two sons: Colin Skelton (born 1904) and Donald Forsyth (1906-1973). Colin Anderson, who was educated at Eton and Trinity College, Oxford, entered the business of Anderson, Green & Co. in 1928 and became secretary of it and of the Orient Steam Navigation Company and, in 1930, was voted to the board of the former company. From then on his interests, particularly in the Arts, developed, whilst he was also chairman of many committees, including:- The London Shipowners Dock Committee (1944-45); the London Port Employers (1945-47); National Association of Port Employers (1947-48 and 1950-54); General Council of British Shipping (1949-50); International

Chamber of Shipping (1949-63); President of the British Employers Confederation (1956-58) and President of the Chamber of Shipping (1949-50).

His interest in the development and encouragement of those practising the Arts has continued and he has been a patron of them for many years. He was Chairman of the Council of the Royal College of Art (1952-56) and Provost from 1967; Chairman of the Tate Gallery Trustees; Chairman of the Contemporary Art Society (1956-60); President of the National Council of Design and Industries Association (1950-53); Chairman of the Fine Arts Commission (1968-76) and a member of the Council of Industrial Design. In 1950 he was knighted and became a K.B.E. in 1969. Sir Colin has many distinctions to his credit but, amongst the most important (and, to me, the *most* important) is his contribution to the art of interior design in passenger liners. He has the uncanny knack of being able to select and guide a specialist in the right way to achieve satisfactory and artistic results. After the merger of the Orient and P. & O. in 1960, Sir Colin, who was also a Director of the P. & O. Company, moved into that company until he retired in 1969.

His younger brother, Donald F. Anderson, was also educated at Eton and Trinity, Oxford, before starting his career in Anderson, Green to which he was appointed a director in 1932, but he resigned in 1948. He had joined the P. & O. Company in 1934 and, with the exception of duties performed with the Ministry of War Transport and the British Merchant Shipping Mission to the U.S.A. between 1939 and 1943, most of his business life was spent with that company. He had a most distinguished career, being knighted in 1954. Sir Donald held the position of chairman of the P. & O. Company from 1960 until his retirement in 1971. He died two years later.

Irvine C. Geddes had three sons, the eldest of whom is Ford Irvine Geddes, who was born in 1913. Educated at Loretto School, Edinburgh and at Gonville and Caius College, Cambridge, where he read engineering, he started his business life with Anderson, Green in 1934 but, when the second world war started, he joined the army as a gunner. In 1940 he was commissioned in the Royal Engineers and served overseas from then on until 1945, becoming A.D.C. and, later,

95. *Sir Colin Skelton Anderson, K.B.E.*

96. *Ford Irvine Geddes, M.B.E.*

Military Assistant to Field Marshall Viscount Gort, V.C. in Gibraltar, Malta and Palestine.

Ford Geddes rejoined Anderson, Green & Co. in 1946 and became secretary to the firm, but was appointed a director a year later. Soon after that time he began to take a great interest in the rebuilding of the fleet and worked closely with his cousin, Sir Colin Anderson, in the activities of the design and building of the new ships, of which one followed closely on another from 1946 until the completion and delivery of the *Oriana* in 1960. During this time three passenger vessels of the 28,000 ton class; one of 40,000 tons and an oil tanker of 24,500 G.R.T. were built, whilst existing ships of the Company were extensively re-fitted after their war service, and an ex-German ship, the *Pretoria*, was re-built as an advanced type of post-war troop-ship for the British Government and re-named *Empire Orwell.*

When the merger between the P. & O. and Orient took place in 1960, Ford Geddes was made a Director of the P. & O. and became deputy Chairman of that company in 1968 and was Chairman during 1971-72. He was also Chairman of Container Fleets Ltd. (1968-71); Chairman of the British Shipping Federation (1965-68); President of the International Shipping Federation (1967-69), was on the Council of the Chamber of Shipping for over fifteen years and also a member of the General Committee of Lloyds Register in 1969. In 1943, he was awarded the M.B.E.

In all my numerous discussions with him, I quickly learned that a point at which to take extra notice was when he started to say something which he prefaced with the words ‘As a layman’, because I knew full well that he was not a layman on technical issues. As with all members of the Geddes family whom I met, he had a quiet and disarming air, but did not suffer fools gladly, and it was my belief and axiom that frankness and honest expression of opinion and feeling was the only sensible and correct way to conduct business with Ford Geddes—as it is possibly the best way to do business with anyone, in fact. If a mistake was made, confess it, and Ford Geddes would help to find a solution, with no recriminations to follow. No one could ask for more.

Ian Irvine Geddes, the second son, was born in 1915 and, when he grew to manhood, after a short experience of office life in Anderson, Green & Company, decided to go to Australia where he became a sheep farmer. He died there in 1978.

Keith Irvine Geddes was the third son of Irvine C. Geddes and was born in 1919. Like his father, he was a keen rugger player, becoming Captain of Scotland in the later 1940's, thus creating what is believed to be a unique instance of father and son being Scottish captains.

During the second World War, Keith Geddes joined the R.A.F. and became a night fighter pilot but, on the conclusion of hostilities, he entered Anderson, Green & Co. and held a position of responsibility when the merger with P. & O. took place but, although he moved over to employment with that firm at the time, he resigned to become a farmer in Buckinghamshire in 1961.

With the recent resignations of Kenneth R. Anderson and Lord Geddes*, the close connection of the Anderson and Geddes families with the business of ships and shipping drew to the end of a long era in which their contributions to the industry had been both very significant and truly admirable. However, if the foregoing story of these two families gives the impression that their success was unaided, it would be one that would be both unfortunate and unfair to many other people of note and ability who took part in the years of endeavour. The qualities of good leadership are usually reflected in the colleagues and staff chosen to assist in running a company, just as a dishonest board of directors will almost certainly have dishonest people in its staff. The history of the Orient Company shows that there were many strong and tough individuals playing important roles in its running, and many stories of their activities have been passed down through the years by the staff, and still enliven conversations between the survivors of the Company when they meet today. Nevertheless, it was the scions of the families of whom I have written who provided the entrepreneural skills and flair which created the Line and so enlarged its scope.

From 1919 onwards, the co-operation of the P. & O. and Orient Companies continued in a clearer way, but each had its distinctive role in its trading and in its ships and, whilst having a family relationship

* Grandson of Baron Geddes (p. 188), he had been involved in tanker operation.

in appearance, also had different house flags and styles which were all maintained until the Orient Company ended and was merged completely into the P. & O. in the 1960's.

The most obvious difference between the ships of the two concerns to be seen by even the most unobservant of people was in the hull colours for, although both had black hulls for a number of years, those of the Orient were corn-coloured latterly (from the *Orion* delivered in 1935) and the P. & O. ships gradually turned to white from the early 'Straths' with yellow funnels, whereas they had been black prior to that time (the Orient were black until 1906 when, running in conjunction with the Royal Mail which had yellow ones, the Company adopted this colour and retained it thenceforth) while the Orient ships also had their funnels fitted with black cowls* on their tops, often called 'Parsons' Hats' by some, and Admiralty cowls by others (the purists!) because the ships of the Royal Navy had for many years been fitted with cowls in this fashion. P. & O. vessels never adopted this style, although some of their later ships (after they had ceased painting them black) did have black tops to disguise the ever-present menace of funnel smuts. The *Arcadia*, of the 1950's, was such a case†. Then, prior to the P. & O. switch to white hulls and upper-works, their superstructures had been painted buff which, with the black hull and funnels, gave them a somewhat sombre appearance within the passenger trade but, at the same time, a certain distinction‡.

The take-over of the Orient Company virtually occurred in 1960 when the *Oriana* was completed and delivered by her builders, but there were stages in this progression. There had been a kind of amalgamation involved in the setting up of the joint running of the Orient-Pacific trading, and there had been an acquisition of the minority shares in the Orient Company in 1960 (by P. & O.), while Anderson, Green, which had been a subsidiary of the Orient Steam Navigation Co. since 1948, was merged into a new organization called P. & O. Orient Lines Ltd., and this latter company managed both fleets of ships from then onwards.

The ships of the Orient Line had been transferred to P. & O. registry by 1965, and their corn-coloured hulls had been changed to white. The following year the name 'Orient' finally ceased to be used.

* See plate 38.

† See also plate 61.

‡ See plate 98.

97. *The P. & O. KAISER-I-HIND, presenting a 'smoke problem'!*

98. *The MALOJA, passing under Sydney bridge whilst it was still under construction, and giving an idea of the appearance of the P. & O. hull colours. (The upperwords were made a lighter shade in the 1930's).*

During the latter half of the 1950's, the P. & O. Group tanker scheme began, in which each company in the group would own some tankers which were to be built. The Orient Company was responsible for the building of the *Garonne* which was delivered in 1959, and it was by no coincidence that this ship's name was that of the first fully-owned steamship of the Orient Line and which, registered in 1878, had first worn the new house flag of the company. It seemed historically tidy that the name *Garonne* should be given to the last ship ordered by the company.*

This new Group Tanker Scheme was not a good thing from the technical management point of view, because the running of oil tankers is a very specialised field of shipping, and it was both wrong and inefficient to involve all the Marine Superintendents, Superintending Engineers and Naval Architects of the many shipping companies of the P. & O. Group in learning this new business. It would have been more sensible and economic to have started a new branch of the P. & O. Group and to have built up its own specialist team.

Ultimately it became obvious that the loss of efficiency and the operating difficulties caused by this arrangement of the Group Companies' tankers were disproportionate to the benefits which had been expected, and an associate company was formed named Trident Tankers, which took over the tankers owned by the various companies within the P. & O. Group.

Apart from their own fleet operation, the Orient Line had managed some vessels for the British Government during both World Wars. A number of Dutch ships, which had fled to British ports when the Germans invaded the Low Countries in 1939, were being managed from the Port of Liverpool, as well as two so-called 'Sam' ships—a type of American-built cargo vessel. These vessels, which are not really germane to the burden of this book, have already been included in the Fleet List.

* Whilst the *Oriana* was the last ship to be *delivered* to the Company, the *Garonne* was actually *ordered* after her.

VIII. CONFIDENCE AND COURAGE

No single book can please everyone, and it is obvious that there are so many facets to the whole business of ships and shipowning that they cannot all be covered adequately in any one volume. Nevertheless, I have read many works devoted to both ships and companies which have left me with the impression that owners had run their vessels almost, as it were, for the benefit of those who would read of their triumphs and disasters: their fine passages or their grandeur, in generations to come, and with total disregard for the objects of the whole exercise of shipowning which, in short, is to make profits. The result is that it is assumed automatically that, because a ship created speed records, outdid her contemporaries in sheer magnificence or otherwise caught the popular imagination, she must have been successful.

In fact, the reverse is very often the case, and investigation of voyage accounts and the like will often demonstrate that the more humble vessels which seldom hit the headlines often produced higher dividends. There are probably three main reasons for this common omission in so many marine histories: first, the voyage accounts are, in so many cases, no longer available (as in the case of the Orient Line, whose main books of account and statistical records were destroyed in the air raids of 1941) and, even if they are available, it is often difficult to isolate the trading results of individual ships; secondly, the majority of people (and I am amongst these) find Balance Sheets and Profit and Loss Accounts to be extremely dull reading and, very often, do not understand them properly unless they have been trained as accountants and, last, there are many instances in which a loss-making vessel has created immeasurable and often imponderable gains elsewhere.

As to the second of these reasons, I do not intend to inflict a mass of Annual Accounts or of figures on the reader, since these, together with the various qualifications required, would fill a book in themselves and, I suspect, make very heavy reading. Accountants would have the advantage that they would understand them, but it is dubious if they would find them the more interesting on that account! I shall, however, endeavour to present sufficient data to avoid this pitfall and, at the same time, demonstrate that the steady increase in the fleet and that its apparent success, as outlined in the previous chapters, was not always reflected in the books of account on the one hand, and also to show the quite exceptional acts of faith which finally put the company on a really viable and profitable basis, on the other.

In this chapter, so far as practicable, firm figures in terms of money are avoided, although they are stated as necessary but, because the value of the British pound has changed so much in terms of purchasing power over the century since the Orient Steam Navigation Company was first formed, the reader must make due allowance for this, since it takes a good deal of imagination to conjure up the implications of—say—half a million pounds in the last century as compared with a similar sum today. For example, the purchasing power of the pound in 1914 was nearly 16½ times of its purchasing power in 1974 and, in the ensuing four years, it lost half its 1974 purchasing power. No doubt this decline in value will be appreciably greater by the time that this book is published. We have already seen this reflected in the prices paid for the post-war units of the Orient fleet, and I have little doubt that this difficulty of achieving fair monetary comparisons is one reason why so many writers avoid treading the quicksands of financial results.

Despite the fact that there are no Orient Line balance sheets prior to 1904, nor for certain years subsequent to that date, a general picture of the results of the firm's trading was compiled many years later by William Fenton Hird (1883-1969). He joined the Accounts Department of the Company in 1900 and, in 1910, he became the Chief Accountant. In 1925 he was appointed Chief Accountant of

99. The ORIZABA in the Thames.

Anderson, Green & Co. Ltd. as well as of the Orient S.N.Co. Ltd., and in 1928 was promoted to the board of the former company. He retired in 1952. His knowledge of the Company over so many years enabled him to make notes on its history—and particularly its financial history—and I have been fortunate in having had access to the notes which he made. Indeed, very much of this chapter is based upon what William Hird had written. It is interesting to note that he was not a director of the Orient Company since, in fact, there were no 'directors', but only 'managers', until it became statutory for every company to have directors and even then, when this was legally necessary, only a few of the senior members of the Company were appointed to the Board.

The Orient Steam Navigation Company Ltd. was incorporated under the Joint Stock Companies Act on 12 February, 1878, with an authorised share capital of £500,000 divided into 5,000 shares of £100 each. The share capital actually issued was £466,350, and each of the two firms of managers was bound, under the terms of the Management Agreement, to hold a minimum of £25,000 in shares. In all probability they took up more than that, and it is certain that, by 1900, the combined holdings were about £100,000, though whether they had bought in on the open market cannot be determined. Thus the two Managing Companies held a maximum of nearly 21½% of the whole at the turn of the century.

At some point, perhaps as early as 1879, the shares were divided into £10 units and the authorised capital may also have been increased by £100,000, although there was no further issue. The bulk of the information concerning the early trading results was compiled from a book started in the early 1900's which gave a retrospective analysis of the Depreciation Reserve, together with the cost of steamers bought and the amount realized when they were sold, together with other relevant information, and this book was kept up to date thenceforth and provides an interesting insight into the fortunes of the Company. Regrettably, a record of the dividends paid by the old company is not available, but the ensuing paragraphs will demonstrate that this is probably not very important in the circumstances, because the depreciation book makes it clear which were bad years, and, indeed, which were the worst, but for other years we can only glean the information that profits were sufficient to meet the full depreciation reserves, and we do not know what surplus there may have been, nor how it was disposed. It is reasonable to suppose that any interim surplus that was not paid in dividend would have been carried forward and ultimately found its way to the Depreciation Reserve.

Under its Articles of Association (the rules under which a Company is bound to operate under its incorporation), the original company was obliged to set aside to the Depreciation Reserve 6% of the First Cost of its steamers annually. Lest anyone may not be clear of the implications of depreciation, let me say, briefly, that if a capital item is purchased, it can be reckoned to have a certain life, after which it must be replaced. Thus, if a man buys a car for £3,000 and reckons that it will be replaced in 10 years, he should put £300 per annum in a piggy bank (or, better still, a Building Society) in order that he could afford a new car when the old one is worn out, and so he should do for

100. The OROYA flying the Blue Peter off Gravesend.

any appliance which he possesses and which will require to be replaced. Few private individuals do this in practice, but live up to their incomes with no depreciation allowance being made (£300 p.a. for the car), with the result that Hire-Purchase Companies prosper, but in the case of a firm it is both provident and, in view of the sums involved, obligatory. Of course, account must be taken of possible inflation and also of such residual value as the item concerned may have when it is replaced.

There are different methods of applying depreciation. A common one in these times is to take a certain percentage of the residual value at each year's end (so that the amount on any item grows less with each successive year, and if it exceeds its life expectation it never quite reaches a value of 'nil'), or one can do as the Orient Managers did, and write down by a fixed amount each year—in this case 6%.

Some readers will already have divided 6 into 100 and realized that the expected life of the ships was thus estimated to be just under

17 years, and will doubtless say that an iron vessel (as the early units of the fleet were) should last for much longer than that, and that, therefore, a fixed depreciation of 6% seems rather high, particularly taking account of the residual value of the ships (or their probable sale price), but there are two facts to be taken into consideration. First of these is that the depreciation also took into account Repairs and Renewals within their useful life and special repairs which, in those days, frequently included the substantial cost of fitting new boilers and, in the second place, the steamers which formed the initial fleet were about seven years old when purchased, and thus not in their first prime.

It would also be a reasonable supposition that the managers confidently expected the technical advances in steam vessels which did, indeed, come about, and that they realized that, if they were to keep in the first flight, their ships would very possibly have to be replaced whether they were 'worn out' or not. If I stress the implications of depreciation, it is because it provides so useful a clue to the early results of the Company.

There is every reason to suppose that the first three or four years of business of the new Company were perfectly satisfactory and, indeed, prosperous, since its fortunes should have followed the trend of overseas trade with and from Australia which, in those years, was steadily increasing. The population of that country was also increasing, and Imports and Exports in relation to population were improving up to 1884. Moreover, the *Orient* was delivered 19 months after the Company was formed, so must have been ordered in its very early days when they had every confidence in the future, and this view is enhanced by the fact that they ordered the *Austral* which was delivered in 1882.

However, although there was a period of relative boom in the Australian trade until 1884, the initial good results of the Company did not extend beyond 1882, largely because of the disaster which befell it when the *Austral* sank in Sydney Harbour. This involved the loss of earnings on £200,000 of new tonnage (which was then nearly a third of the total cost of the existing fleet) until she was back in commission. There would have been other expenses not recoverable

101. The first class dining saloon of the OMRAH.

under insurance policies, and, of course, there was not any question of a 'Loss of Profits' policy at that time. The result was that, in 1883 and 1884, little more than 3% on First Cost was available for depreciation against the 12% (for the *two* years) required by the Articles and, as Irvine C. Geddes wrote in his message to the Staff* many years later, depreciation is an item which must be met before there is any profit. Thus, in those years, there was none.

It is common to think that alternation of 'booms' and 'slumps' have been confined to the period since—say—the first World War, but this is not the case, and it has been a plague of the shipping industry

* See p. 96.

ever since the middle of the last century. (Indeed, one could take it further back than that, although the conditions were rather different). World trade cycles affect most areas, but the Orient Company were the more affected by changes which might occur in Australia itself, and its trade generally declined in 1886 and 1887, while there was, at the same time, an intensification of shipping competition. It is true that, from 1 February, 1888, the Company had a mail contract with the Imperial Government which was worth £85,000 per annum, on a basis of fortnightly sailings, but this benefit also brought its obligations. There was some improvement in the Australian trade until 1891, but the ensuing four or five years have been described as 'catastrophic'. There was a financial crisis in Australia, the details of which need not concern us, but they were of vital concern to the Company at the time and affected their Profit and Loss accounts most adversely.

Gradually, the situation improved and, by 1900, trade was re-established on a satisfactory basis, although any prospect of paying dividends was still remote. In this connection, it must be borne in mind that nearly 80% of the share-holding was held by private individuals or by institutions, who could not have been best pleased at the lack of return on their investments. In the meantime, in 1894, the *Chimborazo* and the *Garonne*, which were 23 and 26 years old respectively, were sold, and at that time their shares in the depreciation fund were insufficient to cover the difference between their cost and their sale prices. Indeed, it was clear that the real value of the Company's assets was less than their book value and did not match the share capital issued. I suspect that readers who have borne with this chapter thus far may be surprised—both by the foregoing facts and by those which follow—since the preceding chapters, which set out the details of the ships; their building, their performances, and so forth, give no more idea of the true financial situation than the majority of books to which I referred at the outset. If they will please read for a little longer, even at the risk of some figures, they will find that the story becomes even more astonishing. Shipowners were never philanthropists, and their object is as surely to make money as to fulfill their obligations to their share-holders. Since this is the whole

102. *The deck lounge in the ORAMA of 1924.*

object of being a shipowner, I feel that it is utterly wrong to ignore it and, by good fortune, the progress of the Orient Line on this front was both remarkable and unexpected.

In the light of the position in 1900, it was decided to reconstruct the Company and, as at 1 August, it was wound up and a new one was formed with the same name (except that the prefix 'The' was dropped) and with the capital in two classes—Preferred and Deferred shares. Share-holders of the old company were offered a choice of either taking up Deferred shares in the New Company at the same face value, or Preferred at 60% of their existing nominal holdings, these latter carrying the right to a cumulative dividend of 5%, the annual payment of which was guaranteed by the managers.

Since no record exists of the dividends paid by the old Company, it is impossible to say exactly how much return the shareholders had received on their capital, but the inference is that, although they would probably have received something in the first 4 of the 22½ years under review, they might (conceivably) have received some small dividend in—perhaps—two of the years 1882-89, and that the chances that they received anything at all from 1889 onwards seem to be extremely remote. Whilst this statement is a little speculative, it is nevertheless a fair inference on the basis of the Depreciation Reserve book because, if the depreciation could not be met in full, there would not have been any dividends. (In two of the years in the 1880's, provision for depreciation was only a quarter of the amount required: in a third the full amount was only provided by drawing on the Insurance Fund; in a fourth, special repairs expenditure exceeded the depreciation provision, . . . and so on.) It seems to be almost certain that the total amount disbursed as dividends was less than the amount of capital written off on the conversion of the old shares into Preferred Shares in the new Company and of those which were redeemed.

The tenor of William Hird's findings for the early days of the Company are abundantly confirmed by an article written in the contemporary journal, *Vanity Fair*, although it was somewhat waspish in its tone, and dealt with the published accounts and Balance Sheet of the Company for the year ended 31 December, 1881. Indeed, these were reproduced and made the subject of some criticism and the writer was outspoken in suggesting that the figures were presented in a misleading manner and that the shareholders found themselves in a disadvantageous position in relation to that of the managers. Tribute was paid to the reputation and respectability of the managers, but attention was drawn to the talents of Elizabeth Garrett-Anderson (who had recently been appointed physician to the Post Office at an annual salary of £1,000) and to her extremely clever sister who was married to Mr. Fawcett, the Post-master General, and the article went on:-

> ' ' *indeed, from all that we have heard of them, we are not at all sure that these ladies combined would not manage any average Company at least as well as the majority of directors with whose names we are familiar; we know, at any rate, that we would rather trust them.'*

This was a much stronger suggestion in the 1880's than it would be today, when women have equal rights with men yet, if the article did shed some light on the financial situation at that time, its tone was such as to make the reader wonder whether its writer was, perhaps, a disappointed shareholder!

The lack of distributed dividends probably accounted for the fact that the majority of the shareholders opted for the Preferred shares, which would provide a certain 5% dividend—and it must be remembered that we are talking about 1900, when 5% was not the low rate of interest which it would seem to be today. Some few of the old shareholders would not assent to the reconstruction, and they were paid off in cash at 60% of the nominal value of their holdings. As for the managers, they took Deferred shares in the New Company in place of their holdings in the old one. Thus the issued capital in the old company was disposed as follows, viz:

Dissentient shareholders paid off	£11,400	£350,000
Converted into preference shares	£339,200	
Converted into Deferred Shares	£115,750	
	£466,350	

The discount on the redemption of the dissentient shares and the reduction in the nominal value of the shares converted into the new

Preferred class totalled £140,240 (40% of £350,600) and this was written off by adding it to the Depreciation Reserve, thereby reducing the book value of the fleet to £490,080, which was considered to be a reasonable figure for, at the time, the new Company took over the fleet of six vessels which consisted of the five which had been built (*Orient, Austral, Ormuz I, Ophir* and *Omrah*) together with the *Cuzco* which was the only remaining second-hand vessel of those with which they had started trading in 1878.

To put this in a better perspective, it should be noted that the subscribed share capital of the old company had not only provided the cost of the four vessels bought from the P.S.N.Co., together with the greater part of the cost of the *Orient*, but, from that point onwards, the depreciation reserves had never been sufficient to cover the cost of new vessels as it became due. Money had been borrowed on debentures: some £110,000 being outstanding in 1880, though this had been reduced to £60,000 by 1900, and it must be assumed that the shipbuilders probably allowed credit in part by accepting bills which could be discounted on the market. In total, the old company had bought nine vessels (second-hand or new) totalling 47,383 tons at a cost of £1,459,896 and had sold 3 of them totalling 11,600 tons which cost £251,999, leaving 6 ships of 35,783 tons in total which cost £1,207,897 which were taken over by the new company and, after the application of the discount on the reconstituted capital, these stood in the books at £490,080. These figures alone demonstrate the buying power of the pound as compared with today, whilst making allowance for the great differences in the qualities of design and building of ships in the 1870's and 1880's.

The Articles of the new Company laid down that 4% depreciation on the cost of steamers should be set aside out of profits before the payment of any (ordinary) dividend and that, if the balance was insufficient for the Preferred dividends, the Managers would make up any shortfall while, if there was no balance at all, the Managers should pay the Preferred Dividend in full. However, although this might seem, on the face of it, almost punitive for the Managers in the light of the experience of the preceding years, in fact, it really meant that they would have to contribute a maximum of £10,176 out of the Orient commissions (which amounted to about £26,000 per annum). In the event of the commissions being greater, the odds were that the dividend would be safe in any case. The Preferred shareholders were only receiving 3% on their *original* investment and, of course, the 5% on their discounted shares was all that they could hope for—however much the Company might prosper in the future. In any case, since the Depreciation reserve had been reduced from 6% to 4%, the payment of the 5% Preferred dividend should be easier to attain, whilst, at the same time, the Managers had become the owners of about 90% of the Deferred Capital—the 'ordinary shares', or 'equity', in more modern parlance. Since the Managers, as signatories to the Memorandum of the reconstituted Company, had subscribed for 7 deferred shares, the Issued Capital thus became:

Preferred shares	£203,520
Deferred shares	£115,820
	£319,340

Although it may not have seemed to be significant at the time, the fact that the Managers did hold this large proportion of the equity was to prove to be a crucial factor in the Company's ultimate advance and success. As it was, the first year passed well enough, with Australian trade improving (as it had been in the preceding two years) and profits were further enhanced, perhaps more by luck than good judgement, by the *Ophir* being chartered for the Duke of York's visit to Australia to open the Commonwealth Parliament. (This charter, a very favourable one, brought about a position in which, for the first and only time in her career, the *Ophir* could be described as a 'profit-maker'.) 5% was paid on both classes of share and a further £30,000 was set aside for reserves. This was unusual, but satisfactory, although this reserve was little more in total than the combined effects of the reduction in depreciation from 6% to 4% and the saving in not having to pay any dividend on the capital which had been written off.

Notwithstanding, it was a good enough start for the new Company, but the next year (1902) was the year of a great drought in Australia, which resulted in a severe down-turn in trade for both that and the following year and, although it recovered and markedly

103. Painted white as a 'Royal Yacht', the OPHIR makes for sea.

improved each year until 1912 (except for a temporary set-back in 1908) this was not immediately reflected in the Orient Line accounts and, indeed, the Managers found themselves obliged to pay a quarter of the Preferred dividend in 1903, 1904 and 1905 and the whole of it, except a mere £100, in 1906, though this was achieved by drawing on the sum set aside for reserves in the first year of trading. After 1906, the Managers never had to contribute to the Preferred dividend again. In 1903 and 1904 it had not been possible to set aside the required 4% against depreciation, and the deficiency was about 2% on First Cost, but the book value of the fleet at the end of this bleak period was not reckoned to be too high.

Thus, after a quarter of a century of trading, the Company—and for purposes of this comment it makes no odds whether one refers to the old or the new, since it was to all intents and purposes the same thing, having only altered in its financial structure—had built up a fine fleet of ships by the standards of the times: ships which were considered by many to be the best on the Australian run and had achieved a name for reliability and popularity with passengers, yet, even in these last years, when the general trade situation had improved, the Company had not been showing good profits, and thus was not achieving its very *raison d'etre*. It is interesting to speculate on the reasons for this lack of success.

The Orient Line had no monopoly on the Australian route, but it was often claimed that they had the finest ships and had run their service in collaboration with the P.S.N.Co. Their nearest rivals were the ships of the P. & O., but there were many other vessels in competition with these three companies* and all of them shared the passengers and cargoes being carried across the seas between Europe and Australia. The collaboration of the P.S.N.Co. and the Orient was not particularly helpful financially to the latter because the arrangement allowed the former company to retain all the earnings of its own ships and, therefore, did not affect the trading results of the Orient Line materially.

The rather unspectacular profits of the Company were probably brought about by a number of causes: the ships may have been too expensive in comparison with their competitors on the one hand and, on another, the Orient fleet was always a small one in terms of the number of vessels owned at any one time. The matter of the *Ophir* must also be considered for, although she was a very advanced type of vessel at the time of her building, being extremely popular with passengers and becoming known as 'The Queen of the Indian Ocean', she did consume some 120 tons of coal a day, and this meant that there was little hope of her being an economical vessel. This one ship, representing 19% of the company's tonnage, not only had no hope of making a profit, but was, to a greater or lesser extent, being subsidized by those units of the fleet which could. Nevertheless, a situation of this sort raises a very interesting point, which is that of 'prestige'. It is easy to say: 'If a ship is not profitable, get rid of her!' In fact, even had the company wished to do any such thing (which is most unlikely) there were

* There were not only British lines involved, but French, German and others. Indeed, the Norddeutscher Lloyd frequently withdrew some of its large trans-Atlantic liners in the slack winter season and sent them out on the Australian run.

104. *Second in popularity to the Orient Line in the Australian run, the P. & O. also ran to the Far East and had a much larger fleet. Here is their NEPAUL wrecked on the Skagstone Rock, outside Plymouth, in December, 1890.*

105. *One of the 'Jubilee' class, built in 1888 (Queen Victoria's jubilee) the P. & O. OCEANA is here seen lying at Circular Quay, Sydney. In 1911 she sank with much bullion aboard off Beachy Head after coming in collision with the 4-masted German barque PISAGUA (which made Dover). It was the PISAGUA's right of way, as a sailing ship.*

other considerations. In the first place, they had their obligations to meet the mail contract, and were obviously in no position to order a new (and more economical) vessel to this end, while the cost of chartering a suitable vessel (which would not have been so easy either) would probably not have improved the situation materially. The fact was that the *Ophir* was a 'prestige' vessel to a large degree, and the consequences of this role are immeasureable and very hard to define. Such ships are, in a sense, tremendously fine advertisements and, although they themselves may operate at a loss, they can bring additional trade to the fleet as a whole.

Only the year before the *Ophir* was built, the Union Company (before its amalgamation with the Castle Line) had launched the *Scot*, which was specifically built to break all records on the Cape route. She succeeded admirably and, with a speed of $18\frac{1}{2}$ knots, her record on that run stood for no less than 43 years! Granted that her service speed was slightly greater than that of the *Ophir*, but she also burnt 170 tons of coal a day! Also, she carried far less passengers (although on a different route), but Donald Currie, her owner, never expected her to be profitable. It is true that there were circumstances of rivalry at the time which probably had an influence on her building, but her very presence enhanced the reputation of the entire Union Line, although the effects could never be quantified.

In the same way, on an international plane, certain grandiose vessels have been subsidized by their Governments, usually on the North Atlantic passenger run, with little hope that their voyage accounts would ever be in profit. There is no question—since her owners were the first to admit it—that when the *Queen Mary* wrested the Atlantic Blue Riband from the *Normandie*, it enhanced their trade in the Mediterranean, *inter alia*. This may seem to be irrational, but life is not entirely rational. The fact was that various governments did pour a great deal of money into their 'prestige' ships and, whether or not they held the Blue Riband, the results were considered to be worth the expenditure.

The almost certain unprofitability of the *Ophir* was not the only factor which had held back the Orient progress, but it must have been a contributory one. Another probable reason lies in the size of the ships. It is true that each successive unit of the fleet had been larger than its predecessor, but the likelihood is that the ships were not big enough to be profitable on so long a route—possibly the longest in the world at that time. Had they been bigger, they would not have been viable because they could not have been utilized to the full—possibly as regards cargo, but certainly as regards passengers. It has been pointed out previously that the most economical vessel is always the biggest, *providing* that she can be fully employed all the time*.

Much bigger ships were being used on the North Atlantic, for example, but this was a trade which was very much more developed and there was a reasonable expectation that they could be employed to maximum efficiency. This was not the case regarding Australia, which was still a developing country and one which did not support the constant interchange of passengers. The P. & O. Company, of course, was a much bigger one in the size of its fleet, and was also running out to India and the Far East, with an assured stream of passengers and freight, and it is not possible to isolate the trading results of that company to Australia from its total operation as a means of comparison with the Orient Company. That is a pity, since such a comparison would be interesting!

No doubt the Orient Managers were disappointed that, after so much effort, there had been so little reward—a feeling that had probably been heartily endorsed by the previous share-holders—but the fact was that they were still in business and still retained an undying faith in the future of the Australian trade. This faith, coupled with almost unbelievable courage, was to be more than justified.

It was at this point that the P.S.N.Co. sold their fleet to the Royal Mail Company, whose chairman was Owen Philipps, later to become Lord Kylsant, and whose meteoric career was involving the swallowing up of shipping company after shipping company until he was, under the umbrella of what came to be termed the 'Kylsant Group', by far the largest shipowner in the world. In theory, the old Orient Line arrangement with the P.S.N.Co. should have continued with the Royal Mail, but it has already been recorded that relations were far from cordial between the Orient and Royal Mail Companies and, on 12 July, 1907, the latter gave the Orient 18 months notice that

* See page 110.

they wished to withdraw their ships from the joint service. An extension of the mail contract, which had expired in January, 1905, to 31 January, 1908, with an annual subsidy of £120,000, was at the core of the matter and, in fact, the agreement between the two parties terminated on 15 May, 1909. In the meantime, a new contract for carrying the mails for another ten years for £170,000 per annum had been negotiated and signed by the Orient Line, which was to be solely responsible for it—the R.M.S.P.Co. having tendered unsuccessfully.

With the benefit of hindsight, it can be seen that the severing of relations with the Royal Mail was probably the salvation of the Orient Company. That Owen Philipps was an exceptionally brilliant man of business there can be little doubt. He was knighted shortly after the break with the Orient and had a most distinguished career, being chairman of some three dozen important companies and on the boards of five others, whilst he had occupied several other important offices. A barony was conferred on him in the 1923 New Year's Honours List in recognition of his public services and he was a man who had consistently gone from height to height. Very tall and of distinguished appearance, he was well liked by both his peers and subordinates.

Finally, in 1927, he purchased the White Star Line at a time when world trade was entering a period of deep recession and when millions of tons of shipping were being laid up, whilst repayments were due to the Government on loans under the Trade Facilities Act. That he had misjudged the swing of the trade cycles in the event, there can be no doubt and, since the circumstances created financial embarrassment to the Kylsant Group, a prospectus was issued inviting subscription to a debenture issue in the parent company—the Royal Mail Steam Packet Co. Ltd. The rest is history.

In 1931 he was brought to trial for issuing a misleading prospectus relating to this debenture issue and, regrettably enough, imprisoned*. A Chairman, like a Government Minister, must be held responsible for such grave errors. It was a sad affair, but it is very relevant to the *contretemps* between the Orient and Royal Mail Companies in 1909 because, although the Orient Line would have superficially retained its identity, there is little likelihood that it would

* Whether Lord Kylsant was a victim of circumstance may be open to debate. The charges brought against him included bringing into the annual balances certain sums of a non-recurring kind and an 'economy of truth', which prosecuting counsel claimed to have falsified the document as a whole, though *the figures were correct in themselves*. Kyslant himself never tried to evade responsibility or to pass it on anyone else and bore the trial with great dignity, while those who knew him felt that there was no criminality in the matter, but that he had taken on responsibilities beyond the capacity of any one individual, and that he had misjudged the economic cycle coupled, perhaps, with a certain recklessness.

106. The third class dining saloon in the ORAMA.

have achieved the successes which followed had it continued to try and co-operate with Royal Mail. In fact, co-operation on that plane was probably impossible, since the alternatives, judging by the long roster of other important companies which came to join the Kylsant Group at one time or another, was either to break adrift (as the Orient Line had) or to be swallowed up. Moreover, after the Royal Mail scandal, the results to the various companies in the group were horrendous, particularly in a time of slump, and the least that can be said is that the Orient Company was well out of it.

No-one could have predicted the events of 1927-31 in 1907-09, but, due to the notice served on them by the Royal Mail Line, the Managers of the Orient Company had to take some action and, equally, they had to take it fast. They were to be solely responsible for the extremely valuable new mail contract and, since the company had been re-organized, had only built one vessel—the *Orontes (I)* in 1902—while both the *Austral* and the *Cuzco* had been sold after giving yeomen service. This meant that their fleet consisted of five steamers, totalling 35,389 tons, of which it was clear that the *Orient* was nearing the end of her useful life. (In fact, she was sold in 1910, when over 30 years old.) To all intents and purposes, the Company had no liquidity in the form of free cash.

The action taken by the managers justifies the title of this chapter—*Confidence and Courage*—since both these qualities were breath-taking in their magnitude. They ordered five ships, of far greater tonnage and speed than any they had owned before:—

Orsova (I)	12,036 tons	Cost £367,691
Otway	12,077	367,674
Osterley	12,129	331,610
Otranto (I)	12,124	327.790
Orvieto	12,133	335.713
	60,499 tons	£1,730,478

For a company which had practically no money, these were astonishing orders, and it is fascinating to appreciate how this operation was funded. At the time—and this was a fortunate circumstance—shipbuilders were crying out for orders and, in consequence, were prepared to grant very easy terms for payment. The prices which they quoted did exclude certain work and equipment for which the owners were to make independent arrangements, but finally the builders undertook to reimburse them for such expenditure and thus to be responsible for the cost of the completed ships.

Despite the amount of money involved, the Company was fortunate in that the cost of these new vessels was relatively low, since the price per ton was only 73% of that of a steamer built in 1902 and, as it turned out—and it may be thought rather remarkable—some 86½% of the price which obtained in 1917, after three years of war. The builders had negotiated payment on the basis of 10% of the total cost being payed in cash on delivery, and 10% per annum thereafter:

the outstanding balance from time to time being represented by renewable bills which could, if required, be discounted on the market.

During the period of construction, the Company may have accumulated some £80,000—£100,000 from surplus earnings but, whatever the exact sum may have been, the Managers could not possibly have had sufficient money to meet the initial cash payments on delivery of the ships. In order to overcome this difficulty, they gave their personal guarantees to the Builders for the liabilities of the Company under the various contracts and, thereafter, loans from its bankers were negotiated.

Whether or not interest accrued on the post-dated bills is not clear, but it is reasonable to suppose that it did. Certainly there would have been interest on the loans from the bank, and it is therefore apparent that the Managers had given their personal guarantee for a sum involving some £2,000,000. Now two million pounds is two million pounds by any standards, but here I must again repeat that the value of money in 1909 had little relation to its value today, and it can be said that they had, in fact, committed themselves to finding a sum or approximately sixteen or seventeen million by 1977 values—and it would be even more by the time this book appears. In 1909 a single million pounds was a sum regarded with a great deal of awe. Indeed, having dealt with the family background of the Company and discussed the trading results to date, one is tempted to wonder how such a sum was to be found in case of need and whether the Managers did not spend many sleepless nights! However, whatever the answers to those questions may be, it is clear that they were able to satisfy their bankers, who would have dealt in collateral rather than in promises.

Certainly the issue of a prospectus inviting subscription to a new capital issue would have had a poor chance of success, because it would have had to confess to a history of some thirty years trading with a very poor record of profit: to having no spare cash and to owing £120,000 in Debentures, whilst the Company then owned five ships written down to a book value of £460,000 which was only some £50,000 in excess of its issued share capital of £320,000. Moreover, for the preceding five years to 1906 inclusive, only the last one had provided enough profit to cover 4% depreciation and the Preference share dividend, although 1907 looked, at that time, as if it would maintain the improvement. This was not a set of facts likely to attract potential investors.

The Managers themselves were still confident in the expansion and development of Australian trade and its consequent benefits to themselves, and of their own capability to exploit this situation with a larger fleet, but this was an assumption which could not be supported by any trading results at that time. Moreover, there were—and are always—risks connected with shipowning. A ship may be lying at anchor and, in effect, minding her own business, when another vessel can collide with her and sink her, with resulting loss of profits. Australia is a country which can suffer phenomenal droughts (as had already been experienced) and also catastrophic floods. These things are unpredictable, but any one of them, together with any other unforeseen disaster, could have caused an immediate recession in the Orient business.

However much research may have been done, any entrepreneural enterprise involves risks. The managers were determined to take this gamble, and were fortified in their ability to make it succeed as a result of the effects of the re-structuring of the Company in 1900. Previous to that date, they had only held about a quarter of the ordinary shares, with correspondingly limited voting rights, and, had that circumstance still existed, it is unlikely that they would have adopted the course which they took. In fact, the Preference share-holders, under the new arrangement, were to all intents and purposes perpetual debenture holders, being guaranteed their annual 5% but without any interest in fluctuations in profits, and only concerned that the Company remained solvent. On the other hand, the Deferred share-holders stood to reap the benefit of increased profits and, since 1900, the Managers had held 90% of this equity. Thus, if the adventure on which they were embarking was to prove to be successful, that success would be for the benefit both of their Management business and for themselves as owners of almost all the equity of the Orient Steam Navigation Co.

Taking account of all these considerations, the Managers determined to pledge their personal fortunes against the future success of this scheme and, of course, the agreement of the other partners was necessary before it could be effective. Concurrently, the Shipyards, who were not receiving their money as the work was done, needed finance to pay their wages, the cost of materials and the like and they, in their turn, must have needed to turn to their bankers for credit facilities. It is a safe assumption that the two sets of bankers—those representing the shipbuilders and those representing the Orient Line—must have conferred together. These would have been financial wizards: men averse to granting long term loans who would have fully acquainted themselves with the history of the Orient Company, and been fully cognizant of the fact that the only security that the Company itself could offer was a charge on the ships of its fleet—which were neither immediately realizable assets nor approaching the value of the sums required. Certainly the new ships, when they appeared, would represent additional assets, but this was in the future, and no-one could state with certainty that they would prove successful. Against all this discouraging evidence, they must have weighed the considered views of the managers about the prospects of the new venture and that they backed that judgement, accepted their guarantee and decided to co-operate with them must rank as a most remarkable testimonial from the Banking community to the Orient Line.

Until this time, the Company's financial year had ended with the calendar year, but now it was changed to 30 June and accounts were produced for the six months ending 30 June, 1909, and the balance sheet at that time shows the position practically at the start of the enlarged business. At that point, the outstanding loans amounted to £1,300,000 and three of the new steamers were actually delivered. Then, in the following February, three months after the fifth and last steamer had been delivered and when all of them were operational, an issue of £750,000 4½% Debentures was made on the Stock Exchange at a discount and, from the proceeds, the outstanding £113,000 was redeemed. After allowing for this and for the discount and the expenses of the new issue, £579,500 became available for the repayment of loans and retirement of bills, and to this extent released obligations to the Bankers.

107. The OTRANTO (I) on speed trials, 1909.

It had been hoped to reinforce the Company's close ties with Australia in connection with this Debenture issue, and that Australian investors might take an interest in the Company's development and subscribe for this issue and, to this end, the half-yearly interest coupons were made payable either in Sydney or London but, in fact, all the interest coupons were presented in London. These debentures were redeemable by 30 September, 1925.

Soon after the start of the new service, the *Orama*, another new vessel, was ordered at a cost of £340,000 and, soon after she was delivered in November, 1911, the *Ormuz (I)* was sold after twenty five years of working. In the meantime, the new service was making a satisfactory start and, of course, the Orient Line had the benefit of that part of the mail contract formerly taken by the Royal Mail. The working account for the enlarged fleet contributed nearly 10% of First Cost for the first complete year; 12% in the second, 18½% for the third and 16% for each of the two remaining years before the outbreak of the 1914 war. These were vastly improved figures, but it is not possible to break them down, even if such figures were to be palatable, since, as stated, the records were lost by enemy action. It is known, however, that the average earnings per voyage of passage money and freight showed an increase of about 40% on those for the preceding years during the first year of operation, and it is thus reasonable to suppose that the improved results were due to the improved load factors of the ships. In fact, the ratio of working profits to earnings for these years was 20.7%, 25%, 31%, 28.4% and 28.5%, which should be compared with an average of 16% over the three years (when trade was improving) before the new steamers came into commission. The overall figures do suggest that the volume of trade was increasing almost concurrently with the delivery of the new ships, and it is doubtful whether they would have been so successful had they been delivered—say—five or six years previously.

The first payments out of the surplus of the working account was made on the interest on the debentures and loans: then the fixed Preferred dividends, and a conventional 5% dividend was paid on the Deferred shares in 1909/10 and 1910/11, but in 1911/12 a larger dividend was made to this latter group. Even after depreciation at

4%, the Company had produced profits of £500,000 in excess of requirements, and this was applied to paying off loans and retiring bills. Reducing indebtedness to outsiders was a prime consideration of the Company but, in 1911/12, a special distribution was made to the Deferred shareholders at the rate of 50% free of tax, though in such a way that would allow the money still to be used for reducing these liabilities.

This was accomplished rather neatly. The Deferred share-holders were invited to subscribe the same sum as that distributed for shares in Orient Underwriting Fund Ltd., which was a newly created Company whose objects included underwriting insurance policies on Orient vessels and lending money to the Company. All the shareholders did this, and thus an effective distribution of 55% was made without any comment being made on the score of excessive dividends, and similar distributions were made in each of the next three years.

In fact, this idea was formulated as a result of a dispute with the debenture holders whose holdings were specifically secured by mortgages on certain of the ships as well as being a general charge on other assets, and the Company had undertaken to keep the mortgaged vessels insured to a total value of not less than 150% (or possibly a little less) of the outstanding bonds. However, as the ships were depreciated, so the insurance values grew less, without a corresponding decrease in the debenture holdings. Moreover, since the Company was increasing 'taking a line' on the insurance (in other words, carrying its own), the debenture holders were perfectly right, and they were finally satisfied when a fractional part of one of the free steamers was mortgaged. They had not been impressed by the Managers' contention that retained profits provided a substantial backing to the firm's insurance risk, but the Managers themselves were impressed by the idea, and so the arrangement came about. In the event, only the first year's distribution was applied for loans to the Orient Co. for, after that, it was not necessary and Orient Underwriting Co. were fully repaid by June, 1913.

By June, 1914, on the eve of war, the whole situation was completely altered, for the shipbuilders had not only been paid off completely, but £175,000 had been paid towards another new vessel, the *Ormonde*, which was under construction and, of course, the Managers were relieved of all liability under their personal guarantees. £70,700 of the Debenture issue had been redeemed and the Company held £147,000 in outside investments. Not only that, the First Cost of the fleet was now increased to £2,845,000 and depreciation had been running at 6% which gave them a book value of £1,500,000 (approx) and working surpluses for the period had been some £2,070,000, which represented an average of some 14.3% per annum on First Cost. Then, after payment of loans, interest, and discount on debentures and Preferred Share dividends, etc. the balance left for the Deferred share-holders over the five years was about £1,150,000 (after tax) of which £200,755 was distributed.

These figures represent an average profit of 200% per annum on the nominal share capital of £115,820 and for dividends an average of 36% per annum. This is the danger of figures when viewing good years in respect of any company with a relatively low amount of issued capital and, if the same figures be applied in terms of working capital—the value of the fleet—the relative figures become 8½% and 1½% per annum. It may be that I have quoted too many figures. If so, I can but apologise to readers, but it must surely be agreed that, when one considers the financial state and return of the company prior to the break with Royal Mail and the ordering of the new ships, with all the risk which that entailed, and then the results of the years' trading immediately after they were delivered, it is difficult to conclude otherwise than that the change in fortune was utterly spectacular and that it more than justified the confidence of the Managers. It is true that the years concerned were boom years in the Australian trade, which was fortunate, but it is impossible not to admire the foresight and courage of the Managers when they proceeded with so bold a scheme—for its success could only be judged with future hindsight — and also by the manner in which they employed their monies to get themselves clear of debt so quickly. It must be one of the most remarkable episodes in shipping history although, as I have said, matters of this sort are so commonly ignored. Of course, as the loans became repaid, the interest needed became so much the less, and the net profits grew in consequence.

These five years of great success were followed by the First World War and, without quoting a mass of figures, it can be stated that, although the ships were mainly in Government service, the working balances were maintained at much the same sort of level and although, as outlined in the chapter entitled *The Orient Line until 1939*, four ships were lost, amounting to some 40% of the total tonnage, the compensation received for them was £1,830,000, which was about £530,000 more than they had cost originally and about £1,426,000 more than their book value. (It should be recorded, in this context, that they had been written down far more drastically than was required by the 4% per annum in the Articles.) Nor were the Company caught by the Excess Profits Duty in respect of abnormal war-time profits since, perhaps by good fortune, their profits had been equally high in the years preceding the war. Royal Mail may have twisted the Company's arm in the period prior to 1909, and forced it to act, but the story would have been different as regards this tax had the new steamers not become operative until just before 1914. In conjunction with previous comments on the value of the pound at different periods, it is an interesting fact that ordinary income tax in those four years of war was 1/8, 3/-, 5/- and 6/- in the pound—6/- being 30 new pence today.

The Share Capital of the Company was altered in 1916, increasing the authorised capital to £3,000,000, but the details are not germane to this theme. In fact, there is little more to tell and the story is best rounded off at the point when Anderson, Anderson & Co. became part of Anderson, Green & Co. Ltd. This came about because, towards the end of the first World War, F. Green & Co. wanted to dispose of their business interests, of which the greatest part was their half-share in the Orient Management. To this end, a private limited company was formed, named Anderson, Green & Co. Ltd. with an authorised capital of £350,000, of which £320,000 was issued, and this company acquired the two separate businesses of F. Green & Co. and Anderson, Anderson & Co: vesting the management of the Orient Co. in a single body instead of in two private firms.

The outcome was not quite so simple as that, because the shares, although all of one class, were divided into 'A' and 'B' shares, each group having equal voting rights in appointing directors and in other matters. The partners of Anderson, Anderson & Co. subscribed for one half of the issued shares of Anderson, Green & Co. ('A' shares) and the other half ('B' shares) were subscribed on behalf of Lord Inchcape. At the same time, the P. & O., through Gray Dawes and Co., bought 51% of the issued Deferred shares of the Orient Company. This arrangement gave the P. & O. Company a voting control, the Agreements being dated 7 February, 1919, although the businesses were sold from 1 January, 1918. Prior to these arrangements, Anderson, Anderson & Co. and F. Green & Co. had each held 15,372 Deferred shares. The first of these sold 7,849 and the second 9,872, when the holdings became:—

P. & O. S.N.Co.	17,721	=	51%
Anderson Anderson members	7,523	=	21.65%
F. Green members	5,500	=	15.83%
Others	4,002	=	11.52%

The P. & O. and the members of Anderson, Anderson & Co. undertook to support Anderson, Green & Co. Ltd. as managers until 31 December, 1938, and members of F. Green gave a similar undertaking to hold good till 31 December, 1933.

This chapter now draws to its close. The story of the Company's ships is told elsewhere, and it will have been appreciated in previous chapters that autonomy did remain with the Orient Managers until their fleet finally came to fly the P. & O. house-flag in the 1960's. The fact is that no-one who reads the bare history of the ships and their fortunes in port and at sea would ever guess how insignificant were the results prior to 1909, and how dramatic they were thereafter and, if a clipper ship or an ocean liner does not have the aesthetic appeal of a balance sheet, the latter is what shipowning is really all about!

Just after the second World War, the Orient Company bought all the Anderson, Green & Co. Ltd. shares, but retained the name of that company. At that time, in about 1948, the Orient Line Board was formed, following the enactment of the new Companies Act which required all Limited Companies to have boards of directors. Previously, all Board functions of the Orient Line had been carried out by the Managers (under the Management Agreement) and the

108. The P. & O. CANBERRA, a passenger liner with engines aft.

Chairman of Anderson, Green & Co. took the chair at Orient Annual General Meetings as Chairman of the Managers—not as chairman of the Orient Company, because there was no such person.

As the Company took back its ships from Government service after the cessation of hostilities, the profitability of each vessel varied but, as is well-known, it depends what one means! If a ship's voyage performance was reviewed at the 'In the Red' meeting, it would usually show a 'black' (*not* a 'red') balance, but if the results were queried in another way as, for instance, 'What was the return on the shareholders' funds?' then, in common with most shipping companies at the time, the answer would be 'Not so good'. However, I can state on good authority that the Orient Line was profitable and efficient to the end.

There were two main considerations in the decision to combine the P. & O. and Orient Companies:— 1) With the imminent commissioning of the two large passenger liners, *Oriana* (1960) and *Canberra* (1961) two high-performance, high capacity and very expensive vessels, coupled with the implications of developing air travel competition, it was obvious that both companies would have a reducing number of passenger ships and that their parallel shore organizations, with duplicated functions, would be under-employed for parts of the year, and 2) Following the successful Orient development of the Pacific route, the P. & O. also wanted to send ships on to America from Australia. With all the goodwill in the world, it was obviously impossible to plan schedules sensibly and fairly, since some voyage dates were better than others, with the two fleets under different ownerships. By 1959 it had become clear to both companies that the only logical and reasonable solution was for P. & O. to acquire the outstanding 49% of the Orient shares.

I will round this section off by recording that the price paid for a £5 Orient share in 1919 was £125 and that, when F. Green & Co. went out of business, they sold part of their holding of Orient shares for £1,234,000 in cash, but retained a holding representing a further £687,500 on the same valuation—all of which arose from an original investment of £50,000 forty years previously! Similarly, the partners of Anderson, Anderson & Co. sold shares for £981,000 and retained a holding of £940,000 from an equal investment. Few statistics could pay greater testimony to their acumen and perspicacity.

109. *The ORIANA off the Needles. Note the position of her boats and that the smoke is rising clear of the ship.*

LIST OF ABBREVIATIONS FOR DECK PLANS AND PROFILE OR ORIANA

A/C – Air Conditioning.
ATE – Automatic Telephone Exchange.
B – Bread Room.
BE – Baggage Elevator.
BgR – Baggage Room.
BH – Baggage Hall.
BIR – Bulk and Issue Room.
BM – Beer and Minerals.
BPT – Brine Pipe Trough.
BR – Beer Room.
BS – Bonded Store.
Bu – Butter.
CB – Captain's Bedroom.
C/B – Cheese and Bacon.
CD – Captain's Day Cabin.
CE – Chief Engineer.
CL – Crew Lavatory.
CH.L – Chain Locker.
CK – Crew's Kitchen.
CL – Crew Lavatory.
CR – Consulting Room.
D – Dispensary.
DK – Duct Keel.
DW – Distilled Water.
E – Eggs.
EDR – Emergency Dynamo Room.
Eng St – Engineer's Store.
EW – Engineer's Workshop.
F – Fish.
FO – Fuel Oil.
FOST – Fuel Oil Settling Tank.
FR – Fan Room.
FS – Flour Store.
FV – Fruit and Vegetables.
FW – Fresh Water.
GDR – Gentlemen's Dressing Room.
GH – Gentlemen's Hairdressing.
GL – Gentlemen's Lavatory.
GR – Gas Generator Room.
H – Hatch.
I – Ice.
IR – Ironing Room.
L – Lift.
LDR – Ladies Dressing Room.
LE – Laundrette.
LH – Ladies Hairdressing.
LL – Ladies Lavatory.
LO – Liason Officer.
LO Dr Tk – Lubricating Oil Drain Tank.
LWL – Load Water Line.
M – Milk.
MT – Meat.
MUC – Manoeuvring Unit Compartment.
NW – Nursing Ward.
OFF – Oil Fuel Filling Station.
OR – Operating Room.
P – Pantry.
PC – Pilot's cabin.
Pots – Potatoes.
PS – Printers shop.
PY – Poultry.
R – Radio Officer's cabin.
Res Fd W – Reserve Feed Water.
SCB – Staff Commander's Bedroom.
SCD – Staff Commander's Day Room.
ST – Store.
ST.CT – Stabilizer Compartment.
TE – Telephone Exchange.
TR – Tobacco Room.
V – Vent Tank.
W – Ward.
WB – Water Ballast.
WS – Wine Store.
WR – Hospital Writing Room.

T.S.S. ORIANA PROFILE AND DECK PLANS

Nº 1

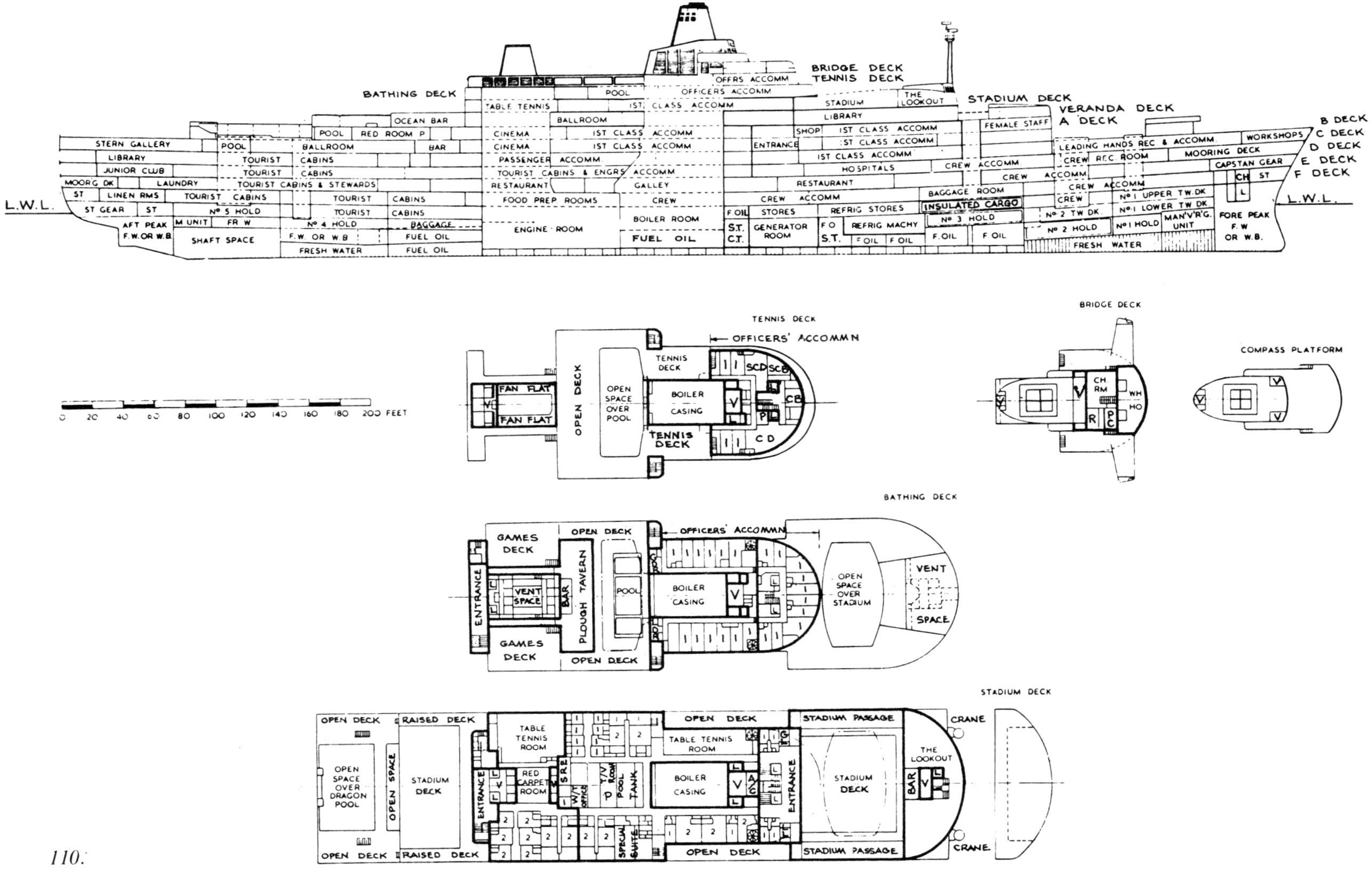

T.S.S. ORIANA Deck Plans

Nº 2

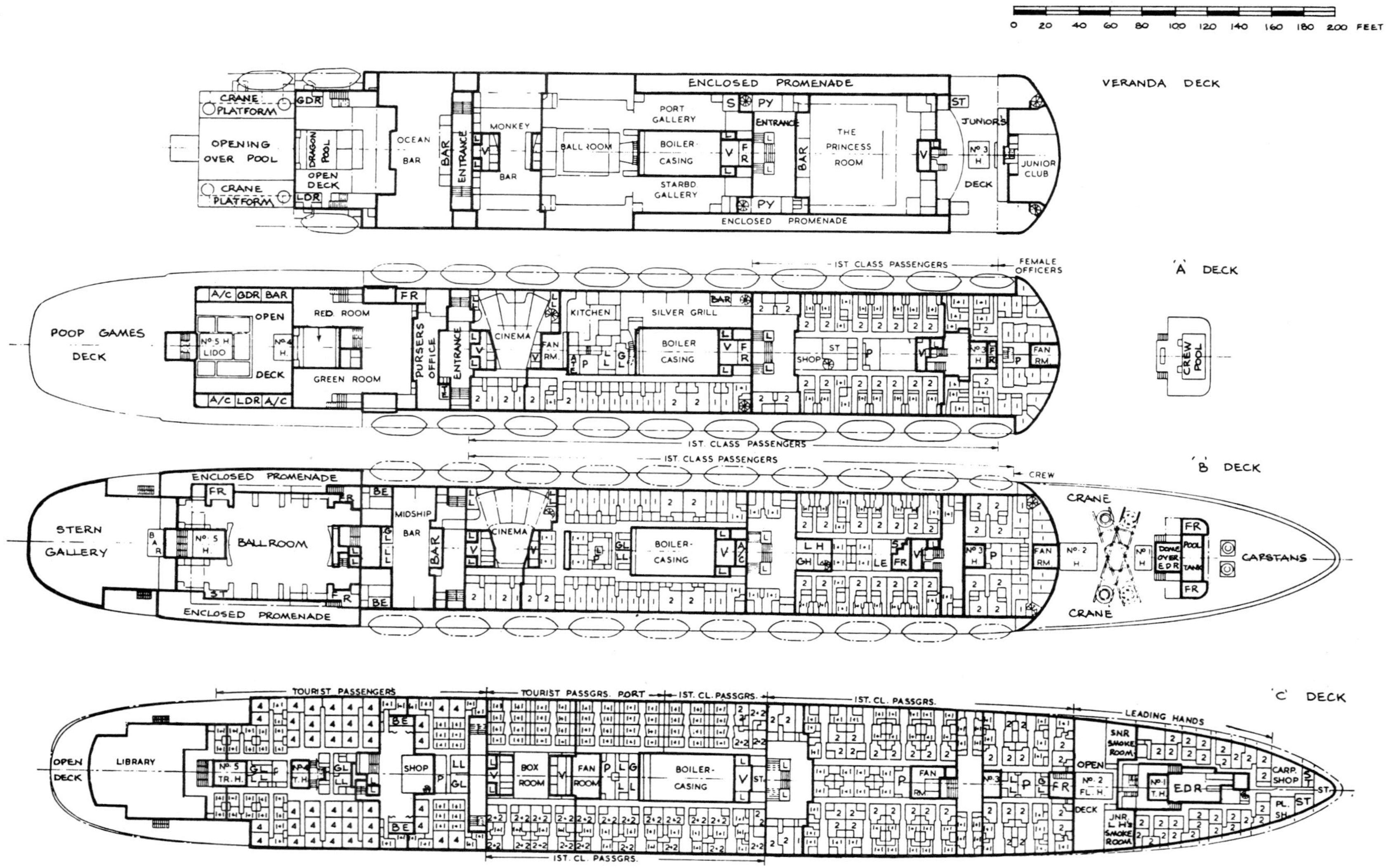

111.

TSS ORIANA Deck Plans

N° 3

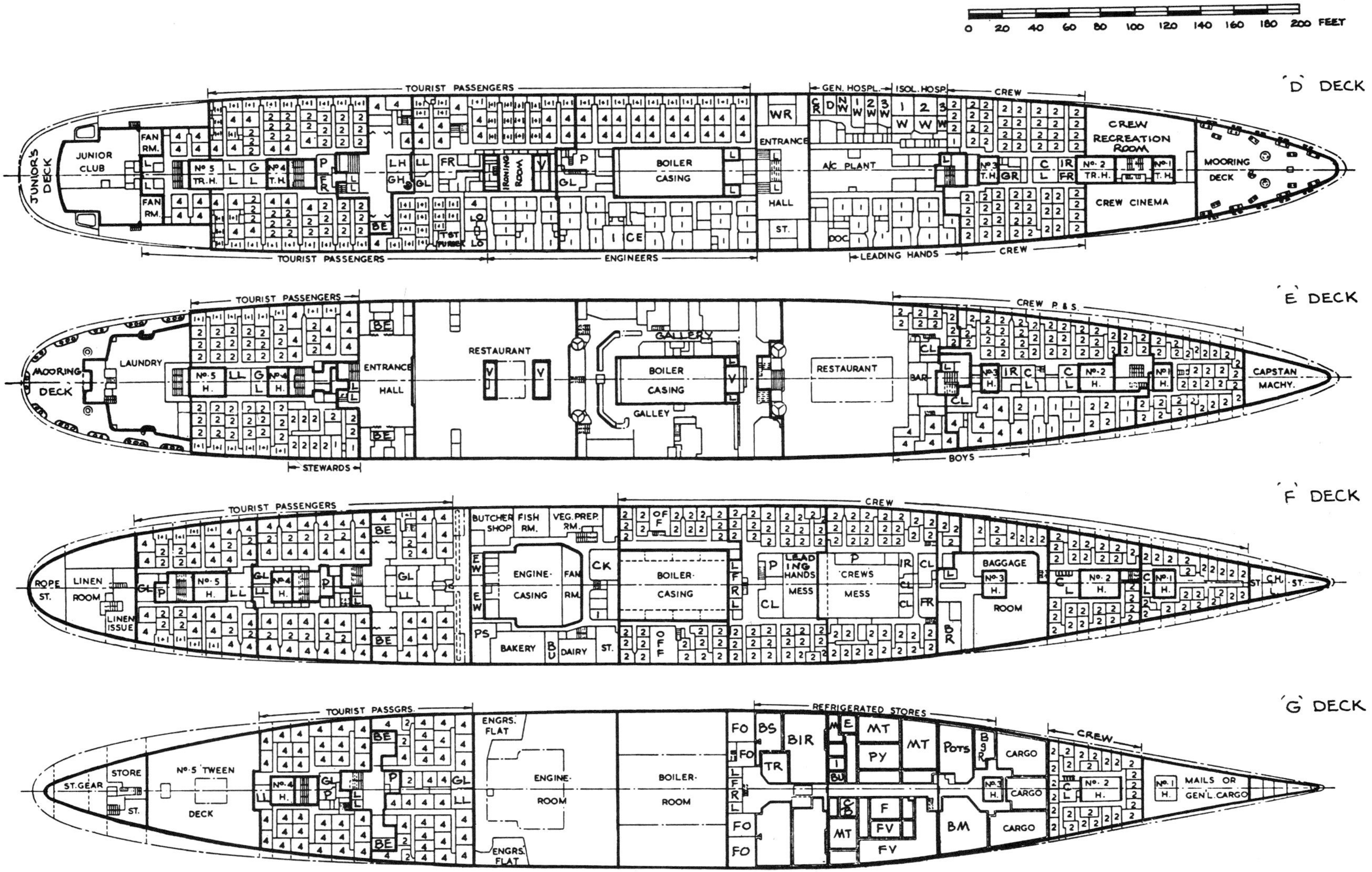

T.S.S. ORIANA DECK PLANS

N° 4

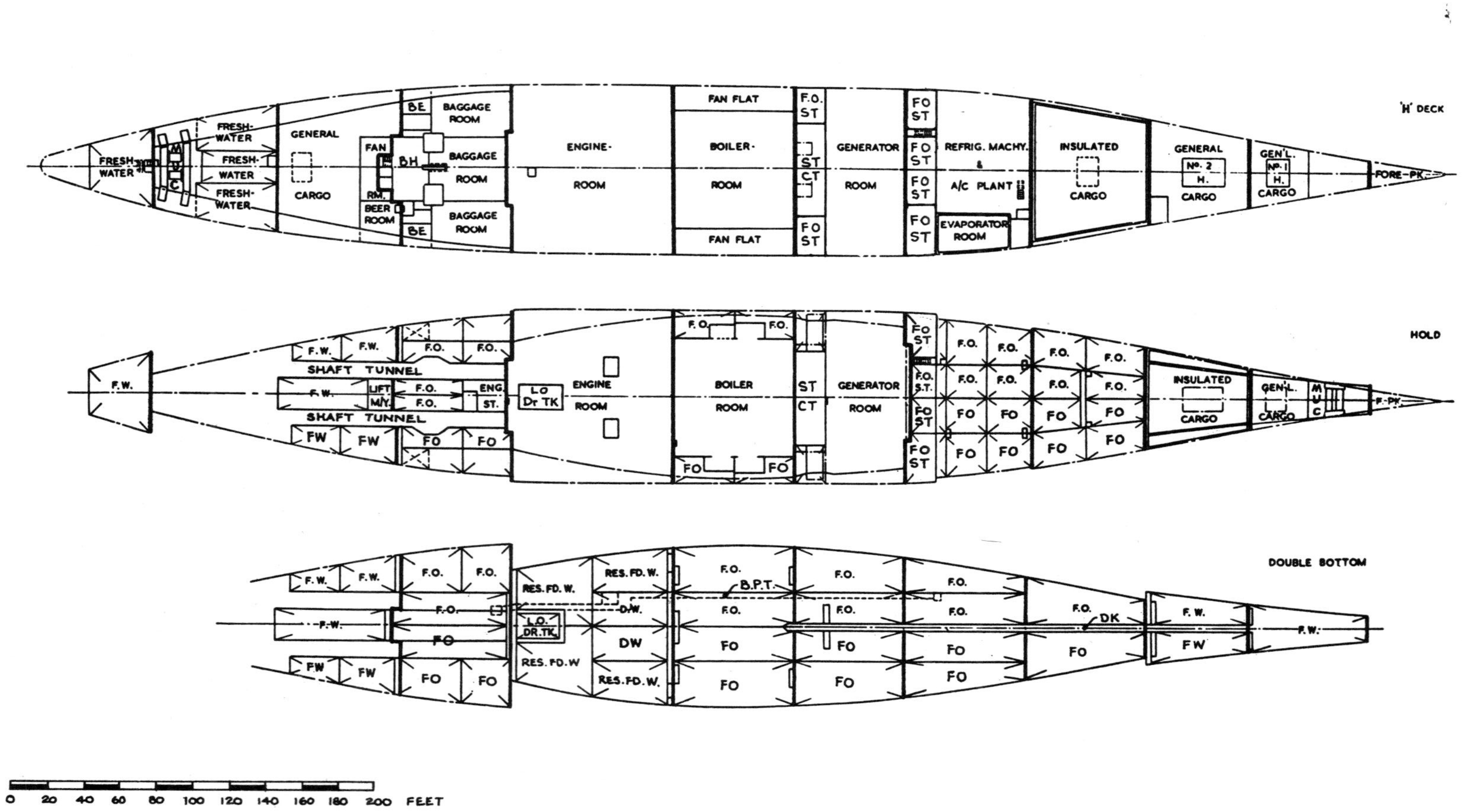

IX. PRIMARY CONSIDERATIONS

THE LAST SHIP to be designed and built for the Orient Steam Navigation Company was the *Oriana*, which incorporated all the knowledge and experience which had been assimilated by the owners and builders of the ship during their long association and, for this reason, she could be claimed rightly to be the best ship ever built for and by them. Although work was not started on the construction of the ship until September, 1957, a great deal of detailed discussion and design work had taken place on the part of both Owner's and Builder's managements and staffs from early in 1954.

Even from the outset the ship was called, facetiously, '*Orbustus*', and letters interchanged between the two Companys' technical departments carried this heading. Sir Austin I. Anderson, the Orient Line chairman at that time, coined this title and, no doubt, because the ship was to be the largest and fastest ever built for the Company, it was to make 'or bust us'. It is true that the Company itself, after the ship was completed, did disappear from the registers of shipping lines, but the *Oriana* was in no way responsible for that occurrence. However, one day it was realized that we should take names more seriously, and an edict was issued that '*Orbustus*' must be discontinued.

The business relationship between Vickers of Barrow-in-Furness and the Management of the Orient Company was one of long standing, great trust and much cordiality, and it had lasted in this way since the *Orama* was ordered in 1922. Because of this relationship, at least one ship was nearly completed there before the contract to build her was signed by the Orient Company. It is also correct to state that a great deal of expensive work was completed by the Builders on the design of the *Oriana* before any exchange of documents took place. The official tender for the ship was not made until after June, 1956.

As has already been stated elsewhere, a simple fact for all manner of transport is that the larger the vehicle of transport, the cheaper it is to carry a unit of load for the same distance and in the same time. The difficulty lies in providing that the quantity of the load to be carried is available when required to be carried. This needs qualification, and none can be better to quote than the late Sir Donald F. Anderson, who stated,

'a) *There is no theoretical limit to the size of a ship but there are practical limits.*

b) *The larger ship is cheaper per ton per mile than a smaller ship, whatever the service.*

c) *Construction costs (of the ship) and operating costs do not increase at the tonnage rate, but not every service can sustain a large capacity unit; e.g. a 60-seater bus is the cheaper unit in a city, but a minibus is more economic for carrying (say) 20 schoolchildren back and forth to school.*'

The foregoing represented some of the important aspects which were considered when the Orient Line Management began thinking about the new ship. They wanted one which would suit the extended service across the Pacific from Sydney and, in order that crew problems would not increase due to long periods away from home, it was desirable that the ship's speed be increased above that which was common to the ships of the existing Orient fleet*. There is another axiom which concerns ships particularly, and that is that every vessel has a speed (which is closely related to her length) beyond which she cannot be economically driven. A short ship cannot be driven fast without using relatively very high and uneconomic power.‡

Another important factor affected the problem of selecting the size of the prospective ship, for the management of the Orient Line did not wish to step up the number of propeller shafts (and their engines) from the two generally used in the existing ships of the fleet, to three (an inefficient arrangement), or four shafts, because this would

* When did we hear of such problems in the days of sail? Ships have changed but . . . . so have the attitudes of their men.

‡ So, in a sailing ship, dependent on wind-power, the maximum possible speed was directly related to her water-line length (L) and lay between 1.25 and 1.45 $\times \sqrt{L}$.

increase initial and maintenance costs. It would also increase running costs due to larger numbers of engineering staff in the ship, and also increase other less obvious unattractive features, such as weight. The maximum power which can be transmitted by a marine propeller of the type used on a passenger liner is limited by the availability of suitable materials for such propellers and the design of them at the time when the ship is being built. For instance, at the time (1945-48) when the *Orcades*, the first of the 28,000 (gross) ton class of Orient Liner, was being designed and built, the maximum power which the Builders could accept on one propeller was 21,250 shaft horse power. In 1954, when the main concept of the *Oriana* was being considered, improvements in design and manufacture of propellers had taken place since 1945, and the Builders could accept 40,000 horse power on each shaft.

The figure aimed at for her of 80,000 shaft horse power was thought to be suitable for a service speed of 27½ knots. Such shaft horse power would also provide a sensible margin for overcoming the resistance due to fouling of the hull in service between dry-docking—the time when a ship's hull is cleaned and repainted: for other resistances or loss of power which take place as a ship ages, and, of course, last but not least, for the uncertainties to be expected from weather. A passenger ship is, in principle, expected to arrive at each port at her appointed time on schedule, in spite of adverse weather and sea conditions. The hull size offered in the design was the smallest which could provide the speed already stated economically.

Another point regarding the size of ship had to be investigated before a decision could be made to proceed further with the design. When the *Orcades* was being designed in 1945, the Marine Department of the Orient Company were asked to investigate whether the harbours to be used would be suitable for such a large liner, whereupon it was found that there were some difficulties; for instance, at Naples the ship enters a rather congested area before tying up at the magnificent terminal for the reception of passengers. On leaving, the ship has to go astern for no less than one quarter of a mile before turning completely about and proceeding out of the harbour. Since this manoeuvre has to be carried out in confined conditions and with many ships in the vicinity, the responsibility laid on those in charge in squally conditions is high. When the *Oriana* was under consideration, with this in mind, the wisdom of increasing the size of the ship was again investigated, but harbour conditions had improved in some places, and the promise of better mooring and manoeuvring arrangements, and the provision for the fitting of a stern anchor, persuaded the Marine Department that all would be well. We never fitted the stern anchor, because the ship proved to have excellent handling qualities.

It is worth noting that the hull was also the shape and size which could just be taken through the tightest of the dock entrances in Barrow, and the section of the ship amidships was shaped a little at the bilges to allow this manoeuvre to be performed.

At this point we should consider a subject fundamental to the design of ships and one which, at the time of the design and building of the *Oriana* and other ships of that period, was occupying the minds of those immediately concerned, to say nothing of those who knew little about the subject, but who liked to talk about, write about, and pontificate about the rather unimportant subject of whether funnels should be positioned at the middle or the after end of a passenger ship. I say 'unimportant' because I believe it unnecessary to fit a funnel aft just for the possible trouble caused by soots. This nuisance can now be reduced to an acceptable level by good design of the funnel. The cause of funnel soots falling to the decks has been touched upon in the chapter *'Ships of the Orient Line'*, where it was explained that the probability of soots falling to the decks of a ship was almost certain if the funnel did not pass up through, and above, the body of turbulent air which moves with a ship, or remains with her if there is a wind blowing over the ship when she is not moving; in other words, when there is a movement of air relative to the ship from whatever cause or direction.

The fashion of arranging the machinery aft in ships is not new, but years ago it was done in many vessels for very good reasons—usually to leave a clear weather deck forward of the machinery spaces, for the working of cargo, or for safety considerations as well as, for instance, in the case of oil tankers. These ships always have a 'trim' problem when running 'light' (i.e. unladen) but, usually, this is compensated by taking ballast on board in suitable parts of the ship, though it must be of an acceptable weight because, as the reader will appreciate, large bending moments on the ship's hull girder can be caused by placing large ballast loads at the sharp end of a ship where there is little buoyancy to support the concentrated weight.

These cargo ships had purpose in the fitting of machinery aft and, furthermore, because generally they had rather small engines driving single propeller shafts to provide the modest speeds of about 16 knots common to such ships latterly, the hull shapes were not so fine-lined as would be found in fast passenger ships, and the drastic bending moments, caused in the faster ships fitted with machinery aft, could be avoided.

There are many good reasons why the normal and traditional arrangement of machinery should be used, and I can think of only two reasons for the fitting of it aft in a passenger ship—neither of which is of great importance:—

a) to shorten the propeller shafts and thus reduce their cost and weight,
b) to reduce the possibility of soots falling on the decks.

The other explanation, not yet mentioned, is as a 'gimmick' to attract the attention of the public, especially those mentioned earlier—the amateur critics.

A most thorough investigation was made into the relative merits of these two major arrangements of the machinery of the new ship. The engines of the *Oriana*, as she was finally built, are as far aft as they can go. Her hull under the water is very finely shaped, there being no parallel body below the water line and her hull tapers quickly from her mid-length to the forward and after ends. The vessels built for the Orient Line after the Second World War had fresh-water tanks fitted between double skins at the sides of the engine rooms, but these were not fitted in the *Oriana* so that the engines could be arranged further aft in the ship. The only way to fit her funnel further aft would have been to lift the boilers up and move them aft over the propeller shaft tunnels. The machinery installation of the *Oriana* was about mid-length of the ship and suitable for the ship's design.

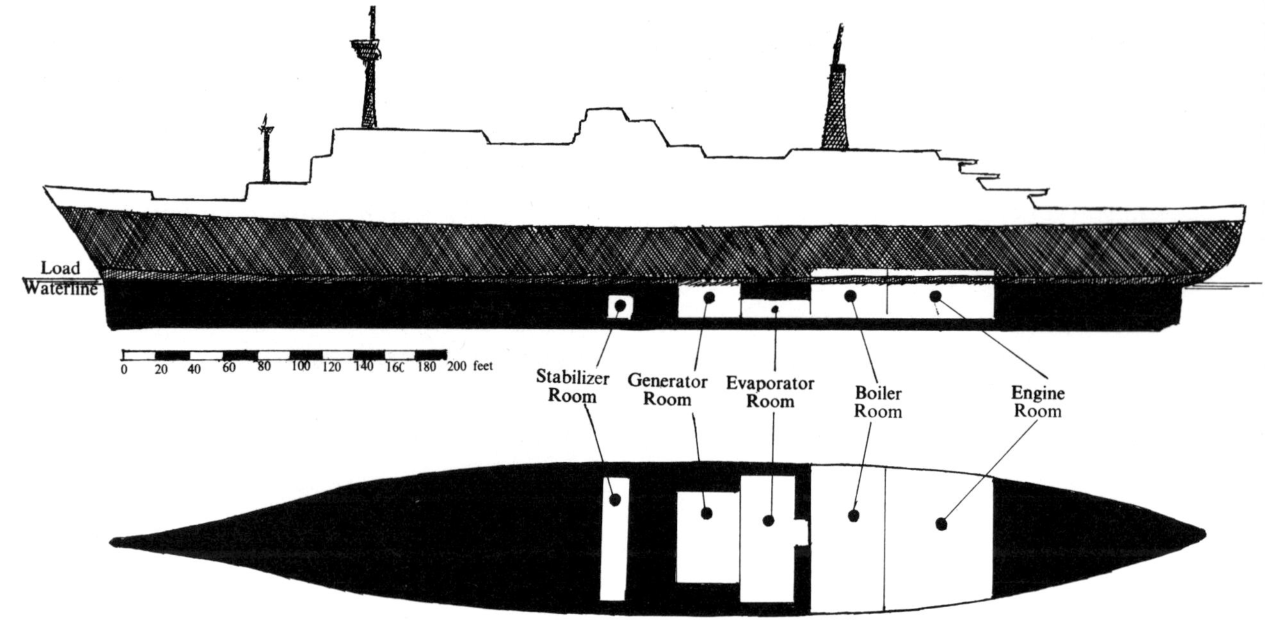

114. Machinery arrangements in the T.S.S. ROTTERDAM.

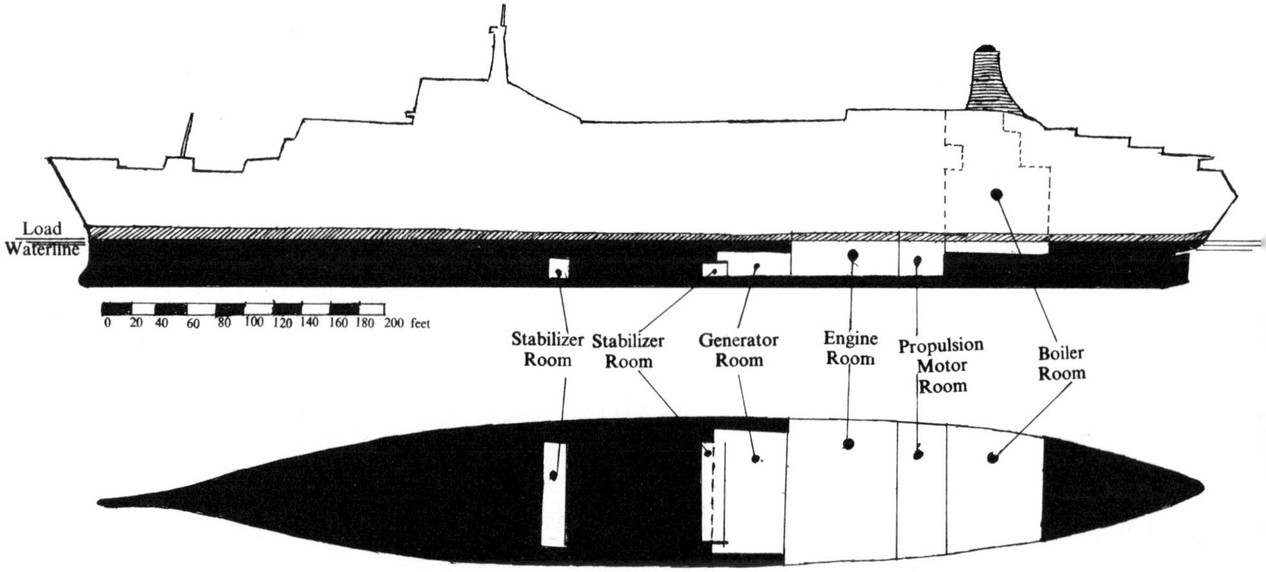

115. Machinery arrangements in the T.S.S. CANBERRA.

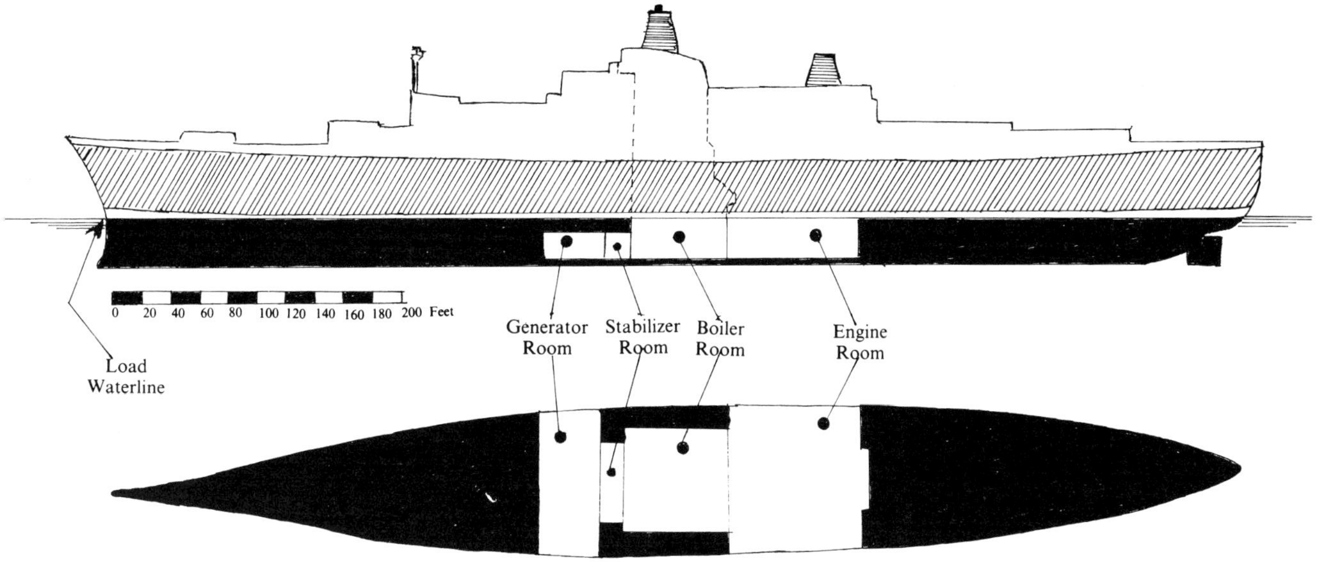

116. Machinery arrangements in the T.S.S. ORIANA.

There have been a few passenger ships with their engines really far aft, amongst them the *Southern Cross* and the *Northern Star* of the Shaw Savill Line and the *Rotterdam* of the Holland-America Line. The *Southern Cross* had problems in regard to her oiling and water-ballasting because special arrangements had to be made to take off the oily ballast immediately prior to her taking on new bunker oil at certain re-fuelling stops on her voyages. There was also some straining of the vessel during heavy weather which caused leaking of windows in the forward parts of her superstructures but, presumably, there was a reason for the design and building of this ship because another similar one, the *Northern Star*, was built soon afterwards.*

The *Rotterdam* was built with a perfectly normal arrangement of machinery; in other words, her boiler room was forward of the engine room and was built at the same level—on the top of the inner bottom of the vessel. She was a large ship of 38,650 gross tons, but was only of

* Though it does not follow that the reason was necessarily a good one.

moderate speed: namely $20\frac{1}{2}$ knots. With a ship of moderate speed the shaft horse power is relatively small and her hull shape is less fine than is necessary in a faster one. This combination of smaller power and less fine lines of the hull make the normal layout of machinery spaces in an after position in the ship more possible.

Investigations have been made by experts in this field of naval architecture, especially in regard to the changes which take place as size is increased in ships having either 'engines aft' or 'engines amidships'. A paper was written and presented to the Royal Institution of Naval Architects on the 10 October, 1962. In it, the authors show that passenger ships of about 25,000 gross tons can have an arrangement of engines further aft than normal but with unfortunate consequences of additional weight and trim problems. The problem of trim with all craft having machinery arranged in an after position varies with the type involved, but in a passenger ship the only weights which can be used to offset the unbalancing effect caused by the heavy weight of machinery aft are those of fuel, fresh water, stores and other consumables, and possibly of cargo. All these are variables and in most cases become lighter as the ship consumes them on her voyage. In order to produce an acceptable condition of trim the Master must gradually take on board sea water as ballast to compensate for weight lost by consumption. It should be noted that an assumption has been made that the machinery is of boilers and steam turbines. This is because large machinery plants for passenger ships have predominantly been of this kind but, even if the machinery were diesel engines or some other type of power plant, the points made in this matter would apply, more or less.

The investigations of the above-mentioned paper also led to conclusions that, as the ships were increased in size from 25,000 gross tons to 42,000 gross tons, and even to 75,000 gross tons, the conditions worsened and the difference in weight between those having machinery amidships or aft became greater. Plates Nos. 114 to 118 show, in a simplified way, the effects of the two arrangements of machinery, in which the ship is regarded as a see-saw with the buoyancy acting upwards as the support of the see-saw and the main weights of the hull and machinery and ballast acting downwards to

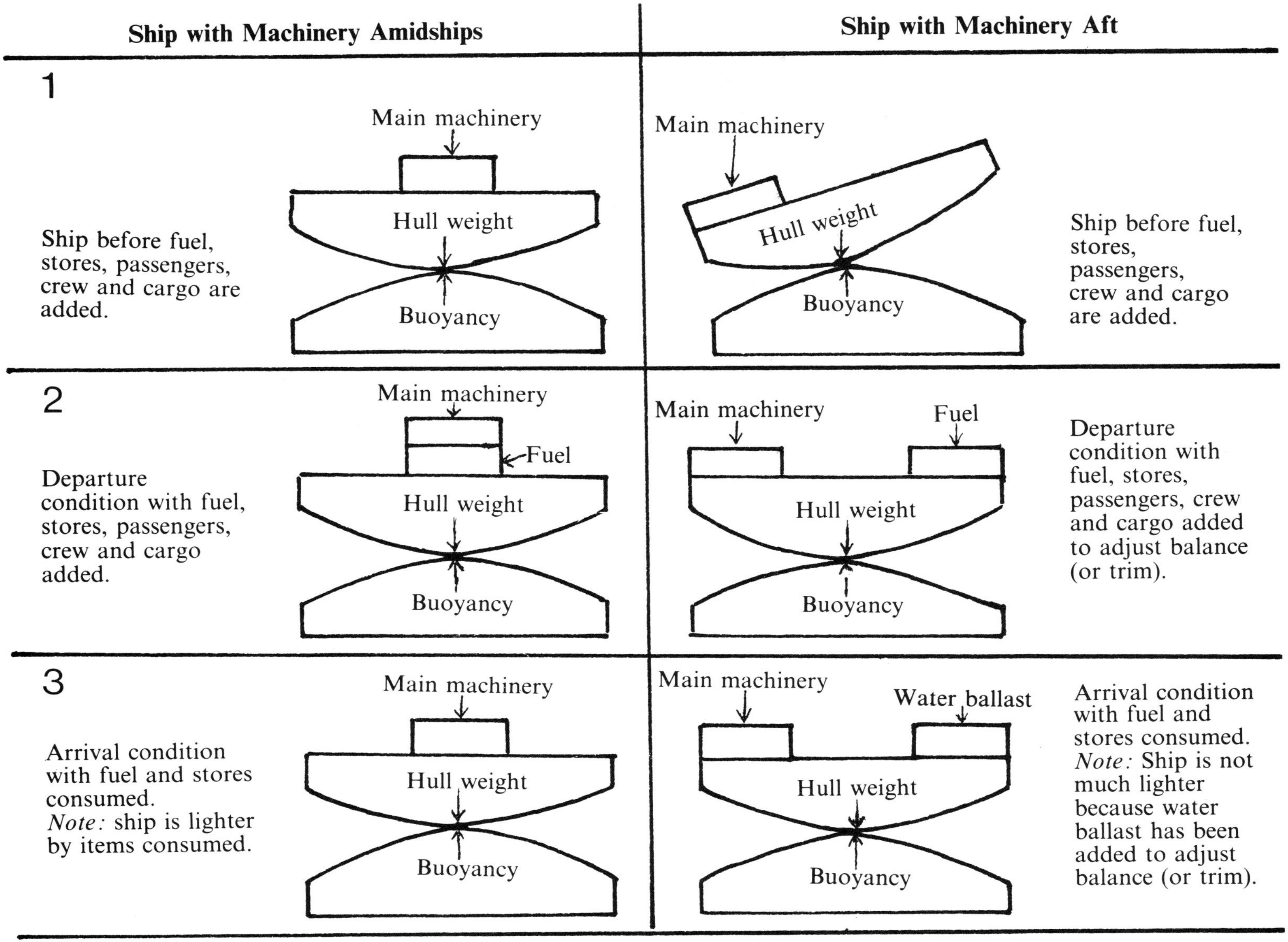

117. Diagram of ships treated as see-saws.

produce level trim or balance through it. Because fine-lined ships do not have much buoyancy at their ends to support weight, the analogy of the see-saw is not too much of an exaggeration. The diagrams show that the vessel with her machinery placed amidships in the hull (or on the centre of the plank of the see-saw) is not subjected to such big bending forces as that of another with machinery aft. Whilst the see-saw of the former arrangement can be loaded evenly along its length, the latter arrangement must *always* be loaded with weight equal in effect to the amount 'x' on the opposite side of the see-saw to the machinery in order to achieve level trim—and 'x' must be fuel, fresh water, stores, cargo or salt water ballast. The weight due to passengers and crew is not large and is distributed fairly evenly about the ship. The machinery represents a large part of the total weight—about 4,000 tons in a ship the size of the *Oriana*—and of this the boiler installation weighs about 1,500 tons. To sum up; the passenger ship with machinery aft must always carry weight to keep level trim, this weight being consumables *or* ballast.

At the time of the designing of the *Oriana* we realised that the increased speed of the ship under discussion, compared with her predecessors in the Company's fleet, could bring other factors into consideration. One of these factors was that of the effect of carrying unnecessary weight in the vessel. Slower ships do not suffer great increase in resistance, and therefore power, when their weight is increased fractionally. It was found that with the new vessel in the loaded condition and at service speed, and taking account of the average price of oil fuel, the cost of carrying an unnecessary ton of weight for a year would be about £17. This figure would be much greater now because of the much greater price of fuel.

When discussing the relative merits of ships' machinery arrangements, this figure of cost per ton for the life of a ship is not to be ignored. Later, the subject of stabilizers fitted in the *Oriana* will be discussed, but when this was being investigated, it was shown that the average displacement of the *Oriana* taken over a full voyage from Southampton to Sydney and across the Pacific was about 88.8% of her normal loaded displacement of 38,400 tons. This meant that her average displacement over the whole voyage was over 4,000 tons less than the normal loaded displacement.

This saving of over 4,000 tons in weight carried by the ship during her voyage can be expressed as a saving in oil fuel costs, using the rough guidance figure of £17 per ton per year, to be about £68,000 for each year of her life. This saving could not be made by a similar ship having her machinery arranged aft because, as she proceeded on her voyage using up oil fuel, stores, fresh water, and other consumables, she would require to have her trim corrected by adding salt water ballast. Such a ship runs at an almost constant displacement near to her maximum draught and, therefore, cannot make the savings from weight reduction which can be achieved by a similar one having her machinery amidships. There are many other points of interest in this comparison, but one last one which is worth mentioning is that the required stability of a ship having her machinery aft is more costly to achieve than that of a like vessel with machinery amidships. The reason is that, having lifted her boilers about 15 feet to position them over the shaft tunnel, and having increased the ship's strength to compensate for this, mostly on the strength deck, it is necessary to compensate for the consequent loss of stability which, as a rule, means making the ship broader, heavier and thus costlier. Drawings of ships to illustrate these paragraphs regarding the layout of main machinery in ships are given in Plates 114-117.

The Orient Line fleet had many ports of call on their route to Australia. The route had changed over the years from that around the Cape to the one through the Mediterranean and Suez Canal but, in all cases, it was necessary to put into various places to purchase fuel, fresh water and stores. After the Second World War and prior to the Suez crisis, the usual ports of call were Gibraltar, Naples, Port Said, Aden, Colombo, Fremantle, Adelaide, Melbourne and Sydney, with an additional call at Marseilles when homeward bound. This meant that some of the ships sailed 25,000 miles in less than ten weeks. These stops had another use, which was very important although, often, not recognized as such. It was a means of allowing the passengers to go ashore to 'let off steam', to have a break and even, sometimes, to get away from the company of those who were 'getting on each other's nerves'.*

* Sailing ship passengers could be 20 times as long at sea and, generally, could adapt themselves to it. Once again it may be observed that people have changed no less than their ships!

The calls at ports were usually made during daylight or evening hours, which made the working of the ships easier, whilst allowing the passengers suitable time to go ashore. There were port leaflets issued to them to enable them to plan their shore visits, and trips were arranged by the ships' pursers' staffs for their convenience. This meant that the programming of the fleet's movements were geared to the arrival of ships at ports in daylight and so, when planning a new one, if her speed was to be higher than previous vessels in the Company, it had to be increased to a speed which would permit arrival at suitable earlier times—usually some hours earlier. To achieve this, the speed had to be increased appreciably.

The service speeds of the Orient Fleet had increased in quite large steps over a period of 70 years from 13 knots in 1877, 16 knots in 1880, 18 knots in 1891, 20 knots in 1924, 21 knots in 1935 and to 22½ knots in 1948. There were other considerations, probably more important than this one of port arrival times, but certainly this one was not inconsiderable in the overall requirements of a passenger ship in the Orient Company.

Having decided that it was necessary to have a faster ship and having also found that 27½ knots service speed was attainable within the restrictions of the number of propeller shafts and the power and the size of the vessel to provide this speed, the next step was to assess her possible earnings and viability. The passenger department gave advice on the proportions of first class to tourist class numbers and the types of cabins to be provided in each class. The freight departments (inward and outward freight) gave estimates of what cargo could be handled in the short 'in-port' periods. A ship is like any other large piece of intricate and expensive equipment, or a large manufacturing works, in that, unless it is employed for most of the time of its existence, it is inefficient and wasteful as a trading medium. A ship should spend as little of her life in port as possible if she is to earn her keep.

For the new ship, which was to cost so much more than her predecessors and to have a much greater service speed, it was even more important to reduce port stays and make it possible to shorten the times taken to load and unload cargo, fuel and stores as well as passengers and their baggage. For this reason, every endeavour was made to incorporate in the design ways and means to accomplish this object. Drawings were made of many arrangements of the new ship's interior, of cabin accommodation and of the other spaces necessary for the comfort of passengers and crew and for the running of the ship. Investigations were made into the employment of aluminium alloy in the construction of the upper works in order to reduce weight and to improve the stability and, as a result, it was found possible to fit an extra deck in the superstructure and so to increase the number of passengers by about one hundred and fifty. This caused a new assessment of the ship's potential earnings.

Another stability improvement introduced at this time was the movement of the lifeboats downwards from their usual position to a level twenty-seven feet lower. This was made possible by the design of a new type of davit about which mention will be made later.

The arrangements planned for the new ship were viewed by all those concerned within the Company, after which the design was sent to the selected Builders for their estimate of cost. When this was received, the Management of the Orient Company made their own investigation into the potential earnings of the new ship and, after a great deal of discussion with the departments in the Company concerned with the project, the decision was made to go ahead and build her.

The service speed of $27\frac{1}{2}$ knots would enable the new ship to cut a day off each of the three long passages of the route, London to Port Said, Suez to Colombo, and Colombo to Fremantle. Comparisons made at the time between the existing newer ships of the Company (the 28,000 gross tons class), and the proposed new vessel showed that

a) Four ships of the size of the one proposed could provide about as many passenger berths per year as six ships of the 28,000 gross tonners.
b) Four ships of the larger size would require an investment of about £8,000,000 less than that required for six ships of the smaller tonnage.
c) Four ships of the larger size would need about 500 less crew than six ships of the smaller tonnage.

d) The saving in cost by the larger ship by spending two weeks less on the voyage from London to Sydney and back to London would be more than equal to the increased cost of steaming faster.

When the decision was made to build the ship to the size, power and speed selected, detailed planning started. Some of the influences which shaped the design of the *Oriana* are of interest.

During the years following the Second World War the living standards of many people throughout the world had been changing and improving, particularly in respect to the material aspects of life. When the new *Orcades* was designed and built, just after the war, the indications were that there would be a great demand for migrant accommodation, i.e. a large number of passengers at minimum fares. Before the *Orcades* was completed, the Management realized that the requirements had already changed and so her berths were reduced in number from 1,046 to 780 in the tourist class accommodation. In the two following ships, the *Oronsay* and *Orsova*, more improvements in deck space and cabins were provided. These improvements had to be paid for by the passengers, and fares were adjusted to suit both the accommodation provided for them, and the rising costs which were taking place after the war. It would seem that the greater part of the travellers in the Orient Line were satisfied that the accommodation, service, and feeding were in accordance with what they required and for which they were prepared to pay.

The ventilation of passenger cabins in the 1920's was very simple and almost useless by modern standards. At that time, air was drawn into the ships by electric fans and distributed through tin metal ducts to the cabins, where it was blown through adjustable outlets to selected parts of the cabin, as the occupants wished. The air could be heated when outside conditions were unpleasant and cold but, because the ships of the Orient Line were often in tropical waters, the requirement for cooling of the accommodation was equally necessary. Unfortunately, under these conditions, the air being drawn into the ship by the fans was already hot, and by the time it had been passed through the fans and distribution ducts it was hotter still. In this state it was then blown into the cabins.

Until full air-conditioning was introduced into the Orient ships in about 1958, the power of the ventilation fans was gradually increased, and the air changes of the cabins became very high, but they produced nothing more than an alleviation of the already very unpleasant conditions, for even a warm draught is preferable to still warm air. Sometimes this state could be aided by the use of a 'wind-scoop', which was a tubular-shaped sheet-metal device which could be pushed out through an open port hole to catch air from outside and blow it into the cabin. By reversing the position of the wind-scoop air could be exhausted from the space. Some of the better cabins in earlier ships were fitted with small portable electric fans, sometimes called 'stir-about fans'. I have been told, on good authority, that in some ships at the beginning of this century an electric fan was offered for use in First Class cabins for 'an extra one guinea'. None of these means of causing the movement of air created very much comfort for the passengers and crew through the heat of the tropics, and real comfort only came with the introduction of air-conditioning.

Air-conditioning means that air is taken from outside the ship, passed through fans, filters, coolers or heaters and de-humidified, if required, before being delivered at the desired temperature and humidity through suitable diffusers into the ship's accommodation. This is an expensive process and, when first introduced, was considered to be a great luxury. The fortitude of those who travelled in sailing ships to places as far away as Australia over a hundred years ago is beyond the imagination of most people today. Travellers in those early days would have no more ventilation than could be provided by wind-sails (pieces of canvas rigged up at suitable angles to catch the wind and direct it into the open accommodation ladderways and doors of the ship). In the 20,000 tonners built for the Orient Line in the 1920's, wind-sails of the sort just described were fitted over the after hatches in hot weather to drive fresh air down the hatch trunks into the passenger accommodation below. When weather was bad and seas were breaking over the ship, there would be little, if any, movement of air within the ship's accommodation and life would be very hard for the unfortunate passengers.

In the early 1950's a paradox arose in connection with the passenger cabins of Orient ships and, presumably, in others about that time, which came about because, for some years previously, there had been a constant and considerable background noise in these cabins due to the increasing volume of air being used in mechanical ventilation.

When air-conditioning was introduced into the Company's ships the volume of air required for ventilation was reduced and the background noise due to ventilating fell markedly. This caused other cabin noises to become more noticeable—(not greater, since they had always been there, but hidden by the overall ventilating noise.) We found, for instance, that telephone conversations could be heard in adjacent cabins. Thus consultations took place with specialists on the subject of insulation against transmission of noise, and a number of full-scale experiments in the construction of cabin bulkheads and linings were carried out aboard vessels already in service, but there were no really satisfactory results.

Nowadays, a ship is virtually a metal box into which the cabins are fitted, while piping and ventilation trunks, usually of steel, in the ceiling and shipside spaces of the accommodation act as conductors of vibration and sound. These sounds are known as 'flanking noises' and are almost impossible to prevent unless very great expense is incurred. Our pursuit of means of reducing the noise of ventilation in cabins had created an almost insoluble problem, so we ceased all further development and even considered the possibility of introducing a noise level in them by the use of the ventilating system! Finally, some steps were taken to improve the construction of cabins to reduce noise between them, but we accepted that we could not really cure the problem without quite inordinate expense.

Incidentally, sails were only gradually discarded in steamships and, even in the 20,000 ton Orient Liners in the 1920's, jibs or foresails were supplied for emergency use. One of these ships, the *Oronsay*, once used her jib sail when one of her engines was out of action in the Mediterranean.

X. THE HULL FORM

THE SHAPE OF A ship's underwater hull to suit the performance required for the minimum power at her designed speed has been the subject of study by hydrodynamicists of general rules for estimating the powering and for the planning of hull forms for the general run of ships, although the full aim of the study has not yet been achieved. Ideally it should be possible to define a hull form for any ship mathematically so as to have minimum resistance for the required speed. So far, after more than thirty years of strenuous effort, the goal has not yet been reached and model experiments are still necessary. The major elements of hull resistance are the frictional resistance of its wetted surface and the resistance created by the wave-making of the hull form. Frictional resistance can be calculated without the use of a model, but the wave-making resistance requires the use of one in an experimental tank unless the hull shape conforms closely with that of another ship and the performance of that ship is known. For the design of large ships of high performance, only model experiments in one of the experimental ships' model tanks, now to be found in many parts of the world, can produce the best design of hull.

Such a tank is that built and owned by Messrs. Vickers Limited at St. Albans, Hertfordshire—the St. Albans Ship Model Experimental Tank. It was built between 1910 and 1913 and, since that time, has become the largest privately owned modern unit of its kind in Europe.

The model tank is about 400 feet long by 21 feet broad, with $11\frac{1}{2}$ feet depth of water. A carriage which is propelled electrically and can be set to tow models at required speeds is arranged to run on rails fitted along each side of the tank and, by specially designed supports, the model can be towed along the tank while readings taken on instruments on the carriage enable data to be amassed about its performance. These supports are designed in such a way as to leave the model free to move and change trim or attitude as dictated by the water through which it is moving, and the smallest possible force is used to ensure that the model follows a straight line down the tank as experiments take place. These 'towing experiments' are the first stage in a long series of tests required for the model of a large specialized ship.

The next stage is the self-propulsion model tests. Miniature propellers near to the required design are chosen from the Tank's standard selection, or other ones made to the special design for the ship are used, and are driven by equipment which records the power required to propel the model. Finally, a model fitted with superstructures is run in the tank in waves of various kinds produced by a wave-making machine to test its sea-keeping qualities. Sometimes it is possible to run these tests and compare them with the behaviour of a model of an existing ship, which can be reassuring to a ship-owner.

The foregoing short description of the testing of ships' models is inadequate and may appear to simplify the extremely complex work required to be done in running experiments of that kind, but it is not the intention of the writer to enter into the maze of technicalities involved.

The making of a ship's model is a long and expensive process, since it varies from between fifteen and twenty feet in length and is usually built of wax. First a mould is made and molten wax is poured into it. This is cast so as to leave it hollow and to provide space for the appropriate ballast weights required and also the for instrumentation required for the experiments. This rough model, after it has cooled, is then carved in a special machine to a shape closely following that of the ship's design and is then finished with tools handled by men experienced in this specialized craft. Finally, the model is floated in the water of the tank and fitted with ballast and instruments required for the long series of experiments. It must be so constructed as to simulate in every way the displacement and weight distribution of the finished ship, so that its model's behaviour during the experiments will closely predict that of the finished vessel. It should be noted that the speeds at which models are run in the tank are not those of the ship herself, but are speeds mathematically related to the comparative speeds of her.

The *Oriana* had a very fine-lined hull, the block co-efficient being about 0.594 including her bossing and other appendages at her designed draught of 31′ 6″. In order to improve her performance, and because her particulars of length to speed were suitable, she was designed with a bulbous bow.* This type of bow enables the designer to 'fine' the lines of the water line at the designed draught. In doing this the centre of displacement at the forward end of the underwater body is lowered and increases the effective length of the ship. This procedure usually shows performance improvements in the ships of higher speeds relative to ship's length. In the case of the *Oriana*, no less than sixteen models were run before a satisfactory shape was found. These experiments were made so as to provide the best underwater form, but additional tests were then required in order to assess the sea-keeping qualities of the ship.

The experimental tank is fitted with a device known as a 'wave-maker', this being built of steel and of the same shape as the tank's transverse section in one plane, but being wedge-shaped when viewed across the width of the tank, having the sharp end at the lower end of the wedge. Mechanism, powered by an electric motor, moves the wedge up and down at pre-selected periods of time and, in doing so, creates waves which move along the tank, breaking on a 'beach' at the other end. By changing the speed and the movement of the wave-maker, waves of the type required can be made and the model can be run at various speeds through them in order to witness its behaviour. From this can be assessed the quality of sea-keeping to be expected from the ship.

This was done for the *Oriana* model and also for a model of the *Orsova*, the previous ship built for the Company. As we knew that the *Orsova* was a well-behaved ship, and as we could compare the behaviour of her model with that of the new one, we knew that we

* Frontispiece.

could expect the *Oriana* to be a good, well-behaved ship when at sea—and this belief has been proved to be correct in practice.

There is no doubt that exhaustive experiments on ships' models in Model Experimental Tanks are necessary and rewarding when carried out for a high-performance ship in a tank of repute.

XI. THE CONSTRUCTIONAL DESIGN

THE ORIENT COMPANY was very fortunate (or, perhaps, I should say very discerning) to have chosen the firm of Vickers, at Barrow, to build their ships after the second World War—particularly the *Oriana*—because Vickers were at that time, in my opinion, the most advanced and skilful builders of passenger liners in Britain and, possibly, in the world. The building of the all-welded hull and aluminium superstructure of the ship could have been disastrous in the hands of lesser builders.

As has already been stated, the investigations into the fitting of the superstructure in aluminium alloy were long and tedious, but the decision to use aluminium alloy was made with the certainty that it would be safe and worthwhile. The Builders carried out many full-scale welding experiments on samples of deck, and only after these proved satisfactory did the work proceed. The cost of the alloy was much higher than the shipbuilding steel it was to replace—about three times the cost of material and labour for equivalent superstructures—but for the purpose of its use in the *Oriana* the decision was correct.

Because so much aluminium alloy (1,040 tons) was to be used in the superstructures and because it was to be so expensive, we were determined to make the alloy earn its keep in every conceivable way. So far as I am aware, no other ship at that time had used the alloy as a 'strength' material when added to the steel hull of a ship in the form of a superstructure. The usual way of adding such a structure was to regard it as a weathertight enclosure for such accommodation as was required to be protected from the elements—something like adding a house on top of the ship—not to help the ship structurally, but to provide protection for the accommodation arranged within it. In the *Oriana*, the steel construction was 'married' to the alloy in such a way as to ensure that the structure worked together as one in resisting the forces arising from loading the ship, from rolling and pitching and from the seas through which the ship was to sail.

To achieve this amalgamation of the two materials, transverse webs were arranged at chosen intervals along the ship's length and were carried from the keel and double-bottom structure through the main steel hull and the strength deck (the uppermost steel deck) upwards through all the alloy decks which were 'fore-and-aft', or longitudinally framed. All the accommodation requirements were subservient in importance to the structure requirements and were adjusted around the need to preserve structural integrity. It will be noted from the figure of the midship section that the superstructure sides (about 12 feet inside the extreme breadth of the hull) were carried upwards through several decks in order to tie the aluminium superstructure structurally to the strength deck.* The aluminium superstructure and the steel hull were all-welded with the exceptions imposed by Lloyds Classification Society—the stringer angle connecting the edge of the strength deck to the sheer strake plating (uppermost plates of the hull and an important strength member of the hull), and a treble-riveted seam of the hull plating at the turn of the bilge plating. These 'crack-arresters' are now regarded by many as being rather 'old hat' and could be dispensed with in favour of (perhaps) special alloy steel. One important piece of structure, which had not featured in Orient ship construction before, was that of forming a turn-out of the shell plating at the strength deck as shown on the midship section. Previous ships built for the Company had an overhang of the strength deck on the top edge of the main hull plating. The effect of this construction had been to form pockets which, in very heavy weather when waves ran up the sides of the ship, trapped the forces of the seas and caused very high pressures, even breaking sidelights and windows, with consequent flooding and danger to cabins and other accommodation. The alarm to passengers was also considerable, so we discussed the matter with the Builders, who

* Plate 119.

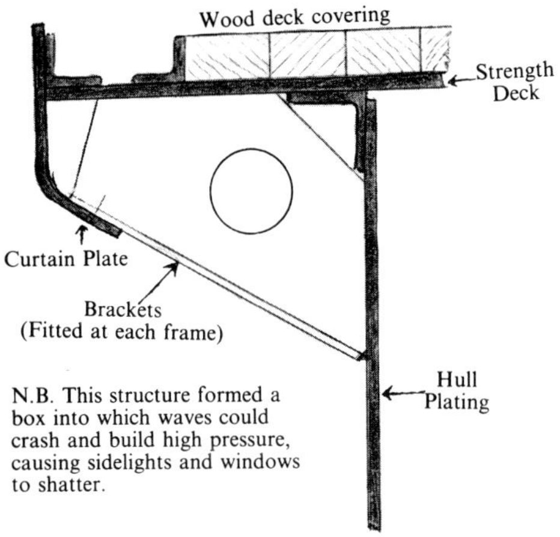

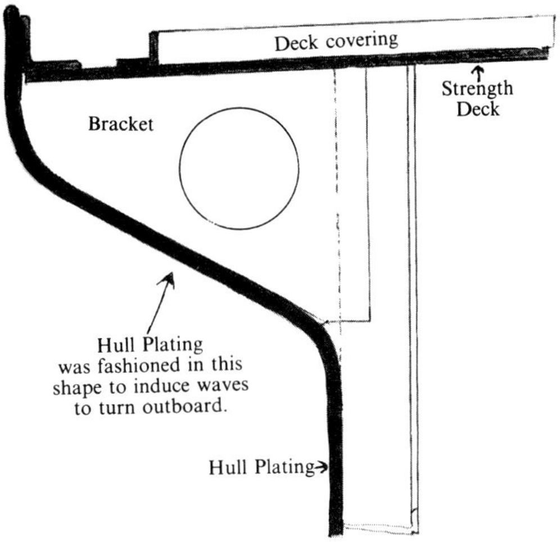

118. Detail of the overhang of the strength deck in the 28,000 ton ORCADES, ORONSAY and ORSOVA.

Detail of the overhang of the strength deck in the ORIANA (See plate 119, marked 'X')

produced an excellent answer in the form of the turn-out of the sheer-strake plating.

In this connection, the reader should note how high the force of the waves had risen above the waterline of these ships—the height above the load waterline of this strength deck is about 35 feet and was usually more in service since, as already mentioned, a vessel of the type of the *Oriana* was only down to her load marks for a fraction of the time.

One other riveted connection which had to be made was that between the steel and the aluminium alloy. The alloy used in the superstructures of the ship was known as a marine type alloy B.S. 1477/NP5/6M for the plates, and B.S. 1476/NE/6M for the sections. Sea water is a sort of electrolyte when associated with the junction of aluminium alloy and almost any other metal—especially bronzes. In such circumstances the aluminium alloy is destroyed by electrolytic action. Great care must therefore be taken with bi-metallic joints in which aluminium alloy is used. How to insulate the two metals in the long horizontal joints between the steel and the aluminium alloy at the

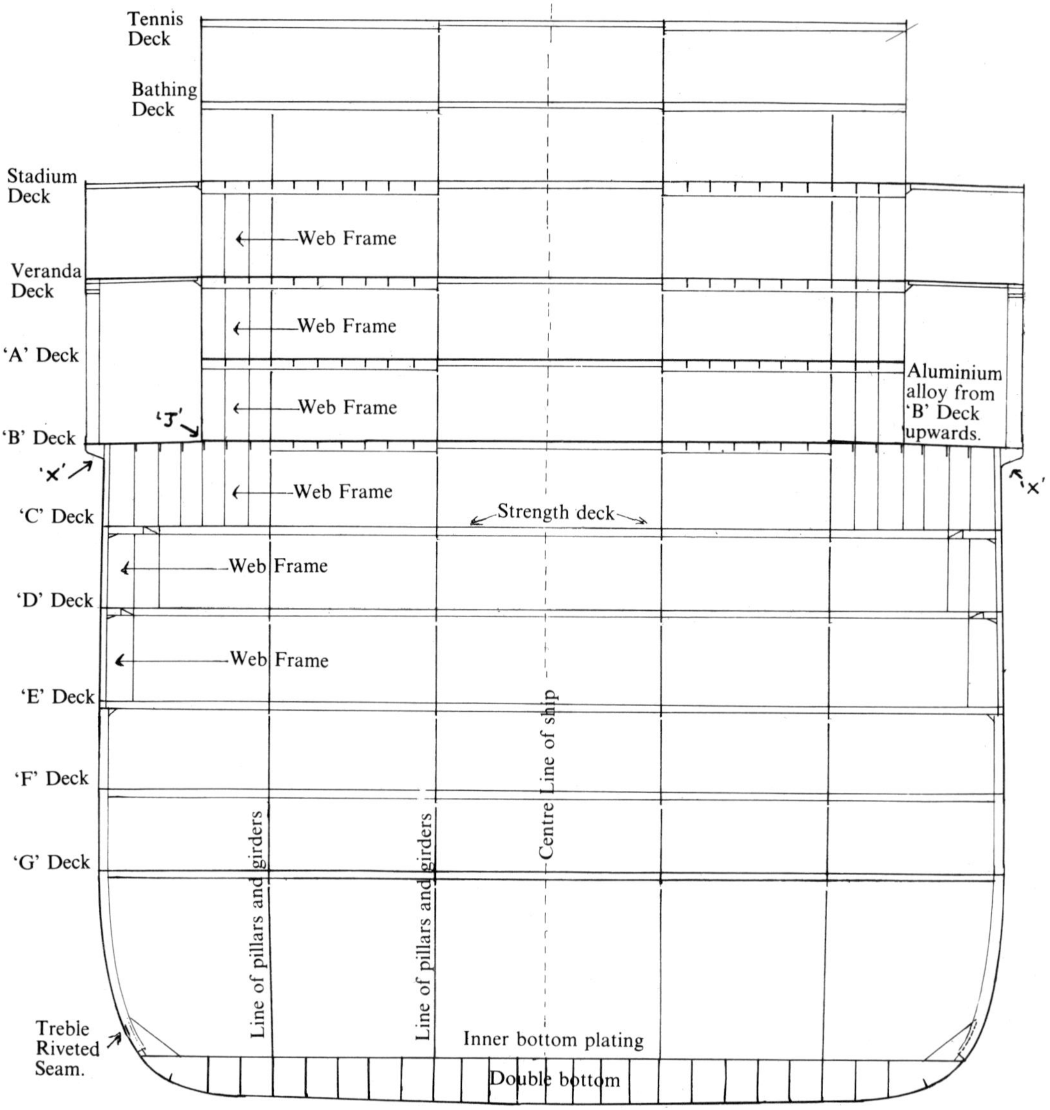

119. The midship section of the ORIANA.

strength deck of *Oriana* caused a great deal of discussion and argument before a settlement was reached. Each joint had to be a 'strength' connection such as had not been featured in ships before. We had inspected many methods used, but none were satisfactory, —most employed plastic sheets to separate the adjoining faces of the two metals, and had stainless steel bolts with plastic ferrules to protect the aluminium against corrosive attack. It must be remembered that the effect of seawater is always present, either as a fluid or in the atmosphere, and if these joints were to break down the ship could become seriously damaged during a long voyage—whilst remembering, too, that her aluminium alloy superstructure also formed part of the ship's hull strength. The riveted connection which was finally selected and used in the *Oriana* is shown in Plate 120. There appears to be very little on which I may comment in this design of joint, but, so far as I know, there has been no failure in it to date, and the *Oriana* is now 18 years old at the time of writing.

In any structure which is to be subjected to high stresses, especially reciprocating, or reversals of, stress, or vibrations whilst under stress, great care should be taken to avoid sudden changes of shape and direction, increases or decreases in area of section, or discontinuities of any description. Holes, especially badly shaped holes with sharp corners, behave like the perforations in stamp edging and cause structures to fracture and tear whilst under stress. These simple facts of engineering are often overlooked even by those engaged in ship designing and building, and the writer has himself been responsible for such oversights. We know what should be done but forget or omit to observe that the mistakes keep happening. There are many stabilizer fins lying on the floors of oceans—fins which dropped off ships because the bolts holding them in place on their shafts were made with sharp changes of section where the bolt heads joined the shanks of the bolts, which were not designed to cater for the abrupt change of section. A number of fins were lost from Orient ships before an excellent change of design was made. That of the *Oriana's* stabilizer fins and shaft connection is especially good and should last the life-time of the ship.

In the early days of the use of welding of ship structures, it was a

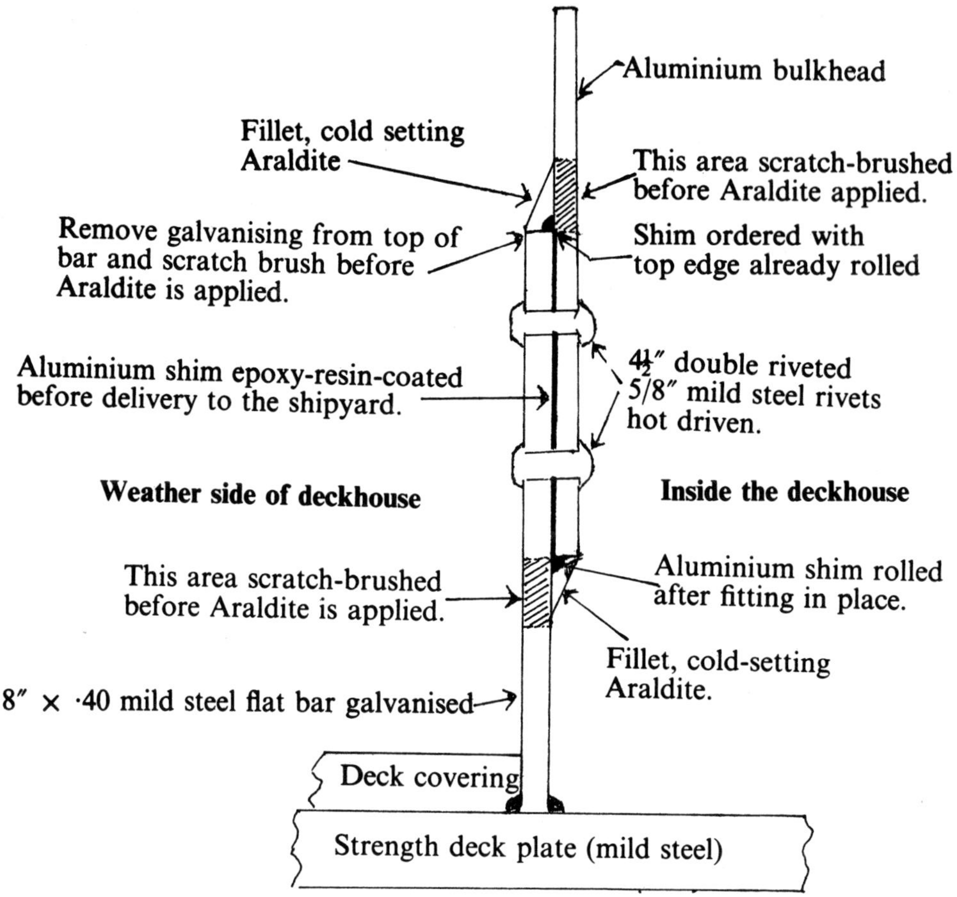

120. Detail of the bi-metallic joints on the Strength (B) deck. For position see Plate 119 – 'J').

commonly held view that welding caused cracking.* The early attempts to weld steel *did* result in fracturing, but this elementary stage was soon passed and the process became reliable. There had always been cracking of steelwork in ships—and probably of the ironwork and woodwork used before steel—which was nearly always caused by bad design or bad workmanship,—or both.

The ship with the heaviest scantlings in the Orient Line's fleet when I joined the Company was the *Ormonde*, built in 1917. I do not

* See page 123.

know why she was so heavily built, but this did not stop cracking of the superstructure. The *Ormonde* was the most cracked ship of the fleet—mostly because of careless design in the details of door openings, window openings and all the simple points already mentioned in this chapter.

The cracking of any structure can be taken as a sign of relieving of high points of stress and often, in cases where such cracking has taken place in a relatively unimportant part of the structure, the crack can be left. This can be done prudently by drilling rather large holes at the ends of the crack to prevent its further propagation and by covering the area with some soft material to preserve appearance. In my experience, if cracks of this sort are repaired, another crack will appear nearby, because the high stress caused by movement of the ship's structure is still there and must be relieved.

The collaboration of the Builders and the Owners in regard to design and construction details of the ships built since 1948 had brought about rapid strides in the use of welding, and resulted in better and lighter ships. Riveting always needs overlapping of plates or flanges of bars to make riveted joints, and the accumulation of all such overlapped plates, together with the rivet heads and points, causes unnecessary weight on the ship. The *Orsova*, built just before the *Oriana*, was the first all-welded passenger liner in Britain, and it was estimated that some hundreds of tons of weight of steel were saved in her construction due to the elimination of riveting. Weight was also significantly saved by the replacement of castings by welded fabrications in the manufacture of rudder frame, stern frame, shaft brackets, bollards, fairleads and hawse pipes.

This principle was applied to the *Oriana*, but even more intensely, and in consequence it is believed that the saving in weight was 300-400 tons as compared with the conventionally constructed ship. The additional saving due to the use of aluminium in the superstructures is very difficult to quantify because, if steel had been used to replace the aluminium alloy, the additional weight would have made the ship (as designed) unstable, and she would therefore have had to be re-designed. Nevertheless, the weight-saving in the *Oriana* was considerable and must have amounted to over 1,000 tons, when totalling the many and various methods used to achieve it.

The saving in weight in the design and building of the ship almost became an obsession, and the Management of the Orient Company issued an edict to the effect that all concerned should endeavour to save it in every possible way. This caused changes to be made in the outfitting and equipment of the ship, which will be discussed later.

It is obvious that there was little point in saving weight by the use of 1,040 tons of very expensive aluminium alloy if the saving was allowed to be frittered away by the careless use of heavy equipment or wrong materials elsewhere in or around the ship.

The design of the structure to incorporate the aluminium alloy as a structural asset was checked at the time of the ship's launch, since this event causes high straining to take place and gives the builders an opportunity to investigate the contribution to the ship's strength made by the superstructure. Hitherto, 'expansion joints' had been fitted into the upper works of Orient ships. These joints allow the superstructure to move as the main hull of the vessel bends when the ship is at sea, or when she is being loaded or discharged, with the result that it is, therefore, not subjected to any major forces created by the movement of the hull. In the *Oriana* the usual 'expansion joint' was omitted and, for the first time in the Company's ships, a superstructure was made to work for its living. I have always regarded 'expansion joints' as a structural crudity and was very glad to be involved in the elimination of them in the *Oriana*.

The Builders invited a team of specialists from the British Shipbuilding Research Association to install instruments and to take readings of stress on the ship's hull and superstructure during the launch, and the subsequent findings of the investigating team were both reassuring and satisfactory. A paper called *'Application of Welding to Ship Construction—with Particular Reference to the Aluminium Superstructure of the T.S.S. ORIANA'** provided information in great deail of the design, use, and constructional problems and benefits of aluminium alloy in the ship. In service, aluminium is a material which can be left unpainted in areas where the charcoal-grey patina it assumes after weathering at sea is acceptable to the shipowner, and this has been done and has saved a large amount of

* By L. Redshaw, M.Eng.

121. Ventilation trunking before installation.

expense, time and trouble in upkeep of the ship. Aluminium oxidises when exposed to the elements, but in doing so it creates a protective skin, coloured charcoal-grey, and, if left, this skin will remain as a natural protection to the surface and will prevent further oxidation. The opposite condition is true of steel, where rust (oxidation) grows and breaks away to repeat the process until finally it destroys the parent material. There are difficulties in the use of aluminium, the most acute being that of bi-metallic effect for, when aluminium is in the presence of another metal, particularly brass or bronze, it will literally disintegrate when dampened by sea-air or sea-water. This disintegration is rapid and, even when some care is taken to protect the aluminium by suitable paint (not lead-based paint which is fatal to the metal), a small 'bridge' of electro-conductive material across the paintwork will cause deterioration and complete breakdown. Aluminium also contracts in cold or expands in heat much more than steel and, therefore, care must be taken in designing structure using these

122.

123. The Deck Heads, particularly in the entrance halls, are filled with pipes, ventilators and wiring.

metals in close relationship to prevent distortion. It is a clean material with which to work and build, but some care has to be taken in the use of pencils or crayons in handling so as to prevent damage to this rather soft material by scratching, indentation, or chemical action on surfaces. Painting with the correct type of paint can present beautiful finishes of lasting quality.

The usual method of building decks with their beams and girders in ships was to rivet, or weld, angle beams to the undersides of the decks in line with the ship's frames and connected to them by beam knees. These beams were of a size to take the deck load imposed on them and were supported by a system of pillars and girders arranged longitudinally along the length of the decks. The girders were deeper and stronger than the beams and suitable in size to carry the loads received from the deck beams. When services, such as of ventilation in particular, or piping and electric wiring, were installed, they often had to be passed through these girders, which were cut away to suit the size of the ventilation trunks or pipes. Compensation for the loss of strength was made by adding suitably fashioned local stiffening. The work involved in doing this was expensive and time-consuming and, in the *Oriana*, the method was changed. A standardized system of fashioning holes in the girders was devised, and they were all cut to this system. This enabled ventilation and piping to be installed more easily, and also made a further reduction in weight possible. There were still some ventilation and piping ducts which were larger than the standard size of these openings in the girders, but these were cut and compensated as required.

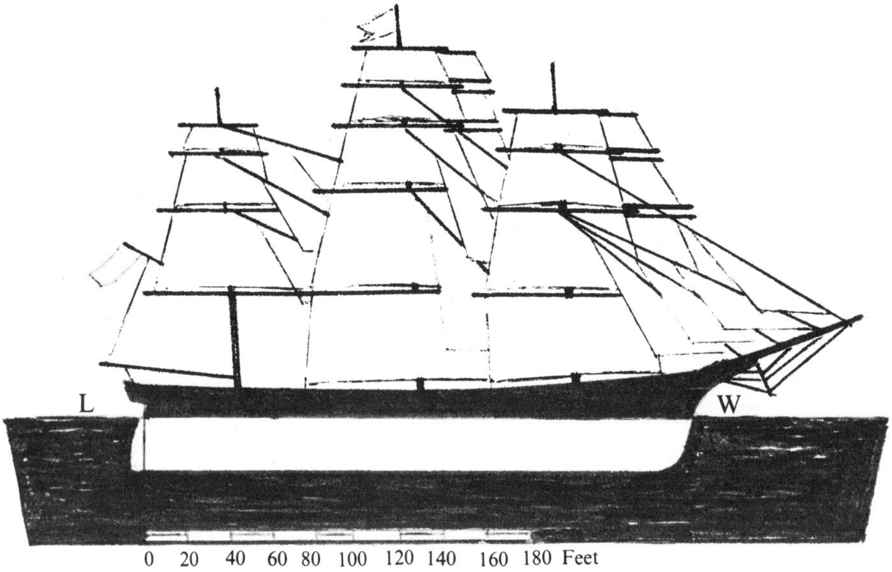

LW = Load waterline

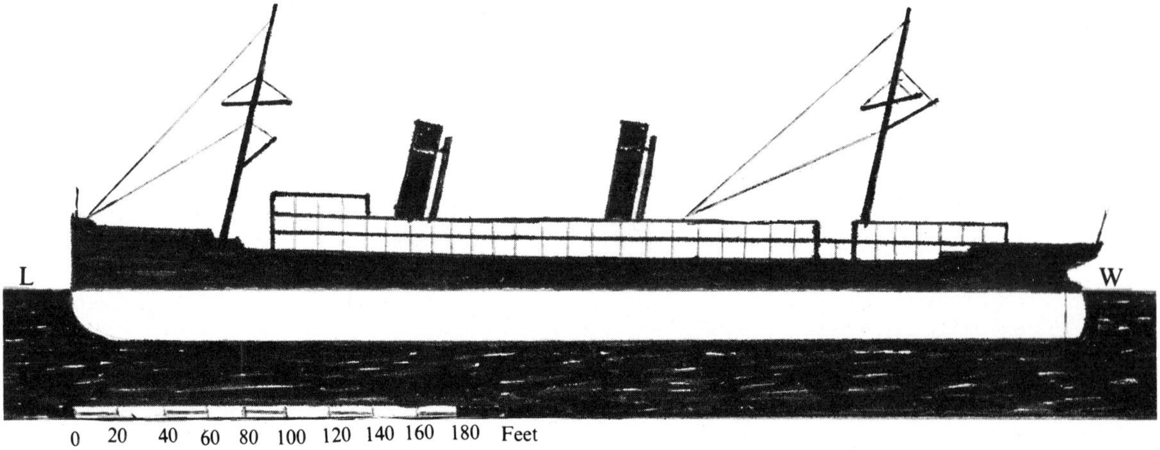

124. *The profiles of the clipper CHAMPION OF THE SEAS (above) and the OPHIR are shown for comparison with plates 114-116. The proportions of the drafts to the heights of the vessels above the load waterlines are of interest.*

XII. MANOEUVRING AND MOORING ARRANGEMENTS

THE MANOEUVRING OF large passenger ships in confined waters, usually on entering and leaving or within harbours, and their mooring, is a large subject in itself. Usually the manoeuvring has to be done at very slow speeds and, as can be seen in the ships' profiles,* the greater area of them is *above* the water and easily influenced by wind. When it is also considered that the power of a rudder to turn a ship is largely dependent on the speed of water over the rudder blade, it follows that a ship is at a disadvantage when travelling slowly in currents and windy conditions. The power of the rudder can be increased momentarily by bursts of speed of the water passing along it caused by the use of the engines and propellers of the ship, but this cannot be done constantly without increasing the ship's speed, which would be undesirable. The use of tugs is an obvious answer to the problem, but there have been a number of occasions when tugs were not available when needed by Orient ships.

The effect of wind on a ship with large and high superstructures is not unlike the effect of wind on the sails of a sailing ship, but the obvious difference is that a large passenger ship cannot adjust the position of her superstructures as a sailing ship can change the number and trim of her sails. However, the ship designer can reduce the height of the superstructures at the ends of the ship, and try to ensure that the profile is built up in a triangular or pyramidical shape so that a reasonable balance of area is presented to the wind. Ships having high stern castles are particularly vulnerable, because the wind blows

* Plates 124/5.

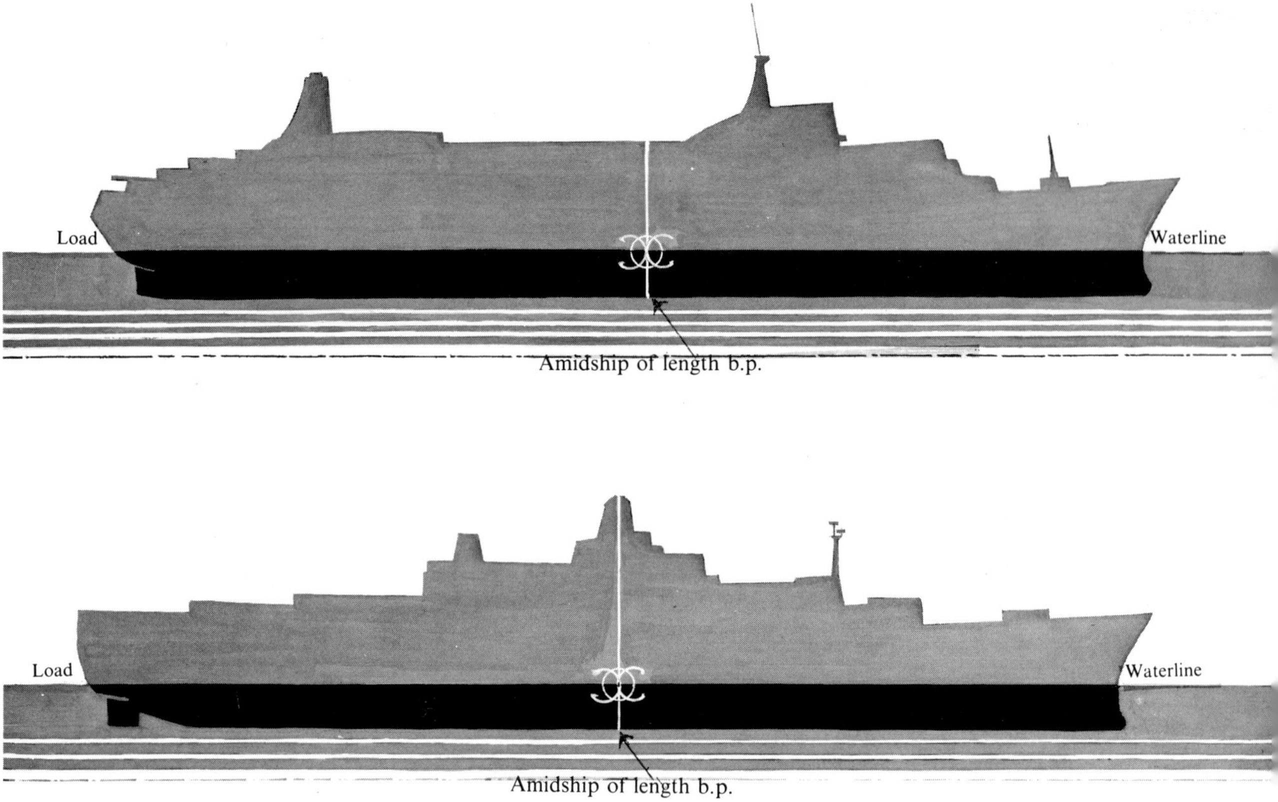

125. Profiles of the CANBERRA (above) and ORIANA, showing areas above and below the load waterlines. The area below the waterline is less than 25,000 sq. ft. and above more than 63,000 sq. ft. in each ship.

the stern off course whilst the ship is moving slowly, and in—say—the mistral, the strong seasonal prevailing wind off the southern coasts of France, a ship of this sort can be hazarded when trying to enter a port such as Marseilles. There are many other areas in the seas of the world where similar winds can be met—there is such a wind which arises seasonally off Genoa and other parts of Italy.

The Orient Company decided that, as the new ship was to be very much bigger in size and value, she should be fitted with better mooring arrangements and with manoeuvring propellers, foreward and aft.

The mooring of a large ship is one requiring feeling on the part of the officers on the bridge, and skill on the part of the officers and men handling the ropes aboard the ship and ashore. The ropes of a large ship are so very heavy and cumbersome to use that lack of vigilance can easily cause accidents to the vessel herself and serious injury to those involved. Hitherto, the ships of the Company had had their mooring arrangements fitted on the forecastle deck about fifty feet above the waterline forward, and on a mooring deck aft situated about thirty feet above the waterline. The heights of quays varied considerably between the large number of ports which were visited by the Orient fleet and it was not uncommon to find that the quay, to which the mooring ropes were to be fitted on bollards, was not more than ten feet above the water. This meant that the ropes had to be run downwards from the ship at very steep angles to the securing points and, in doing so, reduced their holding value.* This was particularly true of the mooring ropes at the forward end of the ships. The mooring arrangements of the *Oriana* therefore had to be improved markedly from those fitted on previous units of the fleet because, being so much larger and heavier, she would present a greater area of superstructure to be affected by wind and this, in turn, would produce large forces tending to break the moorings.

The mooring deck forward was moved from the usual position on the forecastle to a lower deck just over thirty feet above the waterline, while the after mooring deck was arranged in a position about twenty feet above that point. The mooring deck forward had large openings in the ship's side which enabled it to be used as a sheltered deck for members of the crew when the weather was not suitable for them to use the open deck on the forecastle, and when the ship was not being moored.

The mooring of a large ship in the narrow waters of a harbour or anchorage is traditionally done with the help of tugs, but ships are sometimes unable to get the assistance of these and, at such times, are rather helpless, fragile and difficult to handle. Because the Company had experienced this difficulty in recent times, the Management resolved that, at any rate, the *Oriana* should not be entirely dependent

* Plates 126/7.

on towage facilities and, to this end, Manoeuvring Units were devised and fitted. Voith Schneider propellers were considered, but had to be discarded because of difficulties in fitting them in the after position in the ship. Eventually, the answer was found in the fitting of axial-flow pumps (a propeller fitted within a tube to propel the water along the tube).

Tubes about four feet in diameter were sited in the horizontal plane across the ship, two forward, and two aft over the propeller shaft bossings. In each of these tubes was one propeller, each driven by an electric motor developing 550 b.h.p. These produced a thrust from side to side of the ship of about 5 tons from each tube. They were, therefore, equivalent in total to at least two tugs, one at each end of the ship. She could now have instant power sideways equivalent to one tug at each end, and this was better than any real tugs could have been, because the power was there immediately when required and was under the control of the officers on the bridge. The controls for the manoeuvring units were fitted not only within the bridge but also one at each end of the bridge wings.

It should be noted that such sideways-thrusters can only operate efficiently when the ship is not moving in a fore-and-aft direction. They could then be used to turn the ship round on her own centre of length, by thrusting in one direction on the forward installation and in the reverse direction on the after installation. The openings for these transverse tubes were closed when their propellers were not required. The doors on the forward tubes slid vertically upwards against the inside of the ship's skin to the 'Open' position* and the after doors had hinges on their upper edges and opened inwards and upwards as required. These doors were operated by portable electric motors.

Some smaller and slower ships, which now use this device, are not fitted with closing devices on the openings in the hulls and it is conceivable that the adverse effects on the speeds of the ships are not of very great importance. Possibly it could not be shown that closures on such openings in large ships cause reductions in speed or increased resistance. The results from ships' models run in a test tank would almost be worthless due to 'scale effect'. It is known that at least one large passenger ship was fitted with a 'sideways-thruster' or

* Plate 129.

126.

127. Two views of the after mooring deck of the ORIANA. Note the well-rounded apertures for the ropes and their angles.

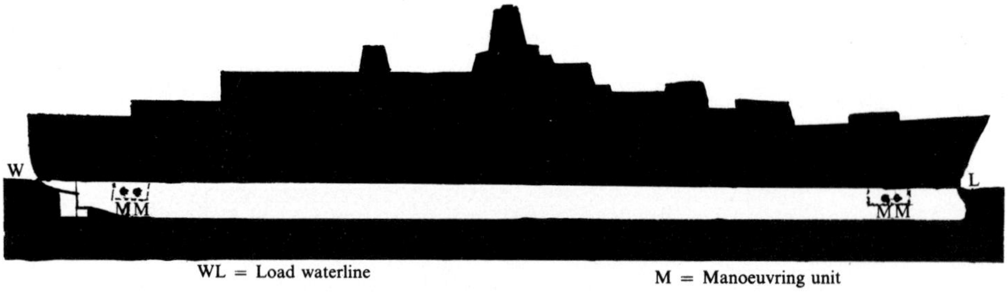

128. Positions of the transverse manoeuvring units.

'manoeuvring unit' which consisted of a rather large single propeller in a tube fitted across the forward end of the hull. No closing devices were fitted to the tube. Some ships, in certain sea conditions, yaw more than others and, if the ship is a large one, the angular sideways swaying motions mean appreciable linear movements, to and fro', at the forward end of the vessel. The large ship fitted with the big sideways-thruster unit was just such a one. By this movement of the bow from one side to the other in a constantly reversing manner, the sea water was forced through the open tube and over the propeller blades within it. This caused big turning forces on the propeller and, although the brakes which were fitted were 'on', the propeller was forced to rotate, first in one direction and then in the other, as the yawing went on. The noise was such as to disturb members of the crew who were berthed not very far away and temporary arrangements were made to stop the propeller turning, by passing steel wire ropes through the tube and around the blades. This was not successful because the wires were cut by the propeller blades. Eventually, the problem was solved for that voyage by the use of chain cable!

The one point made clear by this incident is that appreciable resistance must have been created by the yawing movement of the vessel, which caused sea-water to surge one way or the other in the open transverse tube of the manoeuvring unit. This *must* have affected the speed of the ship.

The *Oriana* was built with strengthening of the structure in an

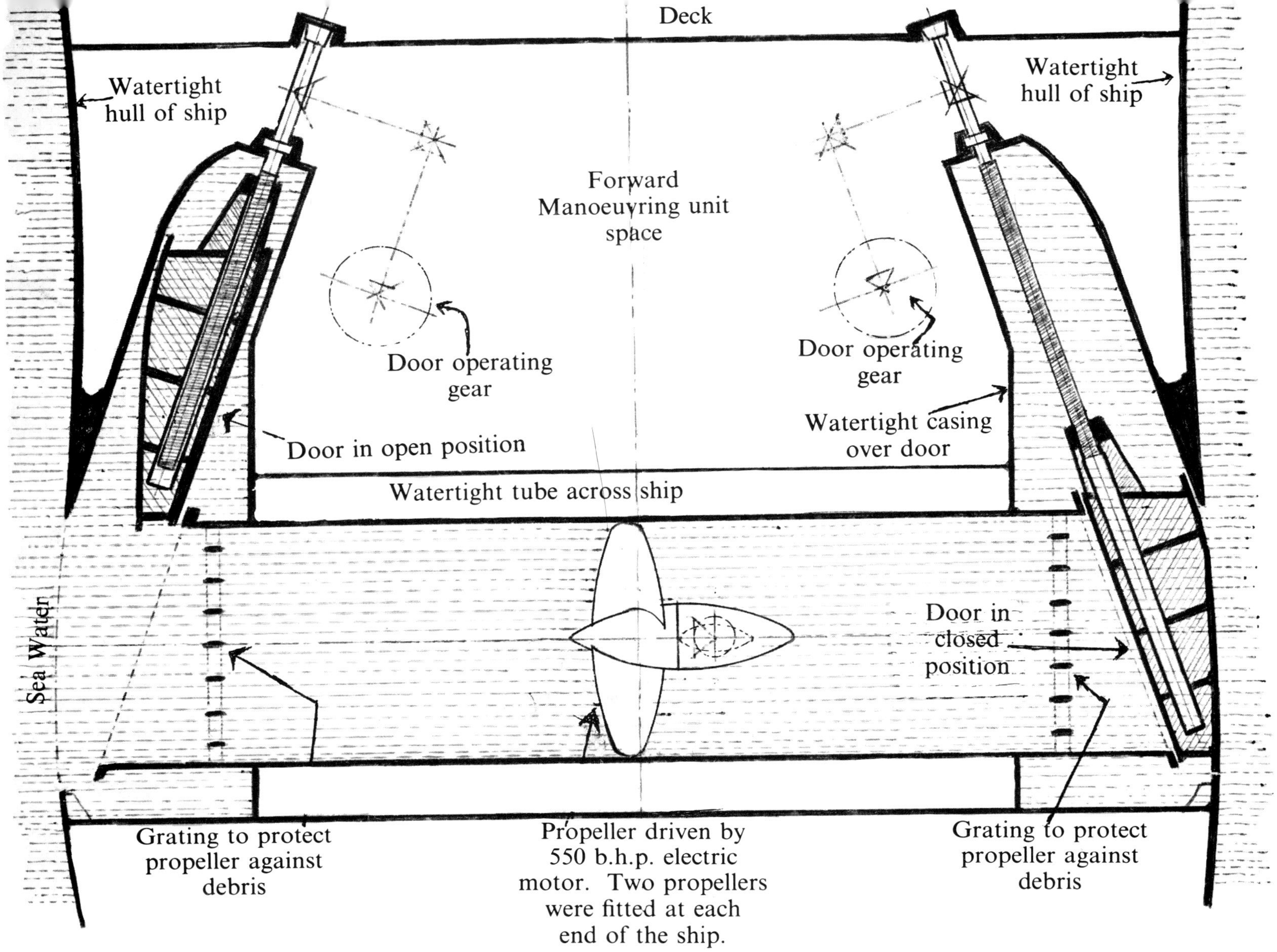

129. ***Diagram**, looking forward through ship at forward manoeuvring space, demonstrating the function of the unit.*

after position to enable the fitting of a stern anchor, if necessary, together with a windlass and other gear required for its use. This was done to satisfy the apprehensions of some members of the Marine Department who felt that this larger ship might require the extra facility of an anchor at the stern of the vessel. In the light of experience of handling her, this possible need for an extra anchor was found to be unnecessary and none was ever supplied.

The bollards, fairleads and mooring pipes were fabricated of rather thick steel plate fashioned and welded to the decks, bulwarks, or shell plating. Because of experience and observations made on other ships, all the shapes of holes through which mooring ropes were to pass were framed with generously curved plating so as to be 'kind' to the rope which ran through them—we had seen many expensive large ropes in new ships destroyed in mooring operations.

To those who have been on board a ship when the anchor was 'let go', it will be no surprise to be told that the anchor cable runs out over the rounded edge of a steel casting or forging. It is no exaggeration to say that the forward end of the ship shudders whilst this takes place. When the *Orcades* was being built in 1947, the Chief Draughtsman of the Ships' Drawing Office, a Scot named Willy Taylor, told me of an idea he had had—and he had many good ones, because he was a man of some genius. The shape of an anchor cable or chain when viewed from its end, is that of a rather thick cross. Taylor's idea was to build a steel wheel, about forty inches in diameter and eight inches thick, which would be mounted on a substantial spindle in a welded steel fabrication over the ship's hawse pipe. A groove would be cut in the middle of the perimeter face of the wheel. This simple device was built and fitted in the *Orcades*, where it proved to be a great success and quietened the whole noisy business of dropping or raising the anchor. This was adopted in all ships built for the Company after 1948.

Some years later, a representative of a well-known maker of anchor windlasses and associated equipment came to solicit my support in regard to an infringement of his Company's patent gear. He told me that Vickers were using a cable wheel which, when he showed me the drawing of his firm's wheel, was almost identical with the one his Company had patented. After asking about the date of the patent, I was happy to tell him that Vickers had fitted their wheel years before that time, and therefore, could not be sued!

The patenting of ideas is very uncommon in the Shipbuilding Industry and perhaps some thought should be given to using the protection and advantages which it offers to brainy people and progressively-minded Companies. In more recent times, I had to work closely with Aircraft Companies concerned with the design and building of hovercraft, and I was amazed to find that they patented the most simple and trivial ideas which occurred to them. I believe this was done to protect themselves against other competitors who could possibly have the same ideas and patent them, thus preventing their use until patent royalties had been paid.

130. The Foc's'le head of the Dutch passenger liner NIEUW AMSTERDAM, with capstans for her anchor cables.

131. Ticker-tape send-off to an Orient ship from Australia.

XIII. CARGO, BAGGAGE AND STORES HANDLING

As HAS ALREADY been stated, a primary aim in the design of this large passenger ship was to reduce the time spent in port to the minimum necessary to load and discharge all the fuel, stores, cargo, fresh water, passengers and their baggage as required at each port. Ideally, all of these requirements should be completely carried out and finished at the same time but, of course, this is impossible, and the best that could be done was to provide the means to enable the work to be carried out quickly and efficiently.

For many years, the cargo of ships of the Company had been taken on board or discharged by means of shore cranes or by derricks mounted on the masts or Samson posts of the ships. Derricks take time to rig, but can be very efficient and quick when handled by skilful men and two are rigged as a 'union purchase'.* The derricks fitted on ships of the fleet were usually capable of lifting about five tons and thus equal to most packages carried by the Company, but one or two of them were capable of lifting ten tons and, occasionally, twenty tons when fitted with special rigging for the infrequent lifts of this sort. Unfortunately, there were some accidents due to faulty rigging of these heavy derricks, and one of these resulted in the death of a bo'sun in Australia. The bo'sun had been responsible for the faulty rigging of the derrick which caused his death but, nevertheless, I was saddened and unhappy that it was possible for such an untoward happening to take place. Cranes had been fitted instead of derricks on one Orient ship built some years earlier and, because these had not performed very

* See Glossary.

well, were not used on subsequent ships of the Company—for reasons which had not been recorded and were not known to surviving members of the staff. When the cargo handling equipment was being considered for the *Oriana*, an investigation into initial costs: maintenance costs; weight, and handling capabilities of derricks and various types of cranes was made, after we had decided that the lifting capacity should be limited to not more than five tons. It was found that, whilst derricks were cheaper than cranes in initial installation, due to differing maintenance costs, they broke even over an assumed life of the ship, and the difference in weight of the two types of installation was not one large enough to influence a decision. The speed of rigging the cranes from their stowed positions to their working positions was much better than the derricks, and they were usually faster than derricks handled in their usual manner. Cranes could be fitted with cabs for the drivers, and another important point was that the element of danger caused in the rigging of derricks did not apply to cranes. It was decided to fit electric cranes made by the A.S.E.A. Company of Sweden and these have been a success in service. The volume and weight of cargo which could be worked in the time that the new ship was estimated to be in each port for other purposes was assessed, and the arrangements and capacities in the ship were made to suit these estimates when using the cranes and hatches feeding the spaces for general and refrigerated cargoes.

The crew and passengers of the 28,000 gross tons class of ship of the Company were a little more than 2,000 in number, but the new ship was to carry 688 First Class passengers, 1,496 Tourist Class passengers, and 899 officers and other ranks, making a total of over 3,000 souls. The cargo to be carried had been reduced in quantity, in order to reduce time spent on its handling in port, but the quantity of stores and baggage required for crew and passengers could not be reduced. This meant that the facilities provided in the ship for handling stores and baggage had to be much better than those in previous ships of the Company if time spent in harbour on these operations was to be equal to, or better than, usual.

The estimated weight of food and drink, apart from fresh water, carried for the needs of passengers and crew of the new ship, was in excess of 70 tons for each week and included over 40,000 eggs, $10\frac{1}{2}$ tons of potatoes, $13\frac{1}{2}$ tons of fresh vegetables, and over 3,500 gallons of canned and draught beers. The store rooms for general and refrigerated provisions were capable of carrying five hundred tons in weight because, of course, they were not being re-stored weekly and some of the stores had to be carried for long periods of time. There were three main methods of taking stores and baggage in and out of the ship.

Two conveyor systems operated through shipside doors, one forward and one aft, on each side of the vessel, while two large stores lifts served these doors on port and starboard amidships; and there were the cranes mentioned above. The conveyors were carried in the ship, and, being mounted on transverse rails, could be used through one side of the ship or the other. They were powered by electric motors and could be angled to suit any level of quay and any draught of the ship. The baggage conveyor aft could deliver from shore to baggage room or in the reverse direction as required. The forward baggage conveyor could deliver or discharge from the forward baggage room or could be used to handle stores into the stores alleyway. The large stores lifts could be used to provision the ship from the quay or to deliver the daily requirements of the galleys from the store rooms—the lifts having entrances in the galleys. The cranes could be used as a supplementary aid to these arrangements, if or when required, because number 3 Hatch Trunk had doors which could open into the stores alleyway, and other cranes could be used on to open decks adjacent to, and opening into, passenger accommodation.

Within the ship, two baggage elevators, powered by electric motors, were fitted on port and starboard near the after shipside doors. These elevators worked vertically up from the baggage rooms to each of the tourist passenger decks and were to be used to distribute baggage to the passengers' cabins. The elevators worked on an 'endless belt' system, having pivoted trays spaced equally and at suitable positions on the belt. Above each tray there was a row of name tabs listing the levels served by the elevator. A steward, when placing baggage on the slowly moving elevator tray, would press the tab naming the level at which he wished it to be delivered, and, in due course, these items would be automatically tipped out and down a chute to the deck selected.

These elevators really work well on the *Oriana*, and are something of a change from one such arrangement which I know to have been installed in a ship. This elevator had trays built of rods—something like the platform of a fork lift truck. On the maiden voyage of the ship, a fault arose in this elevator, with the result that, as each tray was loaded and passed from the sight of the steward loading the baggage into the trays, the trunks and bags and their contents were systematically torn to shreds. This might have been the high-light of a comedy film but was, in fact, a very sad and upsetting affair for some of the passengers in that ship, who were not amused by the incident.

XIV. CARRIAGE OF OIL FUEL

The cost of carrying weight unnecessarily in a ship of the size and speed of the *Oriana* has already been mentioned, but when the quantity of oil fuel to be carried in the ship came up for decision, there were other points to be considered. Oil fuel prices per ton varied considerably and, at the time of the design and building of the vessel, the cheapest oil available between Southampton and Sydney was being sold at Aden, and at San Francisco on the Pacific section of the route.

There was also another factor to be considered. If the rate of refuelling of the ship was not improved from that common to existing ships of the fleet, the time taken in the operation might defeat the savings of time that were being made in so many other ways. Much improved fuelling arrangements were designed to put oil into the rather widely dispersed tanks within the ship, and it has been recorded that the *Oriana* in service took on board 5,400 tons of bunker oil in 3½ hours, which is more than 1,500 tons per hour. This is not high by the standards of oil tanker pumping performances, but is satisfactory for a passenger liner, which usually stays in ports for longer than that period of time.

The oil bunkers of the *Oriana* could take nearly 7,000 tons of oil fuel, and calculations showed that she could steam from Aden with full bunkers to Sydney, and back to Aden, with only a small amount of oil to top them up in Australia. The same was true of her voyages from Aden to London and back to Aden. A voyage to the west coast of America from Sydney and back to Australia could be done in much the same way. It was found that the savings made in purchasing the oil fuel at the cheaper bunkering ports was worth the cost of carrying these large amounts of fuel. Bearing in mind that the consumption of oil when the ship was steaming at her service speed of 27½ knots was about 300 tons per diem, the displacement of the ship would be reduced by 4,000 tons in a little over ten days steaming. The economy in buying oil and carrying it around in the ship had, of course, a 'break-even' point, but we considered that the carriage of nearly 7,000 tons of oil at the cheaper rates was worthwhile.

The positions of the oil fuel tanks in the ship were dispersed in such a way around her as to preserve a good balance of trim if the oil was used from the tanks in a sensible manner. In this way the ship's displacement was reduced by a ton for every ton of fuel consumed during the voyage, and it was unnecessary to take in any ballast water for trim purposes. The only water ballast used in the ship was taken when her displacement was less than about 31,800 tons—a low displacement rarely reached except on long 'legs' of the itinerary.*

* See Appendix 3.

132. *The ORONTES cruising in a Norwegian fjord.*

133. *The ORIANA and the sunrise.*

XV. STABILIZERS

STABILIZERS FOR SHIPS are devices to reduce rolling and make life more comfortable for those on board. Methods of reducing rolling and pitching of ships have occupied the minds of men interested in the subject for generations, but with little or no success until just before the second World War when the Denny-Brown activated fin stabilizer was installed in a number of warships in the British Navy to reduce rolling and so to aid accuracy in gunnery. Although some attempts have been made to reduce pitching by the use of fins, none of them have been successful.

Many ideas have been tried in attempts to reduce the movement of ships at sea. One method attempted was that of building a deck on gimbals, which, in theory, allowed the ship to roll whilst the deck remained horizontal. In practice, the deck rocked about violently and the scheme was a dismal failure!*

Some fundamental ideas for stabilization were based on using tanks built into the ship's sides and which were partly filled with a fluid which was supposed to move from one side tank to the other through transverse pipes, and thus cancel or reduce the roll. To achieve this, the movement of fluid had to be controlled to suit the rolling period of the ship. Some designs incorporated sluice valves in the cross-pipes so that the speed of movement of the fluid could be reduced as required, whilst other designs had the size of the pipes calculated to suit the ship. This method, in its various types, is to be found in many vessels afloat today. It requires no power, but does take up space in the ship, and its effectiveness is not so good as that of

* The *Bessemer*

the activated fin type of stabilizer in ships which are proceeding at speed. Some vessels, such as cable-laying ships, proceed at slow speed for long periods of service and, in craft of this type, the anti-roll tank stabilizer or 'flume-tank' type, is the most suitable because it does not depend on speed for its effectiveness and can operate when the ship is not under power.

Dr. H. Frahm, a German inventor, was perhaps the greatest name to conjure with in the development of anti-rolling tanks, which was carried out at the great German shipbuilding yard of Blohm & Voss at Hamburg, his basis being a large tank, resembling a capital 'U', built athwartships and extending from side to side of the vessel. The water column would oscillate with the number of swings per minute and was sufficiently successful to be fitted in several German and British passenger liners, including the Cunard *Laconia* of 1911, in which the tank was of 320 tons capacity, and the success of this experiment led to a similar tank being fitted amidships in the *Aquitania*.

In the meantime, a Dr. Schlick had been experimenting with the gyroscope to the same end, and his system was fitted to various small vessels including the MacBrayne steamer *Lochiel* in 1908, and the results proved to be satisfactory, but the main difficulty was that, in order to be really effective, the gyroscopic disc should be about 20% of the total weight of the ship which, for obvious reasons, was not generally acceptable.

The characteristics of the gyroscope have now been used during the past half century or more as a means of keeping instruments true in spite of upsetting forces, as, for instance, in the case of torpedo control, aircraft turn indicators and in similar applications where the gyroscope's characteristic of keeping its axis stable in space is vital to the accuracy of the instruments. In the cases cited, the forces involved are very small and thus the gyroscopes, too, are equally small.

In the early 1930's, two large Italian liners were laid down—the *Guglielmo Marconi* (which was launched as the *Rex*) and the *Conte di Savoia*, of 51,062 and 48,502 tons G.R.T. respectively and of speeds of 27½ and 27 knots, being heavily subsidized by Mussolini's Fascist government to enhance Italian prestige, and they were generally

134. The CONTI DI SAVOIA.

considered to have the most luxurious accommodation afloat—if somewhat bizarre. The ships were not sisters, the *Rex* having a counter stern and the smaller *Conte di Savoia* a cruiser stern, while the latter vessel was also fitted with a form of stabilization against rolling based on the gyroscope but, because the forces to be overcome in this case were very large, the gyroscopes were very big.

The designers of the equipment were the well-known Sperry Company, who sub-contracted the building of the gyroscopes to the firm of Vickers-Armstrong, at Barrow. Each revolving disc of these gyroscopes weighed 175 tons and made 910 revolutions per minute, and there were three in each installation, so that the total weight in each of the three installations, including the structural reinforcement required to carry the heavy moving parts, was some 750 tons, and absorbed 2,000 horse-power. Not a great deal seems to be known about the performance of this equipment, but it does not appear that they were ever installed in any large passenger liner afterwards, and the Italian vessel was virtually unique for a vessel of her size in carrying them.

A statement appeared in the press in 1933 stating that the *Conte de Savoia* had encountered gale conditions during which rolling had been reduce from 30° to 4°, 5° and 6° by the use of her stabilizers. It is not clear why these three figures were used, and the reader may take his choice. The cost of this equipment must have been very high but, as often happens in the introduction of new or untried inventions, it is possible that a substantial part of the total cost was borne by the Sperry Company. The weight, running costs and maintenance in service also mounted up to an appreciable liability. A paper was written and presented to the Institute of Naval Architects in London in 1933* and, from this and from the discussions which followed, it is obvious that the subject was a controversial one.

The activated-fin stabilizer appeared as an invention periodically each year for decades (or so it seemed) but failed to work effectively until the Denny-Brown fin stabilizer appeared in the 1930's. It was successful particularly because of the control unit and details of its mechanical design. There are now other types of fin stabilizers fitted in ships, but all depend on the forward movement of the ship, and tilting of their fins, as in the arrangement of the Denny-Brown stabilizers fitted in the *Oriana*†.

In September, 1950, Messrs. Vickers-Armstrong Ltd. at Barrow delivered a new passenger ship, the *Chusan*, to the P. & O. Company. She was a fine ship, but what really distinguished her from all others at that time were her Denny-Brown hydrofin stabilizers fitted to reduce rolling and to make life more comfortable for all on board. Such stabilizers had already been fitted to smaller vessels and to a number of warships for the British Admiralty, but the *Chusan* was the first large passenger ship in the world to fit them. This type is known as the 'activated fin' type of stabilizer and Denny-Brown, at that time, made the only ones of this sort which worked satisfactorily. The secret of their success lay in the control unit which was made by Messrs. Muirhead & Co. of Beckenham, utilizing two small gyroscopes which, through the ingenious use of hydraulic and

* *'Preliminary Calculations of the Sizes of Gyroscopes required to Stabilize a Ship* by Dr. P. Schilovsky, read to the Spring Meeting of the seventy-fourth session of the Institute of Naval Architects, April 6th, 1933.

† Plate 136.

135. The CHUSAN fitted with her Thornycroft funnel top.

electrical power, controlled the movement of the fins to counteract the forces of the waves which would otherwise roll the ship. These fins are something like semi-balanced rudders fitted horizontally instead of vertically, and are placed as near amidships (of the length of the vessel) as possible, because this is the place about which the ship pitches, and therefore will not cause any unnecessary additional force of the sea on the fins, which are fitted near the turn of the bilge: in other words, where the vertical sides meet the flat bottom of the ship.

When the fins are in their operating position, they project about twelve feet out from the hull (in the case of a large vessel), and are about eight feet long in a fore-and-aft direction. They are rectangular in shape and are pivoted about a centre-line approximately one-third of their width abaft the forward edge of the fins. In operation, as one fin hinges downwards, the one on the opposite side of the ship hinges upwards, providing an equal and opposite force. (The 'lift' of the fin is directly due to its area, its angle to the flow of the sea water, and its speed through the water.) This use of them can cause the ship to heel one way or the other when moving forward in still waters, and one can easily understand that, the faster she moves forward, the greater the roll effect that will be created by these fins (or horizontal rudders.)

It can be said, therefore, that the performance of stabilizers of the fin type depends on five major factors, namely:- a) the speed of the ship; b) displacement (that is, the weight) of the ship; c) the stability of the ship; d) the area and number of fins and, finally, e) the control unit.

When the vessel is in waves tending to roll her, the fins are operated to the dictates of the control unit which anticipates the wave magnitude and timing, so that the stabilizers cancel the forces so created by the waves and keep the vessel in equilibrium. This can only be done efficiently when the ship is moving at a speed approaching that for which the stabilizers have been designed but, if she is moving slowly or stopped, they become ineffective since their correcting force is no longer developed by movement through the sea.

The stabilizer fins are mounted on shafts which pass through watertight glands into the stabilizer compartment and, when not required, they are retracted by hydraulic power into recesses in the hull, while they can be put out through the same power by controls on the bridge. The fins are turned up or down by hydraulic rams operating on cranks mounted on the fin shafts, the movement being rapid, as they move from the 'up' to the 'down' position in about $2\frac{1}{2}$ seconds. This is necessary so that they can concentrate their force quickly and stop the roll of the ship as soon as it begins.

There are other details which are of interest, though they might not make interesting reading, but the foregoing remarks give some idea of the working of the activated-fin stabilizer. It does not mitigate in any way the effects of pitching or of yawing of a ship and, to some people, these can be distressing. Pitching is quicker—sometimes twice as quick as rolling and, if one is positioned far from the middle length of the vessel, the vertical movement can be appreciable and, in rough weather, violent. There can be a state of sea in which stabilizers are virtually ineffective, and that is the point when heaving (or bodily

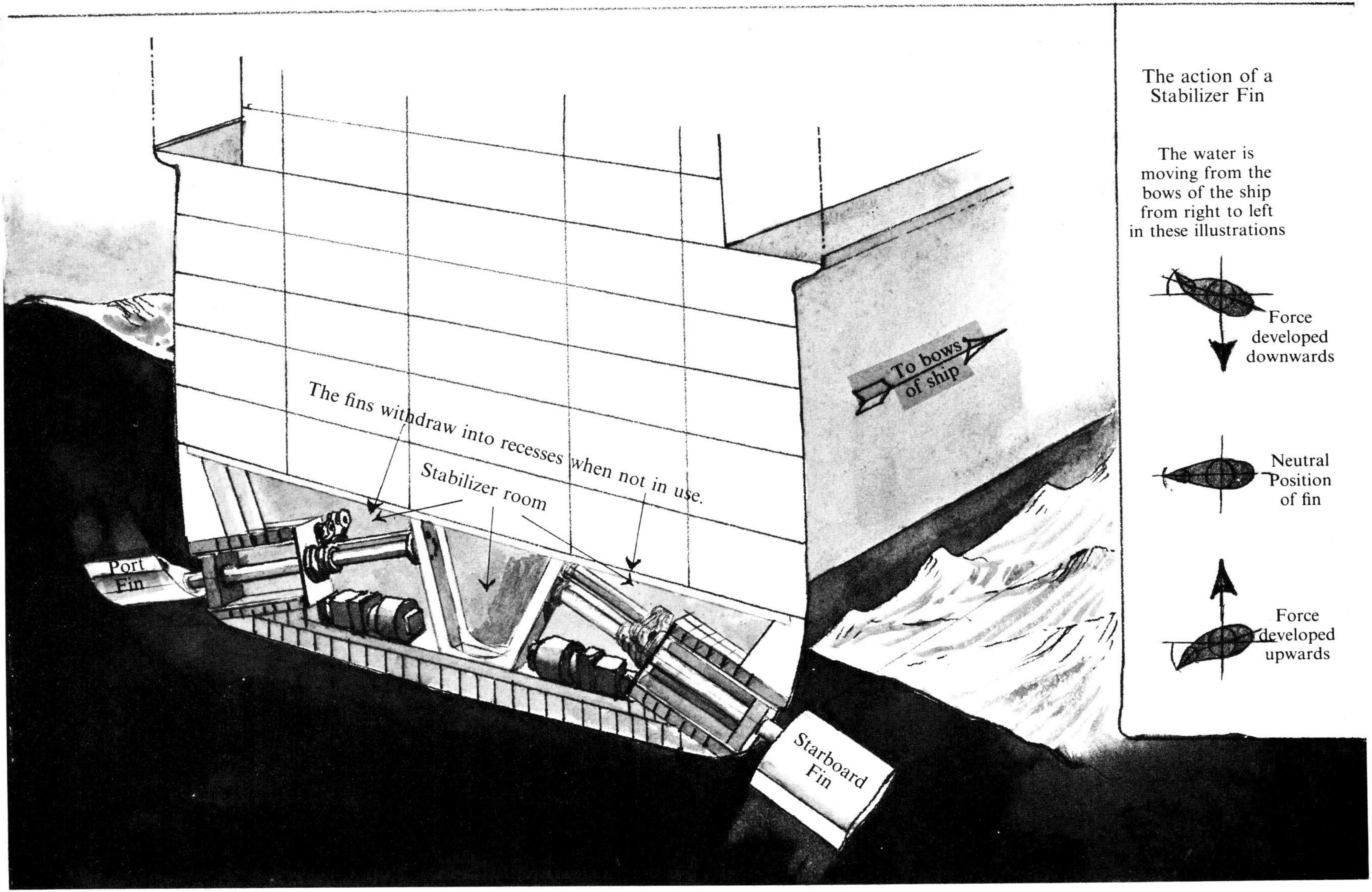

136. Section through the ship showing a stabilizer installation. (For purposes of clarity the fins have been drawn roughly twice their size in relation to the ship).

lifting and falling of the ship) in heavy swell conditions reduce the stabilizing effect of fins to sheer uselessness. I was once aboard the *Orcades* in these conditions in the Bay of Biscay when the stabilizers were working to their maximum output but we were still rolling through at least 18° on each side of the vertical plane. It is true to say that other vessels were hove to at the time, but the *Orcades* had to fulfill a date of arrival at Tilbury in December, 1958, and we just kept going in order to meet that schedule.

To return to the subject of the *Chusan*, I had the good fortune to be aboard her in 1950 when her stabilizers were being demonstrated but, unfortunately, the weather was beautifully calm with a perfectly smooth sea at the time, with the result that there was no hope of utilizing them in their normal role. It was therefore decided to show their effectiveness by using them in reverse, to *make* the ship roll and, to this end, they were started up and, whilst the vessel was moving ahead at 19 knots, the roll was built up very quickly to 25° included angle: that is, $12\frac{1}{2}$° each side of the vertical plane. When the stabilizers were stopped, the rolling stopped within a complete roll period. Two points struck me very forcibly at the time: first, the noise of things falling about within the ship and, secondly, how silly the *Chusan* must have appeared to those in other vessels within sight! However, although there had been no proof of the quality of the control gear in meeting its requirements to anticipate and cancel wave-induced rolling, the effectiveness of the fins as a force to move the ship was abundantly apparent for all on board to see.

In consequence of the effectiveness of the stabilizers in the *Chusan*, the *Orcades* was fitted with them soon after she had gone into service, while the following vessels, the *Oronsay* and *Orsova*, were also built with them.

Although the service speed of a ship is usually quoted in the press and in documents exchanged between builders and owners, as though it were to be constant, it is a variable for a passenger liner operating world-wide routes and calling at many ports. Obviously the speed of the ship is gauged for each leg of the route in order to ensure the right time of arrival at the next port of call and, for this reason, the speeds over the whole voyage vary between ports. The displacement of a ship of this type also varies. For instance, fuel oil in the new ship would be taken at certain ports and, on leaving them, in some cases the ship would be about 7,000 tons greater in displacement. Stores are replenished at other ports, fruits particular to certain countries would be taken on board at some local harbour and fresh water would be taken in at another. Cargo, too, is loaded or discharged at different ports on the route and, as a result of all these variables, the ship's displacement changes constantly and, in consequence of this, the stability of the ship changes too.

The area of the stabilizer fins was usually about eighty square feet per blade, but this was for ships of about 25,000 tons displacement and speeds of about 20-25 knots. These fins operate smaller displacements more easily at higher speeds against smaller figures of stability, but the latter are required by Safety Rules of the Marine Section of the Department of Trade and Industry (once known as the Board of Trade, and, also, the Ministry of Transport) to be not less than a specified minimum for any particular ship. The minimum amount of stability required for a passenger ship is assessed to suit her particular characteristics against possible amounts of flooding, both symmetrical and asymmetrical, which it is assumed (by the Rules) could take place in the event of an accident.

The power needed for the working of the stabilizers is that required to move the fins from one extreme of movement to the other. This operation is done very quickly to enable the fins to produce a correcting force immediately and so counter the build up of energy created by waves tending to roll the ship.

Because there is always a big variation in the magnitude of the forces affecting stabilization of a ship, and also because we knew that the size, speed, and stability of the new vessel were approaching a point where a step would have to be made from one set of stabilizers to two sets, we decided to investigate the problem in some depth.

A stabilizer fin will turn up and down about 10,000 times a day when in operation and, if a ship is only dry-docked once a year, the fins will have moved up and down over one million times between servicings, even if the stabilizers are employed for only one third of the year. This hammering of the steel surfaces supporting the fin shafts causes startling wear to take place and the consequent maintenance on this and other work connected with the stabilizer installations is costly. The Company was very reluctant to take the step of fitting two sets of stabilizers on the ship, instead of one, for a number of reasons.

At that time, although we knew that at least two passengers liners in the course of construction were each being fitted with two sets, we knew also that to do the same would cause large increases in cost in several ways, apart from the approximate doubling in maintenance charges, viz:—

a) The cost of two sets of stabilizers instead of one. This was estimated to be in excess of £100,000.
b) A considerable loss of earnings in the space lost in the ship, estimated to be about 1,500 cubic feet.
c) The cost of carrying about 150 tons of extra weight around the oceans for the life of the ship, estimated to be not less than £60,000, assuming a life of over 21 years.

It is true that two sets of stabilizers for the ship would have cost less than twice the cost of one set of larger ones, but this is taken into account in the foregoing figures.

One other objection to the use of two sets is that, in order to fit them, they must be some distance away from each other in their fore-and-aft positions on the hull. This means that, generally, they would be fitted away from the centre of the length of the vessel, which is approximately the 'fulcrum' position about which she pitches.

The pitching period of a ship is shorter than that of rolling, and is often twice the speed of the roll. Consequently, the linear velocities reached in the constant up and down acceleration of the fins would cause a not inconsiderable amount of additional loading on them and this, in turn, could cause cavitation* on their surfaces, if this was not already present, and the wear and tear on the gear would be greater than in the case of stabilizers fitted amidships.

The stabilizer manufacturers had already told us the size of the largest fins which they were prepared to make, so we then drew three diagrams† showing the estimated displacement on arrival and departure, the speeds between each of the ports on the itinerary, and the stability (G.M.) on arrival and departure from these ports. These

* See Glossary.

† See Appendix 3.

were compared with similar diagrams for one of the existing ships of the fleet, the *Oronsay*, when she sailed from London to Sydney and across the Pacific to San Francisco, for we knew that this was a good sea-keeping vessel and that her stabilizers were satisfactory.

It appeared to us to be promising a successful outcome in that an adverse factor, at one time, was often offset by a factor helping to reduce the fin effort simultaneously. These three diagrams were given to the stabilizer manufacturers for analysis and, after much discussion, the largest size of fins they could make, and the gear to suit them, were fitted in the *Oriana*. These stabilizers have proved to be satisfactory after many years of service.

Of the three diagrams, that showing the estimated displacement on arrival and departure was also interesting to us because it illustrated clearly the saving in fuel and cost which could be made by fitting the main machinery amidships, enabling the ship's displacement to be reduced as fuel and stores were consumed. This caused the average displacement of the vessel to be 88.8% of that fully loaded, with a saving of over 4,000 tons in weight. This subject has been discussed fully under *Primary Considerations*.

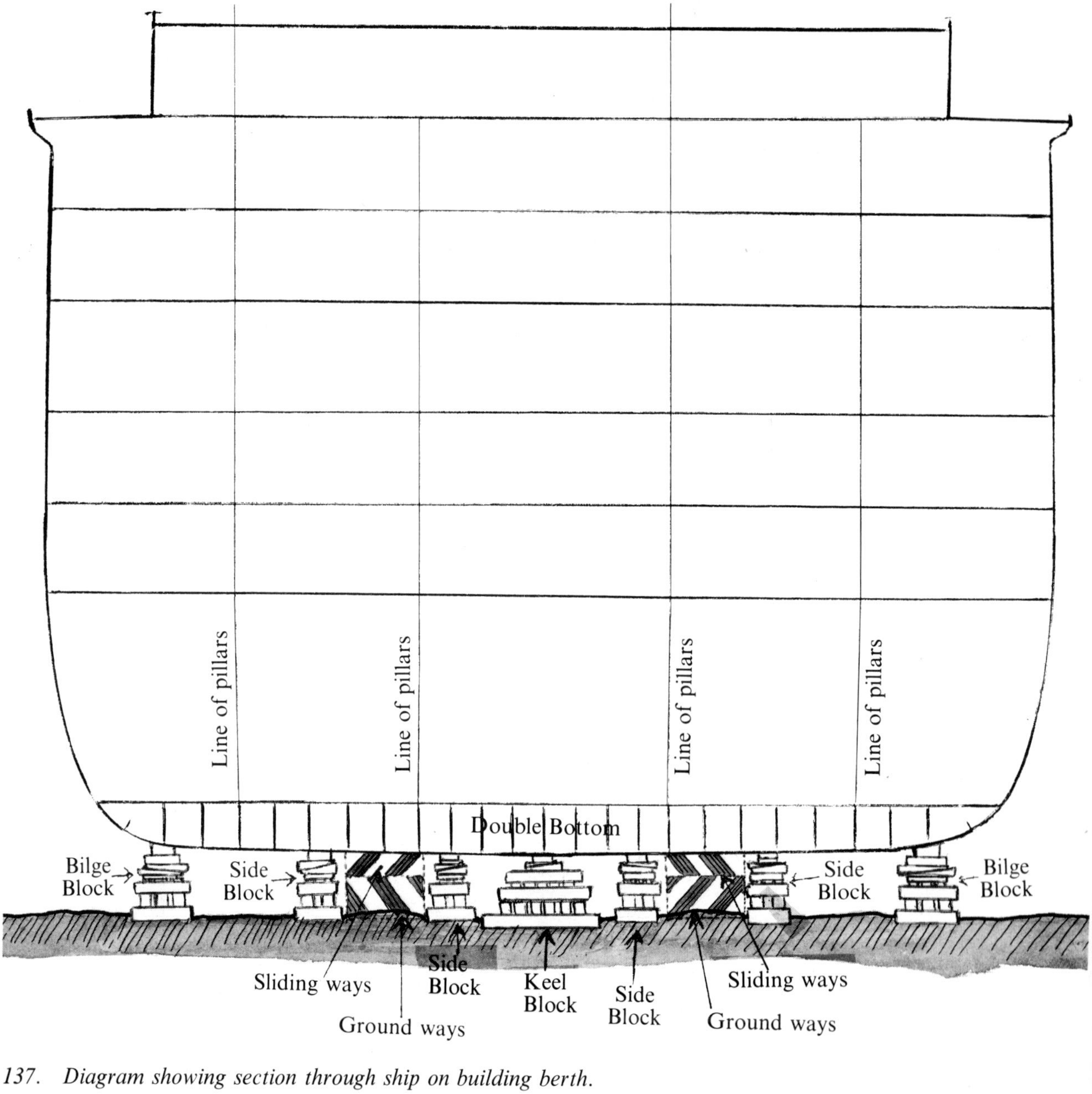

137. Diagram showing section through ship on building berth.

XVI. THE LAUNCH

SOME LARGE SHIPS are built in dry docks which, at the appointed times, are flooded with sea water to bring them into their natural element in a most gentle and undramatic way. This manner of launching is not the usual method, and most ships are launched in the more traditional, exciting and picturesque way: an occasion witnessed by thousands of people and never to be forgotten by most of them because, although many have witnessed launches previously, the next launch is always exciting, breathtaking and different from the previous one. The man who has become blasé about seeing launches is a peculiar and dull fellow or is not yet born. The poet Longfellow was moved to write a poem '*The Building of the Ship*' in which he wrote:—

'And see! She stirs!
She starts,—she moves,—she seems to feel
The thrill of life along her keel,
And, spurning with her foot the ground,
With one exulting, joyous bound,
*She leaps into the Ocean's arms!'**

The most critical period in the building time of a ship is that when she is launched for, when she starts to move down the launchways, she is going through a crisis, never to be repeated, since there is no going back once she has started to move. The *Oriana* was launched in this traditional manner.

The ship is built on a berth sloping gently towards the water into which she will be launched, about six feet above the earth of the berth

* Longfellow was referring to the great sailing ship *Great Republic* in this poem.

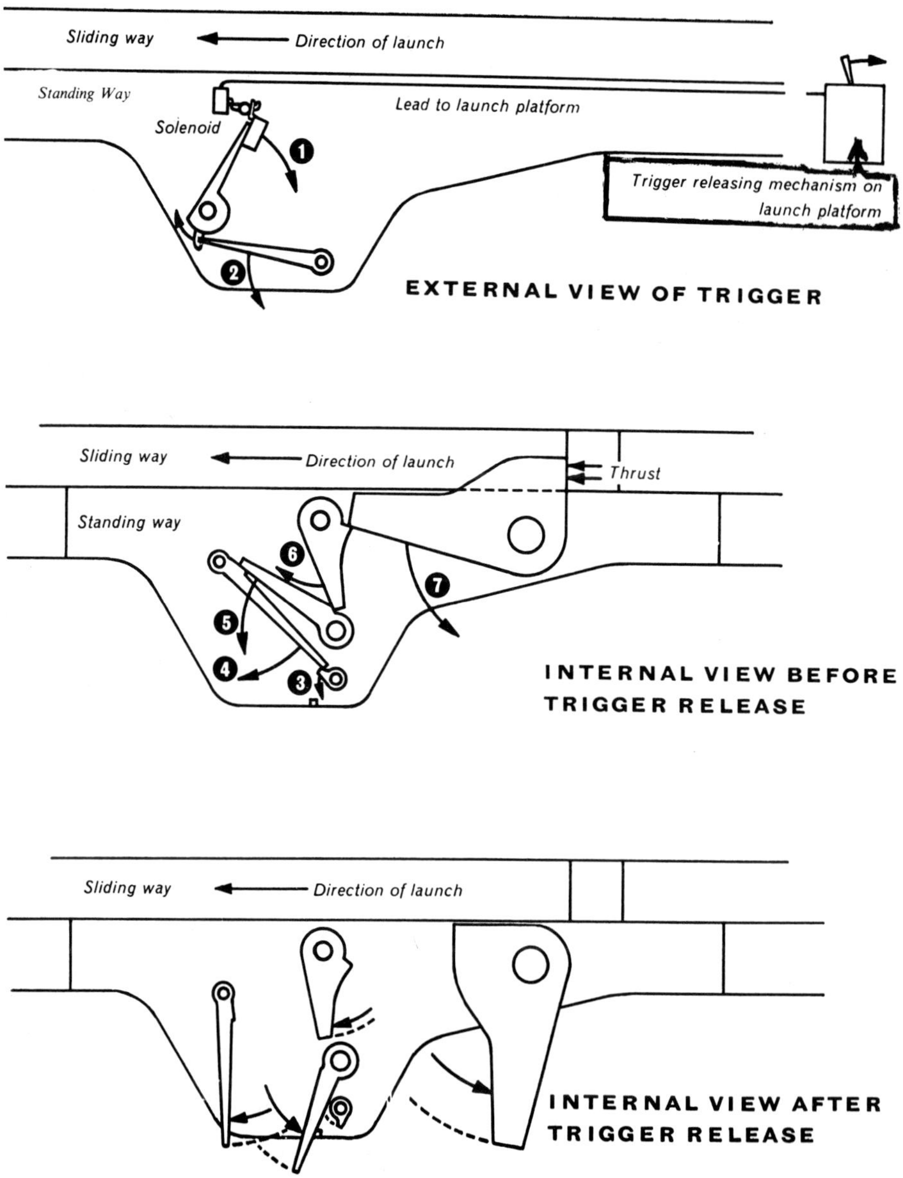

138. *The mechanism of a launch trigger. On release, the levers move in the order of the numbering shown.*

as near as practicable to the water, and is supported by packing of timber and wood shores added as the building progresses.* Eventually, as the time approaches for the launch, the fixed or standing launchways are fitted under the ship followed by the sliding ways with the grease required to lubricate their bearing surfaces.† During this process the launch triggers are fitted,** which are used first to hold and later to release the ship at the time of launching, each taking a load of 187 tons in the case of the *Oriana*, and are released simultaneously by solenoids electrically switched by the lady launching the vessel, in spite of the fact that all she thinks she is doing is to break a champagne bottle!

Until a short time before launching, the hull was held by the existing packing and shores, but these were reduced gradually in number over a period of days as the launch day approached, in order to allow the ship to settle into the launch cradle. On the night before the launch all but a few pieces of essential timbers were removed and nearly all the weight of the ship—15,250 tons—was on the launchways. The triggers are incapable of being accidently or maliciously released before the launch takes place, because they are fitted with locks, and are unlocked just before the launch by responsible personnel, using special keys. A short time before the launch, the last pieces of timber are knocked away, and the ship is then held entirely by the launching triggers.

Meanwhile, another activity takes place over the preceding weeks—the arranging and fitting of hundreds of tons of drag chains with their wires and connections, for a ship is launched at a speed which will take her quickly out into the water and past a rather critical point during the time of the operation. The momentum gathered by the great mass of the ship during the launch has then to be taken off the vessel and in Vickers', as in many other shipyards, this is done by large bundles of chain, called 'drags', which are connected by strong wires to points on the ship's side in such a way as to ensure that the loads of each pair of drags come into action at the same moment and in a progressive way, so as to bring the ship to a stop gradually and without shock. The drag wires are held on to the ship by quick-release connections which can be released as and when required by workmen

* Plate 137.
† Plate 137.
** Plate 138.

on the ship. For the launch of the *Oriana*, there were eight pairs of drags, varying in weight between 140 tons per pair to 110 tons per pair, totalling 1,000 tons of chain in all, and they acted at about twenty feet intervals as the ship progressed down the launchways into the Walney Channel.

A precaution is taken to ensure that the ship can still be launched if she fails to move when the triggers holding her are released by the lady operating the launch lever or switch. Two powerful hydraulic rams are fitted, one at the landward end of each of the two standing launchways, and these bear against the ends of the sliding launchways. Rams are not usually employed but are installed as a precaution against possible sticking of the sliding launchways caused by—say—very cold weather hardening the launching grease or, alternatively, the grease being softened by very hot weather and causing it to be squeezed out by the weight of the ship on the 'ways.

If a ship were launched bow first there would be a serious risk of damage to the rudder and propeller(s) when the ends of the sliding launchways dipped off the ends of the groundways as the ship became water-borne. To obviate this possibility, ships are launched stern first. Plate 147 shows a ship during launching and in a position where the most critical forces begin to assert themselves. As can be seen, buoyancy 'B', increases as the ship slides further into the water and reduces the weight of the ship upon the launchways. As the launch proceeds, the centre of gravity of the ship's weight, 'W', passes the ends of the standing 'ways and creates a moment 'W $\times$ a' tending to tip the ship about them. This is resisted by the buoyancy 'B' pushing upwards, creating moment 'B $\times$ b'. If the ship tipped about the 'way ends, failure of the ship's structure or failure of the 'way ends and their supports, or both, would occur. In any case it would be disastrous and lead to serious structural damage and, probably, to the loss of the vessel. As she moves further down the 'ways, buoyancy increases until the moment 'B $\times$ c' becomes greater than the weight moment 'W $\times$ d' and the stern of the vessel lifts about the fore-poppet, the foremost section of the sliding 'ways or launch cradle*. This item has a special function during the stage in the launch after the stern begins to lift about the fore end of the sliding 'ways. If the

* Plate 142.

139. *ORIANA near Sydney bridge.*

140. *The ORIANA and the Golden Gate bridge at the entrance to San Francisco.*

fore-poppet were built of hard and inflexible material, it would be forced into the surfaces of the standing ways* and slow the launch or, perhaps stop the ship. It is therefore built so that the 'soft packing,' as it is called, in the construction can be squeezed and crushed to allow the high pressures to be dispersed along the length of contact between the launchways. When the fore-poppet reaches the end of the fixed 'ways the ship is nearly water-borne, but the ship's bows are not yet clear of the way-ends. A check must be made during pre-launch calculations to ensure that the ship's bows do not strike the ends of the 'ways as the bows dip on leaving them. This dip of the bows as the ship leaves the ends of the standing launchways is a graceful movement and could be regarded as a gentle curtsy to the lady who launched her. The launch of the *Oriana* took place on a beautiful sunny day, 3 November, 1959, and she was christened by Her Royal Highness, Princess Alexandra.

During the last war, at the Osaka Shosen Kaisha shipyard in Japan, a small freighter was to be launched and a large number of V.I.P.s were invited. The whole work-force of the yard, even including the British and American prisoners-of-war working there, were assembled to witness the event, while a gang of coolies stood ready to rush the keel plates of the next ship on to the launchways as cameramen stood ready to record this minor Japanese attempt to impress the assembled company that they were emulating the mass-production war-time methods of the Kaiser shipyards at Bethlehem, Pa. The Buddhist priest blessed the ship. Speeches were made and the moment to move arrived, but . . . . she stuck fast! Despite the most frenzied efforts, nothing would make her budge! It was most embarassing and the V.I.P.s departed in some bewilderment: the ship finally being eased down the 'ways a couple of weeks later—rather stealthily!

Accidents sometimes take place at the time of launching. There was an occasion on the Clyde many years ago when a ship turned over on her side as she entered the water and dozens of men were left struggling in the river. During a launch from a small shipyard at Wivenhoe in September, 1976, some of the launchways were smashed and splintered, the ship ending up on that day lying slightly to one side

* Plate 143.

of the line of 'ways, and on the concrete floor of the building berth. Fortunately she was of rather heavy construction, perhaps the sort of ship which is designed to 'take the ground' when lying at her berth. Quite a lot of small ships in rivers like the Colne at Colchester Hythe quay, and elsewhere, are aground at low water, whilst taking or discharging cargo, and the bottoms of such ships are built to suit such treatment. This ship, of about 200 feet in length, was not damaged seriously and lay on her berth until means of completing the launch were devised. The reason for telling this story is to describe the method of completing that particular launch, which was unique in my experience. The river Colne, into which the ship was to be launched, is very narrow and very shallow at low tide, but a large floating crane was brought up the river and, after a lifting strop was fitted around the stern of the ship, the crane, at high tide, lifted up the after end of the ship and drew her down into the river.

Some vessels, usually relatively small ones, are launched sideways. When this is done, the ship is built in a position close to the water's edge. When ready for launching the numerous launchways are fitted under the ship, and, on release, she slides quickly down the 'ways and almost falls into the water off the ends of the 'ways. Such launches are both exciting and spectacular, but they look hazardous to the uninformed spectator although, in fact, the wall of water built up by the side of the ship as she quickly slides down into her element, acts as a huge cushion to quell her speed and prevent any possibility of her turning over. I believe ships are launched sideways to suit the narrow waters where they are built, or, possibly, to suit the restricted shape of the shipyard. Large ships have been launched sideways but there is a danger that, when a ship is launched in that way, one end could move away faster than the other and cause twisting and jamming of the sliding ways against the fixed launchways and cause serious difficulties. Brunel's famous ship *Great Eastern* was built near the edge of the river Thames and was launched sideways. There were difficulties at the time of the launch and the ship finally took about three months to reach the waters of the river Thames. This launch is described more fully in '*Origins*'.

An expedient, sometimes used for various reasons, is that of

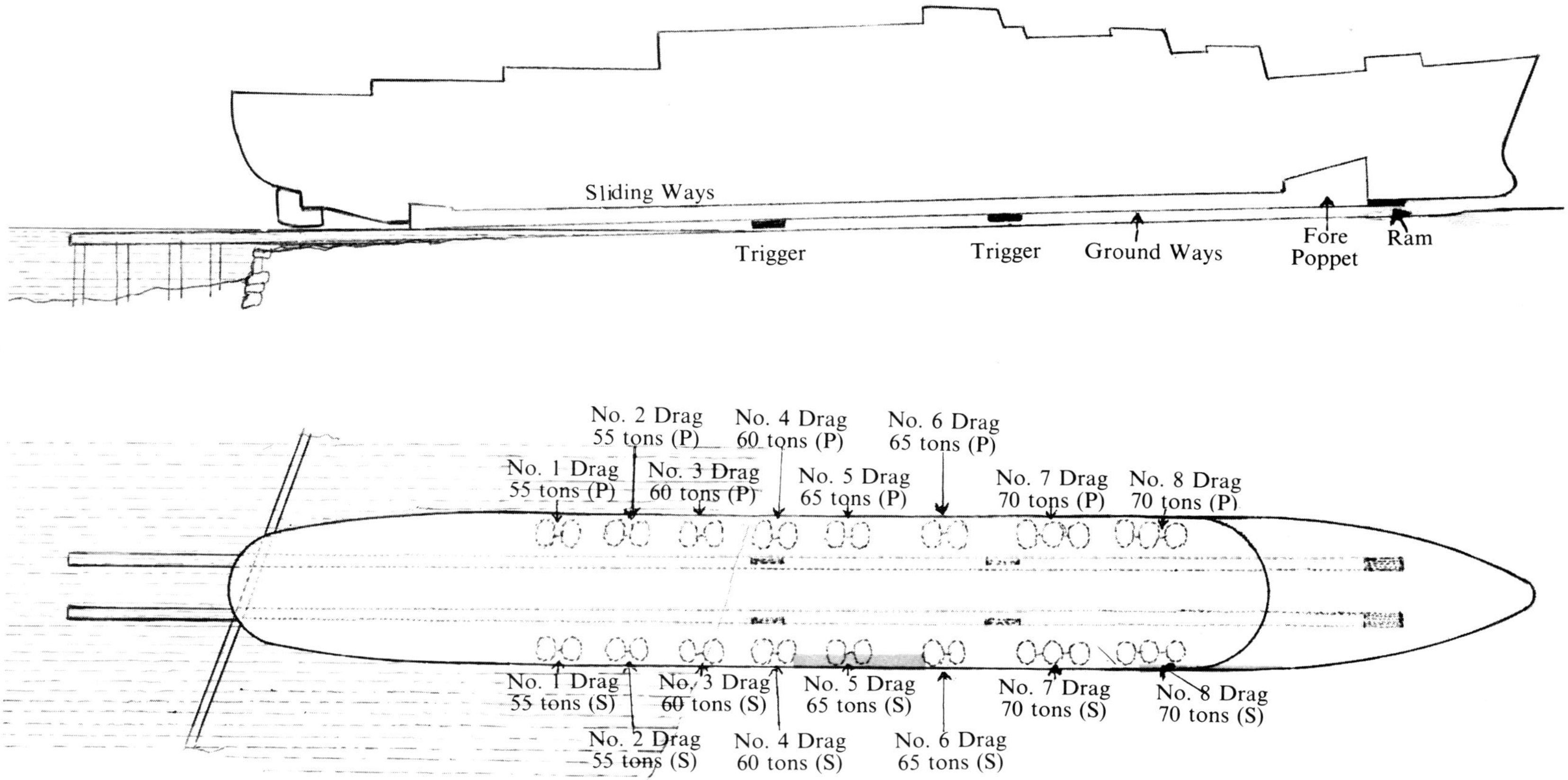

141. Diagram of a ship on her launchways, with drag chains, triggers and rams.

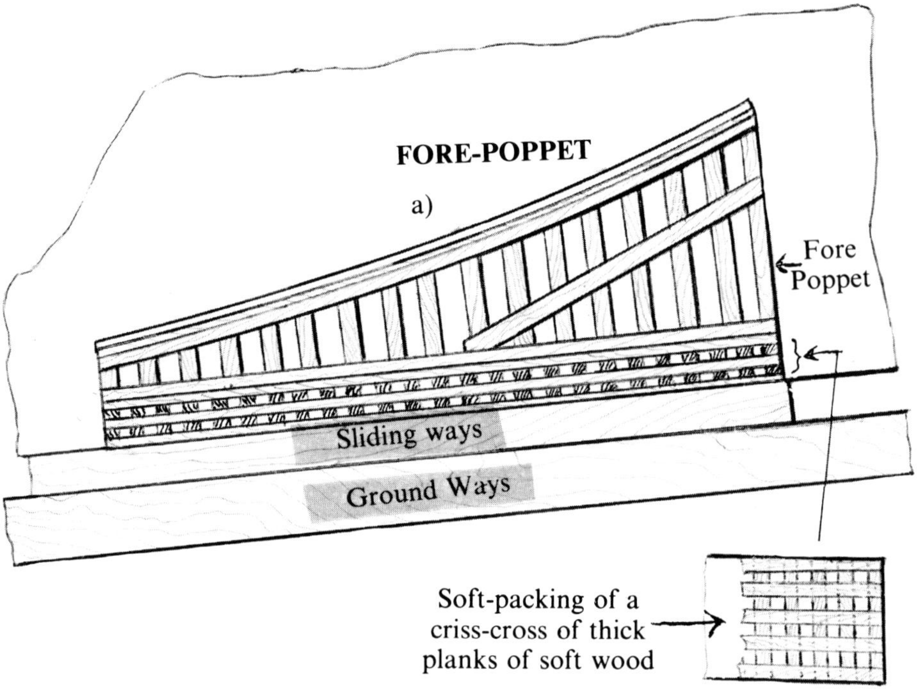

142. The construction of the fore poppet. (a)

building a ship in sections, two, three or more in number, and joining the parts together by riveting or welding in a graving dock, often located far away from the building site. Sometimes this is done to lengthen an existing ship by inserting a new section in the parallel body of the existing hull. Temporary or conveniently situated watertight bulkheads are built in the part or parts of the ship and these are then launched into the water and towed to the chosen graving dock.

This expedient is also used to build a ship too big for the shipyard to build in one piece and, occasionally, to suit the shipyard's method of construction, where—say—the engine room is built in the aftermost section of the ship and is completely fitted out with engine(s),

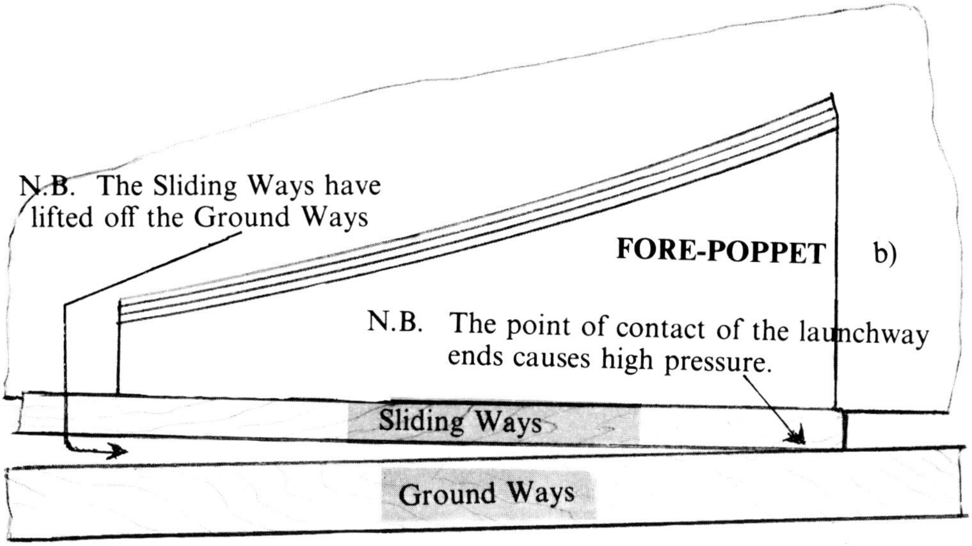

143. Position of fore poppet on ground ways when stern starts to lift. N.B. In this illustration (b), an assumption is made that the fore poppet is rigid and unyielding.

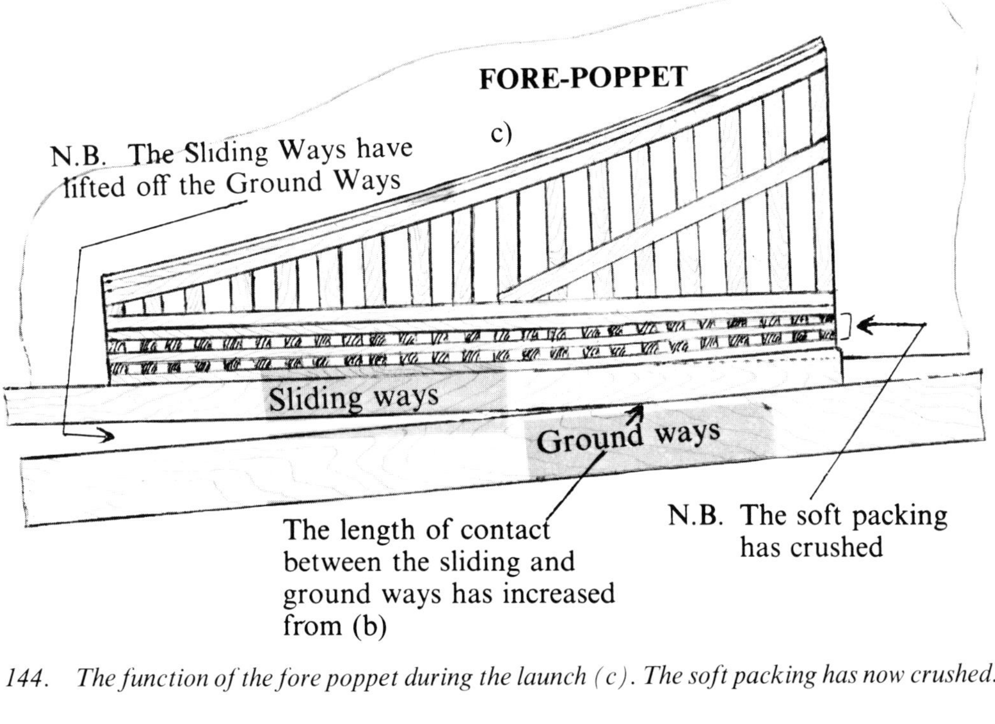

144. The function of the fore poppet during the launch (c). The soft packing has now crushed.

145. Princess Alexandra launching the ORIANA.

propeller(s), piping and systems before being jointed to the section forward of the engine room, which may have been built elsewhere in the yard.*

The methods described have variations of detail in many parts of the world. For instance, the Japanese have launched a ship using ball-bearings instead of the traditional grease to slide a ship into the water. The reason for doing this is not clear to me but, no doubt, there was one! Variations of this sort will take place as time passes but, as has been remarked elsewhere, they are only changes and, sometimes, improvements brought about by availability of new materials or dearth of traditional materials, and the necessity to find substitutes, either of materials or methods.

* On a much smaller scale, triple-screw tank landing craft, of some 330 tons d.w., were shipped out to Egypt in the last war in four sections on the decks of freighters, and joined together out there.

146. The launch is in progress and the drag chains begin to act.

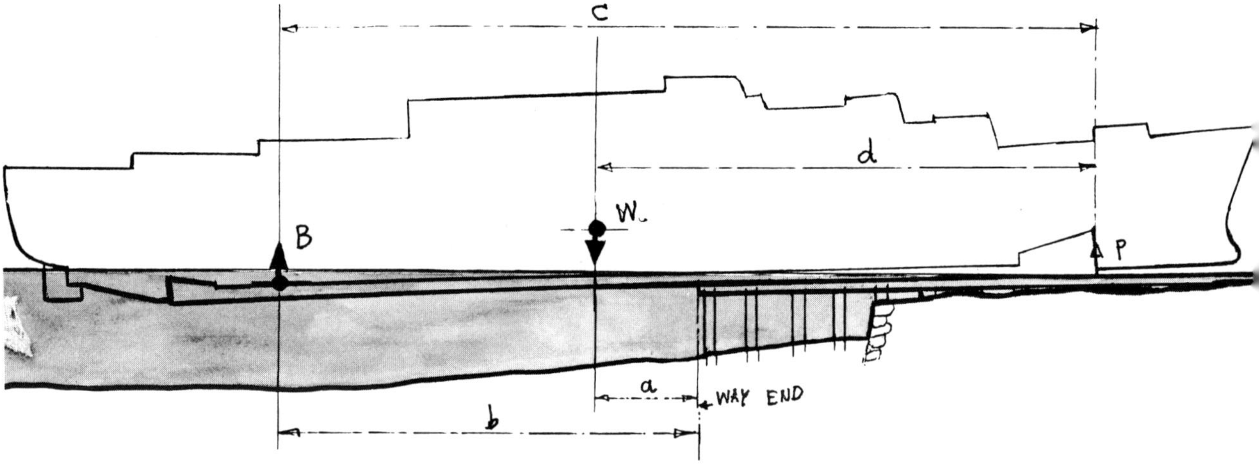

147. *Diagram of a launch in progress, demonstrating the text on pp.306/7.*

XVII. SUPERSTRUCTURE, FUNNEL AND VENT STACK

THE GREATER SPEED of the new ship would create her own winds over the open decks in addition to the natural ones, and a new need arose; to investigate wind behaviour over the deck areas to be used by passengers for deck games and sitting in deck chairs watching the games, reading, watching the sea, or just sleeping in the open air. (Passengers do this for some unexplained reason). We had worked with a team led by Mr. C. H. Burge at the National Physical Laboratory at Teddington for a number of months on the design of ships' funnels for the Orient Fleet, and a very good relationship had been established with them in this matter. The work on the *Oriana* was a continuance of this good team spirit, but what had to be done was now much more extensive and exacting.

The wind tunnel used for the experiments was one which had been used for aeroplane models but, being no longer used for that purpose, was easily adapted for the use of ships' models. The words 'wind tunnel' nearly describe what it is. A large endless duct about six feet in diameter is built of wood and in plan form is the shape of a very large but narrow letter 'O'. A large propeller, nearly the diameter of the tunnel and driven by a variable speed electric motor, is fitted towards one end of one of the straight sides of the tunnel and ahead of the position where models are to be mounted for experimental purposes. In order to straighten the flow of air from the propeller (air leaves the blades of the propeller in a turbulent helical flow) a grid, or grille, of wooden blades fitted at right angles to one another and of streamlined section, is attached across the tunnel downstream of the propeller and upstream of the model position. Access doors are fitted at the point where models are to be hung in the tunnel, and windows for observation purposes are fitted in suitable positions. When the experiments are taking place the tunnel is closed and the air stream from the propeller circulates around the complete 'O' of the tunnel whilst the performance of white plumes of smoke from the funnels of the models can be observed. The air speed of wind over the model, the attitude of the model in respect to the direction of the wind, and the speed of the emission of smoke from the funnel can be adjusted so as to simulate all conditions in relation to the full size ship, her speed, wind speed, and velocity and heat of smoke from the funnel top.

The *Oriana* was to be over 800 feet long and 100 feet in overall width, which meant that one of the models of the scale of $\frac{1}{8}$th inch = 1 foot would be over 8 feet long and 1 foot wide. This model was to be used for tests of the funnel smoke and for the overall observation of the boundary of turbulence over the ship.

This size of model could be manipulated across the wind tunnel as required for purposes of simulation of the effects of winds on the beam or from any other direction. For the purpose of conducting experiments simulating the behaviour of wind over games decks of the ship, larger models were required and these were made to the scale of $\frac{1}{4}$ inch = 1 foot. For this, the model was made in two parts, each about 8 feet long by 2 feet broad. The games decks of these models were divided up into squared areas, by the drawing on them of lines suitably spaced, and air was blown over the deck at speeds and in directions as required. Very small electrical instruments were used to measure wind velocities at each intersection of the squares drawn on the decks, and these measurements were plotted on drawings of the various games decks to record the wind velocities expressed as percentages of the wind velocity over the ship. If unsatisfactory conditions were shown as a result of the experiments, steps were taken to improve the conditions by changing superstructure shapes where possible.

As a result, we were able to ensure tolerable conditions for passengers in many deck areas of the ship. Plate 149 is a typical

148. Model in a wind tunnel, with wind right ahead.

drawing of wind velocities drawn for the aftermost games deck in the *Oriana*.

The design of the funnels of ships has already been touched upon and the design of the funnel for the new vessel followed exactly the same pattern of development. The first step to be taken was the establishment of the height of the boundary of turbulent air at the position of the funnel. Wind from forward of a ship strikes the main hull and is forced upwards over the bows following a rising curve as it moves aft. The forward ends of superstructures and bridges cause further upwards deflection of the stream of free air until it clears all obstructions and starts to fall again as it moves towards the stern. This air movement can be traced by using artificially created 'smoke' from fixed or portable nozzles. When the height of the turbulent air, which moves along with the ship, is known, a model funnel, of the shape required to enclose the various items to be built into it, is fitted to the ship's model. This model funnel is made a little higher than is required to reach the boundary of turbulent air and a tube is put through it of the diameter (to scale) of the inner funnel of the ship.

Artificial smoke is pushed upwards at the correct speed through the tube in the model funnel and observations are then made. Various

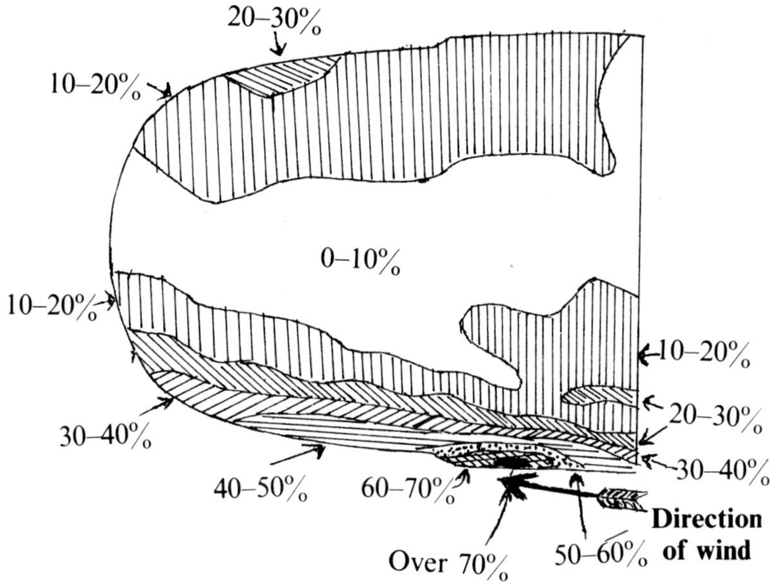

149. Diagram of the after games deck of the ORIANA, showing the velocities of the wind over the deck as percentages of the wind over the ship.

shapes of funnel tops are tried until satisfactory results likely to suit the shipowner are found and also to ensure that soots from the funnel will be carried away from the ship under most conceivable wind conditions to be met in service.

The steaming conditions of the new ship caused new approaches in thought with regard to ventilation of the machinery spaces, particularly the main engine room. The steam temperature was to be 950 deg. F. delivered at an initial pressure of 700 lb. per sq. in., and could create appalling conditions for those working in the engine room unless extremely good ventilation arrangements were made. In ships built for the Company prior to the *Oriana*, the ventilation air had been driven into the engine room by fans through ducts led to suitable positions near the places where engine room personnel were working. The exhaust air from the engine room had then risen up the large trunk leading vertically upwards to escape through the adjacent engine room skylights or the open flaps abaft them.

In the *Oriana*, a large ventilation stack was built over the top of the engine room and this was carried high so as to ensure that the hot air coming from this space was also exhausted into the free stream of air passing over the ship. This vast stack had the look of a second funnel and is today sometimes mistaken for one. Unless this arrangement for the ventilation of the engine room had been made there was a possibility of the hot exhaust ventilation air being drawn into supply fans and forced back into the engine room, whilst there was also the possibility of the hot engine room air making unpleasant conditions for passengers on the open decks.

150. The promenade deck of the Holland Amerika liner NIEUW AMSTERDAM.

XVIII. THE STEERING COMMITTEE

As has been shown in Chapter VII, the family concern running the Orient Steam Navigation Company had an ancestry of men and women of good education and taste and, in the latter years of the 19th Century, the quality of design of the interiors of their ships showed this influence. The Company engaged a relative of the family, an Architect, who had been trained for work on buildings on land and who was later to design works of quality and distinction. He was J. J. Stevenson, F.R.I.B.A., and he designed and was responsible for the decoration of the main public rooms of the Orient Company's steam ship *Orient*, which was delivered to the Company from the builders in 1879. His work must have been considered to be good by the directors because he was retained by them to do the work on the interior decorations of other of their ships, notably the *Austral* (1881), *Ormuz* (1886) and the *Ophir* (1891).

The Orient Line Management had by then decided that they could no longer depend on the rather unimaginative and predictably 'ordinary' interiors of the shipyards of that time and, in due course, another architect was appointed to follow Stevenson in the decoration of Orient Ship interiors. He was Andrew N. Prentice, who was retained by the Company until the completion of the *Orontes* in 1929.

This arrangement of a firm of shipowners employing its own selected Architects to be responsible for the decorative design of the interiors of their ships was at that time unusual, and was pioneering a new conception in this field. The usual method of carrying out the decoration of the interior accommodation of passenger ships was for the shipbuilder to obtain from one or more of the several large Furnishing and Decorating Companies of the period complete schemes of decoration of the public rooms and other spaces of the new ship. These schemes were submitted in the form of artists' highly imaginative coloured perspective drawings and, from them, the shipowner would select those that he considered most acceptable. Having seen some of these schemes, I think it is not unfair to say that the paintings bore little likeness to the finished rooms because they all looked larger and, particularly, much higher than they were to be in reality.

The really difficult part of the work of an architect working on decorating spaces in a ship is to design within the limitations imposed on him by her construction. The low deck height is very restricted as compared with the height provided in large rooms in buildings ashore. There are other difficulties which the good Architect will accept. Pillars, girders, piping, ventilation trunks, brackets, and a multitude of other excrescences cause problems. Sometimes, with the assistance of the Naval Architect and the Shipbuilder, some of these problems can be reduced or removed, but the good Architect working on the décor of ships can adjust to the conditions and work within the rules of shipbuilding requirements and practice.

Probably the greatest difficulty which must be overcome is that caused by the positioning of pillars within a ship. An Architect always wishes to have his decorative design follow a rhythmic pattern of spacing of bays, windows, pillars, lighting features, ceiling panels, etc. As often happens when, say, a dining room is to be built on a lower deck, there are pillars already arranged or positioned to give support to the structures above it and there is every likelihood that these pillars are not where the Architect would like them to be. This is the point where 'give and take' on the part of all concerned must take place. Often the Architect cannot or will not accept that a ship is a structure that moves in every conceivable way when she is at sea and that there is a powerful machinery installation which is sending out pulsations through shafting and screw-propellers to cause vibrations of the hull structure. If a pillar is moved at a position low in the ship and associated pillars above and below cannot be moved to fall into

151. The dining saloon of the OPHIR, designed by J. J. Stevenson.

vertical line with it, a 'spring' has been introduced—and a most effective one too! Passengers should not be subjected to the very unpleasant physical discomfort caused by vibration and possibly, also, to the structural disintegration which usually follows continual vibration in service.

Another difficulty which the Architect has to face lies in the fact that there is little that is straight or which runs at right angles to another plane in a ship. The decks often follow curves of sheer and camber: the ship sides are curved horizontally and often lean outwards or inwards to follow the 'tumble-home' or flare of the hull, and there are frames, beams, girders, pipes, and a multitude of other obstructions which are always fighting against the desires of the interior decorator. The best interior decorators for ships are those who adopt the attitude of 'if you cannot beat them, join them'. One such man, who was an outstanding Architect in the decoration of ships' interiors, was the late Brian O'Rorke, R.A., R.D.I., M.A., F.R.I.B.A. He had already designed interiors for two ships of the Orient Line when I first met him and he had learned much about the requirements of building decoration on to and into ships' structures. He understood what was structurally necessary and, on reflection, although we had differences of views and opinions during our association whilst the building of units for the Orient Line took place between 1945 and 1960, we always reached suitable compromises and understandings, and I am convinced that he was the most excellent and competent interior decorator I have had the pleasure and honour to know. The materials he used for his decorations were usually of a simple and well-tried nature and, often, he also used much less expensive materials than was usual with other decorators employed by the Company. Some of the latter never hesitated to use expensive and often quite unsuitable materials or fittings when cheaper and more lasting materials were available. There could be a reason for the latter course but this will not be discussed, since it was associated with the form of contract made with the decorator.

The employment of Architects to design the décor of the interiors of passenger ships had become fairly common-place by the end of 1930, but the form of this decoration had become monotonously similar, one ship with another, and often followed the fashion of hotel rooms ashore, having artificial fire-places, garish colour schemes and lighting, and sumptuousness of expensive materials but without much taste.

Colin Skelton Anderson became a director of Anderson, Green and Company in 1930 and was twenty-six years of age at that time. His artistic sense was such as to convince him that changes should be made in the design of Orient Ships yet to be built. This conviction, together with the desire of all young people to kick against 'the Establishment', caused him to take action of the right kind—he talked both 'to' and 'at' the other Directors. It is true that he was fortunate in that the Orient Company was a family business and that he was a son of the family. For these reasons he could speak effectively in high places without any of the trepidation that was often felt by those employed at that time in lesser positions in a firm. This is difficult to believe in these days when shop-stewards are so often able to tell their employer how (they think!) he should run his business.

Nevertheless, the Orient Company was fortunate that the Senior members of the Board of Directors were of the mind to listen to him—and to agree. They gave him the full responsibility to find a suitable and sympathetically-minded lay Architect and to guide him in the designing and supervision of the fitting out of the interior spaces of a new passenger ship. Not only was this work to be contemporary in every possible way, but it was to set new trends in interior design. The Architect was also to be made responsible for the design of furniture and fittings, including lighting, in the first and tourist class cabins. The ship's appearance was also to be considered and improved wherever possible. This decision, on the part of the Orient Company Board of Directors, to place such responsibility on the shoulders of a young and untried man, one who was critical of the existing ships and intended to radically change set patterns, was a monumental one. The ship, which was to cost over a million pounds sterling in 1935, was to be the *Orion*, and represented a big venture for a shipping Company to undertake. That the decision was made is to the credit of all concerned.

Colin Anderson set out to find his Architect. It was not an easy task. He did not want one who was too established and set in his ways, since a man of that kind would be unmanageable. He wanted one who was young enough to adapt to a new environment, that of shipyard requirements and practices—and he was fortunate or, perhaps, very discerning, because he found Brian O'Rorke, a young man from New Zealand, but who was working in England.

Brian O'Rorke subsequently had a distinguished career, being responsible for very fine architecture both ashore and afloat. When he came to the Orient Company for the first time, he knew nothing of passenger ship interior design and therefore had a completely fresh and open mind on the subject. For some men this might have been a disaster, but for O'Rorke it was a challenge to be accepted and met. He adapted himself and was responsible for the successful interior designs of the public rooms and spaces and the passenger cabins of the *Orion* under the personal guidance of Colin Anderson. When the ship was handed over to her owners by the builders, Messrs. Vickers Ltd., in 1935 she caused a furore in the press and architectural and shipping papers, because she was entirely different in outward appearance from her predecessors in the Orient Line—or elsewhere—and the interiors were a complete contrast to those of contemporary passenger ships. She was, in short, an outstanding ship. She had a long, successful and eventful career as a passenger liner and as a troop-carrier for the British Government during the last war, and when she was sold for breaking-up in 1963 it was said of her:- '*She will be remembered affectionately, by all those who have known her. Not, though, as a relic of the past, but as a pace-setter of the modern age. She is an old lady now, but can still hold her head high in today's chic circles—which is more than can be said for many of her contemporaries.*'

The success of the team work of Colin Anderson and Brian O'Rorke—although 'partnership' would be a better description—brought about a repetition of the arrangement for subsequent ships built for the Orient Line until, after the building of *Orcades* in 1937, the second World War put a stop to passenger ship-building: losses had to be endured and, amongst them, four large ships of the Orient Line.

After the war the Company again started to design ships to replace their losses. A larger new class of ship was developed which was faster than the previous fleet units of the Company and carried nearly half as many more passengers. Three of these ships were built and were known as the 28,000 ton class. They were called *Orcades (III)*, (1948), *Oronsay (II)* (1951) and *Orsova (II)* (1954) and had a service speed of 22½ knots. The interior decoration of these ships was a much greater task for an architect than that of the somewhat

152. The ORION arriving at Fremantle in April, 1963, on her final voyage before being broken up.

smaller pre-war ships and, although the association of Colin Anderson and Brian O'Rorke was continued, at the request of the latter other architects were brought into the projects. These did work on certain spaces, notably the tourist class dining rooms and special suites of the ships, but there was an over-all supervisory part played by the original partnership in all three ships.

In 1955, a need arose for another ship, which was to be designed to be used for world-wide trading but, to enable her to fulfil new requirements, her speed was to be increased from $22\frac{1}{2}$ knots of the 28,000 tonners to $27\frac{1}{2}$ knots. For reasons explained elsewhere in this book, the increased speed caused the ship to be bigger, and the bigger ship caused a large increase in passenger and crew numbers. The arrangements which had worked hitherto as regards the interior design and decoration of the public spaces and cabins no longer applied. The project was too big! A new arrangement was made in which the whole project would be put in the hands of a firm of Design Consultants but, again, with a benign and benevolent overseeing and control by Sir Colin Anderson, as he now was (having been knighted in 1950). To enable full liason to be maintained, a committee was formed and called 'The Steering Committee.' Its membership was rather loosely fashioned, for all members did not always attend, but only when they were directly involved. My feelings about Committees are expressed at length in *Committees and Conventions*, but this Steering Committee was different. It was really a sort of forum at which all members could learn what was happening in other areas of the overall design of the ship, and thus avoid the pitfalls which ignorance on these matters could cause. It also enabled the members of the committee to hear points of view others had on matters of interest to all its members. Most important of all, the Steering Committee ensured that there was a cohesion in overall design which enabled the Chairman of the Committee, Sir Colin Anderson, to guide the designs so that the finished work provided what was needed by the shipowner for the interests of the passengers.

This arrangement also ensured that there was a 'family' of public rooms and spaces in which intensity of lighting, designs of details (such as light fittings, ventilation outlet terminals, door furniture, etc) were in harmony with each other, even though they may not have been identical. The directional signs and lettering throughout the ship were controlled by the Design Consultant's specialist. That Steering Committee was one of the few committees on which I served and which I liked, approved and applauded. Probably this was because there were no 'passengers' in its membership; no 'professional committee attenders', and because everyone had a job to do and an interest in the work of the committee. Sir Colin Anderson gave the Thomas Gray Memorial Lecture on Wednesday, 2 March, 1966 to The Royal Society of Arts, in which he elaborated on this subject and gave the reasons which led up to the formation of the Steering Committee, the nature of its membership and the work it was designed to do. For complete success and integration of the whole interior design of the passenger spaces, the Committee was the only answer. To quote from his lecture:—

'*So the pattern of control that emerges is this; the client is represented by a Senior Executive, a member of the Board. He is supported by the Naval Architect and by the various other technical people on the Shipping Company's staff whose job it is to run, maintain, keep clean, and repair the ship interiors. This Director, supported by his Naval Architect, will have regular meetings, perhaps monthly, perhaps fortnightly, with the Design Co-ordinator, who is himself an Architect or designer. He will submit the designs, supported by the materials, colours or fabrics proposed by the members of the design team. The appropriate designer will come in person to explain and discuss first his general aims and later his designs and to answer questions about them. In principle the Design Co-ordinator should not allow a design to come forward to his Steering Committee unless he himself is prepared to support it. The normal functions of these meetings will thus be to approve the designs. Their purpose is not to provide a place at which everything will have to be thrashed out from first principles. Even so, they will also provide, in the last resort, the place where the client can excercise his veto if he feels it absolutely necessary to do so, more particularly over matters of cost or efficiency. On another plane there will be many contacts between the Naval Architect and the various designers about the myriads of smaller practical matters.*

'*The importance of removing all responsibility from the client's Board as a whole for the choosing and approving of the various decorative schemes can scarcely be overstressed. The interior design of ships calls for professionals, just as much as the navigation and the catering do, but the member of the Board who presides over the Design Committee is a professional. He represents the people who are paying for the ship in the first instance, and who seek to make her pay her way thereafter. All he has to remember is that, though he is a professional shipowner, he is not a professional interior designer as well. And the same, but in reverse, goes for those who are'.* Little more need be said about the Steering Committee except that it worked well.

153. The ORIANA in Stockholm, being the biggest vessel to visit the port.

XIX. COMMITTEES AND CONVENTIONS

As is usual, the manuscript of this book was read by a number of knowledgeable people to obtain criticism, advice and, above all, correction of mistakes and to ensure that all aspects covered in the final production were satisfactory. On the content of this chapter on committees three gentlemen, whose guidance and opinions have influenced me enormously in my work over many years, had three different reactions. One did not comment on this chapter and so surprised me, for I had expected him to pass some rude comments because he had served on many committees, and was chairman of most of them during his career. Another said what I had expected from the first critic:- in his own words 'You should consider whether this' (the Chapter on Committees) 'does you or the book any good,' and the third gentleman said 'I like this . . . it describes a great deal of the nugatory effort which goes into committee work.' It so happens that these gentlemen have done more than most in work on committees, so each knows much about what happens when they meet—but each had a different attitude to their experiences and to what I had written on the subject.

Obviously the matter is one of controversy and a chapter on it could offend some readers. Whilst I value advice and comment from those I trust and admire, in this instance it had been inconclusive and, therefore, I felt that I should revert to the original intention and write what I feel about the subject. It may give pain to some readers, for which I should be sorry, and interest, or even amuse, others. Having

154. The first class Stadium Games Deck in the ORIANA.

already written about the excellent Orient steering committee for the *Oriana*, this may be a suitable point to discuss the question in its larger aspects.

I suppose that there have always been committees and there is no question that most of them have done, and will continue to do, good and useful work. It is more likely than not that I have been unfortunate in my experiences on the committees with which I have been concerned. Finally, it may be that I am too critical and expect more than is reasonable from them. If so, I apologise for what follows in this Chapter.

First of all, what is a committee? According to my dictionary, a Committee '*is a board elected or deputed to examine, consider, and report on any business referred to them*;' it goes on '*(law) the person to whom the care of an idiot or lunatic is committed*'. I believe the first

155. The Tourist Games Deck in the ORIANA.

part of this definition is not entirely correct nowadays because it does not cover all activities of committees: certainly some are formed to make decisions, although many do not make them. Some of the committees I have known almost encompass the latter part of the definition too! I have also looked up in my dictionary the meaning of the word 'convention' and, in order not to bore the reader with another extract, have paraphrased what it says. A convention is a rather grand committee, doing no more and no less, but usually taking much longer to do it.

I have worked in the City of London for most of my working life and, during that time, have served on many committees, usually by appointment and not by choice. The subjects engaging the attentions of these bodies always had to do with ships or shipping in one way or another and thus my experiences may not be comparable with those of members of committees formed for conducting affairs of business other than shipping—although I believe that they may be similar. Until 1950 the number of committees with which I was concerned was small and seemed to me to be doing useful work.

I was away from London from 1960 until 1966 and, when I returned, there was a noticeable change. The trickle of committees had become a torrent by 1970. Apparently they were being formed for the smallest reasons or on the most trivial of pretexts and, indeed, it seemed that committees propagated themselves, one from another. By now, in large companies, there were professional committee members who were so busy with committees that they had no time for anything else. Many of these listened and said nothing, or, alternatively, talked about very little incessantly. Instances of this behaviour can be seen at certain meetings of the Royal Institution of Naval Architects in London, where members, usually old men who have retired from business, stand up and talk. They are always well known to the others attending the meetings who expect this and are rarely disappointed. To be fair to the old gentlemen, most of what they have to say is well worth listening to but there are some—a few—who always get up to speak, say nothing worthwhile and then prattle on and on because they do not know how to end their speeches. Of course there are those, the majority, who attend such gatherings and never say a word:- like blotting paper, they take in but never give anything. I am one of these and there is every reason for thinking that we do not speak because we have nothing to say, although, in fact, our silence is due to awaiting—often in vain—an opportunity to contribute something constructive.

Some committees are used to enable someone, often the chairman of the committee, to reach decisions which he should be making for himself in his position in the company by whom he is employed and paid. This, in my experience, is a very common reason for the formation of a committee nowadays, and it seems to be a very successful practice. Other committees appear to be used as platforms enabling someone to become a 'star' and to further his personal ambitions. There was one such person who was notorious in the 'City' in the 1950's for shamefully using a large committee in the

156. The ORIANA's first class Tennis Deck.

manner just described. He had the gift of oratory and was an expert at making earth-shattering pronouncements which most of those present were almost certain were either untrue or inaccurate. However, the claim would go unchallenged and the speaker had been noticed by those he wished to impress. Often large committee meetings take place and last for a morning or afternoon and, at the end of the session, do not seem to have decided or to have achieved anything. These are the meetings where the professional committee attenders are at their best.

International Conventions are amongst the worst types of committee meeting I have attended. They are completely democratic affairs where all 'have a voice' whether representing countries having large merchant fleets or only a few ships. Those representatives having no strong views on subjects being discussed can be coerced or talked into favouring other more forceful and interested groups. 'Lobbying' is quite repellent on these occasions and is often done by visits from one large country to other smaller ones prior to the convention taking place. There are also representatives of flag of convenience 'nations' who can use their voting powers to enable undesirable ends to be achieved whilst they usually have no technical help to contribute through their membership. There are also members whose votes can be influenced by their political views. The idea that 'one man one vote' is democratic is one for debate and not a subject for this book but, with respect to IMCO and ILO conventions, it is, in my view, a premise of very doubtful virtue.

These views are entirely personal and may be wrong—but I believe them to be entirely correct. Some legislation regarding ships in recent years has not been good. A number of members of these international conventions cannot be regarded as truly representative of maritime nations at all, but they are nevertheless members of various sub-committees and have voting powers equal to other more knowledgeable and experienced members, thus upsetting the true balance of representation of the real maritime nations. For instance, only a few nations have been responsible for the design and building of passenger ships, but the decisions taken in recent years for the improvement of their safety standards have been largely influenced by pressures from representatives of countries which do not build passenger ships or, at best, only a few. The safety arrangements have been increased unilaterally to the point where I believe that no other form of transport for passengers is as safe. No passenger-carrying aircraft could lift off the ground if its safety requirements were made equal to those demanded for passenger ships. Its passengers may not put any faith in their lifejacket in the event of crashing onto a mountain, but the odds against the machine being able to 'pancake' on to the sea and the jacket being of use are remote in the extreme. A passenger in a liner usually has, for safety, a ship so divided into water-tight compartments that it can remain afloat in spite of two of them being flooded; lifeboats with capacity for all crew and passengers, lifejackets for each person on board and numerous electrical and electronic gadgets to prevent accidents and otherwise communicate with rescuers.

The safety arrangements against fire are much greater than those in passenger-carrying aircraft, but still there are those who strive to increase the arrangements for safety in passenger ships. In days past it might have been argued that these vessels carried many more passengers than aircraft and that, therefore, safety requirements should be greater in the former. The difference in numbers carried is not so great nowadays, and also the question has to be asked, 'Is anybody's life more precious than another's and, therefore, should factors of safety be better for large numbers than small?' A motorcyclist, mountaineer or pot-holer can take what risks he likes but it seems reasonable that anyone paying for transport in a commercial vehicle of any sort should be entitled to equal factors of safety in all of them. If this is so we should look again at standards of safety in both aircraft and ships. These standards should not be reduced to enable a vehicle to operate economically unless the passenger is informed that this is the case. Not only does the British Government turn a blind eye to the differences in standards of safety in ships and aircraft but they, like many other Governments, subsidize the cost of running state-owned aircraft companies which otherwise could not survive. Passenger shipping companies do not benefit from such patronage.

The growth of international maritime convention activities has caused great concentration on ways of improving safety in ships, apparently without cross-ways glances to observe whether other means of transport were equally safe. This has caused passenger ships to be burdened with difficulties of design and construction which now have reached a point where passengers must have become aware of the change in appearances. Gone are the spacious entrances and public rooms with their grandeur of height and space, the splendid open staircases down into dining rooms, in the vessels which were a little 'Ruritanian' and unreal. Perhaps they are no longer wanted anyway, but they could not be repeated today since fire protection rules, subdivision rules, and so on prevent their repetition, even if they were still desired.

Due to international collaboration over some years in connection with ships and shipping there are now understandings and agreements for the measurement of tonnage: safety; strength; load lines; subdivision, crew accommodation and many other standards. In theory, all of this collaboration is good, and even excellent, but I believe there are shipowners of nations which have been signatories to these various agreements who do not observe their own requirements. In regard to tonnage, there were small differences in measurement between those of Britain and countries in Europe which could lead to unfairness to British shipowners. Some years ago a well-known British shipowner of small coasting vessels, which traded around the coast of Britain and to ports in Europe, bought a second-hand ship of this type from a continental shipowner. From memory, this ship was just under 500 gross tons and was at that time entitled to run with a minimum crew associated with that tonnage—and the commercial successs of these little ships was partly due to the size of the crew demanded by this tonnage. I was at a meeting with the then Ministry of Transport when this old shipowner complained bitterly about the outcome of his purchase. After completion of the transaction the British Ministry had re-measured the vessel for tonnage and declared it to be greater than 500 tons gross and that the complement had, therefore, to be increased. This must surely be an injustice? Perhaps there are now changes since I retired; I hope so.

There are stringent requirements for protection of ships against fire and these have been agreed at International Conventions (I.M.C.O.). In the late 1960's, the passenger liner fleet of the P & O Company spent millions of pounds (sterling) in order to bring their fleet up to the standards required by I.M.C.O. fire-protection rules as implemented by the British Ministry of Transport. Some British shipowners at that time found that the cost of doing the work was prohibitive and sold their ships, many of which were bought by foreign shipowners and converted, often into cruising vessels. They were also fitted with fire-protection to meet the latest requirements. One might wonder how it was possible for one shipowner to buy a ship from another shipowner who had found it uneconomic to run, convert it, add expensive fire-protection and then run it successfully.

Because I was personally involved, I know that at least one of these second-hand ships was fitted with fire subdivision in the accommodation using a cheaper, lighter, and, in my opinion, better material than we were permitted to use for the purpose by the Ministry of

Transport at that time. No doubt other anomalies of this kind could be found and so I can only state that my belief is that the carrying out of international agreements in regard to shipping (probably in other respects, too!) can be used to the advantage of the unscrupulous and that the loser is always the one who observes the rules. Whether the good conscience of the one who does right compensates for his financial disadvantage is a matter for conjecture. Perhaps the rules should be enforced more rigorously on transgressing ships when they visit other countries. This is a large and important subject which is seldom aired in an age when, it seems, the great nations must never say a word which might offend the lesser ones.

157. *Two old-timers which escaped the modern regulations – the old MAURETANIA (white) and the OLYMPIC.*

XX. SAMPLE CABINS

When a design is started for a passenger liner, the Management and Passenger Department must provide rough guidance to the Naval Architect of the Company on the types of cabins required and the numbers of them in each of the passenger classes. This enables designs of cabins to be made of all the types required and for discussions to take place between all those concerned. To cite but one obvious instance, it is clear that, if a cabin is to have a private bath, it must take up a greater area of deck than if it did not have one.

In a like manner, there can be a cabin designed for occupying a minimum space, or alternatively for greater space and comfort. When these first steps have been made, the Naval Architect can proceed with the arrangement of the accommodation of the ship and find out whether or not the passenger numbers desired can be achieved. This is never the case, within my own experience! However, a compromise will be found so that no one is satisfied—or so it seems! I shall now gloss over the months of trial and error, and work, which precede the completion of any ship design and pass straight to the start of the contract with the shipyard.

Drawings are made by the Naval Architect of two or three typical cabins for each of the two classes of passenger cabins, together with a crew cabin, showing the beds, wash basins, coat hooks, wardrobes, chests of drawers, dressing tables, baths, W.C.s, and such practical features. Copies are sent to the shipbuilder and to the decorator responsible for the cabins and, after a period of a few weeks, the shipbuilder informs the shipowner that the sample cabins are partly

158. A 'convertible' tourist cabin which could either be four-berth, or two-berth with a shower and W.C.

built and are ready for preliminary inspection. There then starts a long succession of visits to see and criticize them.

The furniture, as detailed by the designer, is built and fitted in the cabins together with light fittings, door furniture, ventilation louvres, hat and coat hooks, mirrors, light switches and sockets, and so on. Finally, lighting is fitted and powered so that it can be used exactly as it would be in cabins aboard the finished ship. Plumbing is also detailed and fitted, but running water is not usually arranged in the sample accommodation.

The visits of the Management of the Company to the sample cabins usually took place about once every month and caused lively discussion. Usually Sir Colin Anderson and Ford Geddes, representing the Orient Line Management, were accompanied by Brian O'Rorke, Professor Richard D. Russell, who was responsible for the

159. A first class two-berth cabin – both in the ORIANA.

design of cabin furniture and décor, or his assistant, and the Naval Architect (myself). The shipbuilders had their own representatives and all criticisms and decisions made during the visits were recorded and those concerned were subsequently given copies of the 'Items Discussed'. As time went by and the detailed discussions and resulting changes in detail were recorded and the sample cabins modified as required, a point was reached when soft furnishings, carpets and wall coverings, and other details which complete the needs of a passenger in his cabin, had been added and they were complete—or so we thought.

I had for many years thought that I was of average height, but had this belief shattered when I went to work in London. The average height of people living there was at least three inches more than my five feet and six inches, but the Managers of the Orient Line were tall men of six feet—and often more—in height. The visits to sample cabins were not always serious affairs: often annoying, but sometimes hilarious. Bobby Wright was the Foreman Joiner—no doubt he would be called the 'Joiner Manager' now*. On occasions, perhaps when the height of a mirror was being debated, agreement would be made when Len Redshaw (now Sir Leonard Redshaw) for the shipbuilders, would call out 'Bring on our average man', and Bobby Wright would appear, smiling as always, and select the correct height for the fitment. He was much shorter than I, being probably five feet and three inches in height, the average height for a lady and, for that reason, a good guide in selecting the height of mirrors, coat hooks and so on. There is one simple rule, a tall person can usually stoop a little to use a mirror but a small person should not have to stand on tip-toe or on a stool. I found my height a difficulty in dealing with some decisions in sample cabins, and the Manager's visits very often high-lighted faults I had not seen.

When these cabins were nearly completed, other Managers of the Orient Line came to see them. This was always a worrying time. One would have thought that the critics who had already seen the cabins would have discovered all the faults and weaknesses, but this was *not* so. A visit by our Chairman, Sir Austin Anderson, always filled me with apprehension, because I knew he would almost certainly discover a fault which had not yet been revealed. He was one who needed complete darkness in which to sleep and he also had had an accident which had deformed the finger of one hand and, if he pulled out a drawer in a sample cabin and the drawer pull or handle was 'different', Sir Austin would catch his finger in that drawer. We did devise a form of light-trap to enable ventilation air for cabins to pass through the openings in the lower part of the doors without letting in light from the corridor at the same time.

The simplest solution to ventilating cabins is used in at least one major shipping company by cutting the doors short of the thresholds, but this permits light from outside passing clearly into them.

Seats in the form of settees and chairs nowadays seem to be built for the 'average' man of six feet. The seats are very often very deep from back to front, and low. The seat designer pre-supposes that the

* In this age when even a dustman is termed a 'refuse officer' and the Gilbertian situation is arising 'when everyone is somebodee, then no one's anybody'!

person to sit in the seat is long in the thigh. If half the people to use the seat are female we can reasonably presume they will be less than five feet six inches tall, in which case they will be short in the thigh and miserable sitting in these chairs and settees with deep seats. I am!

The sample cabins were used to guide all the shipbuilding trades in their work on the ship. The plumber used the cabins to fashion the plumbing to fit the washbasins, baths and w.c.'s; the electrician to run his wiring to the wall switches, wall sockets, light fitting etc., and the joiner to guide him as to the number and position of the hat and coat hooks, wardrobe details and all the multifarious items which a joiner has to fit in his work in a ship.

Vickers used to have a plumber in their employ in the late 1940's who was by nature artistic, if an artist is one who likes curlicues, and abhors straight lines. I do not know what happened to the poor man, but his work ceased to appear in our ships. However I do remember well going on board a new ship belonging to another company and, as often occurred, was following Sir Colin Anderson and another Manager on a tour of inspection of accommodation. The plumbing in that ship was diabolical and Sir Colin remarked: 'Morris, this Shipbuilder must be employing that plumber from Barrow'. About that time a real artist in the skills of plumbing appeared. His name was Harker, a truly fine craftsman, and from that time the plumbing work in Vickers-built ships improved to a point where the work could be called a craft. For the first time the Orient Line could have plumbing made to jigs and standardized. The plumbing behind the panels at the shower-end of the private baths was almost beautiful—but I suppose that I should not prolong my ecstasies about the standardized plumbing of Vickers Ltd!

160. The Captain's Day room – ORIANA.

XXI. CREW ACCOMMODATION

THE STRUCTURAL DESIGN of the ship, for reasons given in some detail elsewhere, had been arranged in such a way as to tie together the aluminium alloy superstructure and the main steel hull so that the two materials would work together as a unit of strength. One feature of this arrangement was to space out evenly, along the hull, transverse webs or deep frames which were fitted on the ships' sides and ran vertically up through the ship to the strength deck and then stepped in and carried on as webs within the alloy deckhouses as shown on the drawing of the midship section.* These webs and deep frames, together with the pillars and transverse deep beams were maintained in the structure, and accommodation arrangements had to be fitted around them.

Due to this paramount need to preserve the integrity of the ship's structure, the cabins for crew and passengers had to be arranged to fit into the spacing of the webs, pillars, deep beams and girders in a way which had never before been done in vessels of the Orient Company. Before the regular spacing of the webs and deep frames was finally determined, schemes were made of various alternative arrangements of cabins envisaged for First Class and Tourist Class passengers and crew. These were examined critically by the managers and senior staff of the departments concerned within the Company and, after general approval was given, the arrangement drawings of the ship decks were made. Perhaps the arrangements of the groups of cabins could be called a 'modular' system, in that they were arranged in regular blocks of identical length to fit between the deep webs along the ship's sides.

* Plate 119.

161. The leading hands' Smoke Room.

The rules governing crew accommodation in the years after the Second World War became stricter as regards the area of cabin floor to be provided for each man and for the amenities and facilities to be provided, but some shipowners were always in advance of the requirements of the Ministry of Transport or Board of Trade, or whatever might be the governing body at the time. The Orient Company was one of those firms which had good relations with the Officers' and Crews' Unions and the Management of the Company knew and consulted with the officials of the Unions on subjects of common interest.

At suitable times in the planning of new ships the Company arranged for representatives of the Unions to call at the Naval Architect's office and scan drawings and discuss details of the new ships in order to ensure that the reasonable wishes of the officers and

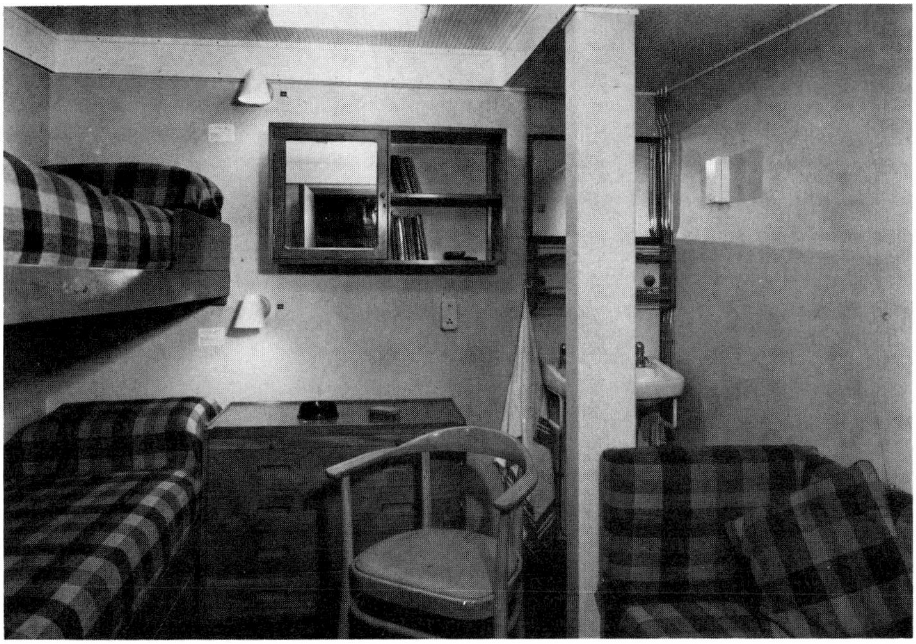

162. A two-berth leading hands' cabin.

163. The crew's mess room – a far cry from the Anderson, Anderson clipper foc's'les!

crew should be met, even if they were a little different from the existing rules.

When the *Oriana* was being planned, the Management decided to make improvements to the crew accommodation and, as usual, the standards to be provided were high. The accommodation of adult members of the crew was single-berth and two-berth cabins and each cabin was fitted with a vitreous china washbasin and furniture of polished mahogany. A few four-berth cabins were arranged in a separate block of accommodation for boys who were being carried as trainee members of the crew. The walls of the crew cabins were covered with a decorative, washable, soft plastic and the design of furniture and soft furnishings was carried out by the same decorators as were employed to do the cabins for the passengers.

The choice of items of furnishing and equipment throughout the ship was made, taking into account the cost and weight of each item. For instance, weight could have been saved by using aluminium alloy bed frames and their spring bases instead of the steel usually used in their construction, but the additional cost was found to be uneconomical when compared with the costs of carrying the alternative weights for the life of the ship—so steel bed frames were fitted. This exercise of comparing the choices of weight and the possible savings in final cost in the ship's life was done for each item of outfit in the ship. Often the investigation showed that it was better to carry the additional weight of the item than to use a lighter, but more expensive, alternative.

There were public rooms provided for the various ranks of the crew and a swimming pool for their use was built on the open deck forward. All the accommodation for the crew was also air-conditioned.

In connection with the decision made by the Company management to accommodate the crew in single or two-berth cabins, it should be noted that, at that time, crews berthed in cabins holding more than two persons were not required by 'rule' to be provided with as large an area of deck per man as those berthed in two-berth or single cabins. This meant that there was an incentive to the shipowner to put crew in cabins holding larger numbers of men in order to

164. *A female officer's cabin.*

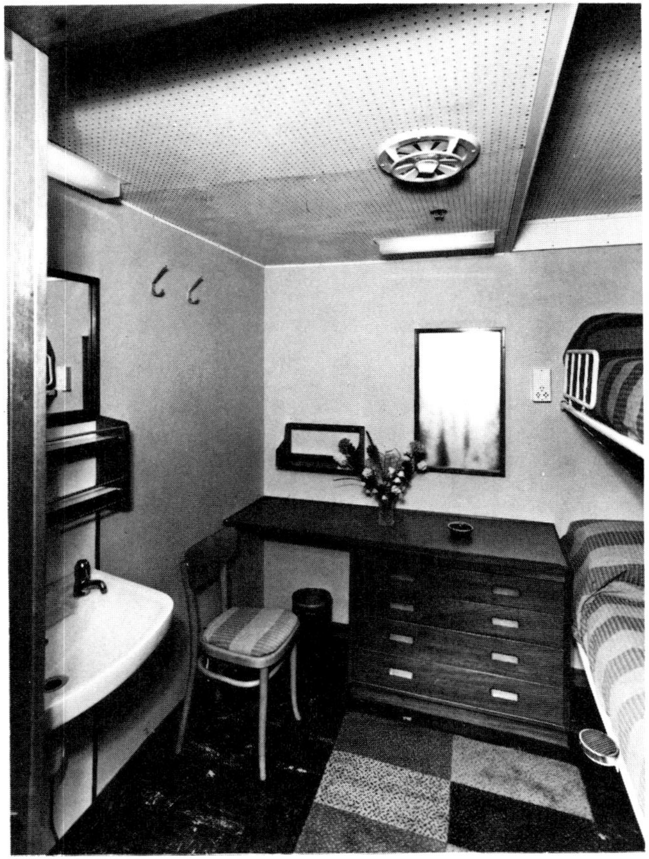

165. *A tourist class two-berth cabin.*

— *The ORIANA.*

reduce the total area used to accommodate the ship's complement. The contemporary picture of the 'grasping shipowner' was not borne out by my own experience, and the quarters provided for the crew of the *Oriana* was at the time in advance of any provided in other new passenger ships in the United Kingdom or elsewhere, so far as I know.

166. First class two-bed verandah suite in the ORIANA.

XXII. PASSENGER ACCOMMODATION

THE CABINS FOR both classes of passengers, First Class and Tourist Class, were built in accordance with the standards of material, fittings and furnishings of the sample cabins, but there were also some fitted in the First Class accommodation which were larger and more luxuriously furnished than the others. The designs for these special cabins were made by architects and decorators employed directly by the Orient Company, and continued an arrangement which had been in force for many years. Sometimes the architects were inexperienced in the special requirements of work on ships and this occasionally caused problems for those who had to maintain them in service.*

One such problem was caused by one of these architects' liking for ceilings made of narrow, polished hardwood planks, each secured by nails in such a way as to ensure that the heads of the nails in each plank were obscured by the next plank to be nailed in place. Good shipbuilders always arrange ready access to spaces behind linings and ceilings in accommodation so that damage or faults can easily be seen and repaired quickly at sea, but our architect had not done this.

On the maiden voyage of this particular ship we had our usual difficulties, but there is always a special one. Soon after leaving Southampton, there was a complaint from passengers occupying one of these special cabins that there was a nasty smell! After the

* It was the policy of the Company to give a number of young men opportunities to further their careers.

passengers had been moved to a 'contingency' cabin (there are always 'contingency' cabins on a passenger ship) we started to investigate. Suspicion at once fell upon the space above the ceiling. There were no access panels to the planked ceiling and this could only be removed one plank at a time—starting at one side of the cabin ceiling. With little imagination one can easily conjure up a vision of the mess caused by the removal and littering of the floor of the cabin with layers of narrow planks looking like a spilled box of large matches. We did find the cause of the smell, but it was not in that ceiling space after all!

The 'knees' of many pairs of my trousers have been worn out whilst I have prayed for Decorative Architects to improve their ways. Some of them would be told of follies perpetrated by others before them, but precisely the same follies would appear again. Once, my Directors arranged that I should fly with a small group of Decorative Architects to Naples to board one of the Company's ships homeward-bound. The purpose of the journey was to help the party, which was to design work for one of our new ships, to understand the problems of fitting decoration into ship structures. These architects had never done work on passenger ships, and, to put it bluntly, they didn't know the 'sharp end from the blunt end'.

During that voyage back to Southampton they were given as much information as I could summon up with regard to the subject and, particularly, I remember telling them of our Company's dislike of sliding doors for cabins or bookcases in ships. This is not a phobia. A sliding door fitted in a ship can jam because of the movement in a ship at sea. Also, if a door is made to slide easily, it will slide by itself with the movement of the ship. Worse still it will be pushed open or shut and crashed into its stops by careless users, causing annoyance to people living around, above and below the place where the door is fitted. Ships are usually built of steel and a deck is enclosed by steel above, below and around its sides. Without going to fantastic lengths in sound insulation of one sort or another, noise and vibration are carried great distances in every direction from the source. Hinged doors can be fitted with stabilizers—a type of friction device—to prevent slamming, but sliding doors are difficult to control, and therefore we did not like to fit them in ships.

167. The special Stadium Deck suite in the ORIANA had a double bedroom: sitting room; dining room, bathroom, shower and lavatory.

All this advice fell on deaf ears! When the new ship was on her trials we ran into an extraordinary storm and the large, frameless glass sliding doors fitted to the library bookcases were smashed to a heap of splinters in a very short time. The movement of the ship caused the glass doors to move swiftly from open to shut, shut to open, and to bang violently against their stops, shattering the glass. Frameless glass doors are attractive but can be very dangerous when used in ships. Even ships fitted with stabilizers move unpredictably during storms, and passengers, who often lack 'sea-legs', can be thrown heavily. Glass partitions and doors should always be fitted with handrails at a suitable height to take care of those who fall about in passenger ships.

Sir Colin Anderson, as already mentioned, is a keen and discerning art lover, especially in the visual arts. He was able to exercise his desire to encourage promising young artists, and those not yet well known, by buying their works for decoration in the Company's ships. He bought designs for carpets for public spaces in the fleet, and commissioned murals and pictures to hang on the walls of public spaces, passengers', officers' and crew cabins and recreation rooms. Many of these works were controversial, to say the least about them, but they were, to use Sir Colin's own expression, 'conversation pieces'. This was certainly true, and I have heard many of these conversations! The subjects of these 'works of art' may not have been beautiful in the eyes of the beholder but, at least, the pictures were not ignored. Quite often 'good' pictures are ignored because they lack inspiration in their conception, and to be ignored may be worse than to be intensely disliked!

There was one 'conversation piece' I can remember very well. It was said by one humorist/critic to have been painted by an artist using a bicycle wheel fitted with its inflated tyre. The technique was very suited to the shape of the picture, an elongated shape about 6 feet long horizontally by one and a half feet high. The description of the artist's method seemed to me to fit the result. The canvas was imagined to have been laid flat on the floor, a variety of oil colours squeezed out of their tubes on to the centre of the canvas, and the bicycle wheel pased backwards and forwards along the length of the canvas in fairly straight lines over the mess of paints, these lines varying from diagonally to horizontally over the whole area. This picture first appeared one night aboard the *Orcades* as she made her way from Belfast to Tilbury, carrying a party of guests. Sir Colin Anderson, who was very much a working Director, arranged to have a picture-hanging party that night, composed of Sir Colin, our hull inspector, Alex Brown, and myself.

After dinner, we foregathered carrying screwdrivers, screws, keyhole plates, and a large parcel of pictures, and proceeded to follow Sir Colin as he passed through the various public rooms and stair halls, and selected each picture for its place and position, all the while being followed by the inquisitive eyes of guests sitting in groups, talking and drinking. At last we came to this 'bicycle wheel' picture, which was to be hung in a large stair hall outside a public room. Alex

168. The tourist class library.

and I took hold of the long picture and stood at each end holding it up against the wall whilst Sir Colin selected its position and, particularly, its height. By this time the inquisitive guests had formed a small crowd of critics who stood behind Sir Colin, making audible and questionable comments. I believe that he had begun to enjoy himself and the situation and, after asking us to move the picture about a little—this way and that—he stated that it was correct and, with a twinkle in his eyes, moved quickly away and left us to the tender mercies of our tormentors. That picture lived up to its name as a 'conversation piece.'

Public rooms are designed for various uses. Some are designed for quiet reading, writing and quiet conversations—or even sleeping, although this is not usually encouraged. Other public rooms are used for dancing, concerts, lectures or other social gatherings, and some for drinking—usually situated near and opening onto games decks and swimming pool areas.

Sleeping in public rooms is a peculiar habit practiced by a minor proportion of the travelling public, but very rarely, except in children, can it be deemed to be beautiful to behold—in fact, in most cases, it can be said to look extremely distasteful to others. Many years ago, there was a long discussion led by the late I. C. Geddes on the design of seating in the First Class lounge for a new ship under construction. The seats, chairs and settees were to be designed so as to provide a degree of comfort, but not so comfortable as to encourage sleepers to use the room. The discussion was long and detailed. Perhaps travellers in the ships did not find the seating as comfortable as they would have desired, but it is possible that a reasonable balance was achieved and that the slumberers were thereby reduced to tolerable numbers. There are some sleepers who are difficult to bear. One young man was recently seen sleeping lying full length along a well-upholstered settee, with his shoes and his feet on the settee, of course. Tolerance has now given birth to intolerable behaviour.

Lighting is a subject which receives great consideration and often causes conflicts of interest. The architects responsible for the design of light fittings and features can increase the electric loading of the generators aboard enormously. In one ship the architects had designed a lighting trough like an inverted wash basin with a light baffle almost covering the bowl, leaving only a narrow peripheral opening around the edge of it. This was thus a type of diffused light and was to be made of reinforced plastic and standardized throughout the public rooms of the ship. Fortunately, before the scheme was finally approved the Engineering Department, responsible for the supply of the electricity generating installation of the vessel, investigated and found that the loss of light through this inefficient design was more than the generators were capable of carrying in addition to their other requirements. The lighting fittings were promptly re-designed!

Strip-lighting is very suitable and desirable for certain positions. It can be used effectively over mirrors in cabins and cove-lighting around the edges of a ceiling in public rooms. The heating caused by tungsten lighting is high as compared with fluorescent lighting. In earlier ships of the Orient Company tungsten lighting was commonly used and was a contradiction of desires in ships operating through the tropics, for its heat increased the problem of improving the ventilation for passengers.

This factor was not so important at that time because the intensity of lighting expected by the public was not so great, but in later ships the heat from the improved lighting became worthy of attention. Unfortunately, fluorescent lighting has its own problems, since it does not give the same sort of light as a tungsten lamp and changes the apparent colours seen by the human eye. When fluorescent lighting first appeared, ladies were disappointed—perhaps 'staggered' would be a better word—by the unfortunate effects of 'make-up' put on under tungsten lamps and then seen in a public room lighted by fluorescent tubes. In the early days of the use of fluorescent lighting, these tubes were of either 'daylight' or 'warm' lighting. The 'daylight' light was a cold blue light not often seen today and the 'warm' light was yellowish in colour.

Nowadays there are many and better colours from which to choose and the problems have largely disappeared. To reduce the problem of 'make-up', fluorescent tubes were fitted over mirrors in cabins of ships after the Second World War, because by then fluorescent lighting was being used extensively in the public rooms. The low intensity of lighting throughout the accommodation of the ships of the late 1920's had several benefits for ships operating through tropical climates, since the load on the generators was reduced, the heating caused by good and high lighting standards was decreased, and there was a psychological benefit, in that very bright lighting brings a feeling of warmth to human beings and, in the same way, quiet and restrained lighting comforts those who are hot.

If tungsten lighting had been used in the public rooms, electrical consumption could have been doubled and, similarly, a considerable rise in temperature caused by the tungsten lamps would have imposed a greater load on the ventilation cooling system in hot weather. The fluorescent tubes, known as either hot-cathode or cold-cathode lamps, varied in length, depending on their use, from twelve inches to five feet. A problem which has always to be overcome in the use of fluorescent tubes for cornice lighting in public rooms is that of preventing black spots in the lighting where the ends of the tubes meet. This was overcome by overlapping the ends of the tubes so as to provide continuous unbroken light in the cornices.

In the 1950's a new fashion in lighting of dining rooms originated in the U.S.A. where lighting standards were reduced to the point where the diners could hardly see each other or the food they ate. This was good for the engineers' generators, the galley staff, and the romantic young diners, but irritating for the not-so-young and poor-sighted elders who no longer cared much about how they looked but were interested in reading the menu, seeing what they ate, and being able to find their way out of the room. Being one of the latter group, I am glad that that fashion has almost died.

In the *Oriana*, the two classes of passengers totalled 688 in First Class and 1,496 in Tourist Class, and the public rooms and deck areas for games, recreation and relaxation were divided up so as to fairly distribute them between the classes. As one might expect, the two classes tended to be distinguished from one another by age as well as by any other differences which could have been noticed—the red-blooded and virile people were mainly to be found in the after end or Tourist Class of the ship. Whilst there was always a furtive movement or infiltration of some Tourist passengers into First Class public rooms, I believe there was also a movement of the more romantically-minded First Class passengers in the opposite direction.

Possibly most of this cross-migration was due to the innate inquisitiveness of human beings and, perhaps, the motivation caused by the feeling that the grass is greener on the other side of the fence; but there was more 'life' and vitality amongst the relatively younger people in the Tourist end of the ship which probably caused a little envy and nostalgia in older passengers. Apparently no great effort was made by the Company to prevent this rather minor movement of passengers although, I suppose, blatant abuse would have brought about corrective measures.

Passenger cabins were fitted out in the ships generally to accommodate adults, but most of the cabins had arrangements so that cots could be added if the occupant or occupants desired to take young children. The cots were of three different types to suit the differing ages involved. In the First Class accommodation a system called 'Telenurse' was fitted in the cabins. A small box-shaped microphone, placed near a child's cot and plugged into the telephone in the cabin, would signal to the telephone operator on duty, by means of a light flashing on the switchboard, that the child was awake and crying. The operator would then contact the parents. This installation enabled parents to take part in the social activities of the ship, whilst being satisfied that the children were safe.

First Class cabins had telephones enabling passengers to call for steward's services and contact friends in other cabins. There was also a telephone service through twelve shore lines for linking passengers to the telephone system ashore when the vessel was in port. Tourist passengers, on the other hand, had a bell service installed in their cabins.

A broadcasting system was available in all passenger and crew cabins with the loudspeakers positioned above the ceilings. The control fitted in each cabin enabled the passenger to select one of two programmes (or switch off) and the volume was also adjustable, although the noise level at full volume was restricted in order to prevent annoyance to fellow passengers. An over-riding control was fitted to this system so that the programmes could be cut out and allow emergency signals and instructions to be broadcast from the navigating bridge. This could be done even if the operating switches in the cabins had been turned to the 'off' position.

A small number of television sets were installed in First Class cabins but about sixty sets were installed in the ship altogether, mostly in public rooms of First Class, the Tourist Class, of the crew, and in some officers' cabins. The programmes could be selected from local television broadcasts at ports of call throughout the world, and from closed-circuit telecine, or 'live' television programmes, whilst the ship was at sea.

In the First Class cabins, electric irons and ironing boards were fitted and there was a third tap over the washbasins providing iced water.

In 1977, I travelled with my wife in the *Oriana* from Vancouver to Southampton, a voyage which lasted over three weeks. This was the first time I had travelled for so long as a passenger aboard, because on previous occasions I had been engaged on work connected with the ship. My wife became friendly with a lady from Scotland who was lost in the accommodation and who asked her for assistance in finding her way about the vessel. The *Oriana* was carrying many passengers who had boarded her in Sydney, Australia, and this lady had joined her there over two weeks before arriving in Vancouver, but still could not find her way from one place to another in the ship. The obvious conclusion is that the lady was dull-witted, but she was not. A great deal of thought had been given (and wasted) about the methods of guiding passengers and to help them to find their way about. Coloured arrowed symbols were incorporated in the deck coverings of alleyways and stair landings which, to quote, '*would be of great value to give passengers quick and easy recognition of fore and aft location.*' They do not and did not do so. The arrows were 'V's' to the average passenger, to whom a 'V' is not an arrow-head! To him, the 'V's' were a form of decoration and had no connection with the message that they pointed forward. The colouring of the deck coverings in the alleyways and landings varied from deck to deck, and, in theory, this was, '*to be unconsciously associated with the passenger's thoughts as to where he was and therefore assist him to find his way.*' Having travelled in the ship and heard the views of many passengers, I am disillusioned and disappointed that this scheme, too, proved over-subtle.

I think we should have done the obvious in all our direction signs and not resorted to psychology—the latter seems to be a delusion in certain applications—and, perhaps, we should have been more cautious and suspicious when salesmanship involving the mention of psychology was put forward as a solution of a problem.

Perhaps the reader will now be saying to himself: 'Why doesn't the Company instruct the passenger by the use of notices in the cabin?' Sadly, it is apparent that passengers cannot, and will not, read notices. I was amazed to discover that most of the passengers to whom I spoke—and I spoke to many—had not read most of what was put into their cabins daily, concerning current affairs such as, for example, the port of call the next day. They expect to be informed verbally of this sort of thing, as it takes less effort on their part to be told what to do next.

The public rooms were arranged in association with each other in a logical manner that had been successful over generations of ships of the Company. The First Class Tavern Bar was built on the Bathing Deck close to the swimming and paddling pools. There were doors and folding glazed screens which opened directly on to the deck against the pools, and the open bar, tiled floor and seating of the room were in harmony with the feeling and usage of the area. As has been mentioned previously, noise and vibration travel far through the structural fabric of a ship and care is needed in her designing stages to locate sources of noise as far away as possible from places where quiet is important.

The noisy sources can be places such as games decks, which are mostly noisy during the daylight, and ballrooms which are often noisy in the evening. The peculiar effect of the sliding feet of dancers in a ballroom can be irritating to those trying to sleep in cabins below. On the Stadium deck, above the main public rooms on the Veranda deck, were the table tennis rooms of First Class and Tourist Class passengers. Noise created by the vigorous activities of the players could only be heard in places which were not likely to be adversely affected. There were also two very large areas for both classes of passengers on the Stadium Deck as well as an attractive room called 'The Look-Out', at the forward end of that deck, for the use of First Class Passengers. This room was glazed by closely-spaced, full-height windows around the semi-circular front and was furnished with large comfortable chairs and a repeater compass and charts to enable passengers to enjoy the view over the sea and plot the ship's position and direction if desired.

Not far aft of amidships on the Stadium Deck and on the centre line of the ship, a room was built and called the 'Red Carpet Room'. For obvious reasons, this room had a beautiful red carpet on the floor. There were a piano and electronic sound apparatus of every kind and any other equipment which might be required in the functioning of the room for its purpose. Musical recitals, lectures, readings, and meetings of all kinds could be held there. Doors were

169. The Red Carpet room – available for musical evenings, lectures, etc.

arranged in such a way that both classes of passengers could have ready access to the area, which was available to them on request.

The Veranda Deck was next below the Stadium Deck and had on it most of the First Class Public Rooms as well as the Tourist Class Ocean Bar situated near, and opening on to, one of the swimming pools for the Tourist Class Passengers at the after end of the deck. On this deck, from forward, were the Junior Club and open deck area for First Class children: the 'Princess Room', a large lounge and library, in which a large and long mural called 'Landscape of the Two Seasons' by John Piper, was arranged across the room to divide it into the lounge area and the library: the Port and Starboard Galleries; the Ballroom, and the Monkey Bar were arranged for First Class passengers. Outside the after end of the Princess Room was a large stairhall and a painting of Princess Alexandra was hung on the centre of the wall opposite to the stairway and lifts. This portrait was painted at Buckingham Palace by the Viennese-born artist Judy

170. The Princess Room, named after Princess Alexandra who launched the vessel.

Cassab, who has lived in Australia for many years. Princess Alexandra, of course, launched the *Oriana*.

On 'A' deck, the next deck below the Veranda Deck; the First Class Silver Grill, a restaurant with its own kitchens, bar and lounge, was arranged on the port side of the ship adjacent to the main stair and lifts. This room was decorated with a motif of silver medallions forming a link with the Elizabethan period. The medallions were about 8 inches in diameter based on medallion seals of the last Elizabethan period—hence 'The Silver Grill'. Like all the Orient Line restaurants, it gave the First Class passengers means of holding private parties, birthday parties, wedding anniversary parties or other special celebrations, which are needed during a long voyage. The choice of food was more extensive than was provided in the main Dining Room on 'E' Deck, and the room, including the bar and

171. Judy Cassab finishing her portrait of Princess Alexandra, which hangs in the ORIANA.

lounge, was extremely attractive. With the smaller numbers of diners and the more leisurely dining and the individual service arrangements, it provided all that could be desired for special occasions.

Dividing the First and Tourist Class accommodation on the port side of 'A' deck was the Cinema, and film-goers could enter its balcony through doors from both the First Class and Tourist Class accommodation. The main floor of the cinema was entered from 'B' deck, again from doors opening on to the two classes of passenger accommodation, and there was a spiral stair connecting the main floor and the balcony inside the cinema. The seating was arranged for more than 300 people, which, from observation of other ships in service, was ample for the numbers likely to attend frequent shows. Many Atlantic liners, fitted with cinemas seating 500 passengers or more, have often shown films to no more than twenty people, and I have rarely seen a ship's cinema with attendances exceeding fifty in number.

172. The tourist class restaurant.

The *Oriana's* Cinema was able to show films to the whole complement of passengers and, because of the attraction of other entertainments taking place at the same time, it was rarely overcrowded. An interesting feature of the Cinema was that part of it was really a hinged hatch cover forming an opening over the engine room to enable major engine maintenance to be done, should it be needed. There was a similar hinged hatch cover in the 'Monkey Bar' on the Veranda Deck and in the 'Red Carpet Room' on the Stadium Deck. If this device of employing hinged hatch covers had not been used, the three rooms could not have been where they were and passenger numbers would have been lost in order to build the rooms elsewhere in the ship.

Abaft the Cinema on 'A' deck there were a Tourist Public Room against the Purser's Office or Bureau, and the largest games deck areas of the ship for Tourist Class passengers. One area had a second

173. The first class restaurant in the ORIANA. It is interesting to compare this picture with plates 35 and 87.

swimming pool and paddling pools for adults and children, and a large games deck extending across and to the after end of the ship. In the after part of 'B' deck there were three large rooms for Tourist Class passengers, the 'Midship Bar', Ballroom and the 'Stern Gallery'. These rooms had doors opening each into the rest so that, on gala nights, the three rooms could be used almost as one very large room. The aftermost room, the 'Stern Gallery', had large full height windows extending all round the after end of the ship, overlooking the sea, and was regarded by many who saw it as the most attractive public room in the ship. It was reminiscent of the stern gallery of old sailing ships. A library was built at the after end of 'C' deck for Tourist Class passengers and, at the after end of 'D' deck immediately below the library, a large room with its own open deck was built for young children. This was fitted with a sand pit and paddling pool on

174. The tourist class stern gallery bar. It will be noted it is on a level with the roofs of the houses. Normally the view would be of the sea.

the open deck and other attractions were fitted inside the room for the entertainment of the youngsters, who were under the supervision of attendants. The main restaurants for the two classes of passengers were fitted on 'E' deck, the First Class Restaurant forward of the galleys and pantries amidships, and the Tourist Class Restaurant abaft the serving areas.

The quality of furnishing throughout all these public rooms was of a very high standard and this quality has been shown through long experience to be the right and most economical way to construct and furnish a passenger liner. It was all a far cry from the early sailing ships of the Company and their contemporaries.

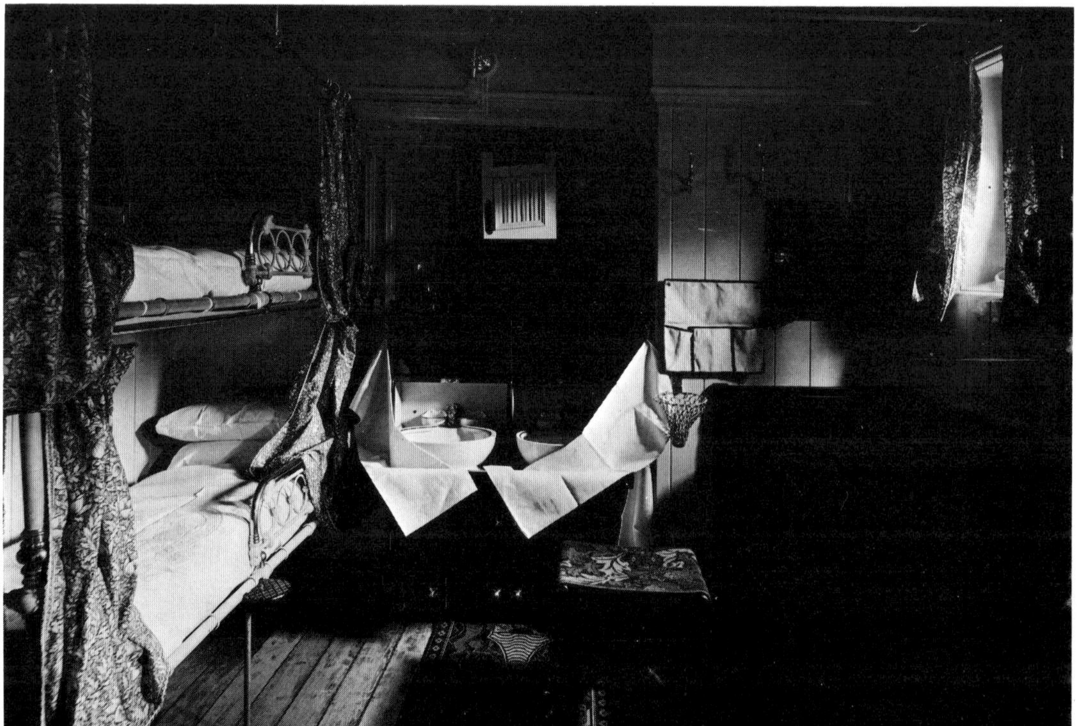

175. A double compactum in the OMRAH (1899). This picture has many details which provide insight into passenger conditions of the period.

XXIII. ABLUTIONS AND PLUMBING

THE IMPROVEMENTS IN amenities for passengers in the fleet from the late nineteenth century onwards continued both in the first class and other grades of accommodation. One of the most important needs for passengers was the provision of bodily cleanliness and, in the early vessels, sea water was generally used for washing, and fresh water only for 'rinsing off' in small quantities, since it was scarce and carried in tanks. No ships made their own, and the first and foremost requirement was for drinking, with washing a very secondary one and only when it was available. Means of washing in cabins first appeared in the form of what was termed a 'compactum', or Folding Lavatory, which was similar to the washing facility fitted in railway carriages for some years before the second World War. It had a top compartment behind a mirror: a mid-height door which hinged downwards to a horizontal position and held a wash-hand basin, sometimes of nickel-plated metal and sometimes of glazed fire-clay. In the bottom compartment was an open-topped tank which received the water from the basin when it was folded up into the 'shut' position while, in the top, behind the mirror, was a small metal tank which held fresh water with a small tap over the wash-basin*. The tap was spring-loaded so that it was automatically closed when its lever was released.

The water tank was filled daily by a cabin steward using a hose from a fresh-water tank fitted in a pantry or place convenient to the cabin, and the drain tank should have been emptied each day at the time that the top tank was filled, but occasionally this was forgotten and resulted in a nasty spillage on the cabin floor. Hot water was

* Plates No. 175 and 177.

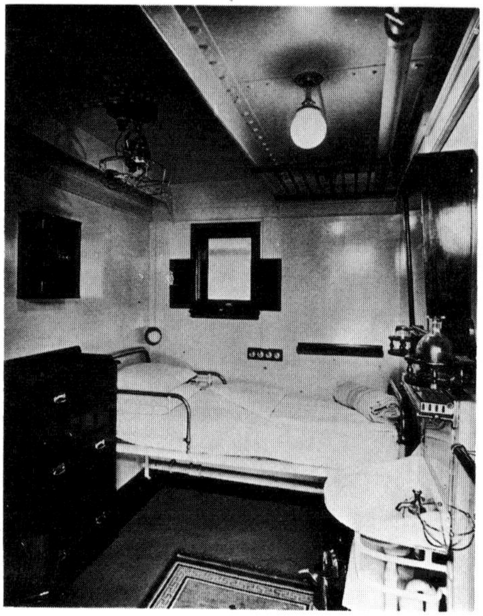

176. View of first class cabin in the OTRANTO (1925). Note: jug, mirror-fronted tank for one cold tap and hot water jug on the deck. (Stir-about fan in the deckhead).

supplied by the cabin steward who would bring it in a small metal jug—usually of brass. I wish I had a few of these jugs today and, even now, they are much sought by antique dealers because, like most such pieces of equipment in those days, they were beautifully made and well-designed for their purpose. The problem of the overflowing of the tanks below the folding lavatories was solved by the next generation of a type of wash basin arrangement.* The tank above the wash basin (which had now become a bulkhead-mounted fixture) was retained but enlarged, and a large mirror disguised its presence, but the most important improvement was the fitting of a wash-basin drain-pipe and trap—an 'S-bend' to some readers. Hot water was still supplied by the cabin steward with a hot water jug. There should have been no more flooding of cabin floors, but passengers could

* Plate No. 176.

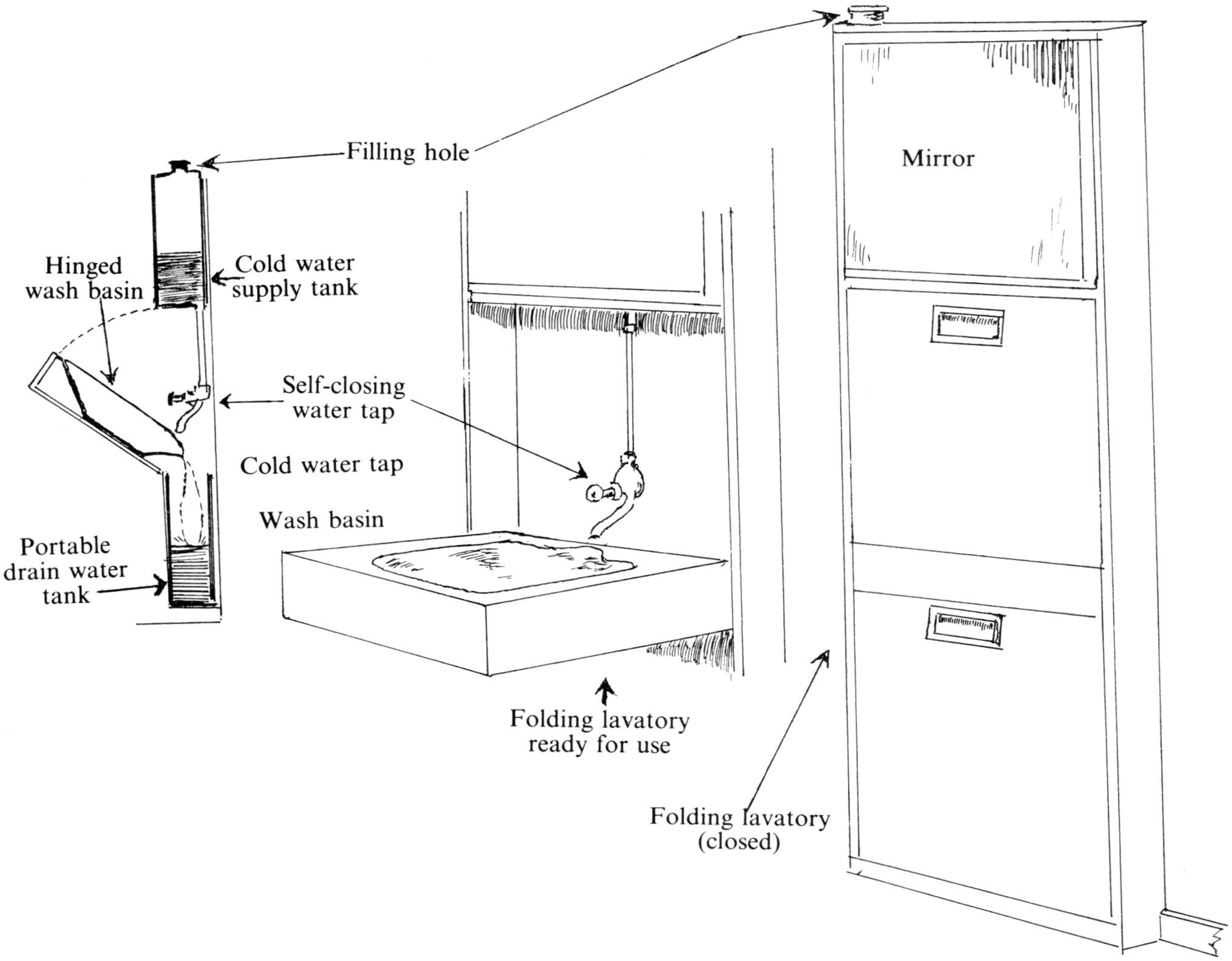

177. Diagrams showing the function of a compactum.

confound almost everyone connected with passenger ship design. No doubt many of them found ways of blocking up overflows and causing the self-closing taps to run constantly, and I know for a fact that many stewards succeeded in doing these things for them with pieces of broomstick and string. Only after 1950 did the supply of hot and cold running water to wash-basins and baths become commonplace in new ships and, soon afterwards, was also being fitted in cabins for the crew. The *Oriana* was so equipped in 1960.

The story of the development of the use of baths in passenger ships was rather different to that of wash-basins. When built-in baths, as distinct from portable tin baths and the like, were first introduced, they were supplied with hot and cold sea water taken from the sea and treated as required. There were very few 'private' baths, the majority being fitted at a suitable spacing throughout the passenger accommodation and attended by bathroom stewards. Because all passengers wanted—or appeared to want—to bath at the same time before dinner, there was a great demand for bathrooms then and, since the stewards' duties included emptying used baths, cleansing them and refilling them for use, it helped them if the water supplies and bath drains were large. The taps were rather like engineers' controls for large machines and the pipes supplying the baths were of $1\frac{1}{2}$ inches bore while the drain-pipes from them were of 2 inches bore so, as may be imagined, the water fairly sloshed in and out!

The baths were supplied with narrow wooden tables which fitted across them to hold small nickel-plated bowls holding hot fresh water which was used by the bathers to rinse themselves down after their baths in salt water. Incidentally, special salt-water soap was provided. A later development was the fitting of small glazed fireclay basins with their own fresh water taps over them at the heads of the baths.

This was only an interim arrangement, which was quickly to be superseded by fresh water baths. Some of these baths of the 1920's were magnificent monuments of the skills of their makers and were of very heavy glazed fire-clay construction but, sadly, often crazed with fine hair-line cracks on the inside surfaces by the extraordinarily hot water which came into them, causing extremely violent and quick expansion of the material around the small areas where the thickness had been increased around the bath-water outlet and the feet of the bath. As the years passed, improvements were made in the provision of fresh water aboard ships, in plumbing and in methods of heating water. After the second World War, hot and cold fresh water was used more generously in passenger ships and the Orient Line, amongst other companies, introduced fresh hot and cold water for public and private baths in passenger, officers' and other ranks' accommodation. Nowadays, new passenger ships commonly have private baths or showers with fresh water supplies in first class cabins, and these amenities are often provided in Tourist class ones as well.

Control of the temperature of the hot water system is difficult aboard most passenger ships because the use of it is not in the form of a steady flow throughout the day. Just before dinner every evening, hundreds of passengers decide to take a bath, and the demand for fresh water 'peaks'. As can be understood readily, less hot water is needed if its temperature is very high, because the baths would be made up of a small volume of hot water and a larger volume of cold. If the hot water temperature is low, not so much cold would be used in a bath, and the temperature is therefore kept high in order to meet the peak demand. Indeed, foolish use of the hot water can cause passengers to scald themselves.

There was—and possibly still is—a problem caused by badly arranged piping systems supplying baths and showers in some passenger ships. Let us imagine that two persons, one taking a bath and the other a shower, are in adjacent spaces: both running the hot and cold taps, and that the shower temperature has been set rather high. If the person in the bathroom, who has been running the hot water fast, turns it off quickly, the hot water flow to the adjacent shower suddenly increases, and the person under it is subjected to an unpleasant shock! We tried many temperature controls for showers but did not find a really satisfactory fitting before I retired in 1971. Perhaps there is such a fitting now.

In the years after the last war, a new concept in providing the pressure in water supply systems aboard ship came into use. Hitherto, water had been persuaded to flow by gravity from large tanks in the space near the base of the ship's funnel, with through pipes leading to the cabins and other points in the accommodation below, and these 'gravity' tanks, as they were called, were kept filled by a float switch which, as required, started or stopped the pump in the engine-room of the vessel. In older installations, this switch often went wrong and caused large quantities of water to overflow on to the open decks. The new pressure system eliminated this problem and operated from a pressure tank in the engine room. We were enabled to provide adequate pressure in the pipes serving the decks at all levels in the new ships, which had not been possible with the old 'gravity' system.

As the older ships aged, the pipes furred up and the flow of water through the taps became very slow. For some years we had experimented with small bore pipes to wash-basins and baths fitted in a section of a deck of cabins in one of the newer vessels of the Company as a result of which, when the *Oriana* was being built, we had enough information and experience from this experimental section of piping to make a decision that the supply piping should be reduced from $\frac{1}{2}$ or $\frac{3}{8}$ inch bore, as in previous ships, to $\frac{1}{4}$ inch bore to wash-basins and showers in the new vessel, and from $\frac{3}{4}$ inch or more to $\frac{1}{2}$ inch bore for bath piping. There were a number of gains achieved by this change. The cabins were improved in appearance because the reduced bore piping to be seen was much neater and less obtrusive than in previous ships, whilst it was cheaper in both cost of material and of installation. Finally, it reduced the weight of piping in the ship and, at the same time, reduced the volume of water lying around in the system, together with the amount of water which had been heated and which cooled whilst lying in the piping ready for use and which had to be run off by each user of wash-basins and baths before obtaining really hot water. Perhaps this is not an important point, but it is a valid one. The improvement of the piping as seen by the passengers was a notable improvement on anything which had gone before it.*

* Plate No. 179.

178. *First class wash basin in an Orient ship of 1935.*

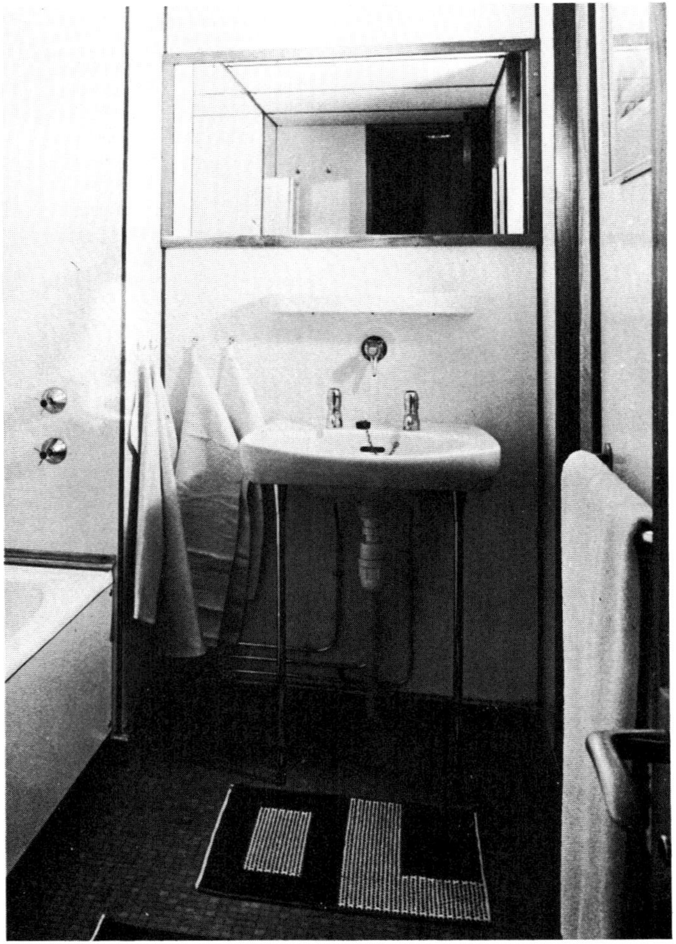

179. *First class wash basin plumbing in the ORIANA, 1960.*

180. *The children's nursery in the ORIZABA (1886) – fortunately in an age before self-resource ceased to be commonplace!*

XXIV. HOSPITALS, CHILDREN'S PLAYROOMS, SHOPS, ETC.

IN SHIPS BUILT for the Orient Company prior to the *Oriana*, hospitals had been built at the after end of the ship. The earlier vessels had the hospital fitted in an individual deckhouse all by itself at the aftermost part of an open deck, thus being situated over the propellers, so that the whole place tended to shake and rattle when the ships were moving at sea. However, this position was not selected to make the patients more sick than they would otherwise have been, but to keep sources of infection as far as possible from the other passengers and members of the crew and, at the same time, to provide the greatest amount of fresh and cooling air when the ship was passing through hot weather.

From personal observation, I have long believed that seamen of all ranks expect and like the noise of things clanking together in ships. Many years ago a colleague and I, when sailing in one vessel in order to carry out some work, were disturbed and annoyed by a noise caused by the vibration of a foot-brake lever on a winch. On investigation, we found that the noise could be eradicated by forcing a small piece of wood between the brake lever and the quadrant. There were members of the crew working about the winch island and, soon after we had left the area, the irritating noise started again. It was obvious that they had removed the wood and must have found the noise to be a comfort of some kind.*

Another incident occurred some time later. There is usually a slight vibration in a ship when she is moving. In the restaurant the tables were set ready for a meal, and in front of each dining chair there

* Might not the seamen have considered the insertion of the wooden wedge likely to be forgotten and best removed against the next time the winch was worked? (Ed.)

181. The children's nursery in the ORIANA.

were about a dozen pieces of cutlery on the table. The noise of clashing knives, forks and spoons was almost deafening and the place sounded as though it would fall apart at any moment. The stewards, the head waiter and his assistants were standing in groups talking and, apparently, quite happy and oblivious of the noise. It appears that a rattling noise carries with it a feeling of vibration because, by separating the items of cutlery, which had moved together on the tables, the noise stopped and apparently the vibration almost disappeared. The design of the cutlery incorporated a collar separating each handle from the blade, fork or spoon bowl. This collar was oval in shape and caused each item to rock slightly to and fro and to progress across the tablecloth until it joined its neighbours and started to rock and clash with them. In a short time the noise was back with us. The simple cure was to grind 'flats' on the sides of the collars and the noise in the restaurant was no more; but such examples make it obvious to me that modern seafarers expect vibration and noise and do not find it distracting.

In the ships built for the Company after the Second World War, the Isolation Hospital and General Hospital were separated; the Isolation Hospital still being built at the after end of an open deck as in previous ships, but the General Hospital and Dispensary were at the after end of the main block of passenger accommodation on the same deck as the Isolation Hospital, in order to help the doctor and his staff in supervision of the patients.

When the design of the *Oriana* was being discussed, the Company decided that this new ship should be totally air-conditioned in the accommodation for passengers and crew. This decision enabled a new concept for the hospitals to be developed allowing them, both general and isolation, to be moved to the quietest area of the ship, just forward of amidships. Each ward of the Isolation Hospital had its own sitting veranda room with a view to the sea, while there was a separate ventilation system for the wards. There were waiting rooms accessible to First Class and Tourist Class passengers and members of the crew, together with a dispensary, consulting room, operating room and all the ancillary needs of hospitals. The standards of furnishing of the hospitals were also raised from those pertaining to all previous ships of the fleet.

Around the ship's accommodation there were arranged clothes—washing, drying and ironing rooms for the passengers' use. These were additional to a large laundry staffed by members of the crew to clean the ship's linen as well as laundry work required for the personal needs of the passengers. This latter service, of course, was an additional charge to be met by them. The rooms for washing and drying and ironing by passengers for their personal needs were equipped with washing and spin drying machines, together with irons and ironing boards. These rooms had tiled floors and walls finished in hard-faced plastics.

Shops for both classes of passengers were arranged to provide their day-to-day needs of toilet goods, clothing, etc., but, additionally, as in most passenger liners, there was an extensive selection of jewellery, pottery, photography equipment, and other goods which could be purchased as presents or for personal use. These shops were associated with well equipped hairdressing saloons for male and female passengers.

The Main Galleys and Pantries were arranged on 'E' Deck, between the Dining Rooms for the two classes of passengers, and preparation rooms for meat, fish, poultry and vegetables, bakery and dairy were arranged on 'F' Deck close to the Main Galley on the deck above.

Meals were served in two sittings in the Dining Rooms and this meant that, in a full ship, over 1,000 meals would be served in one sitting of both classes of passengers. Other pantries for the use of bedroom staff were built in suitably-spaced positions around the passenger accommodation and were equipped to provide an efficent room service.

The radio room was built in a position on the Stadium Deck where it could be visited by any passenger of either class, a service being provided for passengers to contact friends ashore by telegram or telephone.

A printer's shop was designed and equipped for the printing of the ship's daily news sheet, menus, and other printing required for the ship's daily use. It is, in fact, surprising how much printing is required in a vessel of this sort.

XXV. SAFETY PRECAUTIONS AND LIFE SAVING ARRANGEMENTS

THE LIFEBOATS OF the Orient Ships and most passenger liners had been fitted on the Boat Deck (the topmost superstructure deck) for many years but, because of the use of aluminium alloy in the construction of the upper works of the *Oriana*, enabling an extra deck to be incorporated in the superstructure, the lifeboats would have been over seventy feet above the normal waterline if they had been fitted in the usual position. A question came from one of the Directors, 'Why not move the lifeboats to a lower deck?' This was a good question. Eventually, by collaboration with Donald MacLachlan, of the Welin-MacLachlan Davits Company, an under-deck davit of entirely new design was fitted to the underside of the Veranda Deck.

The boats hung from the davits over 'B' Deck at a height enabling passengers to walk along that deck underneath the boats. This arrangement of davits and boats reduced the height of the stowage position to about forty-five feet above the normal waterline. Hitherto, the lifeboats had been made of wood, iron, or steel. Boats of wood were usually built of narrow planks, the best being constructed in teak, laid clinker-wise as a rule. These often hung in the strong sun and, when put into the sea, leaked badly until the wood had swollen again to its original size. If the wood used in the construction was inferior to teak, rot was also a problem.

Iron boats could be long-lasting, but galvanized steel boats were poor unless maintenance was extremely good. Rust attacked the steel in corners where dampness prevailed, and this was usual in ships at sea. Spray often blew along the leeward side of a ship for days, causing decks, on their tops and undersides, deckhouse sides, boats, inside and out, and all outside fittings and surfaces to be constantly and thoroughly wet all the time these sort of wind conditions remained around the ship. The deterioration of paintwork and the progress of rust during such times were costly in maintenance and replacement.

At the time of the designing of the *Oriana*, attention turned to the possibility of using plastics for some exterior parts of the ship—particularly the lifeboats. We enquired about plastics used in ships of other Companies and found that there had been some bad experiences. These seemed to have arisen by using plastics re-inforced by steel or other metals, or by wood. To us, this seemed a wrong method, because the rate of thermal expansion of the two materials would be very different. In any case, we knew that glass-reinforced plastic (G.R.P.) was a very strong material and a structure built of G.R.P. could be stronger than a similar one of the same weight built of ordinary structural steel. However G.R.P. construction was fairly new at that time and had a service history of less than ten years.

The Orient Company then decided to make its own assessment of the value of G.R.P., and representatives visited manufacturers of the basic materials used in its construction in the plastics industry to consult with them on the methods of using plastics by boat manufacturers in Britain. As a result, we found a good boat-builder and, in collaboration with him, designed our own lifeboats, in which the load-bearing structure was entirely made of glass-reinforced plastic. The first boat passed all Ministry of Transport tests very well, and in consequence the whole equipment of boats for life-saving requirements of the ship was built in G.R.P.

Boats for life-saving purposes are hung from davits in such a way as to be lowered by gravity to their loading positions in the event of a ship being abandoned. They are usually ‘bowsed in’ to a firm and safe position automatically as the boat is lowered: the crew carrying out this operation. After the boats have received their passengers they can be lowered to the water and released quickly by special release hooks. Since a few passengers or crew may accidentally be left behind in the possible confusion attending such an event, rope ladders are required by law to be fitted, two to each boat, to enable those still aboard the ship to get down to the boats.

As has already been stated, the distance from the boats to the water is over forty-five feet if the ship is upright in the water, and could be more or less in the case of abandoning ship—but this height is daunting to a man, even if he is young and with a 'head for heights'. Older, less experienced and less able-bodied humans, male or female, could not use such a rope ladder, even in good conditions and in daylight. The possibility of doing the same in stormy conditions and in the dark cannot be contemplated. In previous ships, the rope ladders were stowed in positions above the boats and, to do this, the ladders were rolled up as neatly as possible and put into canvas bags made for the purpose. Finally they were hung in a rather untidy way along the underside of the deck over the boat-loading positions or over the ship's side in similar positions.

One day, Ford Geddes was talking about his own life-saving arrangements in his house in London, where he lived at that time with his wife and young family. He had a gadget called a 'Davis' fire escape apparatus which was hung near one of the upstairs windows. It consisted of a rope passing over a sheave, which was controlled in such a way as to ensure that a person hanging on to the rope could descend at a reasonable speed to the ground outside the building. I understood (at least, my memory tells me so), that Ford was in the habit of exercising this escape gear and I have frequently thought of the consternation he must have caused to passers-by as he landed on the pavement unexpectedly beside them! One day he landed near a passing policeman who, as Ford put it, 'Didn't blink an eyelid.' Our policeman are indeed wonderful. However, we had an idea that this device could be 'marinized' and applied to lifeboats instead of the awful boat ladders.

We devised a foot-stirrup and quick-release belt, as for passengers in aircraft, to be fitted to each end of the rope which was passed over the sheave of the apparatus. This meant that, as one person reached the sea-level, the other quick-release belt and foot-stirrup would have ascended for use by a second person. It would be better than a rope-ladder, because the person using the Longworth descent gear, as it is now named, could fend himself off the ship's side as he swung on the rope, instead of trying to hold on to and move down the wooden steps of a rope ladder. Furthermore, the hazards caused by the swinging of a very heavy rope ladder and its wooden steps are very grave. A man's head could easily be crushed if struck by its heavy woodwork. Moreover it is well-nigh impossible to instil into a lands-man the correct way to ascend or descend a Jacob's (rope) ladder, which is to use both hands on one side, and use it sideways, as it were.

Our next step was to persuade the Ministry of Transport that this would be an improved way of enabling people to get down to a boat from a sinking ship. The talks with the Marine section of the Ministry of Transport did not prove easy. Our strongest opponent was an ex-ship's captain who was so difficult to convince as to be almost implacable. We did point out that all passengers in a liner were not young and fit and, indeed, that many of them are old and infirm and could not possibly be expected to go down a long way using a rope ladder swinging wildly in space. A terrified old lady, for instance, could, in extremity, be fitted into the belt with its foot stirrup and pushed over the ship's side to a waiting lifeboat.

During the discussions and arguments which had already taken place our ace-hand was finally played. 'Was it true that there had been an occasion when, in a sinking and burning troop ship, a soldier had 'frozen' with terror when part-way down a rope ladder, and, because he would not move, the other soldiers had to climb over him to go down the ladder?' With some reluctance our principal antagonist, the ex-seagoing officer, owned that our information was true. It was agreed that, if a successful demonstration could be given on a passenger ship, our proposals would be accepted.

It so happened that the *Orsova* was being refitted at Newcastle and would soon be completed. We arranged that the usual social occasion of a ship sailing from the Builders to her departure port would have an additional event—a demonstration of the Longworth boat descent gear, and that our recalcitrant ex-mariner and his wife should be amongst the guests to witness what took place. When the day came, the weather was calm and rather foggy, but the demonstration proceeded. The ship was stopped and, as a boat was lowered to the

182. The French liner ATLANTIQUE which was broken up after a disastrous fire in the English Channel in 1933. Of 40,935 tons, she was three years old.

water, one or two adventurous souls went down using the Longworth gear. A rope ladder was also released and its end lay in the boat. Some of our Directors went down in the new gear and then there was a stream of girl pursers and other members of the staff, who were thoroughtly enjoying the experience. It was demonstrated that a person going down could stop himself at any point by taking hold of the up-going rope of the gear. Finally, one of the Managers, David Peters, who had been a commando in the Second World War, volunteered to have a race down to the boat, using a rope ladder, and his competitor was another Manager, Kenneth Anderson, using the Longworth gear, which he had never seen until that day. The ex-commando lost the race!

All this had been seen by the M.O.T. ex-mariner, but he would not go down to the boat using either of the methods. Nevertheless we got approval for it and adopted the gear, which was fitted in quick-opening, weather resistant, boxes of G.R.P. hung in their positions over the boats.

So far as I know the only other ship which adopted this method of helping people down from the open deck of a passenger ship to the life-boats or the sea, was the *Canberra*, of the P. & O. Company, and I do not think that the method has ever been written into a Ministry book on 'The Safety of Life at Sea,' which is curious, to say the least.

Fire is the greatest threat to life at sea in passenger liners. Not many people have witnessed such conflagrations, but the experience is one which can never be forgotten, and the risks are there from the moment a ship's building commences. Some fires are caused in ships during building at the 'fitting out' stage, when cabins are being completed, while others break out during the 'turn-round'—the time between arrival and departure of a ship in service. At this time the cabins are being re-furbished and often, in cold weather, workmen switch on electric fires, if they are fitted, to warm themselves and to dry their wet coats. There have been instances of small fires caused by drying clothes which have been laid over theoretically safe electric fires of the convection type. In doing this, the openings in the casing of the electric fire have been obstructed and caused the temperature to rise to the point where combustion of the clothing has started and caused a fire in the cabin.

Some fires are started by cranks and malicious people, and there are always small fires aboard ships during building due to such causes. In the fitting-out stage the ship is very vulnerable to this sort of thing and there have been incidents due to wardrobes in cabins being filled with inflammable materials and deliberately set alight. The Orient Company was the first in Britain to adopt the fitting of sprinklers in the accommodation and other areas of large passenger ships. The sprinkler heads are spaced suitably in piping run in the ceilings and deckheads of the accommodation. The water is fed by pressure from a large water tank for the initial supply of water, but in all ships fitted with the sprinkler system there is a pump, usually powered by a diesel engine, which starts automatically as soon as the water pressure in the system drops below a pre-determined level. In the *Oriana*, because of the extent of aluminium used in her superstructure, the Ministry insisted that two such pumps should be fitted far apart in the vessel so that, if one pump should fail to start, the other pump would cut in—an additional safeguard. The sprinkler head is made in such a way as to release a fierce spray of water when a fire creates a temperature predetermined for the sprinkler head. At the same time, alarms ring on the Navigation Bridge, or other suitable places, to warn staff of fire and to indicate where it has occurred.

The quality of fire protection given by this system is very high and the records of successful fire detection and quenching are numerous and impressive. The method is known to many as a 'fire-fighting system' and has always been favoured by the Orient and by many other large shipping companies. It could be called the British method because, whilst we did not invent it, we adopted it and the equipment is manufactured in Manchester.

The main alternative method is more passive, and could be called 'fire-resisting', or the 'U.S.A. method' (because they produced it) and, to be completely frank, they forced it through all its International legislation. The method presumes that all material used in the construction of a ship is fire-proof, or fire resistant. I have never heard it claimed that all the other materials and substances used in a ship are also fire-resistant and non-inflammable. We know that a ship can have on board thousands of tons of oil fuel, many tons of food fats and other inflammable substances, spirits in the form of nail varnishes, drinks, and so forth, carried by passengers and crew in their cabins where they smoke and are often careless. There are, too, intricate wiring systems and other electrical equipment all over the ship to cause fire but, in spite of this, the Americans favour a system of fire protection which relies on passive resistance backed by various contrived securities which many would declare to give a false sense of safety. I have never been able to prevent myself from being interested in the possibility that the *United States* could have had a major fire, as a result of which we could see the system the Americans favour do its work—without loss of life, of course.

The curious fact about the dislike shown by the powerful maritime authority of the U.S.A. towards sprinklers on board ships is that the sprinkler system was invented and marketed in the States, and fitted in most large buildings there—but not on their ships, which float in the very fluid required for fire-fighting by this method. They have also had some of the worst ship fires. I believe I know why the other

183. Many lives were lost when the American Ward liner MORRO CASTLE was burnt out in 1934. She is beached here at Ashbury Park, New Jersey.

method was adopted by the U.S.A., but will not say more on the subject and thus avoid possible litigation! In respect of this subject of fire protection and, in particular, of the subject of sprinklers, an official of the company which manufactures this equipment in Manchester stated in August, 1978:-

> *'I am happy to confirm the continued success of Marine Sprinkler Systems and so far as we know there is no recorded case of a fully operational sprinkler system failing to control a fire that started in a sprinkler protected area on a ship.'*

Up to October, 1978, the company had provided more than 4,000 Sprinkler installations in Passenger Vessels of all types.

The main machinery spaces in the *Oriana* are protected against fire by the Mulsi-Spray system—a foam producing plant.

The principal material used in what we will now call the 'American method' of fire-resisting was known as 'Marinite', a boarding made in the U.S.A., consisting largely of asbestos, and this was 'pushed' unmercifully on the shipbuilding market some years ago. Nowadays, there are other sorts of asbestos-based boards available to do the same job. The boards are not good material in which to drive screws, and fittings often became loose, unless they were secured by bolts passing right through the boards, with nuts fitted on the other side. I dislike materials of this sort and only used them when obliged to do so by legislation, which was forced on the British by pressures described in the Chapter on *Committes and Conventions*. Unfortunately, the members of some authorities, (although not Lloyds), have been so long away from the real business of building and running of ships that the commercial reasons for which ships exist have been forgotten and, disregarding them, we must constantly make ships safer and safer, even if we finally have ships which cannot earn their keep. The final outcome would be that they are not built at all, because they can no longer be competitive in the business of transport. From these caustic remarks, I exclude many good friends in some sections of the Department of Trade and Industry, with whom I have discussed this subject and from whom I had great understanding and help.

Having gone from the general to the personal, the subject can be changed to another aspect of safety—the holds and some other store places. In order to slow down the progress of a major fire envisaged to have happened in a ship, and which has got out of hand, the vessel is divided into fire zones by heavily insulating the watertight bulkheads which subdivide the ship up to the deck known as the 'bulkhead deck' (the continuous deck to which all of them are carried) except the foremost one—the 'collision bulkhead'—which is taken one deck higher. Fireproof bulkheads are built from the bulkhead deck upwards to the top decks and, as far as possible, these are arranged in line with the main watertight ones so as to sub-divide the ship into separate 'fire-zones.' Any steps required in these bulkheads are also insulated to the same standards as those of the other ones.

The type of detection and fighting of fire in the main holds and some other suitable spaces of the *Oriana* was known as the E.D. Hol inert-gas fire extinguishing system, and it was in 17 cargo spaces, the emergency dynamo room and the battery room. The inert-gas fire extinguishing system, when required, used the oil fuel from the ship's bunkers in a gas-producing plant from which to pump gas into the compartment affected by fire. The attraction of this system is that much of the content of any compartment in which fire had been put out by this method would not have been damaged or destroyed. This fire detection was also monitored on the Navigating Bridge or some other station on board the ship. There are some materials, fortunately few in common use, which are capable of burning in an enclosed space without air because they contain all the ingredients necessary to sustain combustion. The inert-gas system could not prevail against fire in such materials but, notwithstanding, the Pyrene smoke detecting system in the *Oriana* would operate and cause action to be taken by the ship's personnel.

In the event of failure of the electric lighting supply and of electric power to certain essential safety equipment, an emergency generator room was fitted high in the vessel, with an emergency battery room nearby. Two diesel-driven generators each of 200 k.w. 220 volt D.C. power were fitted which would start automatically if the main generators of the ship failed. Connected to the emergency generators was a battery system of 220 volt D.C. 320 amp./hours connected through an emergency switchboard to provide emergency lighting throughout the ship and enough power for steering the ship until the emergency generators could take over the duty.

The *Oriana*, like any other good passenger ship, had all the modern electrical aids to safety and navigation and, from time to time, as was the policy of the Company, these aids were reviewed, improved or fitted, as they became available.

XXVI. THE MACHINERY INSTALLATION

PROBABLY THE FOLLOWING information will only be of interest to technically-minded readers.

Twin-screws were driven through double-reduction gearing by two sets of steam turbines, H.P., I.P., and L.P., of 'Parmetrada' design providing a total normal shaft horse power of 65,000 at 147 revolutions per minute of the propellers. The total maximum designed shaft horse power was 80,000 at 157.5 revolutions per minute of the propellers.

The L.P. turbines were of the double flow mixed impulse reaction type consisting of four single-row impulse stages followed by six reaction stages.

The I.P. turbines were of the all-impulse type, consisting of nine single row wheels. Bled steam for feed heating was taken from these turbines.

The H.P. turbines were of the all-impulse type, consisting of one impulse wheel with two rows of blades followed by eight single row impulse wheels in each turbine.

The H.P. astern turbines were overhung at the forward ends of the I.P. turbines and consisted of one two-row impulse wheel in each turbine. The L.P. astern turbines consisted of two separate impulse wheels incorporated in the forward end of each L.P. turbine cylinder.

The H.P., I.P. and L.P. turbines were designed to run at 4,085, 3,588 and 2,198 revolutions per minute respectively at maximum power, and the astern turbines were designed to provide 65 per cent of

184. The main switch board.

the normal service shaft horse power. The steam for the turbines was supplied to them at 700 p.s.i. gauge and a temperature of 950 degs. F.

The two main condensers were designed to maintain 28 inches of vacuum against a sea temperature of 86 degs. F. Each condenser had 10,100 tubes made of cupro-nickel providing a cooling surface of 32,000 square feet and the total length of all these tubes was 63.75 miles.

The propellers, or screws, were each made from single solid castings 20 feet in diameter, and were made of nickel-aluminium-bronze. Each propeller weighed about 29 tons.

Steam was supplied to the turbines from four water-tube boilers of Foster-Wheeler external superheater design arranged to maintain the superheat constantly at 960 degs. F. at the superheater outlet whilst at sea. The superheat temperature was reduced to 825 degs. F.

185. The main generator room, looking to port.

whilst the vessel was manoeuvring and the outlet pressure was maintained constantly at 750 p.s.i. gauge and the combination, steam-pressure and temperature were all controlled automatically by equipment installed for that purpose.

The air for the boiler was pre-heated to 230 degs. F. by bled steam air heaters and the oil fuel burning installation had four pumping and heating units, only three of which were required to be in use for the development of maximum horse power. Oil fuel had to be heated so that it could be burned satisfactorily in the boiler furnace and the equipment fitted for the boilers maintained the oil fuel at a constant viscosity for efficient combustion. The burners fitted in the boilers were operated with oil fuel at 500 p.s.i. gauge. Each boiler was capable of a maximum continuous evaporation of 200,000 lb. of steam per hour and 160,000 lb. per hour in normal service conditions.

186. Main machinery control console in the engine room.

Steam from these boilers was also used to drive the main turbo-generators. The electrical power was of 220 volts D.C. and, in my opinion, should have been A.C. as fitted in the *Canberra*, and other large passenger liners. At the time the *Oriana* was being designed the subject of A.C. or D.C. power for the ship was being debated, and, because an A.C. installation would have been less expensive and appreciably lighter in weight, I hoped that the decision would have been made in favour of A.C. which I had recommended. However, for reasons which might make complicated reading, D.C. generators were fitted in the new ship, and I now know that this was a mistake.

Nowadays, most electrical equipment is designed to be powered by alternating current and, in consequence, the majority of the electrical equipment in the galleys, pantries, laundry, washing and ironing rooms and elsewhere (which were of A.C. type) had to be

187. Automatic combustion control for the two starboard boilers. There was a similar one for the port ones.

modified to suit direct current or supplied with alternating current through motor-alternators fitted for the purpose, as well as for the fluorescent lighting. If the *Oriana* had had a main electric supply of alternating current, appreciable savings would have been made in the first cost of the installation and, moreover, in the installed weight, quite apart from a reduction in the bulk of some electrical equipment and some improvement in appearance.

The electric power was provided by four turbo-generators, but only three of these were required normally, the fourth being held in reserve. The generators were fitted in line across the ship in a large compartment forward of the stabilizer room, and the generated power was fed into a large switchboard, 65 feet in length, arranged across the compartment. Each generator was 1,750 kW normal rating with an overload capacity of 10% for two hours.

188. The ORIANA leaves her fitting out berth at Barrow for Falmouth for dry-docking prior to her trials off the Clyde, November, 1960.

There was a large demand for alternating current in the ship and this was provided by three motor alternators, each of 250 kW, 230 volts, three phase and 50 cycles. Normally, only two of these would be required, mainly for the fluorescent lighting, but many pieces of equipment, as mentioned above, had to be specially modified in order to work off the direct current supply.

Included in the machinery installation was a group of six evaporators which were capable of producing a total of 650 tons of distilled water every day for the ship's use. This facility was in addition to the 2,958 tons of fresh water which could be carried in the tanks built into the structure of the ship. All fresh water for use of passengers and crew was filtered and treated to ensure its purity for domestic purposes.

XXVII. INTERESTING PARTICULARS ABOUT THE ORIANA

In 1960, when the *Oriana* was completed, she was the largest passenger liner ever built in England as distinct from Scotland.

She cost about £14,000,000 sterling at that time, and was designed to operate from Southampton to Australia, via the Suez Canal, and to cross the Pacific Ocean to Canada and the U.S.A. and, if required, pass through the Panama Canal and back to Southampton, across the Atlantic Ocean.

Particulars given here were true at the time when the ship was new and just delivered by her Builders.

Length overall	804 feet
Length between Perpendiculars	740 feet
Breadth Moulded	97 feet
Breadth extreme	100 feet
Normal Loaded Draught, (designed)	31 feet 6 inches
Normal Loaded Displacement, (designed)	38,400 tons
Depth (Moulded) to Strength Deck ('B' Deck)	68 feet 9 inches
Maximum Loaded Draught, (assigned)	32 feet
Maximum Loaded Displacement, (assigned)	39,020 tons
Gross Tonnage	41,923 tons
First Class Passengers	688
Tourist Class Passengers	1,496

189. The port propeller shaft tunnel.

Crew	899
Total Complement	3,083
Service Shaft Horse Power	65,000
Corresponding R.P.M. of Propellers	147
Maximum Shaft Horse Power	80,000
Corresponding R.P.M. of Propellers	157.5
Service Speed	27.5 knots
Trial Speed using 80,000 S.H.P.	30.64 knots
Contract for Ship placed	12th May, 1954
Ship was laid Down	18th September, 1957
Ship was Launched by Princess Alexandra	3rd November, 1959

Ship was Delivered to her Owners	15th November, 1960
General Cargo (including Hatch Trunks)	150,541 cubic feet, bale
Insulated Cargo	53,520 cubic feet
Insulated Stores	30,051 cubic feet
Bulk Stores	36,305 cubic feet
Mail and Baggage Rooms	32,846 cubic feet

11,598 cubic feet of general cargo space could be used as extra mail capacity, so these figures could be 138,943 cubic feet general cargo, and 44,444 cubic feet mail).

Sundry Store Rooms	60,664 cubic feet
Oil Fuel	6,852 tons
Fresh Water, Domestic	2,365 tons
Fresh Water, Engineer's Feed water	593 tons
Water Ballast (much of this was for alternative use as Fresh Water)	2,005 tons
Weight of Steel in Ship	13,650 tons
Weight of Aluminium Alloy in Ship	1,040 tons
Weight of Ship when Launched	15,250 tons
Length of Piping in Ship	50 miles
Length of Electric Cables and Wiring	350 miles
Length of Trunking for Ventilation, and Air-conditioning in ship	13 miles
Area of Aluminium Alloy Decks and Bulkheads in ship	$\frac{1}{3}$ million square feet
Length of Aluminium Alloy Extrusions in Ship	20 miles
Length of Aluminium Alloy Welding Wire used in Ship	600 miles
Lifts for First Class Passengers	5
Lifts for Tourist Class Passengers	2
Lift from Engineers' Accommodation to Machinery Spaces	1
Other Service Lifts	5
Electric Cranes of capacity to lift 5 tons each	8

190. The electro-hydraulic steering gear.

Electro-hydraulic Steering Gear was fitted.
Stabilizers—with fins, each of 120 sq. feet—1 set.
Sideways Manoeuvring Units, two forward and two aft, each driven by electric motors, each of 550 b.h.p. and each remotely controlled from the Navigation Bridge.
Baggage Handling Equipment, one forward and one aft, comprised overboard mechanical conveyors from ship to shore or vice-versa and the after installation included a long conveyor on the centre-line of the ship carrying baggage into or out of the Main Passenger Baggage Rooms.
Also fitted in the After Baggage Rooms were two baggage elevators to convey baggage vertically in the ship.
Asbestos boards for Fire-resistant purposes 165,000 sq. feet

Air-conditioning Cooling Capacity	22,000,000 B.Th.U. per hr.
Air-conditioning and Refrigeration motors	30 in No. totalling 1,100 h.p.
Fans for Air-conditioning	130 in No. totalling 650 h.p.

A 500-line Manual Telephone Exchange was fitted for First Class Cabins and Pantry.

An Automatic Telephone Exchange of 120 lines was installed for Staff Communications.

About 125 electric clocks were fitted throughout the ship all controlled from a Master Clock on the Navigating Bridge governed by two 8-day chronometers.

About 2,000 electric sockets and 10,000 lighting fittings were fitted in cabins.

About 500 electric sockets and 5,000 lighting fittings were fitted in Public Rooms and Entrances.

Evaporators to produce 650 tons of Fresh Water each day.

Weight of Main Machinery 3,952 tons.

There were fifteen decks and flats in the ship.

Epoxy-type paint was used on the Hull.

The teak wood Decks were only $1\frac{1}{2}$ inches thick secured by special welded screws and nuts to reduce the weight and cost of the installation*.

The steel or alloy decks were levelled with latex underlay before the wood deck was laid.

Soft-plastic decorative coverings were used on the walls of all First Class, Tourist Class and Crew Cabins. This was done to enable colour schemes to be changed from time to time as the ship aged, and for the work to be done easily and inexpensively.

Amongst the systems fitted in the ship were the following:–

Bilge and Ballast Piping; Scuppers, and Dischargers; Cold, Hot, and Iced Water Piping to cabins and pantries; Cold Salt Water Piping; Air and Overflow Pipes; Steam Heating to Oil Fuel Tanks; Sprinkler System; Fresh Water Filling, Gas Smothering and Fire-Detection System; Levelling Pipes; Re-heat Piping for Air-conditioning;

*Plate No. 191.

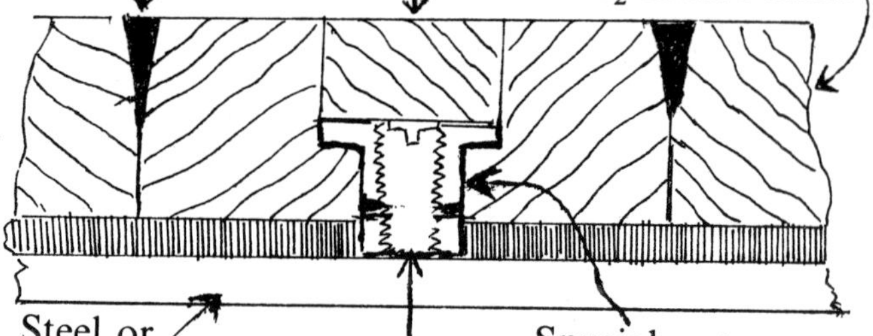

191. Special screws and nuts to secure thin teak deck planks.

Air-conditioning and Ventilating Trunking; Natural Ventilation Trunking; Distant-reading Depth Gauges; Hydraulic System for Watertight Doors; Fresh Water Tank Pneumercator Systems; Steering Gear Telemotor Piping; and many other systems.

About 10,600 square yards of carpet, comprising about 80 miles, of woollen yarn were used in the ship: there were 15 different designs of carpet and the approximate total weight of the finished carpets was 18 tons.

A large passenger ship is comparable with a small town which proceeds at speed from place to place over the seas of the world whilst most of its inhabitants happily enjoy surroundings, food, drink and service superior to that normally provided ashore. The total number of humans which could be carried by the *Oriana* was over 3,000 and caused intense activity within the food-preparation spaces nearly all day long whilst the ship was in commission. At least 20,000 hot meal courses were prepared daily and the bakery and confectioner's shop provided the loaves, rolls and wide variety of cakes required in their thousands each day. Fresh milk and cream was taken aboard at the ports visited by the ship but to ensure that milk was always available a mechanical 'cow' was fitted in the ship's dairy, which was commonly said to be milked with a spanner! There were many rooms, normally unseen by passengers, on the galley deck and the deck below it where activities went on to back up the cooking requirements of the ship—butchers shop, fish and poultry rooms, vegetable preparing space, cold dish and salads service, and the essential plate, dish, cutlery and pan cleaning rooms, still rooms and cruet rooms and other spaces for innumerable jobs to be done connected with the provision of food for passengers and crew. The senior staff responsible for the running of the catering department of a large passenger ship was made up of highly trained people who had had experience ashore in the best hotels in London and other cities of the world, and the service and food and drink provided was, at its best, equal at least to that to be found ashore.

Tableware used in the First Class Restaurant and Silver Grill was called Queen's Ware, made by Josiah Wedgewood and Sons Ltd., using a decoration design by Professor Robert Goodden of the Royal College of Art. The design of cutlery was 'ergonomic' (i.e., of a shape suited to the palm of the human hand), designed by Robert Welch in stainless steel and made by Mappin and Webb. 65,200 pieces were required for the *Oriana*, amongst which were 14,000 table forks, 12,000 tea spoons, 10,000 table knives and fish knives, 1,000 jam spoons, 800 butter knives and 400 pickle forks.

Three dishwashing machines were fitted in the galleys and pantries, each of which was 15 feet long. In one non-stop automatic transit through the machines, the articles passing through would be scraped, washed and rinsed, and finally rinsed again to a high standard of hygiene. All that the galley staff using the machines had to do was load a stainless steel conveyor rack at one end of the washing machine, and take off the cleaned things at the other end.

Four smaller spray-type dish-washing machines were also fitted in the ship.

Provision Rooms and Cold Chambers of the Ship were insulated with Polyurethane, a rigid foam weighing between 2 and 3 lbs. per cubic foot.

192. The BERENGARIA, ex-German IMPERATOR.

193. The AQUITANIA.

Two famous 'Atlantic greyhounds' of the past.

XXVIII. THE END OF THE ERA OF LARGE PASSENGER LINERS AND THE ADVENT OF THE CRUISE SHIP

I HAVE ALWAYS believed that the most important aspects of a passenger ship are the care, comfort and happiness of the passengers, who are the *raison d'être* of the ship's existence and of the employment of her crew. For this reason, all other considerations should be subordinated to them. In recent times this axiom seems to have been forgotten or, perhaps, has lost some of its former importance.

Some years ago, I was a naval architect working for Denny's of Dumbarton, probably at one time the best shipbuilding company in the world specializing in building small ships, principally passenger, car and train cross-channel ferries. Denny's had just started to build a cross-channel ferry for the carriage of passengers, cars and trains. This vessel, the *Aromoana*, was designed by consultant naval architects employed by the future owners, the Government of New Zealand. After we received the contract to build the ship, we were required to make detailed drawings and submit them for approval by the Government Department concerned with this matter. We then received a request from them to move some passenger cabins from a very good position on an upper deck to a lower deck in the ship, and to use the vacated space to accommodate crew cabins which had previously occupied the space now to be used for passengers. This move had been demanded by the seamen's union in New Zealand, and the Government Department had acquiesced to it. This, in my opinion, was a gross injustice to the passengers and a mis-use of the space within the ship.*

There have been other instances of this sort, and probably many more than those about which I have known. The Commonwealth Government of Australia in 1922 started the Commonwealth Government Line by having built five passenger-cargo ships of approximately 14,000 gross tons to carry passengers, mainly in third class accommodation but with provision for a small number of First Class passengers, between the United Kingdom and Australia. The route was from London through the Suez Canal to Brisbane, calling at Colombo, Fremantle, Adelaide, Melbourne and Sydney, with monthly sailings. Within a year, there was considerable reorganization and the name of the Line was changed to the Australian Commonwealth Line. There followed unrest, strikes of seamen, strikes of stewards, and dock strikes, all of which were often about trivial matters but which, together with mismanagement, caused chaos and failure of the state-owned shipping line. The ships were known as the 'Bay' steamers because their names were *Moreton Bay, Largs Bay, Hobsons Bay, Esperance Bay* and *Jervis Bay*, all named after bays in various parts of Australia. The ships were first sold to the White Star Line and then to a Company formed under joint ownership of the Shaw Savill and P. & O. Companies called the Aberdeen and Commonwealth Line and managed by the Shaw Savill Company.

One of these 'Bay' ships made honourable and glorious history. The *Jervis Bay* had been commissioned as an armed merchant cruiser in 1939 and was escorting a convoy in the north Atlantic on 5 November, 1940, when it was attacked by a German 'pocket-battleship', the *Admiral Scheer*. The *Jervis Bay* steamed towards the German warship and diverted its attention and fire from the convoy, which scattered. The commander of the *Jervis Bay* sacrificed his ship and most of her Company, for she sank a blazing wreck, but her gallant action will never be forgotten.

The *Australian Trader*, an Australian National Lines ship, brought into service in 1972, was taken out of commission in 1976. This was caused mainly by the very high wages paid to members of the crew and the annual loss of 1½ million Australian Dollars before

* Some readers will add their own comments.

194. The JERVIS BAY which, as an armed merchant cruiser, fought an immortal action with the pocket battleship ADMIRAL SCHEER.

the ship was withdrawn. It is not claimed that unjust demands and absurd wage awards were the only causes of failure of the *Australian Trader*, but surely they were largely to blame? As indeed, jobs and work are now constantly placed in jeopardy by union executives whose function has sadly changed since their inception.

After the Second World War it was necessary to refit passenger ships which had been used for trooping purposes and, like other companies, the Orient Steam Navigation Company had to rehabilitate its fleet. The *Orion* was the first ship to be released for this work to be carried out, and it took place in 1946. After she was completed with new crew and passenger accommodation, an examination was made of some aspects of the changes which had taken place in the ship. The reader will appreciate that, whilst a cargo ship earns her keep by using the capacity in her holds for cargo, a passenger ship earns most of her revenue from the areas of the decks suitable for the use of passengers. In the former, the relatively small crew numbers can easily be accommodated above the cargo spaces whilst, in the latter, the more space taken by the relatively much larger crew, the less space is available for passengers, who are the money earners for the Company, and, indirectly, for the crew themselves.

It was found that, in the *Orion*, the area of decks given over to the crew's accommodation in the ship had increased above pre-war days by 42%: this being mostly due to improved space for each man carried. The wages and space per man in British ships were increased appreciably after the last war and this trend has continued since then, whilst the time worked per man has decreased. It could and should be said that crew accommodation was generally poor before 1945, but that since that time great strides have been made, especially in cargo ships, where increased space for crew accommodation can be provided without greatly increased initial cost or later costs due to loss of cargo earnings and upkeep. Such considerations are not true of passenger ships. Initial cost is significantly greater and loss of earnings and cost of upkeep both change appreciably and unfavourably. The number of crew members required to attend to passenger needs can be varied by either having:—

a) more men to do the required work and thus have more men with time to kill, since they no longer work the hours that were usual in days gone by, or,
b) less men to do the required work, and to accomplish this by regular overtime.

Either a) or b) requires greater expense but b) requires less crew accommodation to accomplish the work and therefore could allow more passengers to be carried in the ship. The figure of loss of passenger space to crew as shown earlier by increased crew space of 42% in the *Orion* between 1939 and 1946 would be very much greater today if she was still afloat and refitted to modern standards of crew accommodation and requirements of service. In none of the foregoing is the writer 'taking sides'—he is merely stating hard facts and making the point that the plight of the passenger ship in its struggle against extinction by its competitors is not favourably influenced by the changes in crew accommodation, working hours, or wages which have taken place within the past thirty years.

Prior to the use of air conditioning in ships' accommodation, the external appearance of a passenger vessel at once showed the area of the oceans in which she would be used. Ships for the North Atlantic trade, or for similar wild, windy and cold zones, would be closed in with windows around the sides of the superstructures. This arrangement enabled passengers to exercise and walk around the deckhouses, enclosed by the ship's side windows and protected against the cold winds around her. Vessels designed for operation through tropical waters had to have means to induce as much movement of air through the accommodation as possible during the windless and hot conditions encountered during their voyages. The passengers also required large open-deck areas to enable them to take part in deck games and relax in the open air. These fundamentally different requirements for the two main types of trades could be seen by anyone with any knowledge of the subject, but a glance at the deck plans would also show that in the first type of ship the entertainment of passengers would be provided mostly within her by the use of many public rooms, indoor swimming pools, gymnasiums, etc. whereas in the second type of ship the large areas of open deck provided space for deck quoits, deck tennis, open-air swimming pools and so forth. Inside such a vessel the public rooms would not be so extensive, although this latter feature may not be very marked.

The foregoing remarks were true prior to the fitting of extensive air-conditioning in ships. This was first introduced in the Orient Liner *Orion* in 1935 and, at that time, was only used in a few public spaces and some de-luxe cabins in the ship. After the second World War, new passenger ships were fitted with more air-conditioning in their accommodation and, nowadays, almost all newly built ones are totally air-conditioned throughout their cabins and public rooms for passengers and crews.

The average speeds of passenger ships have also risen in recent times and these two factors (air-conditioning and average speed) have brought about changes in those built to operate in hot climates. The need to keep the ship very open to ensure movement of air is no longer valid. Bodily comfort is provided by the air-conditioning. Greater speeds of ships cause greater wind movement over them and reduce the comfort of passengers on the promenade decks, unless they are enclosed, as has always been usual for cold weather ships operating across the North Atlantic. These changes could be seen in the *Oriana*, built in 1960. Her designed operational speed was 27½ knots and this created very strong breezes over the open areas of the ship even when there was no wind. She was fully air-conditioned and, therefore, passengers were encouraged not to open sidelights and windows because, by so doing, the quality of the air-conditioning would be reduced for other travellers.

In the past, a voyage to Australia took a considerable time and, even in the 1920's, would last about six weeks. Although there were a number of ports of call during the passage, there were 'legs' of the voyage which took eight, ten, or more days. Towards the end of such stages, especially if the weather had been bad, the passengers were beginning to feel bored, irritable, and even actively to dislike some of their own number—especially those with whom they had to associate, such as cabin mates, their fellows at table in the dining saloon, and so on. If, in these circumstances there was an unexpected delay such as could be caused by fog, the passengers became very disgruntled. There was one such occasion, when the Orient ship *Otranto* had nearly completed her homeward voyage to Tilbury from Australia about the year 1950. She had had a very happy voyage and the passengers were very contented until the ship started her approach to Tilbury and encountered fog. She lay in the lower reaches of the Thames for two days in one of the very thick 'pea-soupers' which were not uncommon in those days. The passengers became very truculent and, by the time they were able to get ashore, were all convinced that nothing in or about the *Otranto* or her owners was any good, and that the voyage had been a disaster. The moral of this story is that the passenger must be given what he is promised and at the time promised.

The alternative to this is to do what one of our captains, one Captain Whinfield, used to suggest as a good cure for all the passenger problems we encountered from time to time. The ship was to be heavily insulated against heat, all the passenger spaces (and most of the crew accommodation no longer required) were to be turned into large pigeon holes about seven feet long, two feet high and two feet wide. These spaces were to be cooled to a very low temperature and, as the passengers came on board, they were to be deep frozen and packed away in them. There were a number of benefits in Captain Whinfield's scheme.

a) There was no need for a large catering staff to feed the passengers.
b) The passengers, upon being de-frosted, would be happy and contented, and have enjoyed a voyage without sea-sickness or other ills.
c) More passengers could be carried at reduced costs and at reduced fares.
d) Probably the most important point from Captain Whinfield's point of view, he would not have to try to attain the almost impossible feat of creating happy and contented passengers—especially at the Captain's table!

This latter amenity for passengers is not always an easy one to achieve, for a couple of people at 'daggers drawn' at the Captain's table can be a most disturbing and unhappy situation. There are difficulties in carrying out Captain Whinfield's proposal, as many readers will have perceived already, but it is put forward here as something to which serious thought might be given by the young scientists of today. At least a deep-frozen voyage could offer something more attractive than some of the aircraft journeys I have endured.

Incidentally, Captain Whinfield was an interesting man with a fresh outlook on life and was prone to do unusual things which upset some people, but interested the majority. In his youth, he had been in some rather rough ships, and I recall him telling me of some of his experiences in the Black Sea trade in a vessel which carried some passengers. This was in the days when the bunkering was in the hands of the Chief Engineer and the victualling in the hands of the master—usually through the agency of the steward (who needed to co-operate if he wished to keep his job!). This was perfectly common practice, which often led to major abuses, since, if the Engineer could buy coal cheaper than the rate allowed him by the owners, he could pocket the difference, and the same principle applied to the Master and the food. Since the feeding scales, as laid down by statute, were not very good, and since the average owners of vessels running to the Black Sea were generally far from being philanthropists, both the master and the engineer had to exercise considerable ingenuity in order to scrape any 'perks' of this sort.

Captain Whinfield, who was then a junior officer—and these were the days when a junior officer was expected to work on deck during his day watches in the poorer types of vessel—noted that the ship would be turned off course just before meals if there was any sea running, so as to induce the worst rolling conditions and thus cause some of the passengers to feel sick and to lose interest in their food! *Tempora mutantur!*

I was aboard the *Orsova* on her maiden voyage in 1954 when Captain Whinfield was her master and, on the evening of 5 April, we were about to pass the *Gothic* which was homeward bound from Australia with Her Majesty Queen Elizabeth and H.R.H. Prince Philip on board. Whinfield, aware of this, sensed an occasion, and ordered the plumber to make some rocket directors out of pieces of plumber's pipe. These were then mounted on the guard rails at the starboard side of the navigating bridge.

The night was dark, and there was some movement of the ship caused by wind and sea while hundreds of passengers and, I think, of the crew remained on deck to enjoy the occasion. The Captain then sent a cable to the *Gothic*:— *We send warm and loyal greetings to your Majesty and Prince Philip from 1011 passengers en route to Australia and New Zealand* **Stop** *We also wish you both a happy re-union with your children at Tobruk and a quiet leave when you reach home'.*

Then—up went the fireworks! It was certainly effective as it was equally unconventional. Certainly there was no element of distress—it was just Captain Whinfield! It had been interesting to observe what was going on, and I believe that every available light was burning in our ship, while we could see those of the *Gothic* and of her escorting cruiser quite clearly. Then, to the delight of the passengers and

195. The GOTHIC.

surprise—if not consternation—of those more accustomed to the ways of the sea, the *Orsova* was swung towards the *Gothic*, when the ships were still a mile or two apart, though I found this difficult to judge accurately with the naked eye, but readers will be aware of the implications of this manoeuvre but then, as I have said, Captain Whinfield was a man to make the most of such occasions! Almost simultaneously the cabled reply came from the *Gothic*:— *'Please thank your officers, passengers and crew for your kind and loyal message which I have received with great pleasure.'—Elizabeth R.*

At the same time the cruiser quickly took action: increased speed and moved between the two liners, while the *Orsova* resumed her former course and ended a thrilling experience for all on board. It must be left to the imagination what message the captain of the cruiser may have had in his mind!

Until the end of 1960, few people, other than those whose lives were closely involved with the building and running of them, could have foreseen the end of the era of large passenger liners. The end came quickly. There was a sudden fall in the demand for passenger berths and the ships' earnings dropped. Then began the withdrawals from service of ships which had become well-known and popular throughout the world for their standards of comfort and service, and for the famous people who travelled in them. The captains and senior officers of these ships also had names familiar to the travelling public.

The change in popularity of passenger liners started after 1960 and, as an illustration of this change, the port of Southampton, which was in times past one of the most important ports of call for these ships, can be taken. In 1964, over 90 large passenger ships were using the port. By 1969, the number of such passenger ships had fallen to just over 70. This fall continued and in 1972 little more than 40 large passenger liners were calling at Southampton. In 1977 the number had fallen to about 30 and there seems little doubt that this trend will continue. The passenger fleet of 'White Empresses' of the Canadian Pacific Steamship Company is virtually no more and most of the Cunard Line ships, which were well known to sea-travellers over the North Atlantic, have now disappeared within a few years—and so the sorry story goes on. Amongst the many well loved ships which have been broken up, withdrawn from service and laid up or sold are the *Queen Mary* (81,237 gross registered tons), *Queen Elizabeth I* (83,673 G.R.T.), *Carmania, Chitral, Chusan, Carinthia, Sylvania, France* (66,348 G.R.T.), *Himalaya, Iberia, Orcades, Oronsay, Orsova, United States* (55,329 G.R.T.), *Mauretania* (35,655 G.R.T.), and many of the ships which were run by the Union Castle Line, Holland America Line, Swedish America Line, and the ships of many other well known and respected Companies.

Some of these vessels, such as the *Queen Mary* and the *Queen Elizabeth I*, would have been taken out of service because of their ages, but the important point is that they have not been replaced by similar ships. The *Queen Elizabeth II* is mainly used for cruising and has been designed with this function in mind. Some of these ships have been bought when quite old and refurbished for use in other trades. One such a one became the '*Australis*' and, owned by the Chandris Group of Companies, was the '*America*' and owned by the United States Lines, but sailed from Southampton to Australia and New Zealand, calling at ports in the Mediterranean and elsewhere on her voyages, whilst also cruising but, sadly, she has even been withdrawn from this service.

Before the War, not many cruise ships existed and the ships that were being used for cruising were normally passenger liners that were being cruised on their 'off' seasons when the call for regular liner services was less because the demand for berths had become seasonal. There has often been a claim made that cruising was first introduced by the Orient Line, but this claim has also been made by the P. & O. Line. Whichever of them is correct does not really matter, but it is true to say that one or other of these two companies ran cruises many years ago, and was the first in this activity. Certainly cruising was introduced by them to keep the ships paying for their keep instead of having them laid up in some river during their 'off' seasons. The first ships of the Orient Line to do this were the *Chimborazo* and the *Garonne*, when they cruised to the Norwegian Fjords in 1889.

With the introduction and growth of air services and their competition with the sea transportation of passengers, the 'off' season of passenger ships has increased to the point where the use of regular passenger liners is no longer economically viable. Furthermore, the running of them is very much more expensive than it was in many different aspects, e.g. first cost, upkeep and repairs, fuel costs, victualling and crew costs, etc. This point has already been made and needs no more emphasis. In recent years the P. & O. Steam Navigation Company had used its passenger liner fleet, now reduced in numbers, to run cruises in the two hemispheres of the globe and also to make world cruises. These are run at seasons which will provide the best holiday times in both hemispheres. At the time of writing, their cruising takes place from Southampton to places in the Mediterranean and Scandinavia, and as far away as the West Indies for the period between May and the end of September, and from Sydney to exotic places in the Pacific and waters of the far east for the period from December to the beginning of April.

There are periods of time between these two cruising seasons which are used for 'positioning' voyages between Australia and the United Kingdom, when the ships cross the Pacific, through the Panama Canal, to Southampton, calling at interesting and attractive places on their way, and returning seasonally in the opposite direction. The very existence of such passenger ships depends on the imagination, pioneering and inventiveness of the Company which runs them, as well as on the Company's abilities as shipowners in catering for, and running the service. Their success or failure is balanced on a knife edge, and there have been many failures of companies in recent times to prove this. Only the strong and capable companies can survive: little can be left to good luck and changes in planning must constantly be made to improve the services and to attract the potential customer.

Some of the ships which were listed earlier in this chapter were extensively re-fitted to make them as suitable as possible for cruising purposes. The ships had usually been bought by companies speculating in this new business of running cruise ships, which had grown enormously and even alarmingly in the previous few years. Many new areas for cruising ships have been opened up, particularly in the Caribbean Sea, but it could be said that cruising ships will now be found anywhere in the oceans where there are attractive peoples, architecture, scenery, and strange, exciting and interesting things to be seen and experienced. Cruising has now become a highly specialized form of shipping and vessels employed in it should be 'custom' built to suit the requirements of the trade. Many of the ships which were bought and refitted as cruise ships were not very suitable for the purpose and will not be successful, no matter how well they are run. Refits of these ships entailed new requirements for safety of life, especially in regard to fire protection, and were refitted, usually at great expense. Amongst the features which are called for in cruising ships are the following:—

a) Shallow draught and good manoeuvring capabilities to enable the ship to enter and use the small and ill-equipped but picturesque ports which are so attractive for passengers in cruising ships.
b) Good launches and capable crews for them carried in the ship, together with good and safe access to the launches from her, in order to take passengers ashore quickly at small ports where the ship cannot go alongside a landing stage. Passengers are *infuriated* if they are kept waiting to go ashore. Since the ship may be some

distance from the shore, the launches should be capable of a reasonable turn of speed. It should be remembered that many cruise passengers are not only elderly and infirm, but are not active or experienced in nautical matters. Access to boats from the ship and from the boats to the shore should be planned with this point in mind.

c) Wholesome fresh water should be provided either from tanks of generous capacity built into the ship and using reliable shore sources of supply, or by a reliable water-making plant in the ship. The latter is the most obvious answer to this problem.

d) The ship must have generous areas for assembly of passengers who, nowadays, expect to be entertained continuously, particularly if the latter entails little or no effort on their own part. (This is a growing factor of modern life, partly promoted by the insidious nature of the almost universal 'Television'.)

e) To accomplish the requirements of (d) there must be a good entertainments staff which, nowadays, seems to require the attributes of the sort found in 'holiday camps' ashore.

f) The cruise ship often operates in waters far away from ship repair yards, and should have main and auxiliary machinery requiring minimum maintenance. The main machinery can be arranged so that the ship can be kept moving on some part of her total engine power whilst the other part is being overhauled or maintained by her engineers. This is a highly desirable asset in a cruise ship, and is almost a necessity.

'Custom built' cruise ships have been built in recent times in Scandinavia and, less frequently, in Italy and other shipbuilding countries. One such ship had a short life. She was built in Holland for the Cunard Line in 1972 and was called the '*Ambassador*', but two years later was damaged by fire. She was not repaired by the Cunard Line, probably because she was not too successful as a cruise ship, and was sold to the C. Clausen Steamship Company Ltd. of Denmark. The ship was originally designed to carry about 800 rich cruise passengers, but now as the *Linda Clausen* carries 33,000 passengers of a different kind—live sheep from West Australia to the Middle East!* From a photograph published in September, 1976, the ship still

* Cynics might query the difference—numbers apart! [Ed.]

looked exactly like a cruise ship, but was probably then a much better financial proposition than she was to the Cunard Line. It makes a sad story—something like a tramp wearing a 'tail' suit, but it does illustrate that to run a cruising ship must be a difficult trade—unless the trader is clever and experienced, and has a little luck too.

The story of the Cunard '*Ambassador*' could be said to illustrate the vicissitudes of fortune. Like all of us, she was cut down to size, in the same way as I was this morning when I remarked to my wife that I worked harder since my retirement than I ever did before that time. The answer was not unexpected:- 'No wonder the country is in the state it's in'.

XIX. TROUBLES—IN RETROSPECT

In December, 1958, I had the most exhilerating experience of a real storm in the Bay of Biscay, whilst returning to Britain in the *Orcades*. She had an intensive programme of work to be done aboard her—the fitting of air-conditioning throughout the passenger and crew accommodation—and this work was to be done in a relatively short time at the shipbuilding yard of Messrs. Harland and Wolff at Belfast. For this reason the ship was pushed on through seas which had caused many ships to lie-to in the Bay and, although the stabilizers were working furiously, the ship was rolling badly—about 18 degrees each side of the vertical position. When a ship encounters high swell conditions such as this storm produced, she is lifted and falls (heaves) so far as to reduce the apparent effect of stabilizers to the point where passengers plead: 'Why don't they put the stabilizers out?' To tell the truth, I myself thought they were not working on this occasion and went down to the machinery spaces to see for myself.

The dining rooms were not being patronized very much at that time, but we did have a table for six in the First Class dining room which was being used by some very hardy nuns in black habits. They did not miss a meal. The dining room floors in Orient Ships in those days were covered with a very thick linoleum in which designs were laid. Because the ship was fitted with stabilizers and usually did not roll, the dining room chairs were not secured to the floor by the chair chains which were provided. I was sitting near the centre line of the room and the nuns were sitting slightly behind me and on my left, at a rectangular table, the length of which was lying across the ship.

During the meal I had a 'feeling' and looked to my left in time to see a strange sight. The ship had rolled to my left and the ladies, two or three abreast, were sliding quietly away towards the side of the ship, with quaint, rather surprised expressions on their faces. This sliding seemed to go on for a long time (it must have been a second or two) before the legs of the two outboard chairs struck something on the floor and there was an alarming crash of chairs and a most devastating cloud of white under-garments. I'm not very inquisitive on this matter and I am sure I had never asked myself what these ladies wear under those black habits—nuns always frightened me to death—but now I know and am passing this information on. I do not know why the nuns did not take hold of the table edge to stop the movement—but there was no injury, only embarrassment.

After the *Orcades* was refitted, she sailed on her first voyage as an air-conditioned ship towards the end of March, 1959, and I joined at Naples to sail with her through the Suez Canal to Colombo together with other technicians representing various subcontractors who had been engaged on the work of this refit. We had no troubles until the ship sailed out of the Suez Canal into the Red Sea—and then they began. A large fully air-conditioned passenger ship operating through hot and moist atmosphere can condense 30 to 90 tons of fresh water a day from the outside air, depending on the size of the ship, the atmospheric conditions and the quality of the air-conditioning. Some mistakes had been made in details of the work and, as soon as we entered the Red Sea, water started to run in streams from unexpected and strange parts of the accommodation.

One simple error was made in respect of the trays fitted below fan intakes from the outside air. The simple arrangement of ventilation and air-conditioning consisted of several large vertical air shafts, about 20 feet wide by 10 feet in a fore-and-aft direction, with large inlets on the tops of the trunks for atmospheric saturated air. In these shafts, at each deck level, fans were fitted and these had cooling grids to cool the incoming air before it entered the accommodation. The cooling grids had condensed the water out of the incoming air, which should have fallen into the trays fitted below each fan, but the trays were too small and allowed the condensed water to fall like heavy rain in the shafts. As it fell, it leaked through doors on to the passenger decks in the alleyways. I spent one of the hardest weeks of work in my life in the company of the boiler-maker, going around the ship to find means of letting water out of some places into other more suitable ones, where drains could take water to the ship's ballast pumps. Water seemed to be finding its way all over the ship while the boiler-maker and I drilled holes and cut pieces of steel plating with hammers and cold chisels to achieve a measure of success. Meanwhile, a colleague, Sidney Jones, of the Thermotank Company, was trying to channel water in the proper direction from the numerous cooling grids. We had bought a most interesting array of tin-smith's work—large funnels, metal trays, plastic tubing, connections and so on—from shops in various ports on our route and Sidney spent all of his time connecting these oddments in such a way as to help stem the flow of water into the accommodation. Oddly enough, I always found that passengers faced these difficulties with great fortitude and with few complaints whilst they struggled with the inconvenience. They plodded through streams of water along the corridors apparently with a sense of taking part in some worthwhile activity.

Some of the trouble was caused by the use of foam plastic—plastic foamed into cavities which had been made, usually in plywood built around metal trunks, for the purpose of insulating them from the warm air in the compartments through which they were passing. When the ship entered the Red Sea, and the air-conditioning was working hard, the foamed insulation showed how inefficient it was for two reasons: first, the air, or gas cells or bubbles, in the insulation were not complete bubbles but interconnected, and therefore not good insulation and, secondly, the work of foaming had been badly carried out. This method of foaming insulation can be good, if well executed, but if the workman allows pockets of empty space to be formed, the insulation can break down—which happened in the *Orcades*. We removed the plywood covering in several such places as the one described and large quantities of water ran out of the cavities. It is possible that this weakness has now been overcome, but I would be loath to have the cavities in the walls of my house treated by the foaming method just becoming popular in Britain, unless I could be shown how pockets of empty cavities are prevented from being formed in carrying out the work. I left the ship at Colombo to fly home, whilst my colleagues went on in the ship to complete the work.

In October, 1950, the *Oronsay* had been launched and was nearing completion in the fitting-out basin at Barrow. The forward holds of the ship were to be insulated to carry cooled cargoes and the insulation consisted of layers of granulated cork built up to thicknesses of 12 to 18 inches, depending on the positioning of the insulation. Each slab of granulated cork was about 2 feet long by 18 inches wide by 3 or 4 inches thick, and was dipped into a tray of warm pitch or bitumen and applied to the steel of the skin to the ship or to the deck-head or tank top. Additional layers of cork were applied on top of the first layers, and so on, until the desired thickness was achieved.

Each of the three forward holds, Nos. 1, 2 and 3, were being treated in this manner and a large hole about 10 feet by 8 feet had been left in the bulkhead separating Nos. 2 and 3 holds to facilitate doing the work. On Saturday evening, 28 October, 1950, a fire started in No. 2 hold and it was surmised that some molten welding metal had fallen into the cork insulation and had smouldered there for hours before bursting into flame. Unfortunately, the steel hatch cover had not yet been fitted on the top of the hatch trunk serving No. 2 hold and this provided a natural funnel for the fire, while air was fed into the lower part of the hold from the large opening in the bulkhead previously described. All the ingredients for a really good fire were provided: inflammable materials, ventilation into the lower part of the fire and a large chimney (the hatch trunk) to the open air.

Friends told me of the blaze and, when I looked towards the ship from a point two miles away, the flames were huge, leaping at least a hundred feet into the air over her and illuminating the sky. I went on board about 9.30 p.m. and tried to do what I could to help. The fire appliances were arriving from many parts of Lancashire, but there was no real established organization and for a time chaos prevailed. Only the forceful and knowledgeable character of Len Redshaw and his supporting managerial staff prevented disaster. There is an all-important desire by firemen to squirt water on a fire—or so it seemed,

196. The ORONSAY burning through the night.

because as soon as Redshaw had organised the fitting of a large steel plate over the hole in the bulkhead and stopped air feeding the fire, someone would pull it away in order to squirt a pitifully inadequate amount of water on to it. It was obvious from outside the ship that, as soon as the plate was put over the hole, the flames were reduced to a small amount, but this was quickly changed back to the appalling blaze leaping high into the air as some zealot pulled it away again to direct the inadequate stream of water on to the fire. On board the ship, all appeared to be chaos, but behind this was some organization which asserted itself as time went on. Much of the work on the ship was being done in a half-dark state, because the lighting was of the temporary kind usual in a ship in that stage of building.

Inside the ship the heat from the hold was spreading through the steel structure which, in some places, was white-hot and bending and

197. Fighting the fire in the morning light.

twisting as it softened. Accommodation over the hold became incandescent and broke into flames, causing the sprinkler system to operate, but, although this was very effective at first, the heat generated below the accommodation continued in its intensity and overcame the effectiveness of the sprinklers by bursting hundreds of sprinkler heads and causing the force of water to be dispersed too widely. However, the system was effective in that it helped to cool the accommodation.

Firemen on board the ship were hosing bulkheads to prevent the spread of fire from its seat into the accommodation, but the water in the ship was now beginning to make her heel. Fortunately, she listed towards the quay and eventually leaned on it in the worst degree of heel. On a wall of the first class dining room someone nailed a wooden pointer to indicate the angle of heel of the ship and marks

198. The ORONSAY listing heavily against the quay.

were pencilled against the pointer as the night progressed. Gradually the angle moved towards twenty degrees from the vertical and movement around the ship became difficult. Water being poured on to hot areas in the ship ran down to the corners of the outer cabins on the low side of each deck and workmen were called in to cut holes in the ship's side to allow the water to drain overboard. We also removed pipes to allow the water to drain to lower parts of the ship. As the heel grew worse, there came a point when water began to enter the ship through the holes which had been cut to let water out, and there was a minor panic whilst these holes were plugged again.

At about this time there were some crashes caused by the lifeboats, which had been temporarily hooked in position on their davits, falling down on to the quay. These new boats were a sad sight the following day as they lay damaged.

199. A picture showing the angle of heel. It must be remembered that the under-water section of such ships is relatively small.

The list of the ship worsened through the night, but the zealots were still busy. One was seen busily opening a tank-filling plug so that he could pour water into a tank on the high side of the deck and thus (in his view) pull the ship back to upright. As any young student of naval architecture knows, this would have resulted in the ship rolling heavily to the opposite side and, in the absence of the helpful quay, probably capsizing her. As the night progressed, the fire was brought under control and, with the dawn, damping down continued.

The damage was serious and steelwork had to be replaced in the decks, girders, and beams. The cork had been a mixed blessing. Probably there would not have been a fire had another insulating material been used but, since there was a fire, it was found that it could only progress a short distance from the surface of the cork before charring stopped further progress, and thus prevented heat damaging the steelwork of the hull where insulation work had been completed. It was seen that part of the shell of the ship, where the insulation was not complete, was glowing at one period of the fire.

There were lessons to be learned from the blaze aboard the *Oronsay*. Clearly, an organization should be formed *before* a ship fire begins so that it can be fought with a knowledge of what should be done first and *how* it should be done. There must be a central command, and no action should be taken until approval of the command authority has been given. The stability of a ship on fire is one which must be watched constantly and controlled by a naval architect in the control centre. Since the time of this blaze aboard the *Oronsay*, there has been a great deal of discussion on the subject, and methods of dealing with ship fires have been agreed amongst all parties concerned, including the Fire Brigades near shipbuilding centres and ports and the Ministry responsible for the safety of ships. Arrangements for centralized control have been made and, although mistakes will be made in all fires like that of *Oronsay*, the magnitude of the mistakes will be reduced and the subduing of such outbreaks should be more expeditious and less costly. I believe that no person really knows about fire in ships until he has seen one and has experienced the terror and disaster caused by it. It must be admitted, however, that circumstances can alter cases, and that no two fires will necessarily start for the same reasons, in the same places, or follow the same course.

I once had an unusual journey, or, to be more precise, the journey was required for an unusual reason, since I was required to look at the W.C.s fitted in sleeper coaches of the railways in the U.S.A. It was a rather hurried journey too! The plane, a slow but comfortable propeller-driven 'stratocruiser', landed in Idlewild (as it was then called) airport on Sunday, 16 March, 1958. On Monday morning, I toured the railway coaches lying in sidings in New York. That Monday was St. Patrick's day and I found that everything stopped in New York that afternoon. There was the biggest parade I have ever seen, which started about 2 o'clock, and I stood on a street corner for about $2\frac{1}{2}$ hours whilst it passed. There were policemen and nurses in their hundreds in the procession and I doubt if there was anyone left in the city to stop crime or look after the sick. There were dozens of bands and, of course, the drum-majorettes, while the width of the marching columns seemed to be equal to the width of those broad city streets. The banners were many and huge—amusing, like 'Britain, get out of Ireland' and other endearing entreaties, as well as the Lodge banners. At one point I saw the most magnificent negro marching in the parade and wondered from what part of Ireland he might hail. In the evening, I went with friends to have a drink in one of the festive places nearby and saw beer, whisky, gin and drinks of every kind, all dyed green for 'ould Ireland'. The sight of green beer was revolting but the colouring of the spirits was tolerable.

On Tuesday, I went to the Budd Company in Philadelphia. This Company is well known as a manufacturer of very fine railway cars. They were, at that time, developing and building some cars in which the sleeping compartments were made of large plastic mouldings for walls, ceilings and floors. I was very interested in their work but could not see any use for it in our ships at that time.

I returned to New York and flew home from Idlewild at 5.20 p.m. that Tuesday. It was a short visit crammed with interest and, if I had learned what we should not do, at least I had garnered some new ideas for what we could do in our new ship.

Something always happens during the trials of a new vessel, and those of the *Oriana* in mid-November, 1960, were certainly more exciting than usual. She had been dry-docked in Falmouth prior to running her trials and, upon leaving there to make her way to the 'measured mile' area between the Isle of Arran and the mouth of the Clyde, she ran into a fierce storm. In spite of her stabilizers, the big ship was thrown about and both large and small pieces of furniture and other articles, which had not been stowed or secured during the rush to get the ship out of drydock and on her way north through the Irish Sea, began to move noisily about the ship.

The following morning we were able to survey and assess the damage. A very fine and new grand piano had left the entrance to the 'Princess Room', hurtled down the many flights of stairs, and had become a harp framed in matchwood at the bottom of the main staircase. Not many of us receive our harp as quickly as that grand piano! The library bookcases had frameless, sliding glass doors, and these had hammered themselves to shattered splinters by sliding to and fro between their stops. There were also many broken doors, some of which were lying on the decks because the hinges had been torn off. Nor was this the end of it, and we had learnt some lessons about the necessity of securing loose furniture and other equipment in a ship, no matter how great her size, before starting on her trials.

Anyone who had been involved in the trials of a big passenger ship can understand that there are hundreds—nay, thousands—of items which require attention and that human errors and omissions *do* occur. The night when the *Oriana* ran into the storm after leaving Falmouth was particularly memorable because all of our mistakes and omissions were thrown into highlight for the trial guests to see!

During these trials we had another enlightening experience. Many of these incidents were man-made, and this one clearly fell into this category. Flooding of the galley deck in many previous vessels of the Company had been caused by a practice of the galley staff, since the disposal of greasy waste was one of their problems and they had discovered an easy and quick way of solving it. Their solution was to pour it down the nearest scupper in the galley deck, from which they had broken away the trap, whilst it was still hot. The greasy waste would then run along the drain pipes (from the scupper) under the galley floor until it cooled, coagulated, and finally blocked the pipes.

As soon as this happened, the responsibility for the disposal of the offending greasy waste passed from the galley stewards to the unfortunate ships' plumbers, who probably represent one of the most hard-worked and under-estimated departments in a passenger ship. This procedure, which is universally known as 'passing the buck' or 'I'm all right, Jack', is found in every walk of life and, for a very long time, I had tried to help the plumbers to combat this problem and, to this end, had made changes in each new ship. Although yet another new scheme had been introduced into the *Oriana*, I was extremely disappointed to find the galley area awash during her trials. Indeed, it was ankle-deep in water and, to quote Bill Richardson who, at that time, was the Vickers-Armstrong manager in charge of the fitting out of the ship, was 'a limpid clear water lido'!

It was obvious that the new scheme for galley drainage had failed but, as we stood there, we had a stroke of good fortune for once, because a huge inrush of water suddenly occurred from a point behind the lining of a bulkhead near the middle line of the ship, and the cause of the trouble was revealed to us.

Ever since ships were first driven by machinery, I believe that there has always existed a rivalry between marine-engineering and shipbuilding departments in works ashore and also between engine and deck departments afloat. This was certainly evident in the Orient Line, despite the management's continual efforts to eradicate this traditional attitude. During the construction of a new vessel, the Company employed a resident engineer, who was usually brought ashore temporarily for the building and who would return to sea when it was completed, and it was his job to supervise the engineering work of the shipbuilders. Every now and again the enthusiasm of this particular engineer employed to supervise the *Oriana* had allowed itself to take care of his own particular departments to overcome his scruples, and the intermittent flooding of the galley of the ship was an unforgiveable instance of his bias.

From time to time, in existing ships, an overflow of the fresh water-making plants had occurred, to the embarrassment of someone in the engine-room on each occasion, because the overflow pipes were rightly led overboard and thus any overflow could be seen readily by anyone who happened to be standing in the vicinity, including the superintending engineer. The fresh water-making plant of the *Oriana* was capable of producing 650 tons a day (over 145,000 gallons), and this passed along pipes to the storage tanks at a great rate. To guard against possible bursting of full tanks, overflow pipes are fitted, besides alarms to warn engine-room personnel, but the fact remains that mistakes *do* occur and the Resident Engineer took his own steps to ensure that they were not blatantly displayed to all onlookers.

He decided to have the overflow pipes from the fresh water tanks led to, and hidden behind, the lining of the galley bulkheads—another clear case of 'passing the buck'. In recent times, I have been able to discuss this incident with Bill Richardson, who assured me that he had protested to this Resident Engineer about the overflow pipes being led to the galley drainage system, but without avail. It was difficult to inspect all the work being carried out on board a ship during construction, and this kind of deceit was often successfully perpetrated because the level of authority invested in the various representatives of the Shipowners was not clearly defined to the Shipbuilder who, when in doubt, kept his mouth shut!

The *Oriana* had a strange accident in the late 1960's which proved that welded construction is a good and sound method of building steel ships. She was passing through the Panama Canal and was in the hands of a Canal pilot. Almost throughout the world, except for the transit of the Panama Canal, when a pilot is required, he is in charge of the ship although, if there is an accident, the captain is still held responsible. This is not true in the Panama Canal, where the pilot is held responsible for all that happens pertaining to the navigation of the ship.

When a bicycle or car is steered, the front of the vehicle turns in the direction to which the front wheel (or wheels) have been turned and it pivots about the back wheel (or wheels). A ship behaves in a very different way since, when the rudder is put over to steer the ship towards the port side, the vessel will pivot about a point near the middle of her length. Thus, whilst the bows are moving to the port, the stern is moving towards the starboard side, and this movement continues for so long as the rudder is imparting a turning function. Put technically, the ship lies at an angle to the tangent of the circle of turning, the bows being within that circle and the stern outside it. When the rudder is returned to the 'ahead' position, the ship gradually reverts to the straight line of progression. This behaviour, common to all vessels, caused the *Oriana* to suffer the accident I shall now describe.

This ship reacts very quickly to any movement of her rudder and, on this occasion, she was leaving one of the Panama locks homeward bound when another vessel was approaching from the opposite direction. The intentions of the pilot are irrelevant to what followed, but the fact was that he had her helm put over too quickly and the *Oriana* swung much faster than he had expected. As the stern moved outwards, the starboard propeller touched and screwed itself into the bank, causing the propeller and its shaft to be jerked aft whilst the ship was going ahead. The aftermost part of the shafting system, called the tail shaft, is secured to the propeller and passes through the stern tube and through a watertight gland into the shaft tunnel. It so happens that the couplings used on the tail shafts of *Oriana* are what are called 'Muff' couplings—something like a lady's muff—closing over the shafts just as the muff encloses the lady's wrists and hands. Ahead of the tail shafts, the shafting continues through various intermediate shafts along the shaft tunnels, port and starboard, to the engine room. Apart from the muff couplings connecting the tail shafts to the shafts ahead of them, the intermediate ones are connected, to each other, by special bolts through the flanges in the ends of the shaft sections. These special bolts have tapered conical heads and ordinary nuts on their ends.

When the starboard propeller struck the bank of the canal and jerked the shaft towards the stern of the ship, something had to give. If the muff coupling had torn away from the shaft forward of the tail shaft, the propeller and its tail shaft would have been pulled out of the ship and the shaft tunnel would have flooded. The damage to the ship could have been very serious and might have caused loss of life. Marvellously, the muff coupling did not fail but, instead, the bolts through the coupling flanges connecting the intermediate shafts immediately ahead of the tail shaft were torn through the flanges and everything then happened very quickly. The line of shafting moved violently astern, tore away one of the shaft bearings and its supporting seating and brackets, and the huge mass of metal surged astern in the shaft tunnel, being only stopped when the muff coupling struck the stern gland at the end of the tunnel, shattering the stern gland studs and nuts and driving them into the casting of the gland. As a result the shafting and propeller were moved aft about *twelve feet*, and the tail shaft, nearly 28 inches in diameter and of solid steel, was bent through an angle of about 20° from its original centre-line. When it is realized that the propeller weight is nearly 30 tons which, together with the shafting hanging outside the end of the bossing and stern tube, totals over 40 tons, the magnitude of the forces involved can be imagined.

Temporary repairs were carried out and the ship proceeded on one engine and propeller to a port in the West Indies, on the ship's route, where divers examined the damage outside the ship and cut away what remained of the propeller blades. The *Oriana* then continued on her voyage across the Atlantic to Southampton at 14 knots. Upon close examination, the structure of the shaft brackets and bossing was found to be sound and not distorted. If the ship had not been of welded construction, I believe that structural damage and distortion would have taken place together with appreciable leaking caused by torn plate edges and sprung rivets.

This accident happened whilst a Panama pilot was in command and, as a result of his error of judgement, a claim was made against the Canal Authorities for damages totalling £500,000 sterling, which, I understand, was accepted and paid by them.

I was once on board an Orient Liner sailing through the Suez Canal, when she 'took a sheer' and ran aground. If a large ship is sailing through a narrow channel and is allowed to get into a position where one side of the vessel is much nearer to the bank on one side than the other, forces are developed in the water between the ship and the canal sides tending to make her 'sheer' towards the nearer bank.* The Suez Canal Pilot had caused this to happen but, unlike the Pilot in the Panama Canal, he could not be made responsible. Fortunately, the ship was undamaged and could move easily and continue through the canal.

The behaviour of a propeller-driven ship is influenced by the direction in which the screw turns. In a twin-screw ship the propellers usually turn outwards. That is, when the ship is going ahead, the tips of the blades are moving outwards from the ship's sides over the tops of the circles of the propeller diameters. In the 1930's, two sister ships were built for the P. & O. Company by Vickers in Barrow, the *Strathnaver* and the *Strathaird.* The ships had several distinguishing features. Only one of the three big funnels fitted to each ship was a real one. The other two were dummies and, from certain angles and with the sunlight behind the ship, daylight could be seen under one of them. It was said at the time that the extra funnels were fitted because passengers preferred ships with a number of funnels because there was safety in numbers!

* See Plate No. 53 caption.

Evidently tastes change for, after the War, each of these two ships had only one funnel. Another feature clearly to be seen, was the high, rather flat front of the main superstructure. This looked like a cliff and, structurally, was a very poor design. The other two outstanding features, not to be seen by an observer outside the ships, were that the propulsion was turbo-electric (steam turbines driving electric generators driving electric motors) and the propellers were designed to turn *inwards* when the vessels were going ahead. Turbo-electric propulsion provides great flexibility of manoeuvring power, and has keen advocates in the marine engineering world but, whilst it could be a great asset in a ship calling frequently at ports where manoeuvring is required, there is doubt as to whether the extra cost, initially and during service, together with the extra weight and overall reduction in efficiency of the propulsion plant, does not outweigh the gain of better manoeuvring qualities for ships engaged on normal voyaging. Turbo-electric propulsion can provide the same power astern as ahead, whereas the usual available astern power in ships with steam-turbine engines is about 60% of the ahead power.

This is not a very important point but it does have a bearing on a problem which arose during the trials of the *Strathnaver* and *Strathaird.* It is known that there can be difficulties in steering ships having inward-turning propellers when manoeuvring in the shallow waters of rivers, estuaries, and entrances to harbours. In these circumstances poor steering qualities are very undesirable.* The reader can readily understand from the previous two sentences that, if a shipowner wishes to alter the propellers from 'inwards-turning' to 'outwards-turning' in his 'turbo-electric-powered' ship, he can do so by changing over the two propellers from port to starboard and vice versa and, by reversing the rotation of the propulsion motors, go full ahead at about the same speed as before. This being so, the steering properties of these two P. & O. ships could probably have been improved by a change-over of propellers.

Although I have been unable to check the details—(the people involved are now dead)—I do remember, as a boy in the Ship Design Office of Vickers, listening to long discussions by my seniors on some difficulties in the steering of the *Strathnaver* and *Strathaird* during

* See '*Basic Naval Architecture*', by Kenneth C. Barnaby, O.B.E., B.Sc., A.C.G.I., pp. 236-7.

200. *The STRATHNAVER fitting out at Vickers' Barrow yard in 1933. The flat, cliff-like facings to her upper works represent a poor structural design. (From an etching by the author).*

their trials and of the possibilities of changing over their propellers from port to starboard in order to cure the problem. From records, it is obvious that the ships achieved good results during their speed trials, but the reasons why the propellers were designed to turn inwards instead of the usual outwards direction are not recorded and can only be conjectured. Whether the propeller rotation of the two ships was ever changed is very doubtful.

During the mid-1950's, there was an outbreak, fostered by one or two of the younger Directors, of employing 'Consultants' in the Orient Company, and I was affected by two facets of their operations. One concerned the main galleys and the other the ship's laundry. The galley Consultants spent the period of one cruise on one of our ships before designing the galleys for the *Oriana*. As remarked elsewhere, the Orient Management believed that representatives of the various departments of the Company should sail on maiden voyages of ships of the fleet to see and learn how the parts of the ship 'worked' in practice, and I had spent long periods of time over some years studying the way galley staff used their equipment at sea. Much of this time had been spent in the company of the Head of the Catering Department and his staff, and I had drawn a layout of galleys for the *Oriana* in consultation with all the people whom I knew to be concerned in the running of galleys in Orient ships.

These Consultants were given a copy of the galley drawing we had prepared and, after some time, produced their own design. This involved double-banking of ovens and other devices which lost the hot working surfaces galley staff require, together with other desirable facilities, and also involved greater walking distances for dining room stewards. The new design was examined for 'manning' purposes and was found to require a larger galley staff, whereupon the Consultants were asked to think again and, in due course, produced a second design. This was examined again by the Catering Department and was eventually thrown out in favour of a design developed by the Company staff.

The other 'Consultant' design was that of the laundry. This was done by people who had little or no understanding of ships. The main concept was completely faulty in that they had neglected to take into account that the laundry was arranged at the after end of the ship and, in consequence, would have a pronounced sheer or slope on the deck, rising to its highest point at the after end of the area. There is always a large quantity of water running about a laundry—in fact I would call laundry workers 'water-babies'—but one should arrange the water-producing equipment such as washing machines and spin dryers at the lowest point of the sheer of the deck if possible. Our 'Consultants' did not realize this: they thought of floors as flat and arranged the water-spilling machines aft in the high part of the deck and the ironing facilities were arranged at the low end of the space. When the sea was rough, the water on the floor of the laundry found its way into the 'dry' as well as the 'wet' areas of the room, in spite of sills which had been arranged on the tiled floor.

If a Company employs a person to run a department, that person should learn as quickly as he can how to do his work and, as required, discuss with consultants or specialists how best to carry out specific details of the job. If, for instance, galley 'specialists' can spend a fortnight during a cruise and produce something better than the person who was engaged to design ships some fifteen years or so before the time in question, then I think that the latter person was unfit to be retained in his position and should have been dismissed.

I have had the misfortune to be closely concerned with three different brands of 'Management Consultants' during my career, and have now reached the conclusion that they are a modern disease. They are always good-looking and well-dressed men and are equipped with the latest jargon of the day. They are also very self-assured and have an ability to convince employers in the nicest possible way of their incompetence and of the necessity to improve themselves by engaging 'Management Consultants'. It is a 'con' trick that continues to work and expands in its enveloping snares—and I believe that the only people who genuinely benefit are the consultants. Often the first step they take is to dispose of all those they designate as the 'dead-heads' in a Company and I have formed the opinion that amongst the dead-heads are some of the best and most knowledgeable, even if a little elderly, members of senior staff. This view is shared by many whose opinions I respect. I remember one who asked

'Are so-and-so' (consultants) 'in your Company?' He then added, 'If so, get rid of them before they ruin you; we did!' Consultants live richly off the backs of manufacturing concerns and, it must be admitted, do sometimes become wiser as they learn from those whom they are supposed to be advising. I know of one 'throw-out' from a Company who was quickly snatched up by Consultants—he was a good-looking, clever chap, lacking in wisdom, but he had the jargon which is to be found in politicians and in all those who make a living by talking.

During the mid-1950's, there was an 'outbreak', probably a better word would be 'epidemic', in architectural circles. It took two forms. The first and more important one could be interpreted as brutalizing, because the shapes of all buildings, parts of buildings and fittings on and within buildings were rectangular or slab-shaped, and were completely lacking in softness, curves or humanizing qualities of any kind. The use of great slabs of timber to form handrails of stairs, horizontal rails on walls, seats, and so on, was commonplace, and can be seen today in the railway stations, airports and other buildings constructed at that time. The fact that timber was scarce (and contnues to be scarce) and was (and is) expensive, has no bearing on this matter. Fashion had it that we must use timber 12 inches wide by 3 inches thick. The ugliness of fashionable architecture of the period has left its scars throughout our country which only time can eradicate. One can search in vain for any sign of curves; warmth; grace or elegance in most of these buildings and can only sigh for the passing of good standards.

Then there was the other 'outbreak', the 'in' colours. At that time the colours were black, yellow and 'donkey' brown. This colour scheme permeated women's fashions, cars and fashionable architecture, and it seemed to an outsider that there was a little gnome (with a very little head) issuing edicts to everyone in the various areas of design that certain colours were fashionable over periods, apparently in each successive calendar year. It was depressing and rather frightening that mass-thinking (or mass-un-thinking) could be permeating the world of artistic endeavour.

Sir Colin Anderson was sensitive to these things and I have

enjoyed being with him on a number of occasions when he has interspersed remarks in discussions which have helped to stimulate fresh thinking. Once he asked an architect, '. . . and are you going to use some of this "monolithic" type of architecture?' On another occasion, when confronted with an assortment of colours proposed for a scheme, he asked, 'and are these the "in" colours this year?' The one thing Sir Colin did not want was 'in' colours, because the new ship was to last at least 20 years and what was 'in' this year would be 'out' in two or three years after the ship entered service.

Most architects are young at the beginning of their careers, and must start practising somewhere and on something. The Orient Company gave opportunities to a number of these and, as one might expect, not all of them proved to be good at their work. There was one who, in my opinion, was a poor architect. It is true of all who develop new ideas or create works of art that mistakes are made and should be forgiven but, if advice, based on previous experience, is given to a beginner and he ignores that advice, he should not be forgiven for the poor job which may follow. There is no point in writing about this man's mistakes, but one thing he did could cause a smile. He designed some chairs, the frames of which were made of solid steel bars about one inch square in section. They were of the rectangular construction described earlier in respect of buildings and, certainly, no human being is of the shape to sit comfortably for long in such furniture. They were very, very heavy, not light-heartedly to be picked up and carried about, and they were used to furnish a 'Tavern' in the Tourist accommodation of a new ship. Sir Colin Anderson travelled to Australia on the ship's maiden voyage and, as usual, he sent back to the Company reports of the ship's behaviour, shortcomings, and events on board. One report told of a strong drunken passenger in the 'Tavern' who picked up one of those 'unliftable' chairs, swung it over his head, and flung it across the room, tearing tiles out of the ceiling on its way. Fortunately, nobody was in its path, or murder would have been done.*

There were many humorous incidents on 'maiden' voyages but others were not funny and were sometimes expensive too.

If the reader regards this chapter as one of accidents or troubles,

* Readers will be aware that this represented unusual 'passenger behaviour.'

he would be right, and he may suppose that most of them should have been avoidable, together with various other calamities retailed elsewhere in this book. With the benefit of hindsight, such a supposition might be correct, but the incidents have been set forth to demonstrate the great complexity of a modern passenger ship—(the *Table of Interesting Particulars relating to the Oriana* testifies to the truth of this assertion)—and the fact that changes in design of one sort or another are constantly being made in each new ship. The minority of matters which go wrong loom large in the memory, whereas the vast majority of innovations worked perfectly well and called for no comment.

By now, the reader will also have appreciated the great number of people with varied responsibilities who are involved in the different stages of design, and equally that no single one of them is infallible. Indeed, the Company was always sufficiently realistic to understand that a new vessel would be unlikely to work perfectly in every one of her multifarious functions from the outset, and for this reason insisted on some of its technical staff being present on a maiden voyage. Nevertheless, I think that some of the matters which did require attention on these occasions were not only important, but were unlikely to be envisaged by anyone who was not intimately connected with ship design or naval architecture, and it is for this reason that I have included them.

Shipbuilders and seamen have advanced almost beyond belief since the earlier days of seafaring which I discussed briefly in the first chapter. Modern vessels are now extremely sophisticated; highly efficient, complex and infinitely safer than was conceived to be possible a bare century—even a bare half century—ago. Yet—and here I extend the subject momentarily far beyond the strict compass of this book—it can never be said that man has 'conquered' the sea or its elements nor, in the final analysis, that he has overcome his own fallibility. There will always be accidents and disasters, some of which should be avoided (e.g. 'radar-assisted collisions', needless strandings and so forth), but some of which will be caused by exceptional wind or weather conditions or by untoward natural phenomena.

Ships could—and can—be made safer than is already the case,

201. The TITANIC leaving on her ill-fated maiden voyage. Human error cannot be discounted from her loss.

but they must remain functional and viable, yet no amount of built-in safety will legislate for human error. Mankind has set a very high value on human life (so long as the life in question happens to live in the United States or some other progressive and wealthy country). If a large number of people are killed in a disaster in a flying machine, a train or a ship, there is an understandable roar of public sympathy and, often enough, subscriptions are raised for next-of-kin. Yet these peoples' lives are of no more nor less account than those of the far greater numbers who suffer individual disasters all the time, yet which are less worthy of mention in the media. People are being killed or suffering injury every day in their homes and on their highways, to appear as part of various annual statistics. Probably most such accidents result from carelessness of one sort or another on somebody's part.

Of course ships, like everything else, must be made reasonably safe. Perhaps I should say, lest I be misunderstood, that 'they should be made as safe as is reasonably possible', but the operative word must be 'reasonably' since, if they be made *unreasonably* secure, the costs would so escalate as to make them impossible to operate, which has already occurred in some sectors, whilst the comfort and conditions demanded by passengers which, oddly, are invariably much in excess of anything which the majority experience in their normal lives, would suffer accordingly. As I have already expressed myself, I believe that, as a result of foolish decisions, the pendulum has already swung too far in the matter of passenger ships and, even if some existing safety precautions were to be doubled, trebled or even quadrupled, nothing would prevent the ultimate disasters.

I started this book by discussing the early Mediterranean galleys and similar craft, but I am not so naïve as to believe that they were the earliest seagoing vessels. If we believe Plato, Atlantis was a thriving thalassocracy of which the records, apart from those, now lost, at Saïs, were totally expunged by the cataclysms of the times. It is both easy and rational to suppose that the San Andreas fault may, one day not so far in the future, decant Northern California into the sea and create tidal waves which could toss the largest and most powerful passenger liners and very large bulk carriers like mere match-boxes—perhaps far inland.

Some countries have better records at sea than others. Within those countries, some companies have shone as outstanding stars both in their performances and in their records and in this country, with its exceptionally long and distinguished seafaring tradition, the Orient Company, about which I have written, must take an honoured place. Conrad wrote:- *'Ships are all right: it's the men in them!'* Perhaps I may close this book by paraphrasing this well-known truism to: 'Ships are only as good as the people who sail in them', for men, on the whole, have not kept pace with their own technology, but have rather become slaves to it.

The modern passenger, usually cruising, is generally a very superficial person, content to view some port or great city for a few short hours before moving on to the next, whilst being fortified in the interim by dances, more food (than is probably good for him), drinking bars, television screens and the like. He is a far cry from the older 'globe-trotter' who penetrated the tourist veneer of places and was able to draw his own conclusions. Similarly, modern seamen are not 'sailors' in the true sense, albeit men with much greater technical knowledge than their forebears. The officers and crew of the full-rigger *Orient* would be utterly lost and incompetent in the *Oriana*, a bare century later, and, conversely, the officers and crew of the *Oriana* would never sail the *Orient* on such brilliant passages. All else apart, sailing ships and unions are utterly incompatible.

As times change, so ships change too. Some have sneered at the great passenger liners and termed them 'floating gin palaces', particularly those which used to ply the North Atlantic trade. Whether or not passengers really needed the comfort and accommodation they were given in those ships may be a debatable point, when on so short a voyage. Certainly the majority of those being carried to Australia had insufficient self-resource to endure so long a voyage at sea without the comforts and diversions provided for them, despite the ability of their immediate forebears in the emigrant clippers to make much longer voyages in far greater discomfort with equanimity. Perhaps an increase in material standards comes in inverse ratio to self-resource and resolution to face the realities of life. Those who really loved the sea for its own sake, of course, abjured the passenger liner altogether and travelled, when such voyages were still possible, in a 'passenger-cargo' vessel in which the cargo was the basic reason of her existence and in which only a very few passengers were carried.

Speculation on the attitudes and requirements of passengers represents a large and complicated area which leads to relatively sterile conclusions. The fact remains that the demand existed: that it was met and, until the competition of flying machines on the one hand, and the effects of misused union power (in various spheres) on the other, utterly killed it or diverted the ships exclusively into the cruising trade, advances were made steadily over the years to produce a highly manoeuvrable, complex and efficient type of vessel, of which the *Oriana* was probably the last to be built for regular trade. Thus I have set forth much of the tale of her conception and design in this book since, like the carracks and caravels; the clippers and the later sailing-

202. The N.D.L. BREMEN – one of the popular Atlantic passenger liners.

carriers; like the various epochs of the coal-burning steamship and of so many other craft, the great passenger liner will soon be lost in the limbo of past time unless she is recorded now by the men who were immediately concerned with her.

The passenger liner took many and multifarious forms and there can be little doubt that the so-called 'Atlantic Greyhounds' have captured the popular imagination ever since the days, before the nations and the companies rationalized their sailing schedules, when two liners, with or without auxiliary sail, could fall in company and literally race to—say—Sandy Hook with all the zest of racing clippers, while their stokers worked like fiends of Hell below and their passengers cheered on deck, with black smoke streaming to the horizon all the while. Finally, of course, the quest for the elusive 'Blue Riband' made the North Atlantic the race-track of the 'giants'.

The very density of the traffic: the sight of so many huge liners in the terminal ports together; the names of the famous passengers who were constantly using these vessels, the strong under-current of national prestige, quite apart from the matter of the 'Blue Riband of the Atlantic', which was only confined to a relatively few vessels and to which some companies would never admit any aspiration (even when their vessel held it!)—all these things, amongst other factors, led to enormous publicity and interest in these vessels. Of course, they

203. The QUEEN MARY's great rival – the French NORMANDIE.

numbered the most famous passenger vessels of all time—not just in consequence of their Press coverage but due to their very exceptional size; to their splendour and grandeur (so impossible in this age of safety and other regulations) and, in many cases, to their very vulgarity and ostentation. Nevertheless, some of them had enormous character and success, and the North Atlantic passenger run is a tremendous study in itself, but its requirements were very different from vessels carrying passengers to the Antipodes on much longer voyages. Yet, irrespective of changing fashions and regulations; of the realisations that dummy funnels and useless masts do not make a ship better or safer, and whether on the one route or another, conceptions have changed. The *Orion* started a trend, but it is not without interest to observe how the whole approach to the building of a passenger ship has altered in one short generation and to compare, for example, the proportions both above and below the water of such a vessel as the old *Mauretania* with those of more modern vessels like the *Oriana* and *Canberra*.*

This work is about one Company—the Orient Line. It was never a big one in terms of fleet numbers, and it may be felt that it is treated too much in isolation since, for much of its life, it was running in conjunction with, or in opposition to, other firms. I have written the book in this form consciously, since to have extended it beyond the

* Plates 125 and 192.

204. The White Star liner MAJESTIC in the Southampton floating dock.

bounds of the one fleet would have rendered it unmanageable to the reader and altered its form materially. The Orient Company, which has now lost its identity, was one which for long had an honoured and respected name, not only for its reliability, but also for always keeping abreast and rather ahead of its competitors in its quality and design. Having been intimately associated with it for most of my working life, I can write of it with first-hand experience and authority and, since the ships were not only such as they were, but amongst the very last to be built for a regular run, I trust that I may have made some small contribution to recording aspects of the development, problems and design (most of which may be read in a much broader context) of the great passenger liner before she finally vanishes forever from the face of the seas and the ports of the world to become a legend.

APPENDIX I

COMPARATIVE INFORMATION RELATING TO THE FIRST AND SECOND ORSOVA

Item	"ORSOVA" (I) 1909	"ORSOVA' (II) 1954
Length B.P.	536′ 2″	668′ 0″
Breadth Moulded	63′ 0″	90′ 6″
Depth Moulded	38′ 0″	50′ 0″
Displacement Loaded	7,550 tons	32,140 tons, approx.
Insulated Cargo	—	94,060 cu. ft.
General Cargo	259,998 cu. ft.	209,570 cu. ft.
Engines	Quadruple Expansion Steam Reciprocating 14,000 S.H.P.	Steam Turbines 42,500 S.H.P.
Gross Tonnage	12,036	28,790
Net Tonnage	6,831	15,882
Speed on Trials	18.1 knots	26.07 knots

	"ORSOVA" (I) – 1909			"ORSOVA" (II) – 1954	
1st Class Passengers	268	1, 2 & 3 Berth Cabins	1st Class Passengers	681	1, 2, & 3 Berth Cabins
2nd Class Passengers	120	2, 3, & 4 Berth Cabins			
3rd Class Passengers	388	2, 4, 6, 10 & 12 Berth Cabins	Tourist Passengers	813	2, 3, 4, & 6 Berth Cabins

"ORSOVA" (I) – 1909: Folding lavatories in all 1st and 2nd Class Cabins except Special Cabins having washbasins and baths. Communal washing arrangements for 3rd Class.

"ORSOVA" (II) – 1954: Running Hot and Cold Water to washbasins in all cabins in 1st Class and Tourist Class Accommodation.

Deck and Radio officers, Pursers, and Doctor	11	6 Deck, 2 Radio, 2 Pursers, and 1 Doctor	Deck Officers	33	8 Deck, 4 Radio, 2 Doctors, 13 Pursers, 2 Hostesses, 2 Liaison Officers, 2 Nursing Sisters
Deck Dept.	48		Deck Dept.	72	
Eng. Officers	16		Eng. Officers	26	
Eng. Dept.	82		Eng. Dept.	32	
Catering Dept.	134	$\frac{776}{134}$ = 5.8 passgrs/steward	Catering Dept.	471	$\frac{1494}{471}$ = 3.2 passgrs/steward
Total Crew:	291	$\frac{776}{291}$ = 2.66 passgrs/crew	Total Crew:	634	$\frac{1494}{634}$ = 2.35 passgrs/crew

"ORSOVA" (I) – 1909: Senior Officers in 1-berth Cabins, Junior Officers in 2-berth Cabins and ranks of Deck, Engine and Catering Depts. in 18, 24 and 32-berth sleeping spaces at approximately 17 sq. ft. per person.

Total covered deck area given over to the use of crew (excluding officers) = 8,623 sq. ft.

Area per man = $\frac{8623}{264}$ = 33 sq. ft.

"ORSOVA" (II) – 1954: All Officers and a proportion of P.O.s in 1-berth Cabins; Deck and Engine Depts. in 2 and 4-berth Cabins, and Catering in 2, 4, 6, 8 and a few 10-berth Cabins, at 24 sq. ft. per person in 6, 8 and 10-berth Cabins and 30 sq. ft. per person in 2 and 4-berth Cabins.

Total covered deck area given over to the use of crew (excluding officers) = 29,360 sq. ft.

Area per man = $\frac{29360}{575}$ = 51 sq. ft.

205. *The ORSOVA (II) at speed on the measured mile off Arran in March, 1954.*

CABIN AREAS

"ORSOVA" (I) 1909

			Area per Person
1st Class			
B Dk. Single	=	49 sq.ft.	49
B Dk. Double	=	62 sq.ft.	31
C Dk. Double	=	95 sq.ft.	47.5
C Dk. Single	=	56 sq.ft.	56
D Dk. Double (ships side)	=	60 sq.ft.	30
D Dk. Double (Bibby Cabin)	=	102 sq.ft.	51
E Dk. Treble	=	130 sq.ft.	43
2nd Class			
D Dk. Double (ships side)	=	64 sq.ft.	32
D Dk. Treble (Bibby Cabin)	=	114 sq.ft.	38
E Dk. Double (ships side)	=	65 sq.ft.	32.5
E Dk. Double (Bibby Cabin)	=	110 sq.ft.	55
E Dk. 4-berth (ships side)	=	98 sq.ft.	24.5
3rd Class			
D Dk. Double	=	36 sq.ft.	18
D Dk. 4-berth	=	59 sq.ft.	14.8
E Dk. Double	=	33 sq.ft.	16.5
E Dk. 4-berth	=	46 sq.ft.	11.5
F Dk. 6-berth	=	88 sq.ft.	14.7
F Dk. 10-berth	=	144 sq.ft.	14.4
F Dk. 12-berth	=	180 sq.ft.	15

"ORSOVA" (II) 1954

			Area per Person
1st Class			
C Dk. Single	=	95 sq.ft.	95
C Dk. Double	=	147 sq.ft.	73.5
D Dk. Single (ships side)	=	69 sq.ft.	69
D Dk. Double (Bibby Cabin)	=	125 sq.ft.	62.5
D Dk. Double (ships side)	=	89 sq.ft.	44.5
E Dk. Double (ships side)	=	120 sq.ft.	60
E Dk. Double (Bibby Cabin)	=	118 sq.f.t.	59
F Dk. Double (Blind)	=	62 sq.ft.	31
Tourist Class			
F Dk. Double	=	60 sq.ft.	30
F Dk. 3-berth	=	93 sq.ft.	31
F Dk. 4-berth	=	107 sq.ft.	27
G Dk. 2-berth	=	62 sq.ft.	31
G Dk. 4-berth	=	82 sq.ft.	20.5
G Dk. 6-berth	=	120 sq.ft.	20.0
H Dk. 4-berth	=	80 sq.ft.	20
H Dk. 6-berth	=	112 sq.ft.	18.5

APPENDIX 2

COMPARATIVE PASSENGER SPACES IN SOME ORIENT SHIPS 1925 – 1960

SHIP	FIRST CLASS PASSENGERS Space	Area square feet	No. of Persons in space	Area per Person sq. ft.	TOURIST CLASS PASSENGERS Space	Area square feet	No. of Persons in space	Area per Person sq. ft.
OTRANTO 1925	Public Rooms				Public Rooms			
	ex. Dining Room	7,637	540	14.13	ex. Dining Room	2,208	1,168	1.89
	Dining Room	4,640	270	17.20	Dining Room	3,680	584	6.30
	Deck space	30,875	540	57.20	Deck space	21,987	1,168	18.83
OTRANTO 1955	AS ONE-CLASS SHIP =				Public Rooms			
after refit as					ex. Dining Room	8,835	1,416	6.23
as one-class ship					Dining Rooms	8,320	708	11.76
					Deck space	52,862	1,416	37.30
ORONTES 1929	Public Rooms				Public Rooms			
	ex. Dining Room	6,638	463	14.33	ex. Dining Room	2,999	528	5.68
	Dining Room	4,836	232	20.85	Dining Room	3,920	264	14.83
	Deck space	32,580	463	70.30	Deck space	17,770	528	33.60
ORONTES 1955	AS ONE-CLASS SHIP =				Public Rooms			
after re-fit as					ex. Dining Room	9,637	1,410	6.83
as one-class ship					Dining Room	8,756	705	12.42
					Deck space	50,350	1,410	35.71
ORION 1935	546 FIRST CLASS PASSENGERS				Public Rooms			
after re-fit					ex. Dining Room	9,376	706	13.31
in 1947					Dining Room	—	—	—
					Deck space	14,100	706	20.00
ORCADES 1948	733 FIRST CLASS PASSENGERS				Public Rooms			
					ex. Dining Room	9,078	772	11.76
					Dining Room	—	—	—
					Deck space	15,020	772	19.45
ORBUSTUS	Public Rooms				Public Rooms			
(Oriana)	ex. Dining Room	18,570	700	26.50	ex. Dining Room	18,585	1,299	14.30
during design	Dining Room	7,220	350	20.62	Dining Room	9,440	650	14.53
in 1955	Deck space	43,450	700	62.10	Deck space	28,900	1,299	22.25

APPENDIX 3

GRAPHS OF SPEED, DISPLACEMENT AND STABILITY RELATING TO THE ORIANA

The information contained in the three following graphs are of particular interest in considering the *Oriana*, to which they apply, though the same principles apply, in varying degrees, to any passenger liner making a number of ports of call *en voyage*.

The key to the ports is as follows:

Identity letter on graph	Port	Percentage of voyage time from start of voyage
A	Southampton	0%
B	Gibraltar	3%
C	Naples	5½%
D	Port Said	8%
E	Suez	9%
F	Aden	12%
G	Colombo	17%
H	Fremantle	25%
I	Melbourne	29%
J	Sydney	31%

K	Auckland	34%
L	Honolulu	43%
M	Vancouver	48½%
N	San Francisco	51½%
O	Honolulu	56½%
P	Auckland	66%
Q	Sydney	69½%
R	Melbourne	71%
S	Fremantle	75%
T	Colombo	82¾%
U	Aden	88%
V	Suez	91%
W	Port Said	92%
X	Naples	94%
Y	Marseilles	95½%
Z	Gibraltar	97½%
AA	Southampton	100%

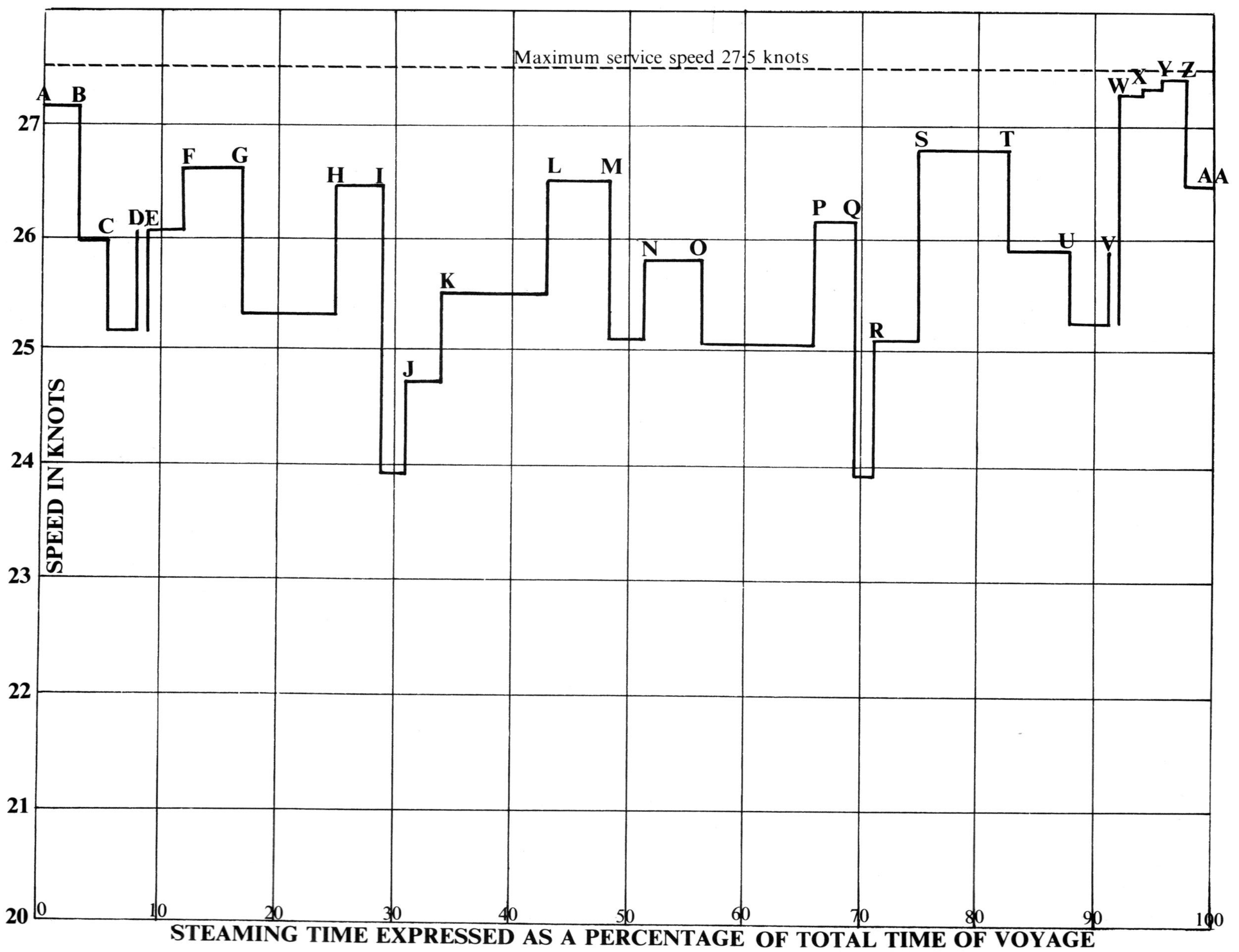
Maximum service speed 27·5 knots
A B C DE F G H I J K L M N O P Q R S T U V W X Y Z AA
SPEED IN KNOTS
27
26
25
24
23
22
21
20
0 10 20 30 40 50 60 70 80 90 100
STEAMING TIME EXPRESSED AS A PERCENTAGE OF TOTAL TIME OF VOYAGE

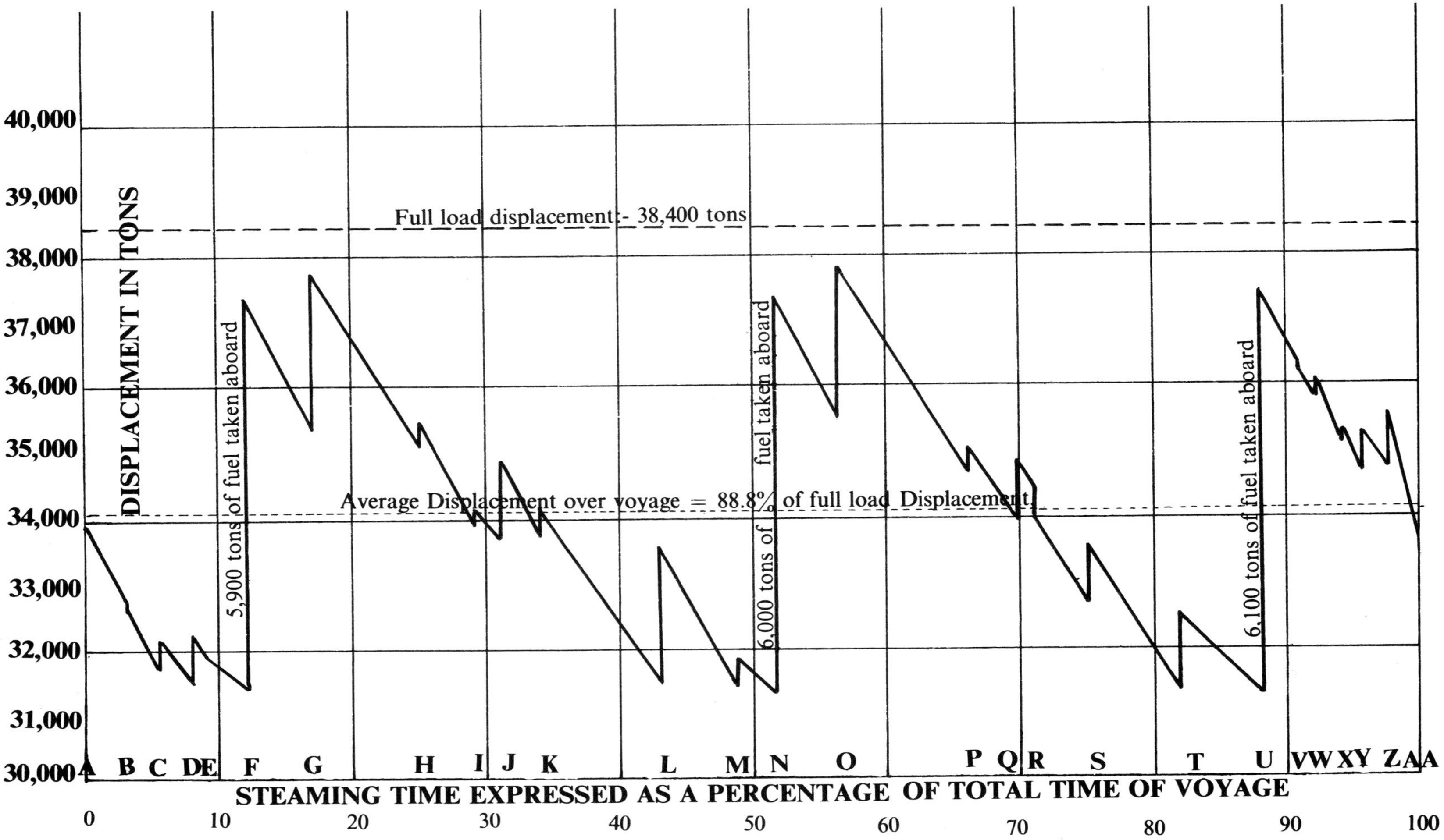
DISPLACEMENT IN TONS
40,000
39,000
38,000
37,000
36,000
35,000
34,000
33,000
32,000
31,000
30,000
Full load displacement:- 38,400 tons
Average Displacement over voyage = 88.8% of full load Displacement.
5,900 tons of fuel taken aboard
6,000 tons of fuel taken aboard
6,100 tons of fuel taken aboard
A B C DE F G H I J K L M N O P Q R S T U VW XY Z AA
STEAMING TIME EXPRESSED AS A PERCENTAGE OF TOTAL TIME OF VOYAGE
0
10
20
30
40
50
60
70
80
90
100

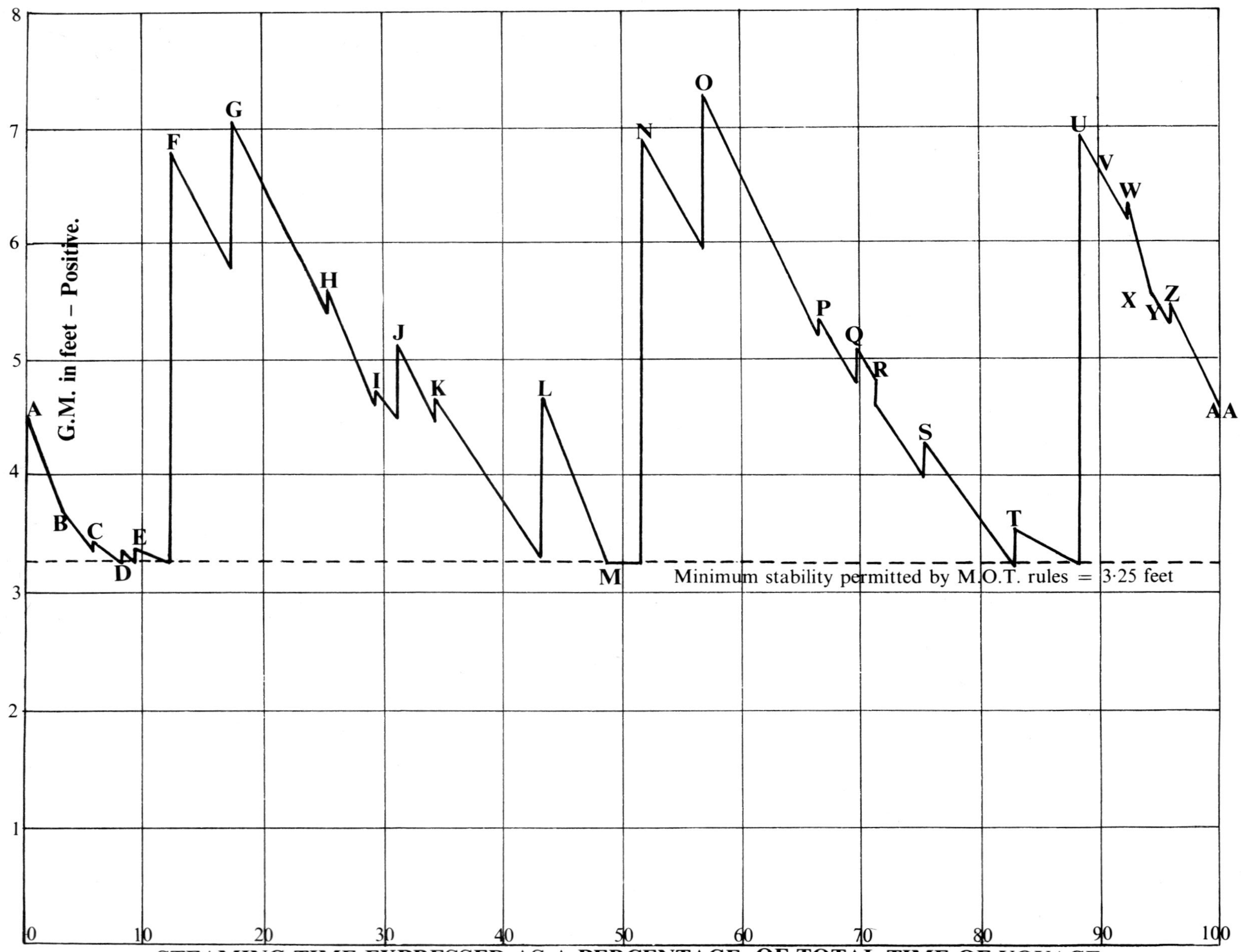

STEAMING TIME EXPRESSED AS A PERCENTAGE OF TOTAL TIME OF VOYAGE

206.
The old IBERIA. Note the davits on her foc's'le head to cat her anchors.

APPENDIX 4

THE BRIDGE OF THE *ORIANA*

SINCE I BELIEVE that most readers have a good idea of the layout of the bridge of a modern passenger liner, I have consciously omitted that of the *Oriana* from the main text. The two sidelights were outside the two wings, which were open, and manoeuvring unit controls were situated near each wing. This open bridge extended somewhat abaft the large midship wheelhouse which was glazed all along its forward side and fitted with clear-view windows.

The wheel was, of course, amidships and fairly far aft of the centre line, and behind it a console incorporating the safety controls for the water-tight doors etc. on the port side and the telephone communication system to starboard, both these lying between lift trunks from below. There were three consoles, which were a new concept on shipboard at the time of her building; one, on the port side of the wheel, concentrated within it all the various engine room controls whilst another manoeuvring unit control was on the other side. A radar display unit was on the starboard side, and another in the chart room which lay abaft the wheelhouse itself, together with a pilot's cabin.

Amongst other equipment was the Sperry-Brown combined gyro hydraulic steering control: course recorders: engine room telegraphs: a gyro compass repeater; a Marconi Seavisa depth indicator with a range of 530 fathoms and a Metron depth-below-keel indicator. There were also the usual smoke and sprinkler detectors, the public address systems and, indeed, practically every modern innovation which could contribute both to safety and to navigation.

207. The bridge of the ORIANA.

208. The OMRAH.

GLOSSARY OF NAUTICAL TERMS AND ABBREVIATIONS

A.C.: Alternating Current. An electrical current which alternates from positive to negative polarity in regular cycles of the required period and power. (See D.C.)

ACCOMMODATION LADDER: a ladder or flight of steps, usually with a platform at each end, lowered over a ship's side for embarkation purposes.

AFT: Towards the stern, or rear end, of a vessel.

AHEAD: A position in front of the ship. To 'go ahead' means to move forward.

AMIDSHIPS: The Middle of the length or width of a ship.

ASTERN: A position to the rear of the ship. To 'go astern' means to move backwards.

ATHWARTSHIPS: Across the ship, at right-angles to the keel.

AWASH: Level with the surface of the water, so that it washes over.

BALE CAPACITY: see CARGO CAPACITY.

BALLAST: Heavy material or water (if ballast tanks are provided) carried low down in a ship to preserve proper stability.

BEAM: 1) The width of a ship. 2) A transverse structural support to (and across) the deck. ABEAM means in a direction at right-angles to the ship's head. (Thus Port beam and Starboard beam refer to the respective sides of the vessel.)

BELAY: To attach or secure a rope by taking 'S' turns about a (belaying) pin.

BERTH: 1) The place where a ship is built. 2) The place where a ship lies in port. 3) A bunk, or bed.

BILGE: Space where drain (bilge) water lies at the bottom of the ship between the keel and the ribs or frames, or at the sides of the double bottom.

BILGE WATER: Stagnant water which collects in the bilges (*supra*) and which should be pumped out regularly.

BINNACLE: Stand on the top of which the compass is supported. Usually with a brass hood with a viewing window. Binnacles for magnetic compasses house correcting magnets, spheres, indoors bar, etc.

BLOCK COEFFICIENT: The ratio of the immersed volume of the hull to the volume of a block with the same length, breadth and draft of the vessel. It can be expressed in various ways, depending upon the measurements used, sometimes to deceive rival concerns.

BOLLARDS: Short posts standing on the deck of a ship or quay to which mooring ropes are made fast, or over which the eye or bight of a rope is taken. Those aboard ship are generally termed Bitts.

BOOT TOPPING: The area between the light and load waterlines of a ship where especially hard-wearing paint is used to resist the scouring effects of both weather and sea—the 'wind and water' area.

BOW: ('o' as in 'how') The forward end of a vessel.

BOWSE IN: Within the context of the text, a boat is bowsed in to its embarkation position by bowsing ropes (or wires) to its stowed position beneath the davit heads. If flat bands of canvas, sennit, etc. are used (usually diagonally across the boat) she is said to be 'griped in'—the bands being known as 'gripes'.

BREADTH (or BREADTH MOULDED): The moulded breadth of a ship is usually taken to be the maximum breadth measured to the inside of her shell or skin plating.

B.Th.U.: British Thermal Unit.

BULKHEAD: A vertical partition or wall made of various materials—steel for watertight bulkheads: steel (insulated) or asbestos board for firescreen bulkheads, etc.

BULWARKS: Raised solid plating (or woodwork in older ships) instead of hand-rails around the deck, helping to keep decks dry and acting as a fence.

BUNK: a bed, or berth, which is built in, and not free-standing. Thus usually enclosed on three sides.

BUNKERS: Compartments for the storage and carriage of coal or oil fuel.

BUTT (of plating): The end to end joining of plates.

CABLE: Within the context of the text, the chain to which the anchor is attached, but can refer to heavy wire or fibre rope. (see CAPSTAN *infra*)

CAMBER: Upwards curvature to a deck between its two sides, to provide good drainage to the scuppers (*q.v.*)

CAPSTAN: Vertical revolving drum used for winding mooring lines or cables in and out. The use for anchor cables is more usual in warships, since merchant ships generally use a special winch for this purpose, called a 'windlass'.

CAREEN: The operation of pulling a vessel—usually a sailing ship—down on her side in order to remove weed and barnacles from the exposed side and bottom, and to repair and re-paint as required. In order to do this, the craft was positioned parallel to the waterfront on a rather steeply-sloping sandy beach and was laid ashore. Heavy equipment, loose gear and armament was taken ashore, and the topmasts sent down. Gunports and other openings in the ship's side had to be made watertight. Tackles were then secured to the lower mast heads and to anchors or other securing points ashore and the ship was then hove down on her side. Relieving tackles were passed under the hull and secured to convenient points on the exposed upper part of the vessel, and were used to control the amount of heel and to return the ship to an upright position afterwards. The other side of the ship was treated in the same way by turning her around and laying the other side ashore. When all was done, the ship was re-rigged and gear was re-loaded. This was not an operation to undertake lightly, except in the case of smaller craft.

CARGO CAPACITY: BALE CAPACITY is the volume within the faces of the sparring and cladding fitted on the faces of the ship's frames and other structures to protect general cargo. GRAIN CAPACITY is the volume within the space into which grain or similar cargoes can flow. (*e.g.* to the inside face of the skin, etc.) INSULATED CAPACITY is the volume within the faces of the insulation and its protective sparring.

CARVEL BUILT: Wooden building (usually in small craft) in which the planks of wood are laid flush with each other, presenting a smooth surface, in contradistinction to 'clinker built' (*q.v.*)

CAULK: To fill the joints or seams of planking to render them watertight—usually with oakum and pitch.

CAVITATION: A phenomenon or condition caused by the fast movement of a body, usually through water or other fluid, at a speed at which the fluid fails to follow the shape of the body, so that cavities containing water vapour form and collapse repeatedly, often causing noise like hammering or explosions. Damage is frequently caused to such surfaces as propeller blades, shaft brackets, rudder and stabilizer fins and similar parts of ships. The holes so made can be extensive and deep, and can involve heavy costs in maintenance.

CENTRE OF BUOYANCY: The point through which the resultant of all the upward forces keeping a vessel afloat in still water are said to act.

CENTRE OF GRAVITY: The point through which the various downward forces, combining her weight and contents, act. If a ship be considered as a see-saw, the Centre of Gravity (C.G.) is her point of balance.

CHANNELS: In older ships, projecting ledges which formed outriggers for the shrouds.

CLINCH PLATES: Plates which overlap at their edges.

CLINKER BUILT: Used of relatively small wooden vessels, in which the edges of the planks overlap, in contradistinction to Carvel built (*q.v.*)

COAMING: Solid watertight raised screen, around hatchway, ladderway, or entrance.

COMPANIONWAY: Stairway, usually with weather-tight door and trunkway following the line of the stairs, from a weather deck to a deck below.

CONDENSER: An apparatus which receives exhaust steam from the main engines, turbines or auxiliary machinery and re-converts it into water, which may then be used again in the boiler feed system.

CROSSJACK: The lowest square sail on the mizzen mast of a square-rigged ship.

DAVIT: (Pronounced 'dayvit') In the text, davits refer to boat davits, and are devices, which have taken various forms, for taking the weight of the lifeboats and for lowering or raising them as required. A gravity davit permits the launching of a boat by gravity when a brake is released.

D.C.: Direct Current. An electrical current, usually of constant polarity and power. (see 'A.C.')

DEADLIGHT: Metal cover for porthole or window, to be used for protecting the glass against possible damage in heavy weather.

DEADWEIGHT: see TONNAGE.

DEFERRED SHARES: Shares and/or stock which rank for distribution after Preference and Ordinary shareholders have been paid.

DERRICK: Spar equipped with sheaves and wires, the heel of which is swivelled to the mast or a samson post. Used for loading and discharging cargo, it can be raised or lowered, and is a form of nautical crane.

DIP (a flag): To lower the ensign half way as a greeting or form of salute. The greeting ship dips: the greeted ship dips and re-hoists, whereupon the first ship hauls up her ensign again.

DISPLACEMENT: see TONNAGE.

DOUBLE-BOTTOM: A structure, sub-divided into water-tight compartments, several feet high, extending from bilge to bilge and usually almost the entire length of a ship. Used for carriage of fresh water: oil fuel, water ballast, etc.

DRAUGHT (Draft): The depth of the bottom of the lowest part of the keel below the waterline. The questions: 'What is the draught?' or 'How much water is the ship drawing?' mean 'How much water does she need to float her?', bearing in mind that a vessel needs more water than the actual depth from the waterline.

DRESS SHIP: To decorate the ship with signal flags and pennants, strung on taut lines from bow to stern via the mast-heads and/or from trucks to deck.

ENSIGN (pronounced 'ensin'): Maritime version of a National Flag.

EQUITY: Shares in respect of which dividends may be paid without limit so long as profits permit. Normally used of all shares except Preference, etc. on which a fixed rate of interest is payable.

FAIRLEAD: A fitting for guiding ropes (usually mooring ropes) around angles or through apertures. Modern fairleads are usually fitted with rollers over which the ropes may run easily and without damage.

FENDER: Pad of rope, cork or of other resilient material, hung overside when going alongside a quay or another vessel to reduce the shock and prevent damage.

FIDDLES: Adjustable raised edges to tables, dressing tables, trays, etc. to prevent objects sliding off them in rough weather.

FIDLEY: Wide air trunk from the boiler room to the open deck.

FLARE: Overhanging curve at a ship's bow, spreading outwards from the waterline. The upper section is known as the 'flam'.

FORECASTLE: (pronounced 'fo'c'sle'). In ancient times, castles were built at the two ends of the ships and were called 'fore castles' and 'after castles'. The word forecastle is still used, but the after castle has become 'poop' (*q.v.*). The crew used to live under the foc's'le, and their accommodation was still given this name even when no longer situated there.

FORECASTLE HEAD: Raised deck at the bow of a ship, formerly termed the 'topgallant foc's'le'.

FRAMES: The ribs of a ship, normally vertical and transverse, which is why Bilbe's method was unusual.* Fore-and-aft or 'Longitudinal' framing is usually a system of framing decks and double bottom structure, where the beams of decks and frames run longitudinally instead of in the traditional transverse direction. The choice of 'transverse' or 'longitudinal' framing is made to suit the type, use and size etc. of the ship.

* See p. 46.

FREEBOARD: Broadly, the height from the waterline to the main deck.

GALLEY: Ship's kitchen.

GANGWAY: Portable bridge or footway, with railings, to give access to and from a ship alongside a quay or tender.

GIMBALS: A system of rings pivoted within each other within which an object (such as a lamp, compass card, etc.) is suspended and enabled to maintain a horizontal position despite the rolling of the ship.

GRAIN CAPACITY: see CARGO CAPACITY.

G.R.P.: Glass Re-inforced Plastic.

GUNPORT DOOR: Obviously a very old term, but still widely used to denote the large doors in a ship's side for use with passenger and crew gangways. Often called 'Shipside doors' today.

GUY: Part of the 'running rigging' (*q.v.*) That is: it is not static but moves. Generally associated with a derrick, being made fast to its head and used to move it from side to side.

HALYARD: Rope running through sheaves or blocks by which flags, sails or spars are hoisted.

HATCH: Opening in the ship's deck to enable cargo to be loaded or unloaded in or out of the hold and 'tween deck.

HAWSEPIPE: Aperture and pipe in the stem (and sometimes in the stern) through which the anchor cable runs (see also SPERLING PIPE).

HAWSER: A very thick rope, usually for mooring the ship or for towing.

HEAD: The forward end of a ship. If a ship is 'down by the head', she has deeper draught forward than aft.

HEAVE: A ship 'heaves' when weather and sea are so bad that she is lifted bodily and falls when the swell passes.

HEAVE TO: To lay a vessel practically head on to the sea (or as nearly thereto as she will comfortably lie) when the weather is too bad for the course to be maintained. Also used of a sailing ship when her sails are trimmed in opposition to each other to bring her to a stop.

HOLD: A compartment in which cargo is stowed. Today a ship is subdivided by watertight compartments and each compartment has a hold number. (Sailing ships had no such bulkheads). Generally used of the space below the 'tween decks.

I.H.P.: Indicated Horse Power.

I.L.O.: International Labour Organization.

I.M.C.O.: Inter-Governmental Maritime Consultative Organization.

INSULATED CAPACITY: see CARGO CAPACITY.

JACOB'S LADDER: A vertical rope ladder, usually with wooden steps, hung over side for use by pilots and seamen. Can be rolled up when not in use.

KEEL: The backbone of a ship along the middle of her bottom. In wooden ships, the keel was either a large piece of timber or several pieces scarphed to one another to form the main piece of construction to which the frames or ribs were attached. With the advent of iron and steel ships, it was a structure composed of heavy bars, usually surmounted by a large double channel bar (the keelson), but in large ships today it is part of a welded fabrication of steel plates, some horizontal and some vertical, and no longer is a 'keel' laid to commence work on the building a new vessel. Often large sections, each weighing 50 tons or more, are put on the berth and welded to similar sections which are prefabricated and positioned by large cranes.

KNOT: A unit of speed. 1 nautical mile (6,080 feet) per hour.

L.b.p.: 'Length between perpendiculars' (of a ship). Perpendiculars are imaginary lines drawn vertically through positions at the ends of the ship, and to which measurements of her length are taken. Usually, the aft 'perpendicular' is drawn through the after face of the stern post, and the forward one is drawn at a point where the forward side of the stem touches the load waterline.

LEE SIDE (or LEEWARD SIDE): Side away from, or opposite to, the wind.

LEEWAY: The sideways movement of a ship from her true course due to wind pressure, and shown by the angle of the fore-and-aft line of the ship and her wake. Today, the effects of tide are sometimes used under this heading.

L.o.a.: Length Overall of a ship. That is, the extreme length of the hull.

LOG: 1) Official journal of a voyage or 2) An apparatus for measuring the speed of a ship or the distance run.

LOAD LINE: (Plimsoll Line) The line to which a ship may be loaded by law. This is denoted by a circle and a horizontal line running through its centre which is cut into the ship's side and painted, on both sides, amidships. Various adjustments are permitted to the draught to take account of the vessel being in fresh or salt water: for the Winter time in the North Atlantic, for different waters of the world, etc.

LOFTING: Also termed LAYING OFF, LAYING DOWN. To draw the lines of the ship in full size on the mould loft floor, to enable templates to be formed for the various shapes required.

MILE (MEASURED): A sea mile is the equivalent of one minute (1/60th of a degree) of longitude on the Equator, or 6,080 feet. Measured miles are used by shipbuilders to measure speeds, usually on trials of ships. Ideally,

209. The Dilemma! The late Stanley Redshaw, Naval Architect of Vickers, the late Capt. Roberts and the author with their stop-watches which showed differences in time during the ORONSAY (II)'s speed trials. Not all of us can use stop watches very well!

they should be situated in deep water, having no currents, wind or tidal conditions to spoil the results. There are several 'measured miles' around the coasts of the British Isles, probably the best and most used being off the Isle of Arran at the mouth of the Clyde. Nautical mile posts are erected in suitable positions on the adjacent shore, two or three posts being lined up with them (so that the ship knows when they are right abeam) and occasionally at two-mile positions. During speed trials these are sighted by specialists aboard the vessel using stop watches. A minimum of two runs for each selected speed is made, one in each direction, but usually the higher speeds are tested using two runs over the distance in each direction. Averages of these speeds are used to provide graphs of power and speed of the ship for future use during the ship's life.

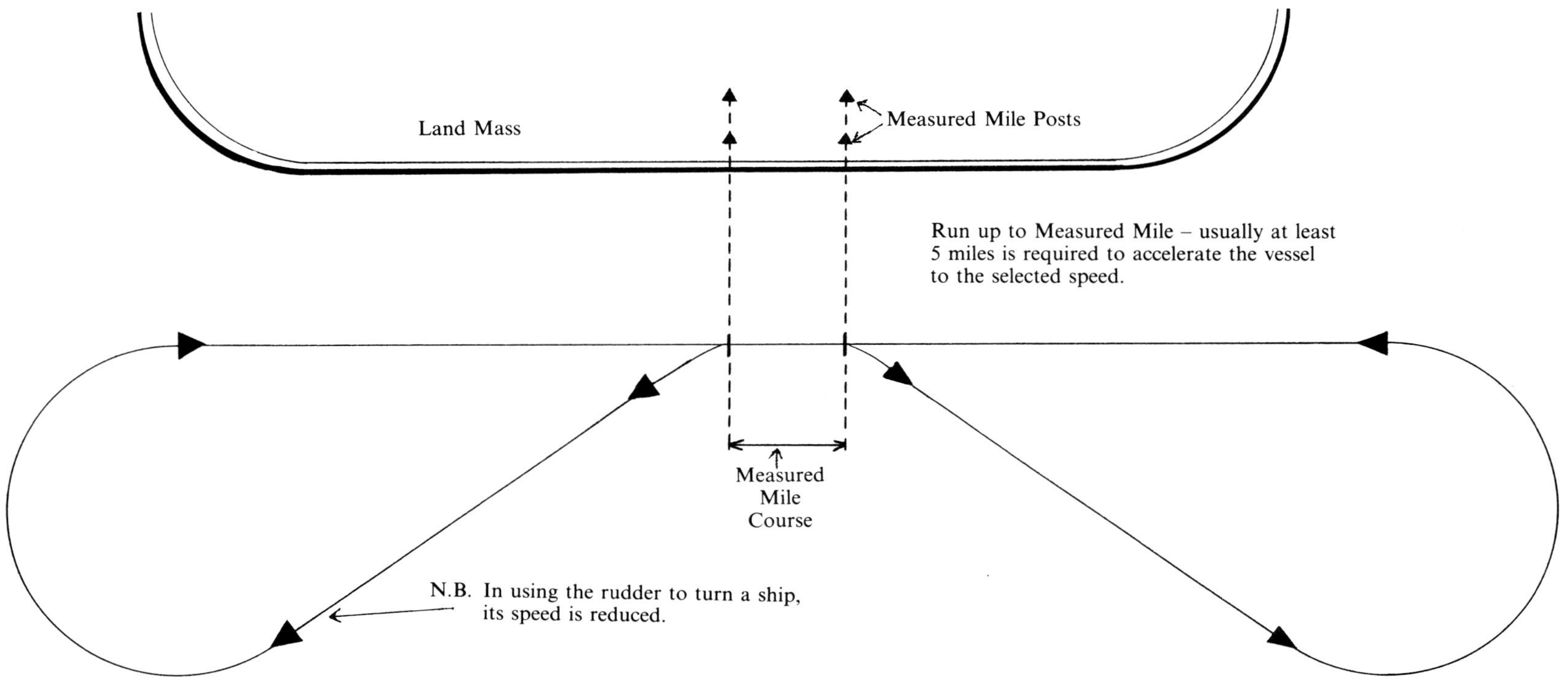

210. Typical course taken by a large ship on speed trials over the Measured Mile.

MITRE: To join two pieces of timber at an angle, so that the finished joint makes an equal angle with each part.

MOOR: to secure, or tie a ship up, to a quay, buoy or another vessel.

MOORING: The action of securing a ship, (see *supra.*)

MOORING PIPE: A metal fitting welded or riveted to the bulwarks, through which mooring ropes can be led to the shore or other securing place.

NOTCH: In connection with welding. In steelwork or other structure, a cut or sharp indentation in the edge of a plate or bar, sometimes caused by poor welding. Such notches can cause weakness or failure by cracking of load-bearing structures, especially if the structure is not 'notch-tough' (*q.v.*)

NOTCH-TOUGH: Metal possessing suitable characteristics to enable it to resist cracking from notches or other acute changes of section.

OAKUM: Tow or combings of rope, oiled and treated for use with pitch to caulk the seams of planks of decks or wooden hulls.

PAY, to: To fill up the gaps between deck and hull planks with oakum and pitch.

PEAKS: The Fore and After Peaks are the watertight compartments in the extreme ends of the ship.

PENDANT: (pronounced 'pennant'). A tapered flag having its greatest depth in the hoist: i.e. next to the halyard.

PITCH: 1) Black resinous material which, when heated and softened, is used together with oakum to caulk deck or hull planking. 2) The rocking motion in which the stern and stem of a ship rise and fall alternately in a fore-and-aft plane due to sea or swell is known as 'pitching'.

POOP: Raised deck at the stern, formerly called 'After castle'. Poop is probably derived from the Latin word *puppis*, which meant the stern of a ship.

POPPET: (Fore poppet, After Poppet). The ends of the sliding launchways which, because of the shape of a ship at her ends, are built to support her and spread the intensity of the forces arising during launching.

PORT: PORT LIGHT, PORT HOLE (Scuttle or Sidelight): Circular window in a ship's side or deckhouse.

PORT: The left hand side of a vessel, when looking forward.

PREFERENCE SHARES: Any security on which the holders are entitled to a fixed preferential dividend before any distribution is made on the Equity capital (*q.v.*)

p.s.i.: Pounds per square inch.

QUARTERMASTER: A seaman who steers the ship under the direction of the navigating officer.

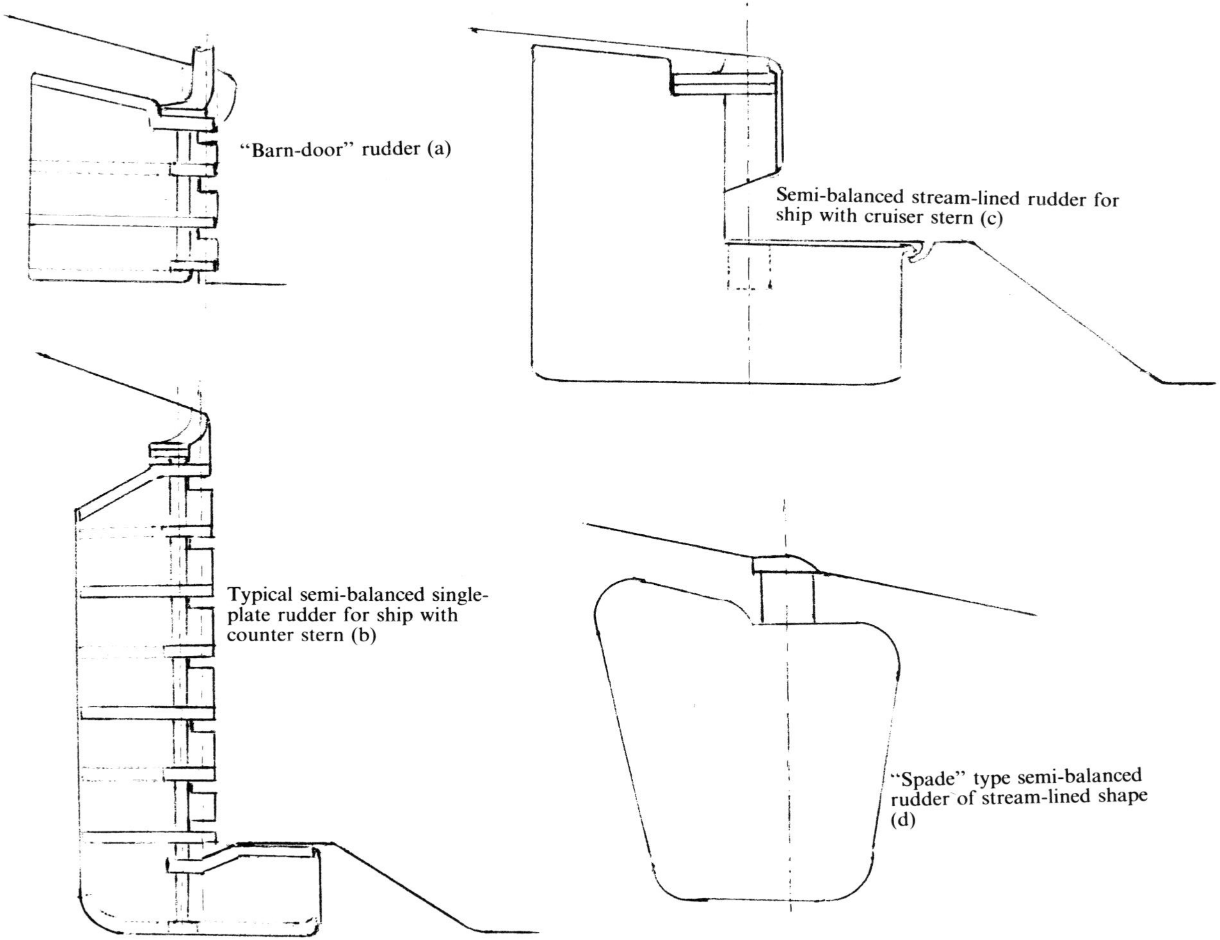

211. Types of Rudder.

RAFFEE: A triangular sail set from the truck of a mast to the uppermost yardarms. Sometimes split into two parts, so that just the weather side can be set.

RIGGING: Standing rigging is the rope, hemp, wire or other material used to support masts, derrick posts, etc. in position permamently. Includes shrouds, stays, etc. Standing rigging is so called because it does not move. Running rigging are those items of rope, wire, etc. which are used to work a vessel—the various lines for the control of sails: for working derricks etc. These *do* move.

ROLL (ROLLING): The rocking motion from port to starboard and vice versa, transversely about the axis of the ship, caused by the movement of a ship relative to the sea.

RUDDERS: There have been many varieties. The oldest form was the steering oar. Next came the type known today as the 'barn-door rudder', which hung like a barn-door from pintles (heavy pins on the forward edge) which fitted into gudgeons (lugs projecting on the after side of the stern post) to provide a hinged effect. As sizes of ships increased, rudders became semi-balanced with the fore part forward of the stern post, first to suit the counter-sterned vessels and, later, the cruiser sterns. (See figure 211 (a), (b) (c) and (d).

SAMSON POST: A short, tubular mast, usually well to one side of a ship's centre-line, and used to support a derrick (or more).

SCALE EFFECT: The resistance of a ship to movement through the water is not entirely proportional to that of a model of her built to scale, and the behaviour of the flow of water over the ship and the model is not entirely similar. This is because of their difference in size. For instance, water will not flow so readily through a small bore tube as through one with a large bore. Model experiments to simulate flow through a transverse propulsion tube in the bow of a model whilst it is moved along in the water of an experimental tank could not be successful, and comparison with the full scale ship would be absolutely unreliable. Indeed, if the tube in the model is very small, *no* movement of water will take place through it. Air flow is very similar to that of fluids when tested through slots or tubes. Hence the term 'scale effect'.

SIDELIGHT: 1) see PORT, PORTHOLE, etc. 2) Green and Red lights, shown at night on starboard and port sides respectively from right ahead to two points abaft each beam.

SHORE: Prop used to support a ship's structure during building.

SOLENOID: An electrically-operated magnetic release mechanism.

SPEED (of a ship): Expressed in knots (*q.v.*) and as 'Design Speed', 'Trial

Speed', 'Service Speed' or just 'Speed'. Design speed is not a precise term and is often used to mean different things by different shipbuilders, but often means the speed which the designer hopes to achieve on trials. Trial Speed is a misleading term, because the ship may not be fully laden during her trials and the power used for the speed achieved may be the maximum possible. These factors are seldom realized in service. The Service Speed is a figure derived from Builder's and Owner's statistics, together with the Trial results, and takes account of the weather and sea conditions over the operating route of the ship; the growth of resistance of the hull during the periods between dry-docking and cleaning of its surface, and falling of performance in service.

SPERLING PIPE: Pipe from abaft windlass to chain locker.

SPRITSAIL: 1) A four-sided, fore-and-aft sail, spread by a spar (sprit) extending from the heel of the mast to the upper corner of the sail on its after edge. 2) A square sail set beneath the bowsprit—fore-runner of jibs.

STABILITY: Basically, the tendency for a vessel to return to the upright position if she is displaced from it. To do so, she must be 'stable'. Were the vessel unstable, she would heel until she recovered enough stability or she would capsize. This can take place if—say—cargo has shifted or flooding has taken place. A stable ship is one in which the centre of her weight is below her metacentre, which is a point established by her under-water shape and mathematically calculated during the design stage. If a ship (usually a freighter) is loading a very heavy cargo which does not occupy all the space in her holds, much care must be taken to distribute the weights correctly. If too much is too high, she will be tender, and possibly unstable. At best, she will give long, slow rolls, and almost pause each roll as though deciding whether to roll back. If too much is too low, the ship will be 'stiff', and will give very quick, jerky rolls. This can cause damage. The whole question of ship stability is a large one, which cannot be covered adequately in a glossary.

STABILIZERS: See text, pp. 291 et seq.

STAND ON: To maintain course.

STARBOARD: Right-hand side of a ship, when looking forward.

STEAM, bled: Steam taken off a steam system at a suitable place, as regards pressure and temperature, to suit the use to which the 'bled' steam will be put.

STERN: The aftermost part of a ship. The most usual stern used in sailing and steam ships of the 19th Century was known as the 'counter' stern. This was an extension above the stern post, on which the rudder was hinged, and the lines of the upper part of the ship were widened and carried abaft the stern post to form an overhanging extension to the ship, which was elliptical or half-round in plan form, and which protected the rudder (and screw, if fitted) from damage when the ship was alongside a quay or another ship. Towards the end of the 19th Century, another type of stern was introduced—presumably by the British Admiralty, because it was—and still is—termed the 'cruiser' stern. In profile, the overhanging end of the ship is carried down towards the waterline in a gentle curve which finally turns in a forwards direction near, or on, the waterline, and then runs forward horizontally until it reaches the main part of the hull at the rudder and the sternpost. As in the Counter stern, the plan form is very rounded at the upper deck, to afford protection of the rudder and, to a lesser extent nowadays, the propellers. The first Orient liner to be fitted with a cruiser stern was the *Ormonde*, delivered in 1917.

STOW, to: To pack away in a suitable place on, or in, a ship.

STOWAGE FACTOR: of a commodity is the number of cubic feet occupied by 2,240 lbs. of that commodity.

STRAKE (of plating): is a continuous line of plates riveted or welded end to end, which is also attached in the same way to strakes on both (or only one) side, to form a ship's deck or shell. A strake runs in a fore-and-aft direction—not vertically.

STRINGER ANGLE: The angle bar fitted at the edge of a deck to enable the deck and shell plating to be connected by riveting.

STRINGER PLATE: A plate fitted at the edge of a deck, enabling a connection to be made to the shell plating. For strength purposes, it is often thicker than the rest of the deck plating.

SURGE: A momentary movement of the ship caused by waves or currents, additional to her average movement.

SUPERHEAT: When steam is heated to a higher temperature than is necessary for its formation at a given pressure, it is said to be superheated. Modern marine engines utilize superheated steam to increase their efficiency.

TEMPLATE: A pattern (or mould) made to the exact size of a piece of work which is to be fashioned on which rivet holes, overlap, apertures, etc., are shown. Usually made of a light board or even thick paper.

TENDER: 1) Craft to carry passengers to and from a ship when she is in the stream. 2) See STABILITY.

THWART: Cross seat in a ship's boat.

THWARTSHIPS: see ATHWARTSHIPS.

TONNAGE: a) Deadweight tonnage is the weight of cargo, fuel, stores etc.

which bring a ship down to her load line from a light condition. That is, when 'down to her marks' the total weight of the ship and all she contains, less the weight of the ship herself and of her equipment.

b) Displacement Tonnage: The weight in tons of a ship or equally the weight of water which she displaces, being associated with a stated draught. (i.e. Light draught: Loaded draught: 20′ draught, etc.)

c) Gross Tonnage (G.R.T.) Gross Registered tonnage is a figure of capacity expressed as 'tons' and, in very broad terms, is the total internal volume in cubic feet of the ship divided by 100.

d) Net Registered Tonnage: The Gross tonnage, less spaces used for accommodation of crew, machinery, etc. In other words, the measurement (on the same basis as G.R.T.) of the earning capacity of the ship. In a passenger ship, passenger accommodation is included: officers' is not.

Net and Gross tonnages are used to compute port charges, Canal dues, Dry-docking fees and the like. There are other forms of tonnage which are not germane to this book.

TRANSOM: A transom counter is a type of stern which is flat and somewhat shield-shaped, generally with a slightly curved surface. Very usual in many wooden sailing ships. Transom also refers to the structure about the stern.

TRIM (of a ship): a term defining the arrangement of weights in a ship which produce her forward and after draughts. A ship is generally loaded to be a trifle 'down by the stern'.

TRIM (of sails): When sails are hauled round to take the best advantage of the wind, they are properly 'trimmed'.

TRIPLE EXPANSION ENGINES: A multiple expansion steam reciprocating engine. The expansion takes place in two stages, since there is one high-pressure cylinder, one of intermediate pressure, and one or more low pressure cylinders.

TUMBLE-HOME: The inward inclination of a ship's side between the waterline and the upper deck. The opposite of Flare (*q.v.*). A ship with 12 inches tumble-home would be two feet wider at her maximum breadth than at the upper deck.

TURBINE: A form of engine in which the kinetic energy of steam is transformed into a direct rotary motion through steam jets which act at high speed on rotary vanes. Since the power developed is very smooth and quiet, and can also be very high, it is ideal for passenger ships intended to have high power and speed. The turbine reduces vibration, but is not reversible. Thus separate turbines need to be used when going astern, usually of much lesser power. Various initials, etc. have been used in connection with turbines, as follows:–

D.R.G: Double reduction gearing.
H.P.: High pressure.
I.P.: Intermediate pressure.
L.P.: Low pressure.
PARMETRADA: Parsons and Marine Engineering Turbine Research and Development Association. (Designers of turbines.
S.R.G: Single reduction gearing.

UNION PURCHASE: When two derricks are in use, the one centred over the hatch and the other over the side, with their runners shackled to a common hook, cargo can be handled quickly, since the derricks do not need to be moved. (The 'runner' is the wire connected to a winch which hauls up or lowers the cargo.)

UN-SHIP: Remove or displace.

VISIBILITY: On a clear day, the curvature of the earth is a limiting factor. The distance of the horizon is $1.15 \times \sqrt{\text{the height of the eye}}$ in feet so that, from the upper passenger decks of Orient liners, which are—say—50 feet above the water, the horizon is distant $1.15 \times \sqrt{50}$ which is fractionally over 8 miles. The upperworks of a similar ship could be seen at twice that distance.

WATERWAY: Deck gutter.

WAY: Forward motion of the ship. To have 'way on her' means that she is moving forward.

WEATHER SIDE: (Windward side) The side of the ship towards which the wind is blowing and the side over which no sailor would ever throw rubbish, etc.

WEIGH (anchor): To raise the anchor—*not* to record its weight! Once the anchor is off the ground, the vessel is under 'way'.

YAW: A ship is yawing when she is swaying on either side of her course.

INDEX

Subjects which are mentioned very frequently are not necessarily listed below in cases where the reference is merely *en passant.*

Names of ships are shown in *italics.* *n* denotes footnote.
References to illustrations are shown in **bold.**